305.8
BAN

D1458558

This b...

70 NOV 1996

RACIAL AND ETHNIC COMPETITION

91204

MODERN REVIVALS IN SOCIOLOGY
Series Editor: Professor Chris Bryant

Chris Jenks (ed)
The Sociology of Childhood: Essential Readings
(0 7512 0044 1)
Zygmunt Bauman
Hermeneutics and Social Science: Approaches to Understanding
(0 7512 0045 X)
Howard Parker
View From The Boys: A Sociology of Down-Town Adolescents
(0 7512 0046 8)
Nicholas Spykman
The Social Theory of Georg Simmel
(0 7512 0047 6)
Daniel Lawrence
Black Migrants: White Natives. A Study of Race Relations in Nottingham
(0 7512 0057 3)
Peter Halfpenny
Positivism and Sociology: Explaining Social Life
(0 7512 0059 X)
William Outhwaite and Michael Mulkay (eds)
Social Theory and Social Criticism: Essays for Tom Bottomore
(0 7512 0073 5)
J D Y Peel
Herbert Spencer: The Evolution of a Sociologist
(0 7512 0094 8)
Michael Mulkay
Functionalism, exchange and theoretical strategy
(0 7512 0103 0)
Michael Mulkay
Science and the sociology of knowledge
(0 7512 0104 9)
Michael Banton
Racial and Ethnic Competition
(0 7512 0110 3)

RACIAL AND ETHNIC COMPETITION

Michael Banton

Professor Emeritus of Sociology
University of Bristol

Gregg Revivals

© Cambridge University Press 1983
© Michael Banton 1992

All rights reserved

First published in Great Britain in 1983 by
the Press Syndicate of the University of Cambridge

Reprinted in 1992 by
Gregg Revivals
Gower House
Croft Road
Aldershot
Hampshire GU11 3HR
England

Gregg Revivals
Distributed in the United States by
Ashgate Publishing Company
Old Post Road
Brookfield
Vermont 05036
USA

A CIP catalogue record for this book is available
from the British Library

A CIP catalogue record for this book is available
from the US Library of Congress

ISBN 0 7512 0110 3

Printed in Great Britain by The Ipswich Book Company

for Marianne

'There is something reasonable about trade to all men, and, you see, the advantage of it is that, when you first move among people who have never seen anything like you before, they naturally regard you as a devil; but when you want to buy and sell with them, they recognize that there is something human and reasonable about you' – Mary Kingsley in 1898.

(Gwynn, 1932:79)

'In my view the ideal society would be one in which each citizen developed a real split personality, acting selfishly in the market place and altruistically at the ballot box . . .'

James E. Meade (1973:52)

Contents

Figures

Tables

Acknowledgements

Completion of this book was assisted by the University of Bristol which gave me study leave so that I could teach and work at the Australian National University for the second semester of 1981 and at Duke University, North Carolina, for the spring semester of 1982. Visiting appointments of this kind can be very helpful in providing an extended period relatively free from distractions, and the stimulus of students who approach the subject with different assumptions. To mention by name the colleagues and students at these and other universities from whose comments I have benefited would be too difficult a task, but it would be wrong not to acknowledge how much I learned from those who worked with me when I was part-time Director of the Social Science Research Council's Research Unit on Ethnic Relations from January 1970 to July 1978.

MICHAEL BANTON
April 1982

1

Introduction

On 10 November 1975, the United Nations General Assembly voted by 72 votes to 35 to adopt resolution 3379 which 'determines that Zionism is a form of racism and racial discrimination'. The principal speaker in favour of the resolution was the representative of Kuwait. He referred to the International Convention on the Elimination of All Forms of Racial Discrimination (resolution 2106) according to which 'the term "racial discrimination" shall mean any distinction, exclusion, restriction or preference based on race, colour, descent, or nation or ethnic origin'. He presented this as being 'the total definition of racism adopted and espoused by the United Nations'. He went on to refer to the Israeli Law of the Return, permitting a Jew who had never been in Palestine to 'return' and to the policy prohibiting a Palestinian from returning to his actual home; these he saw as concrete practices which had 'the effect of excluding some people on the basis of their being non-Jews and including others on the basis of their being Jews – Jewishness being decided officially by Zionism as an ethnic and not strictly a religious definition'. The Kuwaiti ambassador added 'there is one "ism" that comes to this platform to proclaim: "Hands off! If you criticize me you are criticizing a religion. If you criticize me, you are expressing hatred for a people!" ' To such arguments he objected, insisting that Zionism was not synonymous with Judaism.

The ambassador failed to persuade his opponents who did indeed see anti-semitism behind the resolution, and who thought it betrayed a serious and perhaps wilful misunderstanding of Zionism. The procedural status of the resolution was also important. It came after two resolutions about the implementation of the Programme of the Decade for Action to Combat Racism and Racial Discrimination and the convening of a 'world conference to combat racism and racial discrimination' in 1978, which was to carry forward international action in this sphere. The west European countries, together with the United States, Canada, Australia, New Zealand, Fiji, Chile, Uruguay, Kenya, Liberia and Zambia wished to support the first two resolutions but explained either that they could not do so if the programme was to be widened into a platform for action against Israel, or that they felt

1

obliged to abstain on the Zionism resolution in order not to jeopardize the Programme for the Decade. Their apprehensions were justified, for, although a conference was held in Zambia, the adoption of the Zionism resolution wrecked the Programme.

The positions adopted by governments in connection with the 1975 debate were influenced by overriding political objectives, but the question of the meaning given to the word 'racism' is nevertheless of importance. After all, those who drafted the resolution chose to use it, presumably because it would assist in bracketing the Israeli state with the government of South Africa as responsible for a crime against humanity and for policies constituting a serious threat to international peace and security. The 1975 debate shows that 'racism' is now an accepted expression in the highest international forum. Though its first use in a United Nations' document dates only from 1968, within seven years the diplomats had come to use it with few protests about any imprecision in its meaning; indeed more speakers questioned the definition of Zionism.

Words that end in '-ism' have a special attraction to those who want to cut corners in argument. The United Nations had earlier condemned 'the unholy alliance between Portuguese colonialism, South African racism, zionism and Israeli imperialism'. Whenever there is armed conflict within a state, the government is ready to refer to the opposing force as one of terrorism. Racist, terrorist, fascist and colonialist are used as epithets with little regard for accuracy. It was open to those who drafted resolution 3379 to specify the actions and policies of the Israeli government which they thought worthy of condemnation, but they chose to pitch the debate on a level of high abstraction and rhetoric.

One of the duties of the intellectual is to press the awkward questions. He, or she, should probe the arguments that are advanced in support of the good causes as well as the bad; should reveal any inconsistencies, and disturb the complacency which can affect those who advocate apparently progressive movements as well as those who defend the established order. It is usually easier for a writer to question the assumptions of those who are seen by the peer group as opponents than to expose the weaknesses in causes to which the writer lends support, but it is not the intellectual's duty to follow the crowd. The meaning given to the word racism has changed from its original 1930s sense of a doctrine about racial superiority to one that is much less coherent but more comprehensive, yet it remains a term of extreme opprobrium. That it is now employed so readily increases the need for scrutinizing its use.

A further reason for not accepting a vague use of words like 'racism' is that the loose thinking which can hide behind them may affect programmes intended to rectify real social evils. What the international programme to combat racism and racial discrimination might have consisted of is now a matter just of speculation, but in many countries there have in recent years been numerous programmes designed to improve community relations. Those who have joined them have regularly been committed workers, yet the level of achievement has been disappointing; some training programmes have been counter-productive; neither the dedication of individuals nor the money has been employed with the effect that was expected. This surely suggests that accurate diagnosis is as important to anyone seeking to remedy the ills of the body politic as it is to the practice of medicine. The comparison of different countries' experiences in the effort to reduce discrimination could have formed a useful part of such a programme.

One starting point for this book is the belief that loose-thinking about racism should be subjected to constructive criticism, which means trying to formulate better diagnoses. A crucial weakness associated with many of the words ending in '-ism' is that they single out a set of beliefs, practices, or relations, and present them as if they have an existence apart from the beliefs, practices, and relations of particular individuals in particular times and places. Once people slip into the assumption that racism or capitalism or communism exist in the sense that, say, influenza exists, then they are led into one trap after another. One such error is to overlook differences between historical periods. Thus Ruth Benedict (1942: 103), after referring to the way the Old Testament prophet Ezra preached against intermarriage with Ammonites and Moabites and had the wives and children of mixed marriages deported, concluded: 'Fanatical racism therefore occurred in Israel long before the days of modern racism', as if confident that she was identifying the same phenomenon. When racism is defined as a particular kind of doctrine it is relatively easy to say whether or not this doctrine was being advanced at a particular time, and to decide that the prophet Ezra was *not* advancing such a doctrine. (Though in many cases it is far from easy to decide just which arguments belong in doctrines identified as '-isms', like social Darwinism, Marxism, functionalism, and so on.) When racism is defined as a practice, such as the practice of racial discrimination, either the word is redundant (being already covered by the definition of racial discrimination) or it mystifies the issue by presenting the practice as the expression of some elemental force deep in the human psyche or forming an integral part of the foundations of a particular kind of social order. This has led to a vain search for the historical origins of racism.

It is perhaps easiest to approach the historical problem by listing first the principal possible resolutions. If it is thought that racism was absent from ancient Hebrew society and from classical antiquity, then its appearance might be associated with the 'discovery' of the New World and the Pope's action in partitioning it and its people between two European nations (the so-called '1492 school of race relations'); for Englishmen, it might be linked with the period after 1660 when they first involved themselves to a significant extent in transporting enslaved Africans across the Atlantic for sale, and presumably required some justification for treating them as goods since they had previously professed to abhor the trade in human flesh; it might equally well have been needed about the 1770s when the slave trade started to be threatened by criticism from within European society; the British parliament forbade participation in the slave trade in 1807 but slavery in the British colonies ended only in 1832 and in the United States in 1865; it might be thought that if doctrines of racial inferiority arise to protect or advance economic interests, racism would be systematized when slavery was abolished and an ideological rationalization was sought to replace a legal institution; on similar grounds, research workers might start to look for the beginnings of modern racism in England after 1874 when imperialism first became an electoral issue and a new social structure was forming on an industrial and urban foundation.

The historical evidence does not identify any of these periods as the one in which racism originated. Nor is it certain that racism is a European invention. Throughout history all the peoples of the world have been prone to make ethnocentric judgements, that is, to judge others by the standards of their own culture without allowing for the possibility that others' actions may be guided by the values of a different culture. But, when members of the two cultures concerned are physically distinguishable, what would otherwise be called ethnocentrism may be labelled racism, though the justification for doing so is at least debatable. Whether the word can properly be applied to some kinds of group relations in the Far East is also a matter for careful consideration. The Japanese people go to great lengths to avoid being identified with people of non-Japanese origin, even when the difference in ancestry cannot be detected from speech or appearance. It has been estimated that 70 per cent of Japanese parents employ private investigators to enquire into the ancestry of any prospective son- or daughter-in-law to make sure that he or she is not of Korean or Burakumin descent. Any marital alliance with a non-Japanese, even a white American or European, is considered demeaning if not polluting. Chinese attitudes towards marriage with non-Chinese are often little different, while there is corresponding hostility towards the Chinese in some parts of Southeast Asia. Some of these attitudes resemble those called 'racist' in North America, but they are unlikely to be quite the same since the cultures differ, and a marriage between two individuals will not identify their kin groups to the same extent. Each society has its own forms of ethnocentrism, while some place more significance than others upon criteria of descent.

The historical evidence also suggests that the attitudes and behaviours which today are called racist have changed and developed over time to become more complicated in our own generation. It seems as if in the nineteenth century a new quality entered relations between European and non-European peoples, reflecting the technological and economic superiority of Europe but making the differences seem greater and more permanent than they really were. Surveying the tremendous changes in their country, many Victorian English writers appeared almost intoxicated by discovery of new sources of power which seemed to promise an even greater future and to testify to the superiority of their own people. They spoke of their own people as a race and argued, in effect, that knowledge of another's race was an important clue to his or her character. The meaning of the word underwent an important change.

The Europeans' belief in their inherent superiority found its most systematic expression in the doctrine of racial typology according to which the human population consisted of a limited number of permanent human types with distinctive characteristics. This doctrine shattered the Christian image of the relations between God and his world; it denied the Christian ethic which judged men's actions in terms of their intentions, claiming instead that nature set limits to the capacities of the different types and that morality must be relative to race. The intellectual pretensions of the doctrine were destroyed when Charles Darwin's discoveries showed racial typology to be an error in biological science, but typology had a simplicity and popular appeal that Darwinism could never attain and so it lived on to become the source of the Nazis' racial doctrines. Their misuse of the evidence about the nature of differences between human stocks became one of the twentieth century's greatest scandals.

Since many people who rejected the Nazis' ideas nevertheless continued to employ a pre-Darwinian conception of race and to assume that the cultural differences between nations must ultimately be explicable in biological terms, it was necessary to explain to a popular audience just how science had moved forward from a typological conception of race. One of the most successful popularizers of anthropology was Ashley Montagu (1964:xli) who drew a parallel with 'phlogiston', a substance supposed by a late-seventeenth-century chemist to be present in all materials and given off by burning. A hundred years later Lavoisier demonstrated experimentally the processes of combustion and proved that there was no such substance as phlogiston, but nevertheless some distinguished scientists were for a long time unwilling to abandon this useless supposition. The proposition that humanity was divided into a limited number of distinct races was no more valid or useful as an explanatory principle. So Ashley Montagu concluded that 'race is the phlogiston of our time'.

It might now be better to say that race was the phlogiston of anthropology for a period of about 100 years starting around 1850. Those who today wish to see populations of different colour kept apart are less likely to base their arguments upon supposed biological differences and are more likely to emphasize differences in culture and way of life. The media of mass communication, especially film and television, have taught their audiences that the physical nature of man is everywhere similar but that human cultures display a fascinating diversity. There is an emerging understanding that 'race relations' are not a separate class of phenomena and that the basic concern must be with inter-group relations. Just as skin colour has served as a marker of group membership in Mississippi, so has identification as a Catholic or a Protestant in Northern Ireland. Relations between groups identified by skin colour, by religion, and, in countries like Belgium, by language, have features in common that are independent of the particular kind of feature that designates the group. Expressed succinctly, inter-racial relations are not necessarily different from intra-racial relations. The contrary belief was an error in social science. How that error came to be made is still the subject of dispute, but the issue is important because the diagnosis of how the mistake came to be made must imply a prognosis about how to avoid similar mistakes in future.

The necessity of comparison

Some universities in the United States offer a course in 'Comparative Race Relations'. Such a title implies that it is possible to study these relations in a manner that is not comparative. Unquestionably, the relations between black and white Americans can be examined in a course about the history or social organization of the United States, but such an examination will be conducted within an American frame of reference, taking for granted American popular conceptions of the nature of race. It cannot show what is special about American assumptions. This can be done only by comparing present-day United States beliefs about the nature of race and its social significance with the beliefs and actions of people in other countries and historical periods.

In support of the concentration upon a single country it can be urged that beliefs about race bear little relation to the facts of biology, so that the only way to study them is within the social context that has given them shape and significance. Yet on this argument there can be no study of comparative race relations, since the relations to be studied vary in essential respects from one country to another. It would be easier to defend the view that the best way to study racial relations is within a framework provided by the history and sociology of particular countries were it possible to contain people's ideas within such frameworks. This is patently impossible. Americans interpret information about black–white relations in Britain or in southern

Africa in terms of their experience within their own society. People in Britain and southern Africa do likewise. Moreover, members of minority groups within each society have perceptions of race relations overseas which differ from those of other minority groups and, in certain respects, all minority members see some things differently from majority members.

The Zionism resolution at the United Nations assumed that racism in one country could be equated with racism in another. If the relations between people who are physically different have any special characteristics, only by comparison is it possible to control the biases built into interpretations grounded in the assumptions of particular societies and generations. Scholars who work in those sections of the humanities most sceptical of sociology now increasingly recognize that it can offer a perspective which gives students a deeper understanding of any society and its history. To succeed in this it needs to employ concepts which are sufficiently culture-free for them to make comparison illuminating.

Any framework for comparing racial relations in different countries must allow for the ways in which racial groups are constantly changing. One significant feature is that the defining characteristics of such groups change less easily than most other aspects of human culture. During the twentieth century the cultural distinctiveness of the peoples of the world has been reduced at ever greater speed. Patterns of mass-production and consumption have taken Coca-Cola, jeans and pop music across most political boundaries. Technological changes have hastened this process. For example, in communication between air traffic controllers and pilots the world over, English has for several decades been the universal language. The use of computers, automobiles, transistors and the like has created standardized modes of thought and communication. Sports have been internationalized, so that many new states, in quite different climatic regions, have thought it important to field soccer teams able to uphold their national honour. The driving force behind such changes has been not political ideology but consumer demand.

This trend towards cultural uniformity is slowed down at several points. Where membership of a group is identified by the physical signs of race, there are psychological, economic and social factors which cluster round the physical difference and channel the direction of change. In the latter part of the last century this misled many observers into believing that race (in the sense of physical type) was a culture-free concept essential to the explanation of historical trends. This was how the expression 'race relations' entered the language. Critics have been able to demonstrate that this was an error without being able to replace the expression with a better one. Misleading though it may be, people will go on talking of 'race relations' for a long time to come.

One of the tasks of sociology, however, is to discover a way of overcoming the consequences of this historical error by finding better ways of conceptualizing social relations between peoples who are physically distinct, and of transcending judgements rooted in the experience of particular groups.

Differences in people's appearance and behaviour have in all societies served as signs indicating that a person is a stranger or someone of a particular nature and therefore to be treated differently. Physical characters may be used to assign people to membership in a particular social category; they are then expected to behave differently and others believe that they themselves should behave differently towards them. When this happens, how is the relationship between race as a physical classification and as a social classification best expressed? In a previous book (Banton, 1967:57), the author argued that while race as a biological category did not in any significant way determine people's behaviour, it influenced their behaviour by serving as a role sign. Differences of race, like those of age and sex, were used in the division of labour as a way of creating and identifying social roles. This was a statement of the interactionist perspective which sees racial relations as relations between individuals influenced by their group affiliations. While it was an improvement upon previous formulations it did not go far enough in separating the various elements involved in social classifications as they are used in everyday life. People do not perceive racial differences. They perceive phenotypical differences of colour, hair form, underlying bone structure, and so on. Phenotypical differences are a first-order abstraction. It is these differences which are used as role signs and they can be the bases for structures of inequality without the society having any concept of race. It just so happens that Western European culture in a particular phase of its history has ordered phenotypical variations in what have been known as 'racial' classifications. In this sense race is a second-order abstraction. The comparison with the social significance of age and sex is still valid, for people are also identified as young or old, male or female, by physical signs like wrinkles, gait, hair colour, length of hair, bust size and so on. The signs that say roughly how long ago someone was born are interpreted culturally in terms of beliefs about age – at present a relatively uncontentious set of ideas. The signs that indicate whether someone is male or female are interpreted culturally in terms of beliefs about what is appropriate to men and women, that is, to gender roles. Some aspects of gender classification have become almost as contentious as racial classification.

Signs indicating a person's expected role are significant both in the eyes of others and to the individuals themselves. A man of Jewish descent who rejects the Jewish faith may wonder whether he wants to identify himself as Jewish. If he has a distinctive name he can change it to one without Jewish associations. However, remembering the persecution to which Jews have been subjected, he may choose to present himself as Jewish even though he does not need to. An Afro-American who has the opportunity to be accepted as white may nevertheless prefer to identify himself or herself as black. Should the time come when in the United States it matters little whether people are considered black or white, many Afro-Americans will continue to identify themselves with people overseas of similar complexion so long as differences of skin colour are indicators of differences in social position in any part of the world. It will, on the most optimistic outlook, take many generations to overcome the present identifications of social in-equalities with differences in physical appearance.

Group differences are maintained by two processes that are often complementary. When people form a group they bind themselves together by processes of inclusion; in so doing they set apart others as non-members by processes of exclusion. Such processes can be discerned in all societies and historical periods. Their operation does not depend upon people having words in their language by which to designate them. In those societies in which people are defined as inferior on grounds of race the social pattern depends upon there being a word for race in the language and upon people being conscious of the significance attributed to race in that culture. Equally, for people to be patriotic or to count themselves members of an ethnic group, there have to be names for the nation or group in question and sets of beliefs about the importance of belonging to them. The conventional view in sociology is that the adjective 'racial' designates physical character-istics like skin colour when these are used to identify a group or to serve as the bases for group identity. In parallel, the adjective 'ethnic' designates cultural characteristics like language, customs or religion when these are used in a similar manner. The main disadvantage with this practice is that a racial minority or group may also have its distinctive culture and possess an ethnicity. If the same set of individuals can be both a racial and an ethnic group there needs to be some principle to provide guidance about when they are to be designated by the one name and when by the other. As was remarked earlier, identification as a Catholic or a Protestant in Northern Ireland has served as a marker of group membership in a similar way to skin colour in Mississippi. Signs which in India reveal that a man or woman belongs to a particular caste may have similar consequences. This points to the desirability of distinguishing between the rule which assigns an individual to membership of a group and to the consequences of such membership.

Accordingly, the practice in this book has been, in the first place, to describe the physical or cultural characteristics which result in individuals being assigned to particular groups; in the second place, to assume that social groups are created, maintained and changed in the course of activities by which individuals seek their own ends. It may be advantageous for them to come together in a group, either to advance or to defend their shared interests. The form of any group then results from the inclusive processes by which people bind themselves together and the exclusive processes by which others are shut out. In the third place, it is held that individuals utilize the knowledge of their generation in the pursuit of their goals. They have drawn upon and elaborated beliefs about racial differences to exclude others from their privileges and to increase the solidarity of their own group. Ideas of shared ethnicity have been used in a similar way, but, whereas beliefs about race have mostly been used in processes of exclusion, beliefs about ethnicity have been used to promote inclusion. Membership in an ethnic group is usually voluntary; membership in a racial group is not. The distinction is more complicated, particularly in urban societies, because some members of excluded groups based on racial characteristics do not identify themselves very much with the group to which they are assigned. Their lives are affected mainly by the exclusion to which they are subjected. Other members of these groups identify strongly and struggle with their fellows for greater equality, strengthening the inclusive and ethnic bonds. Their lives are affected both by exclusion and by the inclusive processes which arise in reaction to it.

In American English it has been customary to speak and write of 'race relations'. In British English several authors have preferred 'racial relations' but the tendency of late has been to conform to United States practice. If, however, racial and ethnic relations are to be regarded as a pair of terms reflecting the exclusive and inclusive processes, there is the advantage of symmetry in using the adjectival forms for both terms, and writing of *racial* relations.

Seeking to avoid judgements anchored in the cultures of particular societies, this book starts with a chapter on red, white and black in the New World, describing the patterns of relations between people from those continents that developed in different regions of the New World. It starts not with a conception of race but with the varied use made of phenotypical and cultural traits. Since people in different parts of the hemisphere have made quite different use of the idiom of race to identify groups and features of their relations, it would be wrong to present them from the outset as 'race' relations. Quite what race means, and the consequences of using it as a marker of group membership, is not known in advance; it has to be discovered anew in each context.

Just as people look at the societies in terms of their experience of their own society, so they look at other historical periods in terms of their understanding of their own time. Those accustomed to a racially divided society may perceive 'race' relations in centuries before the word race was invented and before people had any conception of it. They frequently overlook historical changes in the meaning of the word. Chapter 3 offers a corrective to this. It ends by explaining that when the word 'race' is used in legislation against discrimination it must be defined in a way that will be effective in the arguments of a courtroom; when it is used in a population census it must be defined in a way that is effective in the context in which people complete their census forms. These two definitions will differ from the definition of race in zoology. Different fields of activity will all require slightly different definitions of race, each tailored to the purposes and contexts of the field in question. Sociology, too, may need its own formulation.

The tensions associated with racial differences in recent years have influenced those who set out to study them. The lessons to be learned from comparative study have often been neglected. Many teachers concentrate on the subject-matter which helps them and their students develop the approach to which the teacher is committed. Since this commitment reflects the teacher's political philosophy, there is a political and intellectual struggle over which are the right questions to study and teach in the later part of the twentieth century. On the one hand there are those who stress 'relevance' and believe that social scientists should concentrate on the questions they see as politically important to minority advancement, even when hard evidence is lacking for the conclusions which they draw. On the other hand there are those who wish to develop the existing theories by examining the sorts of problems that can lead to firm conclusions and which can provide the sort of intellectual training expected from an undergraduate education. This book can be identified with the second viewpoint. It is written in the belief that, when teachers and students of sociology concentrate upon improving the available theories for explaining patterns of racial and ethnic relations, differences of political philosophy and personal commitments can be subordinated to an intellectual discipline and rendered more easily manageable. It advances a new theory of racial and ethnic relations. Not everyone will be attracted to this theory, but those who reject it are invited to consider what sort of theory they think should be preferred. Chapter 5 attempts to systematize such theories as other authors have advanced in the attempt to explain the origin and maintenance of racial boundaries. No one can today simply reject all the available theories without being under an obligation to explain what might be put in their place which would be more satisfactory.

The present work is therefore very different from the one entitled *Race Relations* (Banton, 1967). That was theoretically eclectic, reviewing what was then known about the subject in a fairly loose framework provided by an account of 'six orders of race relations': contact, acculturation, domination, paternalism, pluralism and integration. Some writers still find merit in this scheme, but, while it is easy to select cases which fit such a typology, others can be very problematic. Patterns of racial relations vary on so many dimensions that it may be preferable to start at the other end and see if a better theory, and a better conceptual framework, can be constructed by beginning with the actions of individuals pursuing their interests in historically defined circumstances. Their actions modify the pattern of group relations and alter the circumstances which face their successors. Orders such as domination, pluralism and integration are then seen as the end-products of relations conducted at the inter-personal level.

Racial and Ethnic Competition seeks to move on from the position reached in *Race Relations*, and to benefit from the shorter study of the growth of knowledge in this field presented in *The Idea of Race* (Banton, 1977) by analysing the main topics of discussion in terms of a single theory. It is called the Rational Choice Theory of Racial and Ethnic Relations since it presupposes that in inter-group relations, as in other spheres, individuals try to make the best use of the available resources in order to attain their objectives. When they miscalculate or act irrationally this carries them off course. To understand their behaviour it is necessary to pay every bit as much attention to the alternatives open to them in their situations, so an application of the theory may have to spend much longer analysing how the alternatives have been structured than in discussing the kinds of choice which are possible.

The central argument can be stated very simply. It is that competition is the critical process shaping patterns of racial and ethnic relations. Competition varies in both intensity and form, since much depends upon the nature of the units which compete and the kind of market in which they compete. When members of groups encounter one another in new situations the boundaries between them will be dissolved if they compete as one individual with another; the boundaries between them will be strengthened if they compete as one group with another. In competition, people seek to realize the values of their groups. Some of these values may, in the eyes of non-members, imply prejudice, but they are subject to modification and social science can illuminate the processes by which they change.

The exposition of the theory in Chapter 6 is followed by two chapters which discuss in greater detail the processes associated with individual and group competition. To try to cover the whole vast range of work in the field of racial and ethnic studies would be a difficult if not impossible task. Nor would it be worthwhile, since the present need is to find better ways of interpreting what is known. In the present state of knowledge, one of the best, and certainly the simplest, ways of organizing information about racial and ethnic relations is to see them as a part of the history of particular societies. To draw upon the strengths of historical presentation, the chapters on competition are followed by three more on South Africa, the United States and Great Britain, which set out the main sequences in the development of racial and ethnic relations in those societies. They are written from the standpoint of a Rational Choice conception of the determinants of boundary formation, maintenance, and change, but they cannot prove that standpoint superior to any other. Only in the more detailed examination of events in the present time is it possible to approach the conditions in which sociological theories can be properly tested. The following chapters, dealing with discrimination in housing and employment, state the case for the Rational Choice Theory more fully by showing how it can be applied in these fields.

Another contention of this book is that the error of race in its social application has called forth an opposing over-simplification. In some quarters it is not race but racism that is the phlogiston of our time, a supposedly elemental force which is never clearly located in human psychology or social structure and which offers only circular explanations of racial discrimination. To label someone or something racist is to express a strong condemnation. In present-day industrial society racial inequality can result from a long chain of fairly ordinary activities so it is difficult to decide who, if anyone, is responsible for the outcome. This does not excuse the result. To call a complex set of relations, or a whole society, racist, may seem to cut the knot. It expresses a rejection of certain consequences of the mode of organization. But in reality it solves nothing and the knot still has patiently to be untied. If the incidence of discrimination is to be reduced its causes must first be understood, and, since inter-racial behaviour is not a special kind of behaviour, that means it must be seen in its context. To understand racial relations in a London hospital it is necessary first to understand how a hospital works, and this is a very complex matter involving a knowledge of the technical requirements of medicine in different fields, of the organizational arrangements for staffing and provisioning the hospital and of the various academic disciplines concerned with explaining organizational behaviour and inter-personal relations. Only when sufficient progress has been made with understanding these matters can the research worker then turn to considering what difference it makes if the consultant, the registrar, the administrator, the pharmacist, the ward sister, the nurse, the dietician, the radiographer, the cook, the receptionist, the porter, or the patient is white, brown, black or yellow, Catholic, Hindu or Muslim, someone looking forward to promotion or someone who feels that his or her horizons are limited by race or ethnicity. To understand how these issues affect relations in the hospital it may be necessary to go back to a study of the characteristics of the group to which a minority member belongs: to understand why he, or his parents, came to London, the expectations which other members of his group have of him, the experiences they have of other groups in London society and their feelings towards it. The pattern is complicated because people from many different racial and ethnic groups may be found in a single hospital and they may be concentrated in particular positions within a hierarchy. Relations within a single ward, or between just two people, may reflect events crossing half the world and the accumulated experiences of several centuries. If the subject is so complicated, it cannot be successfully studied without carefully defined terminology. The pre-liminaries may be irksome but they can trip up the impatient research worker who tries to jump over them.

To understand social behaviour in any setting it is necessary to discover how people see the alternatives before them. An elementary lesson in sociology and social anthropology is for students to learn to avoid making ethnocentric judgements. Some of the most valuable research studies have been those which demonstrated the existence of sub-cultures within industrial societies and have shown, for example, that the behaviour of deviant youths can be understood only in terms of the values of their groups and their beliefs about how the wider society operates. To understand the behaviour of those who discriminate racially it is necessary to do the same, and the research worker must try to sympathize with his (or her) subjects' values. At a later stage of the research he (or she) may wish to argue that those values have undesirable consequences and to discuss ways in which they might be changed, but it is counter-productive to define that behaviour from the outset in ways that hinder the task of interpretation.

The ultimate objective of study and research in this field must surely be the accumulation of knowledge and skill that will contribute to the elimination of prejudice and discrimination based upon ethnic and racial origins. Since the forms which prejudice and discrimination take vary from one society to another, and between historical periods, it is necessary first to examine the big issues of racial distinction in history, and to clarify what has been involved, so that the variables relevant in the analysis of small-scale situations can be related to a larger framework. The activist who wishes to combat discrimination in some present-day society will want to get on with the job and not bother with the mistakes of the past, but it is better if other people do bother with those mistakes and see what can be learned from them. Everyone's approach to a social problem is influenced by his or her upbringing and the ideas of the groups with which he or she is associated. No one can throw off or succeed in ignoring the past, and only if its influence is examined can its power to mislead be corrected.

2

Red, white and black in the New World

European settlement in the New World brought together three major population groups from the sixteenth century onwards: Amerindians, Europeans and Africans. Members of the three groups differed in their appearance, their language, their religion and their ways of life, notably in the goals they sought and the skills they possessed. In Massachusetts the whites had come in search of a land where they could enjoy religious liberty. To Mexico and Peru the *conquistadores* came seeking souls and treasure for the Spanish Crown. In Virginia, Brazil, and some other parts, the settlers wanted land, produce, and any treasure they might happen to find, but they sought it for themselves rather than for their home governments.

The European settlers differed in their military strength relative to the Indians and in their ability to control and exploit the territory. This depended on the ease of communication, the density of settlement, the value of the produce they could sell by way of international trade, and so on. In the United States the Europeans were relatively powerful: in many areas they slaughtered the Indians and by the middle of the nineteenth century they had confined nearly all of them to reservations. In Latin America the Indians were too numerous and the terrain too difficult for the Europeans to be able to take possession of all the land. In some parts of the New World the land could be used to produce valuable crops for the European market but the white settlers were unable either to clear the land and grow these crops themselves, or to find sufficient local workers to produce them under European direction. So they looked for a new source of labour. It would have been little use bringing in free workers to labour on the tobacco and sugar plantations, for free men would not long have been willing to undertake such work for wages. They would have wanted to make farms for themselves and work on their own account. In many places land was plentiful but labour scarce. The relatively large-scale production of tobacco and sugar therefore required a labour force that could be bound to plantation, that is to say, it required some form of servile labour. The answer was found in the importation of Africans to work as slaves in the United States, the islands of the Caribbean, northeast Brazil, and the parts of continental central America where there was this kind of labour demand. Wherever peoples meet they mate, and children of mixed ancestry make their appearance. The rate of admixture may be higher when one group is more powerful than another, particularly, as in Brazil, if that group is predominantly masculine. Once mixture starts, its effects are likely to multiply. If two people, one conventionally 'black' and the other 'white', have several children, they are likely to be of different complexion: some may be quite dark, others quite light. Whereas the inheritance of eye colour is fairly straightforward from the standpoint of genetics, the determinants of skin colour are complicated and only partly understood. The natural colour of human skin is decided by the amounts of three chemicals: melanin producing a black appearance, carotene a yellowish one, and haemoglobin a reddish one. The quantities of these substances in skin cells are determined by genes, and by hormone action (cf. Banton and Harwood, 1975:47–55). Because of the variability in body chemistry, mating between people of different stock rapidly produces a great range in shades of complexion; no distinctions of skin colour can be drawn that are as clear as those between people of blue eyes and brown.

As Europeans settled in the New World and introduced Africans, mating occurred between people originating in three continents, resulting in the transfer of genes from one group to another and the creation of new intermediate groups. It would be simple to refer to this as a mixing of populations, though that can be misleading since the three original stocks themselves varied in physical characters. But it is sometimes possible to examine the frequency with which a particular gene is found among the people living in a particular locality and in this way to measure the introduction of genes that have originated in another continent. For example, there is a chemical familiarly known as PTC (phenyl-thio-carbamide) which can be tasted by only a minority of Europeans (33 to 50 per cent) but can be tasted by all Amerindians. Brazilian research workers have tested people from northeastern Brazil, who have settled in São Paulo, in respect of this and some other genetic markers, and have concluded that their ancestry is 11 to 16 per cent European in origin (Saldanha, 1962; Elston, 1971). Since blood-group frequencies also vary from one region to another they too can be used to calculate the flow of genes from one population in the formation of a new one. The genes of a black American in the United States usually are partly of European origin. In the South figures vary between 6 and 10 per cent; elsewhere between 13 and 31 per cent; while one of the most reliable studies, in Oakland, California, came to an average of 22 per cent (Reed, 1966). It has also to be remembered that a substantial number of partly black Americans have 'passed for white'; in particular, children of European appearance but partly African heredity have been brought up as whites and have introduced African genes into the 'white' gene pool. It has been calculated that approximately 23 per cent of the persons in the United States who were classified as white in 1960 had an African element in their biological make-up (Stuckert, 1964:195). Such considerations indicate that it would be unwise to regard a group socially counted as 'black' or 'white' as being biologically distinctive. In almost all circumstances there will be tendencies to reduce biological differences, but social classifications will not change in step with the biological shifts. Social classifications, as this book will seek to explain, are influenced by social determinants and serve purposes of their own.

Three kinds of classification

According to the anthropologist Charles Wagley, the main differences between Amerindians, Europeans and Africans in the New World from the sixteenth to the eighteenth centuries can be summed up as those of ancestry, appearance, and socio-cultural status (Wagley, 1959).

The Europeans expected an Indian to be of Indian appearance, of Indian ancestry, and to lead a conventional Indian existence; an African was supposed to be of black appearance, of African ancestry, to be illiterate, superstitious and childlike in the way they thought Africans were; a European was expected to look like a European, to be of purely European descent, a Christian, and to behave like a European. The three groups were thought of as distinct on each of the three dimensions. The Europeans' expectations mattered because, being in positions of relative power, they were able to make them come true. The more important places in society were reserved for Europeans because they could trust only those with whom they had shared interests. In North America at least, they concluded fairly early that little could be gained from making slaves of the Indians since it was difficult to make them work in the way the Europeans wanted; such action would increase the likelihood of their being attacked by Indian tribes and these attacks could be more dangerous if there were Indians inside as well as outside their settlements. The Europeans learned about Indians and Africans within the frameworks of particular relationships, the Indians as members of separate societies with strange cultures and the Africans as servants. Those relationships moulded the images of Indians and Africans that the Europeans built up and they tended to reinforce the assumption that these groups were quite distinct and had to be kept so.

Yet even from the earliest years there must have been many reasons for doubting such a simple view. The Europeans were very conscious of differences of status among their own population, for their societies were more rigidly stratified in the seventeenth century than they are today. There were major differences in literacy and social skills. The Europeans knew that Indian and African societies were also stratified and could perceive similarities in the positions of rulers and aristocrats across cultural boundaries. In the small-scale settlements of the early decades they would have been very much aware that, in some contexts, skills, reliability and moral worth were attributes of individuals and not of population groups. From early years mating occurred between reds, whites and blacks, producing an increasing number of individuals who did not fit neatly into any of the three categories. It will have been in the interest of some, or all, Europeans to treat some at least of these intermediary people as Europeans, but circumstances must have varied. How was the threefold structure to adapt to the pressure generated by people of partly European appearance and ancestry who were wholly European in their manner of life?

Two solutions were possible, and the extent to which either was adopted was reflected in the terminology employed for referring to people who could not be assigned unequivocally to one of the three original categories. The first solution was to recognize a range of intermediate social categories; the second, to make the anomalies fit in the nearest appropriate category. In most of the New World the first solution was adopted for a period; and the number of social categories multiplied to reflect the various possible degrees of mixed ancestry. The Spaniards, who placed great emphasis upon genealogy as a mode of social placement in their homeland culture, developed some very complex schemes of classification, but they seem to have borne little relation to social patterns as they existed in practice (Mörner, 1967:58–9). One of the difficulties resulting from the recognition of new categories was that the degree of mixture in a person's ancestry was not necessarily reflected in his appearance (which could be more red, white or black than expected) or in his socio-cultural status (for example, a man of mixed ancestry who was the son of an influential white settler, or who had been successful on his own account, might be richer or more powerful than a man of pure European descent). In general it was considerations of power which were most important. In Spanish-speaking countries it was sometimes possible for a person of mixed ancestry to obtain a legal declaration certifying that he was white, while the Jamaican legislature in the eighteenth century sometimes passed private bills to confer the legal rights of whites upon persons of mixed descent. Appearance could be more important than ancestry when there was doubt or room for argument about the latter. Therefore a scheme of classification based upon ancestry and resulting in a range of intermediate categories was likely to become unmanageable. There would be too many people intermediate between even these categories since, as has just been pointed out, physical variation in complexion, hair form, facial features, etc., is continuous and provides no basis for sharp differentiation. It must also be remembered that classifications are used only when it suits peoples' interests. If a man is seeking a favour of someone of uncertain social status he will do nothing to draw attention to that uncertainty lest it affect his chances of success; he is more likely to support whatever claim the potential benefactor makes to status.

By the late eighteenth century, according to Wagley, the pressures upon these classificatory systems were causing them to break down in most New World countries. Ancestry, appearance and socio-cultural status could not be kept in line. Each region came to emphasize that mode of distinction which was most effective in its circumstances as a way of dividing people up. The United States made ancestry the primary criterion; continental central America emphasized socio-cultural status; Brazil and parts of the Caribbean put the main stress on appearance.

Appearance

There are reasons for thinking that the Portuguese and Spanish colonists in the New World were more ready to mate with women of Indian and African origin than the colonists from northwestern Europe who settled in North America. The Portuguese and Spaniards came from a region which had known much intermingling with the Moors. The Moors had frequently been a match for the whites in battle and formed part of a civilization covering much of the known world, a civilization with its own universities and a religion of which Europeans had some knowledge. The Portuguese and Spaniards were Catholics; they acknowledged the authority of their priests to declare what their religion demanded of them, while that religion stressed the observances of the church rather than the individual conviction of the Christian. The Portuguese and Spaniards were accustomed to a legal system deriving from Rome which recognized the status of the slave and provided legal protections for anyone in that status. Thus it can be said that the colonists who came to the New World from the Iberian peninsula were better prepared to live in a society which included reds and blacks as well as whites. The Portuguese and Spaniards might have been as proud and brutal as the English and Dutch, but they did not see the gap between themselves and the other groups as being so great, and when they mated with women of Indian and African origin they were less troubled about the morality of such unions.

Because many of the Portuguese and Spaniards came to the New World as agents of their home governments, rather than as settlers, they brought few of their own womenfolk, which increased the frequency with which they mated with other women. In Brazil the Europeans were dispersed over wide stretches of territory; local government was weak relative to the central control of the Portuguese state and the Catholic church. The Brazilians' relations with world trade were the fitful ones of a boom-and-bust economy. But particularly important for social categorization was what Carl Degler has called 'the mulatto escape hatch' whereby mulattos secured a special niche in the socio-economic structure as the agents of the whites in supervising slaves (in agriculture and mining), pursuing those that ran off, making war upon Indians and escaped slaves, serving as urban artisans, shopkeepers, boatmen and cattle herdsmen (Degler, 1971:226). In times of economic recession masters emancipated their slaves since it was not worth their while to maintain them, so that the population of free blacks and browns grew. Emancipation came late but gradually; it was impelled by a recognition that slave labour was much less productive than free labour, by the desire to free the capital frozen in the buying and administration of slaves, and the wish of inland estate owners to get hold of the labour controlled by coastal slave-holders. In a country with relatively low population density and poor communications, local community life was the more important, so that, outside the main towns, it will have been impossible to maintain the original expectation that whites and blacks were to be distinct in appearance, ancestry, and socio-cultural status; nor would it have been so easy to draw a sharp line between positions reserved for whites and those suitable for mulattoes alone. There will have been growing pressures to allocate positions according to the competence of the individuals who might fill them. In this way health, education, and respectability became more important than colour, especially in northeastern Brazil. (In the southeast around the industrial city of São Paulo there has been continuing white immigration and a dark complexion is more of a disadvantage, but the social pattern is still very different from that of North America.)

Studies conducted in northeastern Brazil shortly after the Second World War reported a variety of words used to describe people whose appearance showed differing degrees of European and African admixture. The word *negro* was rarely used unless the speaker wished to be insulting; someone with a very dark complexion was called *preto*, but the *pretos* ranked themselves according to fine distinctions of shade and features. Thus, in one locality, the following descriptive terms came in gradual transition: *cabra, cabo verde, escuro, mulato escuro, mulato claro, pardo, sarará, moreno, louro*, and *branco da terra* (someone who was completely white to outward appearance but might have some other ancestry) (Hutchinson, 1952:28–30). These studies did not investigate the extent to which people agreed upon the order in which these terms were to be ranked or the extent to which people agreed that a particular individual was appropriately identified by one rather than another. Those questions were investigated by Marvin

Harris (1964b) in a fishing village 25 miles north of Salvador. He found a family in which there was a baby girl with a light skin and straight black hair who had two sisters both of whom were much more negroid in appearance though they had the same father and mother. Photographs of the three girls were shown to 100 neighbours and relatives who were asked how they would describe their appearance. They used 8 different terms for Iará, the most caucasoid sister, and 12 for Toninha, the most negroid. On the assumption that the previous studies had accurately defined the rank order of terms for this region, the terms employed to describe the sister can be listed as follows:

	Iará	*Toninha*	
Branca	56	1	*Branca*
Louro	2	1	*Clara*
Clara	8	1	*Sarará*
Sarará	1	1	*Canela*
Morena clara	16	4	*Cabocla*
Morena	6	7	*Morena clara*
Mulata clara	6	44	*Morena*
Mulata	5	14	*Morena escura*
		7	*Mulata*
		9	*Mulata escura*
		10	*Escura*
		2	*Preta*

In another section of the research nine other portraits were shown to a different sample and 40 different terms elicited. Since the disagreement about the ranking of these terms was very great, six of the major ones were presented to a third sample, who proved unable to agree upon anything other than that *branco* was the lightest and *preto* the darkest. In follow-up interviews, it was found that quite heated discussions could be generated by asking a group of fishermen whether *mulatos* were darker or lighter than *morenos*. The confusion was such that when someone was asked again about the use of these terms two weeks later a different answer might be given. The use of the terms varied from individual to individual and from situation to situation, reflecting the egalitarian social patterns in the fishing industry upon which the life of the community depended. In parts of Brazil with a different economic structure there may have been a stronger pressure for identifying all brothers and sisters, or members of one family, by a common term, but the Brazilian pattern in general is one in which terms for variations in skin colour etc. apply only to the appearance of individuals.

In some islands of the Caribbean, like Jamaica and Barbados when under

British rule, there was a continuous social gradation. Fair-complexioned people were mostly placed towards the top, and dark-complexioned towards the bottom. In certain islands there was a white population so long as sugar was a profitable crop, but when world markets changed the whites left. Circumstances varied from one period to another, but the nature of Caribbean agriculture favoured a two-class structure of land-owners and labourers, and this limited the growth of any continuous scale of ranking based on appearance. The niche for an intermediate group of traders, supervisors and artisans was very small. H. Hoetink (1973:21–40) has concluded that where and when there were few whites relative to blacks, the whites tended to accept the mulattos socially; where and when there were many black or mulatto freemen there was more tension between them and the whites. He finds evidence of a three-tier structure of this kind in many of the British, French, Dutch, and Danish islands, and in Surinam, but Cuba and Haiti require a more detailed characterization. In Trinidad, Guyana, and some other parts of the region, the nineteenth century saw a substantial immigration of brown people from India and a smaller one from China which increased the diversity of physical appearance.

Socio-cultural status

The Spanish government was particularly concerned that Spaniards in its colonies should remain distinct in appearance, ancestry and socio-cultural status. If the Crown was to keep hold of its overseas possessions, and extract treasure from them, it needed to control those of its subjects who ruled these colonies, and to prevent their establishing any breakaway regime. In the early period, even aristocratic Spaniards were willing to marry Indian women, but their children were not able to hold high office in the colonies since the Imperial government reserved such offices to persons born in Spain. Even Cortes, after his return to Spain, was denied the position of governor lest he should be involved in any move against the Crown. Such policies reinforced the emphasis which in Spanish culture was placed upon ancestry as a determinant of social status. Concubinage between Spanish men and other women was tolerated. It was not sexual relations between people of different groups that troubled the Spaniards so much as the fear that, if such persons were allowed to marry, the children would be able to claim Spanish ancestry and the calculation of their social rank would be too problematic.

The colonial status structure came under pressure with the growth of an intermediate population deriving partly from inter-group mating and partly from other streams of immigration. As early as the seventeenth century, labourers from the Philippines and China were imported into Mexico. The pressure to recognize an intermediate stratum consisting of 'the *castas*' was strongest in those parts of Spanish America, like nineteenth-century Cuba, with a competitive economy oriented towards the world market in sugar. Cuba moved in the Brazilian direction, towards a form of society in which terms describing differences of complexion were used simply to distinguish the appearance of individuals. In continental Spanish America economic growth was slower and there was less importation of African labour. Mexico, Guatemala, Ecuador, Peru and Bolivia moved towards a situation in which the main social division was one of socio-cultural status. This was a pattern made up of two main groups. On the one hand were people involved in government, the professions and trade, of either Hispanic or partly Hispanic origin, the latter being called *ladino* in Guatemala and mestizo in most of the other countries (Pitt-Rivers, 1969). On the other hand were Indians engaged in traditional cultivation but subject to taxation and therefore concerned to market some of their produce. Some members of the first group could not be clearly differentiated from Indians in respect of appearance or ancestry; it was their way of life that distinguished them.

The Indians have continuously adopted elements of Spanish culture, especially in the realm of religion, so the Indian identity has changed. At the same time some individual Indians have abandoned their traditional identity to become mestizos or *ladinos*. To make this change they had to live and dress as the mestizos did, speaking Spanish, adopting a Spanish name and attending a Christian church. In Mexico self-identification is sometimes the only factor which now differentiates the mestizo from the Indian, and whole communities have changed over when; given their current pattern of living, this has seemed advantageous. Someone who has changed over may be called an *indio revestido* (redressed Indian) while in the Andean region there is a special term *cholo* which is applied to 'civilized Indians' having an ethnic status intermediate between that of the Indian and the mestizo. In Guatemala the word *raza* is used *both* to indicate whether a man lives as a *ladino* or an Indian, *and* when classifying him by appearance. Thus a *ladino* can also be described as a Negro or as 'looking Indian' (Pitt-Rivers, 1973:13–14). Groups are distinguished by socio-cultural status, but within the groups individuals are distinguished by appearance.

In general, mestizos do not create difficulties for the Indian who, as they see it, wants to become 'civilized', but the position varies. In parts of Mexico Indians are challenging the mestizos for local political power; in such circumstances Indians are less likely to want to change their identity and the reaction of the mestizos will reflect their political interest. In some parts of Guatemala there are quite large towns where there are almost no *ladinos*. Positions in the division of labour which elsewhere would be occupied by *ladinos*, like traders, shopkeepers and artisans, are filled by Indians. Members of the Indian upper-class, powerful and respected in their own communities, speaking Spanish and knowing enough of Hispanic culture to be able to hold their own, have had no reason to change their status for that of a low-ranking position in a *ladino* community they did not respect. In Quetzaltenango, the second-largest city in Guatemala, an Indian commercial class continues to speak Quiché as well as Spanish. Its women mostly wear Indian dress and the *ladino* commercial class complains bitterly that the Indians are running them out of business. In Mexico City the social order – at least in a visitor's eyes – resembles instead that of classification by appearance: people occupying the higher social positions tend to be of Hispanic, and those in the lower positions of Indian appearance. It is the structure of society which decides what social positions there will be, and the terminology has to identify and differentiate those positions. Different parts of the New World have their own classifications and people in each part look at other regions using the categories with which they are familiar, as if expecting social structures to conform to cultural categories.

Socio-cultural status is more likely to be the main mode of social classification in countries in which two or more sections of the population live relatively independent lives so that there is little competition between them. This is to be expected in the earlier stages of contact between peoples, especially when neither group is completely dominant. The Spaniards in Mexico were much more powerful than the Indians, but they could not subjugate all of them or put all of them to work producing goods for the world market. Indians could contrive to live for centuries within a culture of their own, and the question of classification arose only when they moved into zones in which they were interacting with Hispanics and mestizos. As market relations develop and extend, bringing more Indians into relation with others, the mode of classification is likely to move towards the more individual one that emphasizes appearance. Social mobility tends to increase the size of the mestizo group and *mestizaje* provides a basis for national identification.

Ancestry

The English settlers in North America were ill-prepared by their culture and previous experience for creating a society which could include red and black people as well as white. Their religion emphasized the faith of the individual believer; it led some of its adherents to see the distinctions between peoples as ordained by God, and to concentrate upon building up exclusive communities. Their law did not recognize any personal status other than that of the free man, so that, when legal institutions came to take account of the existence of slavery within English communities, the slave was regarded as an article of property. Their culture was already individual- istic, competitive and market-orientated. Whereas the Portuguese and Spaniards had known the Moors as opponents to be respected, English attitudes may have been moulded by the disastrous experience of Ireland. In 1565 the English government, determined to assert its claim of sovereignty over Ireland, sent out a series of colonizing parties involving many of the same West Country gentlemen who were to be leading figures in the earliest projects for settlements in North America. These parties were concerned not so much to establish English rule over Irish peasants as, in some places at least, to replace them with Englishmen. The Celtic Irish were to be displaced because they were savages. This has led George M. Fredrickson (1981:20) to distinguish an English ethos or ideology of colonization from a Dutch one. The former implied the seizure of land, the expulsion as a group of those presently occupying it, and the establish- ment of a territorial claim. The latter implied trade with the native peoples and an acceptance of cultural differences without large-scale conquest of territory.

The English plan was, by negotiation with the Amerindians, to obtain land for their own use. It provided for the preaching of the gospel to infidels and savages, but no schemes for subordinating them. Those members of the colonizing party who could not pay for their own passage undertook to serve a merchant or his assignees in a particular colony for a period of time calculated as sufficient to repay the merchant's costs and allow him a profit. Thus a skilled worker had to contract for a shorter period than an unskilled man. On arrival in the colony the merchant or his representative sold this contract to a planter or farmer. The contractor guaranteed the servant his maintenance and certain 'freedom dues' on its expiry; at any time before this, the right to the servant's labour could be sold to a new master for the balance of the term (Galenson, 1981). The discovery of a new source of labour must have been an unexpected development. In 1619, at a time when the Virginia colony was twelve years old, a Dutch vessel appeared off Jamestown which wanted to dispose of some 'negars' captured from a Spanish vessel. The colonists acquired twenty 'Negars' but on what terms it is impossible to tell. It would appear that some were required to serve for a fixed period, like indentured servants. When a child was born in Virginia to one couple from among this group, the child was baptized; since there is no record of the parents' being baptized it can be inferred that they had been converted to Christianity before coming to Virginia.

In 1624 a Negro named John Philip was accorded the status of a freeman and allowed to give testimony in a court case because he had been

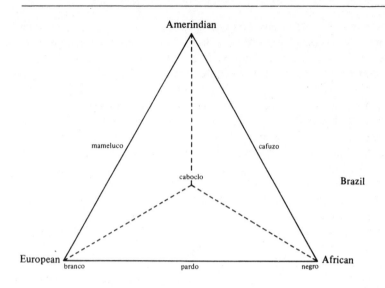

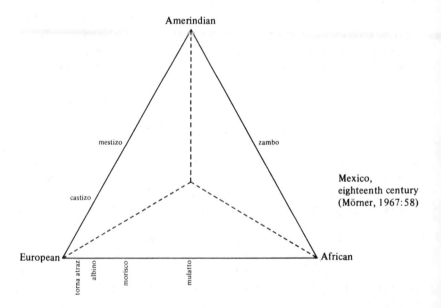

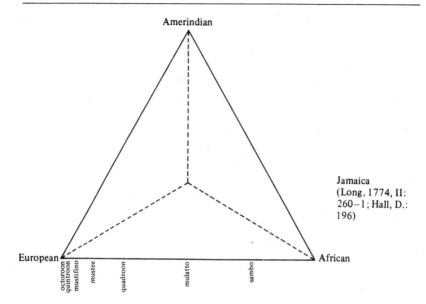

Figure 1 Terms used to identify people of mixed ancestry

'Christened in *England* 12 years since'. This suggests that the early colonists may have thought it unlawful to hold baptized Christians in perpetual slavery; it helps explain why, in the 1630s and 40s, some of the Africans in Virginia and Maryland were regarded as slaves and others not. It makes less strange one of the many ironies of Afro-American history, that the first recorded case of a black man going to court to claim that he was being unlawfully held in bondage, should have been one in which the defendant was also a black man.

The evidence from Virginia is particularly interesting because it suggests that the English did not from the outset assume that Europeans, Indians and Africans were distinct in appearance, ancestry and socio-cultural status and had to be kept so. Quite possibly religious status was as or more important than appearance or ancestry; certainly the colonists in this period used at first to refer to themselves as Christians rather than as whites. The assumption that Englishmen were free and Africans were slaves was created in the 1660s at a time when the purchase of slaves became a better long-term investment for the planters than the acquisition of indentured servants. As Fredrickson (1981:78–9) says, the important decision of the 1660s was not that there could be slaves, for there already were, but that converted slaves could be held in bondage. It was not until 1682 that the last loophole was closed by an enactment making slaves of all those arriving 'whose parentage and native country are not Christian at the time of their first purchase . . . by some Christian'. This meant that a Christian could be held as a slave because people in Africa were not Christians.

From this time forward blacks were identified as slaves and slaves assumed to be black. There were exceptions, at least to the first of these assumptions, but free blacks were increasingly seen as anomalies and were subject to restrictions. In 1670 the Virginia legislature had barred them from owning white servants, but such legal handicaps were probably less burdensome than pressures that had no statutory backing. There were parts of the United States where distinct communities of people of mixed origin were formed (most notably in New Orleans after the purchase of Louisiana in 1803) and terms were used to describe varying degrees of mixture, like mulatto, quadroon, octoroon and mustee (see Figure 1 for a comparison of terms used in three countries, though it should be noted that those used in English-speaking countries for persons of mixed European and mulatto ancestry varied from one locality to another). The closer people of mixed ancestry approached being white, the finer were the distinctions that were drawn, because it was proximity to the whites that determined status. In South Carolina too, there was a significant mulatto class and the courts there were unwilling to equate its members with the blacks.

At the end of the eighteenth century in the United States it seemed as if the economic circumstances were unfavourable to slavery and might lead to its abandonment in the South as in the North, but the boom in cotton brought a boom in slave-holding. This strengthened the identification of a dark complexion with the slave status, though not without a succession of struggles. With the growth in the number of persons free and unfree, of fair complexion, and the existence of a class of free 'persons of colour' who in their cultural attributes were superior to many poor whites, there were forces all over the south which worked in favour of a three-tier social order. These forces were held in check by the unavailability of any distinctive sector in the economic structure which the intermediate group could secure for themselves, and by white hostility, especially from the white working class. From early times the Southern state legislatures had restricted the power of slave-holders to give slaves their freedom (witness the way Thomas Jefferson had to petition the Virginia legislature in his will that certain of his slaves might be manumitted), and, with the growing tension, these states tightened their many controls over the free blacks. Indeed, at the end of the 1850s radical legislators in many Southern states pressed vigorously for laws to re-enslave all free blacks who would not leave those states (Berlin, 1974). The South came to emphasize ancestry as the main criterion of status and the entire country moved towards a two-category system in which people were to be classified as either white or black; those with any recognizable degree of African ancestry were assigned the black category. Words like mulatto for people of mixed ancestry dropped out of use. The terminology had to reflect political realities which, by the end of the century, meant that when a fair-complexioned person was assigned to the black category he usually lost the right to vote and was denied equal treatment in public services, in the economic sphere, and before the courts. The implications of the United States mode of classification were more drastic than those of Brazil and Mexico.

Comparisons

Of the three methods of classifying people, the main contrast is between the Brazilian use of individual attributes among which appearance is but one, and the United States use of ancestry to ascribe people to one or other of two opposed categories. The problems posed for social science by the three modes of classification will be further explored in Chapter 4 and the underlying social processes analysed in Chapter 6, but for the present it may be helpful to compare the Brazilian and United States forms as a contrast between two modes of appraisal. Imagine that when one person meets another he obtains an impression about the other's education and wealth, that he makes a judgement about him from his mode of dress and his complexion, and that he gives the other marks out of 10 in respect of each of these. Imagine that in Brazil the other man is a dark-skinned lawyer; he might score 9 on education, 6 on wealth, 8 on costume and 1 on complexion, an average of 6; he would rank above a fair-complexioned bank clerk who scored 5, 3, 4 and 8 on the four scales. In the United States a similar pattern of assessing people usually obtains within white groups and within black groups but in many situations of contact between whites and blacks the decision about whether the other person is white or black is separate and distinct from the appraisal of status within the category in question. The Brazilian pattern is that of a continuous scale of social status; in the United States there have been two categories which usually have not been allowed to overlap.

In the United States the criterion of ancestry was used to assign people of mixed origin to the black category because it suited the more powerful white section of the population to do it that way. But it could be equally logical to use the same criterion, in a two-category system, to ascribe people of mixed origin to the white group. There could be situations in which the whites wanted to increase as much as possible the relative size of their group and chose this as one way of doing it. The nearest example to this may be the way that, in the Netherlands Indies in the nineteenth century, many people of mixed ancestry were accepted legally as Europeans, and in the

Netherlands today such 'Indonesians' are counted as white even though their complexions may be fairly dark. But a more general response, in the Netherlands Indies as in southern Africa, was for the whites to use multiple criteria of ancestry to buttress their position by creating a three- or four-tier structure. To belong to the top tier, predominantly white ancestry was required; while mixed ancestry conferred membership in an intermediate group. Ancestry in a population group distinct from that of the subordinate group, as with Indians in South and East Africa, has also been used as a principle for assigning people to membership in an intermediate group. Among white South Africans one of the themes of political discussion over many years has been the argument that it is in the interest of the white group to make allies of the intermediate groups. The ideology of apartheid can be seen as an attempt to keep the three dimensions of classification congruent so that whites, Cape Coloured (or browns), Indians, and blacks, remain distinctive, and it is not necessary to emphasize any one dimension of difference more than the others; nevertheless the practice of apartheid, being based on white interests, places most stress on the white/non-white distinction, pushing the Coloureds and Indians towards the blacks and depriving the whites of potential allies.

The mode of classification has implications for the number of classes, or categories, in the classificatory system. The use of ancestry as a criterion tends to result in a small number of categories, as in the two-category system of the Deep South. Where socio-cultural status is used, there will be at least as many categories as there are ethnic groups in the population; if two groups are in active competition there can be two clearly defined socio-cultural categories, but the pattern is likely to be less stark than where ancestry is employed, and there will be more recognition of varying degrees of status. Where classification is by appearance, the categories will be variable and will rarely form the basis for the formation of social groups. Thus, with classification by ancestry, the dominant group will assign an individual to a category, ascribing to him or her a status as difficult to alter as assignment to the male or female gender. With classification by socio-cultural status there will, at the margins of groups, be opportunity for self-assignment to the group identity which the individual prefers. With the third mode, classification by appearance will be one component in an appraisal of status on an individual rather than a group basis.

European expansion into the Americas, Africa and Asia has been only one of the great population movements that have led to the appearance of what whites have called racial relations. The other great movements of expansion have been those of the Chinese and Indians (in which are to be included the inhabitants of what are now Pakistan, Bangladesh and Sri Lanka). The Europeans for the most part moved into slightly populated territories and established themselves as masters. When they have lost their supremacy most of them have left, though in a few countries, like Kenya, significant numbers of whites have accommodated themselves to black rule. The Chinese for the most part expanded into Southeast Asia as independent traders and businessmen, keeping their ties with the sending society through lineage organizations and secret societies. Since they have been economically successful and they maintain their distinctive culture, they have been in sharp conflict with indigenous groups in Malaysia and Indonesia. The Indian expansion occurred in a framework of political weakness, since they were recruited as indentured labourers for agricultural work in Burma, Ceylon, Malaya, Mauritius, South Africa, Guyana, Trinidad, Fiji, and elsewhere. In several of these countries the Indian population expanded and its members succeeded in business, so that they have challenged the political predominance of the native population and obtained a powerful position in the country's economic life. The principles governing modes of social classification in the New World should be applicable to the structures arising from the expansion of the Chinese and Indians as well as of the Europeans. Though this book starts with the Europeans in the New World, it develops modes of analysis that can be applied to the results of contact between all human populations.

3

Changing conceptions of race

Amerindians, Europeans and Africans in the New World differed from one another in many ways, physically and culturally (especially in language, religion, and technical abilities). Some whites all along maintained that the only distinction that really mattered was that between people who were Christians and those who had not yet been brought to that faith, but this viewpoint was never taken seriously outside a small minority. In other parts of the world where there have been encounters between peoples of different appearance and the dominant group has been Muslim, religious distinctions have sometimes over-ridden those of physical appearance (as in one period of Malaysian history). The opposition between groups has been sharper when it could be identified with physical differences, but the significance attributed to such differences has varied.

It is of the greatest importance to appreciate that relations between reds, whites and blacks in the New World were not described in racial terms until the latter half of the nineteenth century. To begin with, the various groups were identified by labels which related to their cultural or physical characteristics; they were called Spaniards or Indians, blacks or mestizos. Then groups of common ancestry were referred to as races, but the word 'race' was used simply to designate the group and played no part in any attempt to explain the nature of the individuals who were members of it. That came later. In the nineteenth century, especially in North America, blacks and whites were called races and it was assumed that the biological nature, characteristic of each group, influenced the relations between members of the two groups. Later still, with the rise of sociological explanations, it was argued that the relations between members of two such groups were primarily determined by the political and economic structure within which, as part of a historical process, they were brought into inter-relation.

This chapter seeks to explain how the meaning of the word race changed over time, how it came to be applied to reds, whites and blacks in the New World, and to their inter-relations, and what the social consequences were of representing the differences between them as racial rather than as national, cultural or politico-economic differences. It would be better if this could be done comparatively. The way in which differences between peoples were represented in European languages and cultures might be compared with corresponding representations in Chinese and Indian languages and cultures, and the variations related to differences in the overseas expansion of European, Chinese and Indian peoples. Unfortunately it is well-nigh impossible to make such a comparison in the present state of knowledge about the cultures and histories concerned.

Presentism

Students of the social sciences are taught to recognize ethnocentricism as a form of bias. They are less frequently taught to recognize its partner, which might well be termed 'chronocentrism', but is coming to be known by the simpler designation of 'presentism'. This is the tendency to interpret other historical periods in terms of the concepts, values and understanding of the present time.

The historical study of racial thought and attitudes has often been flawed by an unreflecting presentism. Earlier writers are held up to scorn without any adequate attempt to locate their understandings within the context of the knowledge available to their generation. Modern writers all too easily neglect the shifts in the meaning attributed to the word race. This chapter will outline the main shifts, contending that, as new modes of explanation of human variation have arisen, so the word race has been used in new ways, but the old usages have often continued alongside the new ones. 'Race', and its associated words suggesting commonality of ancestry or character, were developed into popular modes of thought and expression in many European languages in the eighteenth century so that they constituted an idiom in which people related themselves to others and developed conceptions of their own attributes. In the nineteenth century this idiom was extended through the identification of race with nation (and *Volk*), and the rise of potent beliefs about national character. Where previously there had been an emphasis upon supposed innate differences between persons distant in social rank, the stress was changed to differences between people of distinct nations. Political circumstances helped mould these changes but they cannot be fully appreciated without taking account of changes in scientific understanding.

Possibly the most notable feature of race as a concept is the way it has inveigled observers into assuming that the main issue is that of the nature of differences between populations, and that they should concentrate upon what 'race' *is*, as if this would determine the one scientifically valid use for the word. Physical differences catch people's attention so readily that they are less quick to appreciate that the validity of 'race' as a concept depends upon its value as an aid in explanation. From this standpoint, the main issue is the use of the word race, both in rational argument and in more popular connections, for people use beliefs about race, nationality, ethnicity and class as resources when they cultivate beliefs about group identities.

The failure to allow for changes in the sense in which the word race has been used has important consequences; those who misunderstand the past of their society are likely to misunderstand the present, since people judge the present in the light of what they believe the past to have been. If changes in the significance of words are not appreciated, the past will not be properly understood. The historian (or sociologist) judges his predecessors, but will himself be judged by a later generation because he is not standing outside history. Since the limitations of his knowledge will bemuse his successors, he should be charitable in assessing the limitations of his predecessors.

Phenotypical variation

Confronted with others who looked so different, people must constantly have asked: 'Why are they not like us?' If some exaggeration may be permitted in order to present the argument in its simplest form, it can be suggested that the educated European in the middle of the eighteenth, the middle of the nineteenth, and the middle of the twentieth centuries, would have offered different explanations of the reason why Europeans, Africans and Asians looked different. Moreover, these explanations of human variation would have corresponded (though not precisely) to the kinds of explanation acceptable in the biological science of their time. If 'race' was used as a term in that explanation, then the significance attributed to the word would have been different in the three instances. In the eighteenth century it might have been said that Africans and Asians looked different because they were of different descent, and 'race' might have been used to designate a line of descent, as in writing of 'the race of Abraham'. In the middle of the nineteenth century such explanations might well have been considered unsatisfactory and it might have been asserted that the outward differences between Africans and Asians were part of a more general pattern of variation in the mental abilities of groups and their suitability for living in particular regions of the world. In the wake of this mode of explanation 'race' came to be used as a synonym for 'type', which was on occasion defined as a primitive or original form independent of climatic or other physical influences. Types were thought to be permanent, so the theory of racial typology left no room for the modes of explanation introduced by Darwin and Mendel.

The educated man addressing himself to these questions in the middle of the twentieth century would not have been satisfied with either of these explanations. He would, or should, have said that Africans and Asians looked different because they inherited different genes. In the African gene-pool the genes determining such physical features as skin colour, were different because the process of natural selection had operated in favour of genes conferring an advantage in the environment in which people had to live. He would have explained that physical variation could not be accounted for by reference to a postulated range of pure types, but was the product of adaptation by selection and had to be studied statistically using the methods of population genetics. In this scheme of thought, the word race can be used as a synonym for sub-species, that is, a sub-division of a species which is distinctive because its members are isolated from other individuals belonging to the same species. Because of their isolation, its members mate with one another and so reproduce their distinctive features, but if, through migration, their isolation were reduced and they mated with others of the same species but not sub-species, their distinctiveness would disappear.

This chapter seeks to explain the main variations in the use of the word race by relating them to these modes of explanation. It argues that throughout the three centuries 'race' has been used both as a taxon, to designate categories of mankind, and as an explanans, to explain certain of their characteristics, but the relation between designation and explanation has varied. When 'race' has been used to identify a group of people of common descent it has often been a synonym for 'nation'; it has served to identify a population but there has been little suggestion that by so identifying it, any special characteristics of the population have been explained. When 'race' has been used with the implication that it designates a permanent zoological type, its claim to explanatory power has been much higher. When 'race' has been used as meaning 'sub-species', the implication has been that the individuals so designated have something in common biologically though, without further investigation, this may explain relatively little about them.

Reference to Figure 2 may be helpful to clarify the distinctions which are required to sort out the confusions surrounding the word race and its history. The first column serves to indicate that humans in all periods of history and in many regions of the globe have differed in complexion, hair form, physique, and so on. Scientists today, whatever their nationality, can recognize the expression 'phenotypical variation' as a suitable designation for these differences. To explain such variation they use the concepts of population genetics. These are analytical concepts with a technical significance independent of the popular understanding that the man in the street in Tokyo, Lagos or Atlanta has of the cause of variation. Popular theories which seek to answer the question 'why are they not like us?' utilize

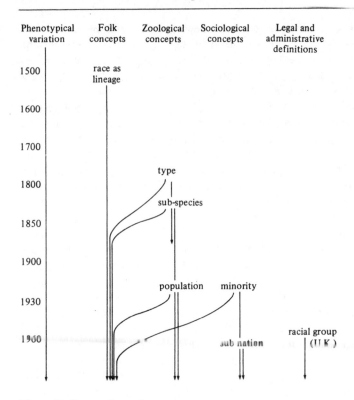

Figure 2 Conceptions of race

folk* concepts which usually have little scientific value, but since people organize their lives by using folk concepts, they can affect human behaviour. What the man in the Atlanta street or the foreman down the South African mine has believed about the nature of race has often been more influential than what the biologist has demonstrated. The second column records the entry of the word race into the English language as one

---

* A folk concept is a term in a popular as opposed to a scientific explanation. For example, in 1952 the author was living just outside a West African town. One night there was a great din, sounding as if half the population had turned out of their houses in order to beat the bottoms of saucepans or other drum-like objects. After half an hour or so it subsided. On enquiring next morning he was told that the moon had been getting smaller because the Devil had been eating it, but the Muslims had made a noise and frightened him off. Science would refer to the event as a partial lunar eclipse, an analytical concept, and would explain it in terms of scientific cosmology. Those who made the noise acted in terms of a folk cosmology which saw events in the sky as resulting from action by spirits, and the Devil was the folk concept they employed to explain the eclipse. There are, of course, plenty of Western folk explanations, such as the readiness to interpret individual characteristics of temperament as inherited from particular ancestors.

used in common speech to refer to a line of people of common descent, with the implication that their similarity of appearance or temperament was the result of shared ancestry. In the eighteenth century, botanists, most notably Linnaeus, developed systems of classification, or taxonomies, to identify the various forms of plant and animal life. A taxon is a class or category within such a scheme; it classifies but it does not explain unless it is part of a theory. The third column represents the way that 'race' came to be identified with zoological theories that attempted to account for phenotypical variation. The fourth and fifth columns make reference to sociological concepts and official definitions introduced because the popular under-standing of 'race' was too unreliable for use in these contexts. Many people in twentieth-century Europe and North America who have an understanding of why peoples differ physically believe it acceptable to use 'race' as a convenient synonym for phenotypical variation. That is a matter of judgement. But to interpret an eighteenth-century statement about differences between peoples as if 'race' meant to the writer the same things as it does today would be a bad example of presentism.

As has already been mentioned, the English settlers in North America were at first inclined to refer to themselves as Christians, and to Africans as Negroes. In the middle of the seventeenth century they began more frequently to call themselves 'English' and 'free', and then, after about 1680, as 'white'. They scarcely ever used religious designations, like 'heathens', 'pagans' or 'savages' for Negroes; instead, the descriptions 'blacks' and 'Africans' came into use by the eighteenth century. Winthrop D. Jordan, in *White Over Black*, his very substantial study of American attitudes towards the Negro between 1550 and 1812, refers at times to 'the races' but it is important to remember that during this period it was unusual for the people themselves to employ the idiom of race in ordinary speech and writing. It comes into use occasionally in a literary context, as in a South Carolina poem of 1732 which remarks upon 'dark Beauties of the Sable Race,/ (Stained with the Tincture of their Sooty Sin)'. Apart from this poem, a reference to Phillis Wheatley as 'the Phoenix of her race', and uses such as 'there is not a Race of Men on Earth more False Liars . . .', Jordan furnishes no examples of North Americans using 'race' before 1776 to designate sections of the population. Nor do ideas of racial inferiority, as a modern reader understands them, very often make an appearance. Blacks are disparaged because they are slaves, the descendants of slaves, or the issue of improper unions (as in the reference to stain in the verse just quoted). At this time, even in the egalitarian United States, blacks were placed at the bottom of the social scale primarily because they were of dishonourable descent and this was supposed to be proven by their slave condition. There is plentiful evidence that whites well knew that, if slavery was to be maintained, it was necessary to preserve what one colonial governor called 'a decent distinction' between the descendants of Englishmen on the one hand, and free Negroes and mulattos on the other, but this was stated as a political requirement rather than as something biologically required or justified. In this period any such implication was more likely to be expressed in terms of the purity of blood rather than race (Jordan 1968:95, 127, 146, 165–7).

In the Spanish-speaking countries of the New World these characteristics of language and thought were more strongly marked. From the fifteenth century there was in Spain increasing concern about 'purity of blood', perhaps in some measure in reaction against the mixing of stocks that had occurred in the preceding period. The Spaniards were anxious to obtain spouses of good lineage when they married within their own group and they projected this concern onto unions with non-Spaniards. In the New World mulattos were stigmatized not because of their non-European ancestry but because they were descended from slaves. When, in 1778, the Spanish government extended to its overseas possessions certain regulations concerning marriage, they excluded mulattos, Negroes and other castas. When the Council of Chile received this instruction it replied concerning Indians that 'their origin is not vile like that of other Castas'; the Council of the Indies agreed, and Indians were given the same standing as Spaniards in the marriage regulations (Mörner, 1967:38–9). Discrimination by whites against non-whites in the eighteenth century may look as if it were motivated by the same attitudes as those familiar to a twentieth-century observer, but the appearance is deceptive.

Race as descent

It is a serious misconception to assume that the idea of race was generated in the interaction between whites and blacks in the New World. The word was introduced as a literary expression for designating a class of beings, particularly a class formed by common descent. In this sense such little explanatory power as the word could muster derived from the genealogical mode of reasoning embodied in the Bible.

When John C. Greene's book *The Death of Adam* (1959) asserts that Adam, as the first man of history, began to die in the minds of scholars about the time of Newton, the reference is not just to the declining acceptance of a Biblical story but to a whole paradigm of explanation. It also dates the change a little earlier by referring to the beginning of the process and to the most advanced thinkers of the period. As Greene remarks, 'before the seventeenth century no pressing need had been felt to group plants and animals into species, genera, orders, classes, and the like'. John Ray, the pioneering natural historian of the late seventeenth century, declared 'the number of true species in nature is fixed and limited and, as we may reasonably believe, constant and unchangeable from the first creation to the present day'. The criterion of species was common descent, presumed or actually observed. 'A species is never born from the seed of another species and reciprocally', he stated. This meant that, regardless of differences, individuals belonged to the same species if their descent from the same ancestors could be proved or reasonably inferred.

Up to the eighteenth century at least, the dominant paradigm in Europe for explaining the differences between groups of people was provided by the Old Testament. It was the story of God creating the world, and, on the sixth day, of his making Adam in his own image. The Old Testament provided a series of genealogies by which it seemed possible to trace the peopling of the world and the relations which different groups bore to one another. Thus Augustine derided the idea that there might be men in unknown lands on the other side of the world because the suggestion that some of Adam's descendants might have sailed there was 'excessively absurd'. Many writers attempted to ascertain the date when the world had been created by working back through these genealogies. Others attempted to explain the assumed inferiority of black people by reference to a curse supposedly placed by Noah on the descendants of Ham, decreeing that they should be servants of his sons Shem and Japheth; or by relating it to the dispersal of peoples after the fall of the tower of Babel. Implicit in such arguments is the assumption that differences are to be explained by tracing them back to particular events, the consequences of which are then transmitted genealogically. This is also a view of the world in which God is likely to intervene to punish or reward particular individuals and in which men are therefore less motivated to develop and improve classificatory concepts like that of species. As the quotation from John Ray indicates, a species was seen simply as the product of an arbitrary action by the Creator.

Within a paradigm of explanation in terms of descent there were several possible ways of accounting for physical variation. Firstly, it could be held that differences of colour and such-like were all part of God's design for the universe; perhaps, as in the hypothesis about the curse on Ham's descendants, they were the result of divine judgement; perhaps, though, they were a part of God's plan that had not yet been revealed or that man could not properly understand. Secondly, it could be held that physical differences were related in some way to climate and environment and were irrelevant to the important questions of man's obligations to do God's will. Thirdly, it was sometimes argued that since the differences between Europeans, Africans and Asians were repeated in successive generations they must have had separate ancestors. It was hazardous and perhaps unnecessary to challenge the story of Adam directly, so the doubters suggested that the Old Testament account was incomplete: Adam was the ancestor of the Europeans alone. The debate about whether mankind consisted of one or many stocks had to be cast in terms of the dominant paradigm and therefore it was phrased as a choice between monogenesis and polygenesis.

The use of 'race' as a term in explanations of this kind is reflected in the first major definition of the word given in the *Oxford English Dictionary* (1910), *viz*: 'I. A group of persons, animals, or plants, connected by common descent or origin'. This is the principal sense in which the word is used in English in the sixteenth, seventeenth and eighteenth centuries, and it continues to be used, though rather less frequently, in this sense. But already in the sixteenth century the notion of likeness because of descent was generalized and 'race' was used to denote instances of likeness without any claim of common descent, like Dunbar's reference in 1508 to 'backbiters of sundry races' and Sidney's of 1580 to 'the race of good men'. As the *Dictionary* records, this use continued into the nineteenth century, as with Lamb's reference to 'the two races of men': the men who borrow and the men who lend; thereafter it was less frequent.

While this literary use of the word was becoming established, natural-historians wrestled with the problems of classifying living things and of getting agreement upon the names by which the classes were to be designated. This work reached a peak in the writings of Linnaeus, and in particular in his *Systema Naturae*, the first edition of which was published in 1735. He proposed that creatures should be identified by the last two categories, the genus and the species, in what is sometimes called the binomial system. An example might be *Canis familiaris* for the domestic dog. The nomenclature adopted for birds adds a third term to identify the sub-species (or variety) and if a species is not divided into sub-species the species name is repeated; if a genus is not divided into species the genus name is repeated. Thus among the titmice the British Coal Tit is named *Parus* (tit) *ater* (black) *britannicus* (British); the House Sparrow is *Passer domesticus domesticus*; the Wren is *Troglodytes troglodytes troglodytes* (or *Troglodytes*[3]).

Linnaeus began his classification with 'Mammalia: Order I. Primates'. One subdivision was *Homo sapiens*, divided into Wild Man, American, European, Asiatic, African, and Monstrosus. This presented blacks and whites as different sub-species and not as different species. Since 1735 the taxonomic enterprise has flourished so that the modern reader who wishes to know how man stands in relation to the birds, and consults the *Encylopaedia Britannica*, proceeds within the Animal Kingdom through the following taxa: Sub kingdom 2, Branch C, Grade II, Section c3B,

Phylum 21, Sub phylum 3, before reaching Class 7 Aves and Class 8 Mammalia. The latter then divides into Sub-class and Infraclass before reaching the Order: Primates; and from there into Superfamily and Family before reaching the Genus, *Homo.* Modern man is named *Homo sapiens sapiens* to distinguish him from *Homo sapiens neanderthalensis.*

It is worth pausing over the classification of the dog, *Canis familiaris.* All domesticated dogs belong to the same species despite the obvious differences between the German Shepherd, the Spaniel and the Poodle. The latter are not sub-species or races but breeds. Their distinctive characteristics are maintained by the action of humans who control their mating. If the dogs were let loose they would interbreed and the distinctive characteristics would be lost. This draws attention to what creates a distinctive species or sub-species. In the time of Linnaeus the criterion of species was fertility: a horse and a donkey were accounted separate species because if they interbreed they produce mules which are infertile. Currently a species is defined as 'an evolved or evolving, genetically distinctive, reproductively isolated natural population' whereas a sub-species is 'a subdivision of a sexual species with all the attributes of the species except that reproductive isolation is partial rather than complete'. A species divided into sub-species is called a polytypic species. Japanese, West Africans and Eskimos are sub-species of *Homo sapiens* who maintain their physical distinctiveness from one generation to another because, from geographical isolation and cultural preference, they mostly mate with themselves rather than with Koreans, Europeans or Amerindians, but they belong to the same species since they could mate with other sub-species and produce fertile offspring. The distinction is important because in the nineteenth century the main dispute about race centred upon whether blacks and whites were different species of one genus or different sub-species of one species.

The change in the use of the word race that can be detected in the writings of Thomas Jefferson may seem very slight but it gains significance as a step towards these later developments. Jefferson is noted for advocating the abolition of slavery; as President of the United States he acted to stop the slave trade and to restrict the spread of slavery in his country. He also stood out among southerners in publicly doubting whether blacks might not be 'inferior to the whites in the endowment both of body and mind', while adding that 'whatever be their degree of talent, it is no measure of their rights'. Yet Jordan (1968:481) concludes that: 'His derogation of the Negro . . . constituted, for all its qualifications, the most intense, extensive, and extreme formulation of anti-Negro "thought" offered by any American in the thirty years after the Revolution.' Jefferson gave the word race new associations and significance, for he equated it with species, bringing together white perceptions of black Americans and the conception of an

ordered universe of the kind natural historians were describing. He
hesitated over 'the blacks, whether originally a distinct race, or made
distinct by time and circumstances' but there was 'a real distinction which
nature has made' which he bolstered, remarking that 'different species of the
same genus or varieties of the same species, may possess different
qualifications'. The prejudices of the whites, the recollections of the blacks
of their injuries, and this real distinction combined to 'produce convulsions
which will probably never end but in the extermination of the one or the
other race'. Thus he implied that the differences must be permanent and
wanted the slaves sent away to some country where they could be 'a free and
independent people' (see Jordan, 1968:429–90).

These opinions have to be set against the background of the contemporary
debate about the causes of barbarism. Why had some societies advanced to
a civilized status and not others? Those who approached this question
within the intellectual framework developed by the Scottish philosophers of
the eighteenth century stressed what they called the moral causes of
progress. Today they would be called cultural or environmental causes.
According to this school some societies had progressed because they
enjoyed the happy combination of a favourable environment and social
institutions which promoted individual liberty and political stability.
Writers of this school often believed in monogenesis: that all men were
descended from Adam and Eve, but had developed differently because of
climate and circumstance. This view was opposed by writers who stressed
the physical causes of inherited dispositions and capacities. They believed
that some societies had progressed more rapidly because they were
composed of men and women of superior talent. These authors were more
likely to subscribe to polygenesis: the doctrine that the differences between
human populations were permanent and could be traced back to separate
ancestors. Jefferson endorsed neither side. His *Notes on Virginia* in effect
advanced both arguments, suggesting that it was not necessary to choose
between them. He drew upon the literary use of 'race' to designate people of
common descent but identified it with the assumption that the people so
designated constituted a taxon in a natural classification and that their
special characteristics could be understood as a consequence of their place
in this wider order.

Race as type

In Linnaeus' view, natural history consisted of describing the various
productions of the earth, their appearance, their habits, their relations to
each other, and their uses. Implicit in this conception of classification as the
goal of science was the belief that nature had been constructed on a pattern

discoverable, at least in part, by human reason. It was man's duty to study nature diligently so that he could come closer to God, could better understand his purposes, and could glorify him in his works. At the heart of the conception of nature to which Linnaeus came was the idea of an *oeconomia*, a rationally ordered system of means and ends. The earth, with its delightful variety of climate and topography, was populated with an equally varied assemblage of living beings, each perfectly adapted to the region in which it lived. The economy of nature lay in the balance between its constituent elements. Linnaeus never tired of describing the mechanisms which maintained the adaptation of organism and environment and the equilibrium of species (Greene, 1959:134–7). God had created not a series of individual species but a self-regulating system. He did not need to intervene in the day-to-day affairs of his creation.

The man who more than anyone else extended the method of Linnaeus to the study of the animal kingdom and, though only in outline, to that of man, was the French comparative anatomist Cuvier. The system which he hoped to discover by relating animal structure to conditions of existence was the 'great catalogue in which all created beings have suitable names, may be recognized by distinctive characters, and (are) arranged in divisions and sub-divisions'. Cuvier's method of classification rested heavily upon the conception of a type (defined by the *Oxford English Dictionary* as 'a person or thing that represents the characteristic qualities of a class; a representative specimen'). If the right representative specimen was chosen, the essentials of the category could be understood. Cuvier divided man into three main sub-species (which he called races): Caucasian, Mongolian and Ethiopian, which were further sub-divided. He stated that they were all one species but they had been separated by some great natural catastrophe. He presented the three races as differing permanently in ability because of the biological differences between them that were as yet little understood. Thus the earlier physical-cause interpretation of human variation was given a new foundation.

Cuvier's influence was immense, and, during the course of the nineteenth century, the notion of type was extended to the analysis of poetry, aesthetics, biography, personality, culture, social movements, and many kinds of difference other than those of interest to biologists. Sociologists recognize it in Max Weber's concept of an ideal type. Cuvier's teaching was one of the principal factors behind the emergence, in the middle years of the nineteenth century, of an international school of anthropological thought. It is important to note that the conception of type was independent of the Linnean classificatory system. A zoological type could be a genus, a species, or a sub-species. Critics therefore protested that the notion of type was redundant since the Linnean classification sufficed. As the usual criterion for a species was that its members could breed with one another, and since the races of man engaged so frequently in interbreeding, *Homo sapiens* must be one species. The typologists criticized the orthodox definition of species. Prominent among them were Charles Hamilton Smith, Samuel George Morton, Joseph Arthur de Gobineau, Robert Knox, Josiah Clark Nott, George Robbins Gliddon, James Hunt, and Karl Vogt. They are often identified as proponents of 'scientific racism' but their central concept was not race but type, and their key proposition was that types were permanent. Therefore their theory is better designated 'racial typology'. Giving it this name has the advantage of reducing slightly the diverse significations of 'racism' today, but it should be stressed that typological thinking has been the core of most racist thought and doctrine for over a century.

Though there were variations from one writer to another and Vogt at least changed his opinions significantly, the typologists more or less agreed in presenting man as a genus divided into types which in effect were species. They believed that each type was permanent and was suited to a particular zoological province of the earth's surface; just as kangaroos were found only in Australia, so Australian Aborigines were a distinct human type forming part of that province. At the same time they recognized that the actual races of the contemporary world were all mixed; they accounted for this by arguing that hybrids were ultimately sterile so that though, because of human foolishness, races might deviate from their type, nature kept the deviation within bounds (see Banton, 1977:32–55).

The Typological Theory can be summarized as holding that:
1 Variations in the constitution and behaviour of individuals are the expression of differences between underlying types of a relatively permanent kind, each of which is suited to a particular continent or zoological province.
2 Social categories in the long run reflect and are aligned with the natural categories that produce them.
3 Individuals belonging to a particular racial type display an innate antagonism towards individuals belonging to other types, the degree of antagonism depending upon the relationship between the two types.

The typological mode of explanation differed from the previous one in being agnostic about origins. The typologists rejected earlier beliefs that the earth was about six thousand years old. Whatever might have happened in earlier epochs, within the period for which there was anatomical evidence, types appeared to have been constant. One of the main attractions of typology was that it offered a theory of history purporting to explain the differential pattern of human progress. The record of history also contributed to the theory by revealing the special cultural attributes of types that went along with the physical differences. Since changes were the outcome of the essential characteristics of types in relation to particular environments, the theory attributed little significance to purely contingent events like the reputed curse upon Ham's descendants. Though the Typological Theory could be reconciled with a belief in polygenesis it was really of a very different kind. It asserted that a person's outward appearance revealed more than his descent; it was an indicator of his place in a natural order that changed only slowly.

Asked to account for the three patterns of racial relations in the New World, someone who subscribed to the Typological Theory would have asserted that the settlement of persons of European and African origin in new zoological provinces could not succeed. Hybrid forms would prove infertile and the territories would ultimately revert to the indigenous type which alone was suited to them. In the short term, however, the sharper distinction between blacks and whites in the United States was because the innate antipathy between Saxon and the Negro was greater than that between any two other types; the Portuguese was less averse to mixing, but the outcome would be no different in the end. Gobineau would not have argued thus, since he did not believe in the infertility of hybrids, but he would have represented the differences between American regions as short-term consequences of variations in 'historical chemistry' as mankind declined to a state in which all men would be of similar physical appearance and cultural mediocrity.

Long before the Typological Theory was proclaimed, there had been white writers who disparaged the abilities of blacks. James Walvin's documentary history of the Negro in England collects a variety of extracts from books and pamphlets from the sixteenth to the nineteenth century in which the authors speculate about the origins of differences between blacks and whites, speak for and against the slave trade, and dispute about the industry of blacks in the West Indies. Apart from the egregious Edward Long, hardly any author uses the word 'race'. Even Thomas Carlyle in his notorious *Occasional Discourse on the Nigger Question* of 1849 neither used it nor attempted to explain why Negroes were as incapable as he maintained. In the later eighteenth and early nineteenth centuries, especially in the United States, there were plenty of statements asserting the inferiority of blacks, but they did not necessarily claim that the differences were permanent. They tended to be particular statements, related to the speaker's experience. The political significance of the doctrine of typology was that it lifted such statements onto a plane of greater generality and offered an explanation. To assert that blacks were inferior might convince some people, but to say that blacks were one racial type out of a limited range and that the same principles which explained the whole range of phenomena also explained the particular characteristics of blacks was to advance a thesis of much greater intellectual pretension.

It will be apparent that typological explanations of social patterns could easily be manipulated so as to appear plausible to members of the general public. Indeed, the area of racial theory provides many illustrations of the importance of Sir Karl Popper's contention that it is easy to find confirming evidence in support of a theory: the main task is to test a theory by seeking disconfirming evidence.

Race as sub-species

Charles Darwin's *The Origin of Species, or The Preservation of Favoured Races in the Struggle for Life*, of 1859, cut the ground from under the feet of the typologists by demonstrating that there were no permanent forms in nature. Each species was adapted to its environment by natural selection, so that people of one racial type who migrated to a new habitat would there undergo change. The ups and downs of history could therefore not be explained in terms of the qualities of particular types. In the *Origin* Darwin recognized 'geographical races or sub-species' as local forms completely fixed and isolated, but concluded that since they did not differ from each other in important characteristics there was no certain way of deciding whether they should be considered species or varieties. He employed the word race primarily when referring to domestic races as the outcome of human breeding, and presented them as incipient species, for, as his subtitle suggested, it was by natural selection that favoured races became species (Darwin, 1859: 62–3, 73).

Darwin's revolution was so complex (Mayr, 1972) that it took decades for even the specialists to appreciate its implications. In the 1930s, more than seventy years after the publication of the *Origin*, new lines of reasoning and research in biology led to the establishment of population genetics. Human variation was to be comprehended statistically in terms of the frequencies of given genes within the gene pool of the relevant population. This meant that, for biologists, 'population' was the successor concept to the discredited notion of racial type, and that race could be legitimately used only as a synonym for sub-species, as explained above.

Yet the first adaptations of Darwinian thought to social affairs preserved much of the older mode of explanation, in part because the reorientation demanded of people was so great, and in part because of the particular circumstances of the late nineteenth century. That period saw unparalleled technological advances which helped knit together the peoples of Europe in larger, more effective units, and to increase the gap between them and the peoples of most other regions. Social evolution was therefore pictured not as adaptation to changing environments but as the story of man's progress to superior modes of living. Sociologists represented it as a process in which men first lived in small bands, then successively as members of clans, tribes, peoples, states and empires. Groups designated as races were often thought to belong somewhere in such a scale; skin colour and similar traits served as signs of membership in groups that had progressed in different measure, and therefore functioned as boundary markers. The emphasis was upon the way social processes exercised a selective influence upon inherited biological variations.

Social theories deriving their inspiration from these new forms of explanation are commonly referred to as Social Darwinism, but this is a misleading expression since it is so difficult to identify any coherent and readily distinguishable body of thought that corresponds to this label (Halliday, 1971). It is less confusing to speak of a Selectionist Theory, such as was stated most clearly by Sir Arthur Keith in 1931 (Banton, 1977:100). This theory holds that:

1 Evolution may be assisted if interbreeding populations are kept separate so that they can develop their special capacities (as in animal breeding).
2 Racial prejudice serves this function and in so doing reinforces racial categories in social life.
3 Therefore racial categories are determined by evolutionary processes of inheritance and selection.

Someone who favoured the Selectionist Theory might well believe, with Keith, that racial differentiation is a process making for the improvement of mankind. Where the typologists inferred that pure races must have existed in the past, the selectionists see racial purity as something constantly advanced as men adapt to new circumstances causing their groups to evolve. A people's determination to decide its own destiny, which itself derives from natural selection, can dictate what the major social groups will be. This determination, a Selectionist might say, has been strongest among white Americans, for they have done most to maintain racial boundaries, but can also be discerned among mulatto groups when they come to feel a distinctive identity. In such a way each group develops the abilities which will be of most use in its particular environment. Selectionist theories have been refined and developed recently within the new school of thought known as sociobiology (see, e.g., Reynolds, 1981:27–34) by the use of concepts of inclusive fitness, kin selection, and reciprocal altruism. Early formulations of the theory of natural selection presented biological fitness as dependent not upon the physical and mental powers of an individual but upon the number of offspring he or she left. Fitness was a matter of differential reproduction. But, since a person's brothers and sisters have many of the same genes, these can be passed on as well through one sibling as another. When it is a question of a group's survival or expansion it is the inclusive fitness of the group that counts rather than the relative fitness of individual members. When animals or insects related by kinship help one another this gives their common genes an advantage in the selection process. For example, among hive bees the workers are sterile females and, since sisters are more closely related genetically than are parents and offspring, the worker bees favour the reproduction of their own genes most efficiently by helping their mother the queen produce more sisters for them by a kind of factory farming of the queen bee. Kin selection is the outcome of their social organization. The behaviour of the worker bees is a kind of altruism, since they forgo the possibility of reproducing themselves in order to maximize reproduction by the queen and in so doing maintain the hive as a society. Among other examples of altruism are the emission of alarm calls which help others of the same species but attract dangerous attention to the one giving the call. There are birds which will feign injury when their nest is threatened, attempting to attract the predator's attention to themselves, and there are animals which forgo reproduction under environmental conditions that are adverse to their group. Such forms of apparently altruistic behaviour are now seen as ways of optimizing the production of common genes. When the same process is extended to non-kin it is called reciprocal altruism; this amounts to a willingness to help others if they in return will help the first animal in any way that will help it reproduce.

The Selectionist Theory may be regarded as a biological rather than a sociological theory. Its proponents would consider this irrelevant, since what matters most is a theory's ability to explain observations. Pierre L. van den Berghe has applied sociobiological reasoning to the study of racial and ethnic relations, arguing that ethnicity is an extension of kinship and that the sentiments associated with it are of the same nature as those encountered between kin, although diluted. He combines inclusive fitness and kin selection by writing of nepotism, and adds two other determinants of social organization: reciprocity and coercion. If by reciprocity he means only those forms which assist reproduction, this is not explicitly stated, but coercion is described as the use or threat of force which enhances the fitness of those able to exercise this power. Van den Berghe (1981:37–8) states that while the general paradigm is that organisms behave so as to maximize their inclusive fitness, human behaviour is also influenced by an individual's assessment of the relative costs and benefits of particular transactions, though in the last analysis successful competition over scarce resources is converted into reproductive success.

It is certainly possible that our behaviour is determined by our genes to a greater extent than we realize, but speculation about possible determinants is, by itself, of little value. Charles Darwin, after having written out a sketch of his theory of natural selection, devoted eight years to an examination of sexuality in barnacles as the most expeditious way of subjecting his ideas to empirical test. Van den Berghe asserts (1981:240) that the genetic basis of the tendency to favour kin is clearly shown by the ease with which parental feelings take precedence over racial feeling in cases of racial admixture. It should not be difficult to compare the strength of feelings expressed for their children by natural parents, adoptive parents and foster parents, but apparently it has not been done. When someone has identified the sociological equivalent of Darwin's barnacles, and conducted tests that produce positive results, it will be easier to consider such extravagant claims.

The crucial question concerns the extent to which the explanation of social behaviour can be reduced, *without remainder*, to the terms of a biological explanation. Van den Berghe seems at times to equivocate (1981:5, 239) since he holds both that human behaviour 'must be analysed at three distinct but interrelated levels: genetic, ecological and cultural; and that ethnicity is a special basis of sociality, irreducible to any other'. He contends that some, but not all, observations at each level can be explained in terms of factors operating at the next lower level, but he exaggerates the extent to which this is possible and neglects the problems of explaining the observations which constitute the remainder, particularly at the ecological level. He claims that his theory 'accounts better for the appearance *and disappearance* of racism in various times and places than competing theories that attribute racism either to ideological factors . . . or to the capitalist mode of production' (1981:32, italics added). His theory is impossible to test. It could be suggested that the relative fitness of reds, whites and blacks is assessed by their relative rate of population increase, ignoring the different average duration of life in Stockholm and Calcutta and the quality of life available to people in those cities. If in the future vast numbers were to die either in Scandinavia or India, from whatever cause, this too could be interpreted in terms of differential fitness. The theory would serve simply to sanctify the events of history. If the theory is advanced to explain 'the appearance of racism' it is first necessary to define racism. Has it appeared in Brazil? If it is to be found in the United States but not in Brazil where is the explanation of the difference? If there is racism in Brazil, and everywhere else that blacks and whites have encountered one another, then racism is simply a feature of such encounters and cannot be independently explained. A consideration of the historical evidence about 'racism' in different countries surely shows beyond doubt that there are variations from one time and place to another. Just because these various kinds of thought and behaviour are sometimes identified by a single name does not permit a scholar to assume that it can be treated as a unitary phenomenon for the purpose of comparing the power of competing explanations.

The difficulty with all evolutionary theories is that of determining whether particular developments have an evolutionary function or not. If everything has such a function the argument becomes circular and it is no longer a theory. If some things do not have such a function, can this be established at the time or only long afterwards? Human societies develop values which help people cooperate with others in ever larger units, but can they not also develop dysfunctional values like a desire to exploit others politically, economically, or sexually? Is it to be asserted that every form of vice serves an evolutionary function? If not, by what objective criteria can it be determined whether racial prejudice is a vice or a virtue? Those who speak for selectionist theories tend to see socio-cultural evolution as a mode of evolution which enables humans to evolve more rapidly than other species. It is seen as an extension of biological evolution and human culture is regarded as a part of nature. Yet it is equally valid to argue that socio-cultural evolution has been responsible for the emergence of modes of consciousness for which there are no parallels among species affected by biological evolution alone. What are considered social virtues may have functions in socio-cultural evolution which can in no way be understood if they are seen solely in the context of biological evolution.

The theory of evolution as this is understood by biologists is complicated and not easily grasped by those without a specialist training, but within biology it is certainly a falsifiable theory. Unfortunately, appeal is sometimes made to Darwin's authority by those who advance conjectural schemes about how human societies might have developed. Since there can be no test of how they would have developed had circumstances been otherwise, this is not within the realm of theoretical discourse but in that of the philosophy of history. The social scientist has other tasks to get on with, for when groups are in competition their members display in-group solidarity and out-group hostility in ways that can be studied scientifically. The understanding of what is involved in these situations can be better advanced by studying these problems than by presenting them as the outgrowth, at several stages remove, of evolutionary functions. The Selectionist Theory cannot be disproved; it is simply less powerful as an explanation of the detailed features of inter-group relations.

Folk concepts of race

Race was first used in English as a folk concept and began to acquire an analytical or scientific aura only in the nineteenth century when it was used in the way that an eighteenth-century scholar, writing in Latin, would have used *genus*; or perhaps it was used as a synonym for species. But even so this practice was vigorously disputed, for if race was a synonym for species it was redundant (Banton, 1977:30). Nevertheless, it gained ground, being used (as has been seen) in the sub-title of Darwin's *Origin*. English writers employed it frequently when elaborating their philosophies of history, for it was widely believed that the growing economic and political strength of the European powers sprang from qualities inherent in the white race, or races, and that these promised continuing European supremacy. For example, Sir Charles Dilke in the book *Greater Britain* which was first published in 1868 but went through many editions, wrote primarily in celebration of the positive qualities of the English stock rather than to disparage the people of other stocks. (See Biddiss (ed.), 1979, for other examples of the varying senses in which the word race was used.)

In the latter half of the nineteenth century and the first quarter of the twentieth, an interest in race was associated more strongly with radical than with conservative political philosophies. The radicals looked to science for a more rational way of organizing society. Race seemed to offer a key to the interpretation of human history and a weapon for attacking the Church and the superstitions it defended. Knox and Vogt were both radicals, while Nott and Gliddon loved 'parson-skinning'. Marx at one time thought 'the common Negro type is only a degeneration of a much higher one' and Engels that the lowest savages had regressed to a more animal-like condition. Both accepted every contemporary stereotype of the Jews; they agreed that the Czechoslovakian peoples and South Slavs were 'ethnic trash', while Engels disputed the claims of Czechs, Serbs, Croats and Ruthenians to independence from Habsburg and Turkish rule on the grounds that they were peoples 'without any history', lacking any natural capacity for self-government and doomed to be ruled by more advanced nations (Paul, 1981; see Challoner and Henderson, 1975; and Watson, 1977:129–30).

Though appeal to race could easily be used in the service of imperial expansion, the experience of the South African War of 1899–1902 was a salutary check upon assumptions of British power, not only overseas but at home. It came as a shock to discover how physically unfit were the men who lived in the big-city slums. Of 11,000 Manchester men who volunteered for the armed services, 8,000 had to be turned away and of the remainder 2,000 were declared fit only for the militia. Concern for the physical efficiency of the population became intermingled with the problem of the declining birth-rate. In 1905 Cecil Chesterton, then a Fabian socialist with Tory leanings (after the manner of Bernard Shaw), was writing 'in the last resort, the empire, all efficiency, depends upon the kind of race we breed'. The need for national efficiency became a slogan crossing party lines and most of the

Fabian leaders were at one time or another attracted to the Eugenics movement and its fear that Britain was breeding a race of degenerates (Searle, 1971:60–1).

Sidney and Beatrice Webb, leading representatives for progressive thought in their day, were convinced of the inequality of races. So too was E. D. Morel, a man of impeccable liberal credentials who had done so much to expose abuses in the Belgian Congo. The Webbs were impressed, indeed alarmed, by the efficiency of the Japanese. Writing in the *New Statesman* in 1913 on 'The Guardianship of the Non-adult Races' they were explicit about the child-like character of Britain's wards: 'the child is growing up . . . whereas it used to be only seven years old, it is now fourteen'. They maintained that 'as regards many parts of the British Empire it would be idle to pretend that anything like effective self-government can be introduced for many generations to come – in some cases, conceivably never'. Moreover they suspected that only parts of the Anglo-Saxon race possessed those qualities most conducive to the development of socialism. In July 1914 Beatrice foresaw an 'impending catastrophe' by racial invasion 'by outcasts from Southern Europe, mongrels from Algeria, and coolies from China'. This, she wrote, 'seems to me a bigger tragedy than any hypothetical defeat by an army of Germans' (Winter, 1974). When, after the war, the French used African troops in their occupation of the Rhineland, E. D. Morel published scare-mongering articles in the Labour Party newspaper, the *Daily Herald*, edited by George Lansbury who was later to become leader of the party. One was headlined 'Black Scourge in Europe. Sexual Horror let loose by France on Rhine. Disappearance of young German girls.' Morel's campaigning about the 'Black Horror on the Rhine' (the title of a pamphlet he wrote) was favourably received in left-wing circles. He saw the African as a child of the tropics unequipped to survive modern capitalist exploitation (Reinders, 1968). Racial thinking gained a remarkably firm hold upon almost all shades of political and social thought in Britain during the first quarter of the century (as it did in many European countries). Only with the rise of Nazism did the critics start to gain ground.

The older literary use of race in the sense of lineage has persisted in English though it seems increasingly quaint. Book I of Sir Winston Churchill's *History of the English-speaking Peoples* was entitled 'The Island Race'. In 1957 he could still write, about the early twentieth century, 'meanwhile in Europe the Mighty strength of the Teutonic race, hitherto baffled by division or cramped in lingering mediaeval systems, began to assert itself with volcanic energy' (1958:Preface). There cannot now be many people left who believe that the ups and downs of nations are a reflection of racial qualities rather than technological skill and the possession of material resources, though this is not a question that has been thought worthy of detailed investigation. From a political point of view the important feature is that there exists an elastic folk concept of race that can be utilized in ways that lack biological or social scientific justification. This folk concept draws heavily upon the Typological Theory which has been superseded in science but is not easily expelled from the popular mind because of its appealing simplicity and the ease with which it can be twisted to deal with conflicting evidence. New names can be found and employed in academic discourse but they are too complicated for ordinary conversations.

As an example of how new words can be coined which bring with them unfortunate associations, consider the origin of the word 'miscegenation' which has passed unremarked into the vocabulary. This was introduced by two journalists working as the contemporary equivalent of the Democratic Party's dirty tricks department during the United States presidential election campaign of 1864. Under this title they published a little book arguing that mating between persons of different racial stocks produced superior stock, in an attempt to insinuate that it was the policy of the Republicans to encourage such unions. From that time onwards the word miscegenation came into use where previously people had written or spoken of amalgamation. It is a word to be avoided, not because of its origins, but because its use tends to reinforce pre-Darwinian assumptions about zoologically discrete populations. Yet what word is to be used instead? To speak of 'mixed marriages' is no more satisfactory because the genetic differences between a bride and groom belonging to the same 'racial' group could be greater than between a couple considered to belong to different ones. Since it is the social assignment that matters it is preferable to speak of inter-group marriages, but such an expression is unlikely to catch on among a public for most of whom the Darwinian conception of race as sub-species is too complicated.

Race as an administrative category

One reason for the popularity of race as a folk concept has been its elastic quality. It can be used in many senses and there is no pressure upon people to be exact. When official statistics employ race as a category there have to be rules about how individuals are to be assigned to categories. Marvin Harris (1964b:23) has described a case involving a caucasoid woman who conceived an illegitimate child by a caucasoid man. In the third month of her pregnancy she married a negroid man who visited her in hospital when she was confined. The attending nurse was obliged by law to assume that the Negro husband was the father of the child and to register the child as Negro on the birth certificate. Subsequently arrangements were made for the child to be adopted by a white couple, but the court denied the petition on the grounds that the child was a Negro. This was contested, and Harris was called as an expert witness to testify about the race of a little boy with blue eyes, straight blond hair and a distinctly pallid skin colour.

The drafting of laws against racial discrimination and the collection of statistics at census time also require precise definitions so that it can be determined whether or not a given individual is of a particular race. Such definitions are fashioned by the need to meet administrative ends and must rely on simple procedures that can be operated by people lacking technical expertise. Therefore they bear no necessary relationship to scientific definitions, though both administrative and scientific definitions influence the use of race as a folk concept.

In Great Britain legislation penalizes both discrimination 'on racial grounds' and the imposition of requirements which put at a disadvantage persons of another 'racial group, i.e. a group of persons defined by reference to colour, race, nationality or ethnic or racial origins'. One provision of the 1968 Race Relations Act that has since been repealed permitted an employer to turn away job seekers belonging to a racial minority if he did so in order to maintain a reasonable racial balance in his work force. For this purpose group membership was determined not by origins or cultural identification but by place of upbringing, so that a dark-skinned person with a Jamaican father and an Indian mother who was mainly educated in Britain was to count as a member of the British racial group. It was thought appropriate in terms of public policy not to count the children of immigrants as immigrants and this affected the definition of racial group. It is one example of the way that an administrative definition may differ from a zoological or sociological one.

Another example of careful definition is provided by the 1976 Act, section 26, which permits an association whose main purpose is to cater for 'persons of a particular racial group defined otherwise than by reference to colour' to discriminate in its selection of members on the basis of race but not colour. The intended meaning is apparently to permit discrimination on the basis of ethnic origin in these circumstances only. Thus the Indian Workers' Association need not admit English or Pakistani applicants, and a bequest to establish an old people's home for Jews may still be given legal effect. It is, however, impermissible to establish a scholarship fund for whites only, since in this context being white is not a 'race' but a 'colour' (Lustgarten, 1980:76).

In social life racial classifications overlap with cultural classifications, whereas in law they may have to be distinguished. It has been argued that Sikhs are a 'racial group' within the meaning of section 3(1) of the 1976 Race Relations Act. They are said to be a racial or ethnic group within the larger Indian racial group. In 1982 the Court of Appeal held that this reasoning could not be applied in the case of *Mandla v. Lee*; in this case the headmaster of a private school had refused admission to a Sikh boy whose father insisted that he should wear a turban. The Court concluded that the headmaster's objection was not to the boy's race but to the turban, and that there had been no unlawful discrimination. By no means all Sikh men in Britain wear the turban, but to the religiously orthodox it is a vital badge of group identity (this   overturned on further appeal, see 1AER 1983: 1062–72.)

A court can take its time and have the benefit of expert advice in determining the racial and ethnic identity of a person but a census needs to employ quicker and cheaper methods. Above all, it is dependent upon the willing collaboration and the understanding of the people to be enumerated. In the 1970 United States census the answer to the question about 'colour or race' was missing for one person in ten. Write-in responses included many unclassifiable responses such as 'American', racially uninformative national origin, hyphenated designations presumably reflecting mixed parentage, and other problem replies. A sample of those who replied unambiguously were interviewed later; about 18 per cent of those who originally reported Spanish origin or descent reported otherwise on the subsequent occasion, while 23 per cent of those who identified themselves as Spanish at the interview stage had not recorded themselves as Spanish in the census.

Another complication for the census-takers is lobbying by ethnic pressure groups concerned to get as high as possible a count of their group. The civil-rights legislation and executive orders of the 1960s established the principle that each minority was entitled to a share of jobs and services proportionate to its share of the population. Therefore, the larger a group's total in the official statistics, the greater its entitlements. Hence the desire of ethnic spokesmen that their groups be separately listed rather than have their members left free to write in an answer in the 'other' category. Those who speak on behalf of ethnic groups concerned to improve their public image often argue that their group should be known by a particular name, and since not all members of the group agree about this, the name used on a census form may affect the returns. In 1930 the Bureau of the Census classified Mexicans as 'non-white'; this evoked such a storm of protest that in 1940 they were classified as 'persons of Spanish mother tongue'; in 1950 and 1960 they were 'white persons of Spanish surnames'; in 1970 there was a category 'persons of both Spanish surname and Spanish mother tongue'; in 1980 they could, if they wished, record themselves as 'white', or use the 'other' category to identify themselves as Mexican, Puerto Rican, etc.

There were many minorities which wanted to be separately recorded in the 1980 census, and many were disappointed. Ethnic enumeration has become so important a political issue that the Federal Office of Management and Budget has imposed a uniform system of ethnic accounting on all federal agencies, including the Bureau of Census. Lobbying may well have influenced the selection of groups listed in the main ethnic question in the 1980 census:

4. Is this person –		
	○ White	○ Asian Indian
	○ Black or Negro	○ Hawaiian
	○ Japanese	○ Guamanian
	○ Chinese	○ Samoan
	○ Filipino	○ Eskimo
	○ Korean	○ Aleut
	○ Vietnamese	○ Other – *Specify*
	○ Indian (Amer.)	
	Print tribe	

Although only one choice was allowed, the entries were not mutually exclusive, as the many white Hawaiians will have discovered. Supplementary to this question was another about 'ancestry' which offered the possible reply 'Afro-American' but not 'Black' or 'Negro', and a third enquiring specifically about Hispanic origins.

One commentator (Lowry, 1982?) infers that the Bureau regards an individual's ethnicity as whatever he says it is, and sees its own job as being to group replies into categories which will assist civil-rights enforcement agencies to satisfy vocal ethnic lobbies and provide as much continuity as possible with previous practice. Its duty to provide valid and reliable information gets a lower priority. Anyone who uses it should be warned that the information about ethnic identities was supplied by whichever member of the household completed the form; that the schedule guided respondents towards Hispanic identifications; and that for some minorities response consistency is not much over 60 per cent.

Experience with the British census shows some points of similarity with that in the United States. In 1971 information was collected on the country of birth of the individual and his or her parents, a procedure which had many advantages but was likely to be less useful with the growth of the British-born population of West Indian and Asian origin. At one stage it was thought that the 1981 census might include a new kind of question:

Race or Ethnic group. Please tick the appropriate box to show the race or ethnic group to which the person belongs or from which the person is descended.

1 ☐ White   7 ☐ Indian
2 ☐ West Indian   8 ☐ Pakistani
3 ☐ African   9 ☐ Bangladeshi
4 ☐ Arab   10 ☐ Sri Lankan
5 ☐ Turkish   11 ☐ Other –
6 ☐ Chinese

This was criticized for inconsistency. There are white West Indians and Africans; most of the categories are nationalities, so why not ask simply for nationality? (see White, 1979, for a careful analysis). Other difficulties arose because the Census requires people, where practicable, to complete their own forms and therefore the categories have to correspond with those that members of the public understand and regard as acceptable. To use a colour category like 'white' in a form which people are legally obliged to complete would also have led to dispute, so trial studies were undertaken with other kinds of question. If a person was of European 'race', he or she was to tick a box labelled English, Italian, Greek or Polish, etc. If a person was non-European, there were boxes labelled West Indian, African, Indian, and so on. Alternative trial questions approached the subject from a different angle, asking: 'Does this person belong to, or is he or she descended, or partly descended, from any of the following ethnic groups? Yes/No. If Yes, please tick appropriate box.' These trials exposed many further difficulties. Adults who were ready to classify themselves as West Indian did not want to classify their United Kingdom-born children similarly and, in the absence of any category 'black British', put them down as English or Welsh depending upon their birthplace. Some Asians wanted to be enumerated by religion rather than national origin. Misunderstandings abounded and cooperation was low (Sillitoe, 1978). Whether there should be such a question, and the form it should take, became political issues, and the government eventually decided against its inclusion.

Conclusion

The word 'race' is currently used in several quite different ways, as Figure 2 illustrates. There are three contexts in which people try to use it in a precise way: the biological use of race as sub-species, the sociological attempt to define the characteristics of racial minorities, and the legal or administrative uses of categories like racial group. Then there are folk concepts of race which probably vary from one group to another; they draw upon the old literary sense of race as lineage or descent and take a powerful impress from the nineteenth-century sense of race as type, though they are now also influenced to some extent by developments in scientific and administrative practice.

This chapter has explained how in the New World the Europeans were the first group to have to consider how they should designate themselves. The Spaniards and Portuguese identified themselves by their nationality. In the United States the European settlers, though originally all English, were more diverse, and they came to identify themselves as whites in opposition to the Negroes, but, up to the nineteenth century, 'Negro' was simply a way of designating people with some measure of African descent. It came to imply more than this only when 'Negro' could be seen as a name for a category in an inclusive kind of classification which hinted at a more powerful explanation of human variation than could be gleaned from the Bible. Whereas there had been many whites who believed Negroes inferior, the appearance of the Typological Theory furnished a new and more powerful explanation. Typology subsumed the doctrine that whites were superior to blacks and made it part of a more general theory that claimed to account for variations in all forms of animal and plant life in the different geographical provinces.

The Typological Theory was advanced by writers in Europe and the United States but appears to have had no counterpart in the rest of the New World. It is sometimes suggested that the theory was put together because the ruling classes in Europe and the New World had for some time provided encouragement for any authors who formulated theories that assisted their material interests. Thus Typology could be seen as justifying the enslavement of blacks in the United States and the expansion of European imperialism. In these crude terms, there is no merit in such an argument. The defenders of Negro slavery in the United States relied more upon the Bible than upon any doctrine which appeared to conflict with it, and it was primarily after the ending of slavery that Typology became politically significant as the white upper and lower classes united at the expense of the blacks. Nor were the European powers anxious to expand their empires in the 1840s, 1850s and 1860s. Domestic opinion at this time was opposed to expansion, which started to pick up only later in the century. The social and political developments which stimulated the European typologists were the events occurring within Europe, like the revolutions of 1848. The men who advanced the Typological Theory were a very varied collection of persons and, while it would be misleading to examine their work solely within the history of science, it must be emphasized that their doctrines (and, indeed, many ideas in current thought which derive from them) cannot be understood apart from the history of science. The growth of scientific knowledge is influenced by the structure of the society in which the scientists work, and the people in power can have a short-term influence upon scientific research (as the case of the Soviet geneticist Lysenko illustrated), but a powerful group cannot force scientific advance to follow a path that happens to suit them. The reader who searches for evidence of social and political influence upon conceptions of race will not find very much before the early years of the twentieth century.

Theories about race did not begin to appear in other parts of the New World in any significant form before the end of the nineteenth century. Then they came in Darwinian costume, appealing to the authority of a major scientific breakthrough. The Selectionist Theory offered a more powerful explanation of racial differences than the Typological Theory had been able to do, since it explained these differences by referring them to principles of heredity and selection which appeared to account for differences within races (like height, eye colour and I.Q.) as well as differences between races. It was a more comprehensive theory, accompanied by better supporting evidence, and it could be used as a justification of imperialist expansion far more effectively than the Typological Theory.

After the Civil War it became more common in the United States to refer to relations between whites and blacks as 'race relations' and this terminology was later extended to other regions. It spread the assumption that race relations arose from contact between individuals who acted at all times as the representatives of zoologically distinct groups. The physical nature of the groups determined the kinds of social relations that were possible. Quite apart from the mistaken biological premises they left aside as irrelevant any view of all individuals of whatever physical type as responding in similar ways to social incentives and sanctions; they also ignored the ways in which any person's attitudes towards strangers are an outcome of the social and political relations with the other group.

The consequences of representing the differences between reds, whites and blacks in the New World as deriving from biological differences, changing slowly if at all, are fairly evident. Such a presentation of the nature of these relations implied that little could be done by political action to change the situation. It made the boundaries between the groups appear impermeable and inflexible.

4

Studying 'race' relations

The expression 'race relations' crept into the English language without anyone noticing quite what it entailed. An early example of how the issues were perceived can be seen in Lord Bryce's 1902 Oxford lecture entitled *The Relation of the Advanced and Backward Races of Mankind.* By 'relations' he meant not the relations between persons, but the relations between races as units in a global process of evolution, as is evident in his conclusion that 'for the future of mankind nothing is more vital than that some races should be maintained at the highest level of efficiency ... It may therefore be doubted whether any further mixture of Advanced and Backward races is to be desired.' While other writers than Bryce, in the United States as well as Britain, wrote of 'relations between the races' the first use of the brief form 'race relations' as an apparently conventional designation of subject matter may be that of the Chicago Commission on Race Relations appointed to investigate the riot there in 1919.

American and British usage

A moving spirit in Chicago at that time was the sociologist Robert E. Park who used the expression in the 1920s and made major advances towards the clarification of the issues involved. Yet when the text book by W. D. Weatherford and Charles S. Johnson, *Race Relations: Adjustment of Whites and Negroes in the United States* appeared in 1934, a great deal too much was still taken for granted. The book opened with the statement 'The United States is not the only spot in the world where race friction is found' but, after an initial discussion of 'the philosophy of race relations' devoted its quite appreciable bulk to the consideration of only American Negro slavery and the status of the Negro and his relations with whites in the United States. It was a book written for college courses in the United States and it could comfortably assume that blacks and whites were two races without bothering about the processes by which individuals came to be classed as one or the other, or the significance of these processes for an understanding of what 'race relations' really were.

Any reader who feels that there is little progress in sociological understanding would benefit from studying some of the early works in this field and from trying to identify how things that today are taken for granted were not apparent fifty or sixty years ago. Much of what now seems like confusion was concealed by loose terminology, notably by the frequent use of 'problem' without specifying just what, or whose, the problem was. Something of the flavour of concern in Bryce's generation can be seen in the Universal Races Congress held in London in 1911. The sessions, spread over four days, attracted an average audience of over one thousand, and the contributions were published in a volume bearing the title *Papers on Inter-Racial Problems* . . . (Spiller, 1911; see Biddiss, 1971). This word 'problem' was a key term governing the discussion of racial relations for the first half of the century at least. It reflected the white reading public's political anxieties and influenced scholars to define their work in similar terms. It is to be found in the title and substance of J. H. Oldham's *Christianity and the Race Problem* of 1924, and again in another collection of purely scholarly essays, E. T. Thompson's *Race Relations and the Race Problem* of 1939. Ironically, though Gunnar Myrdal argued that the United States had to deal with a 'white problem' rather than a 'colour problem', the sub-title of his great work *An American Dilemma*, was nevertheless *The Negro Problem and Modern Democracy* (1944). In Britain, later still, when Penguin Books decided to commission 'a study of racial relations' they insisted, to the author's disquiet, on giving it the title *The Colour Problem* (Richmond, 1955; see Drake, 1956).

There were writers like Basil Matthews who, in *The Clash of Colour*, argued in 1924 that the race problem was created by the expansion of Europe which led to conflicts that were economic and political in essence even if they seemed to be racial, while the world domination of the white man was a recent development unlikely to persist for very long (1924:23, 124, 136). Yet it was those who appealed to the authority of science who had the initiative, and they tended to present racial relations as arising from contact between individuals who acted at all times as the representatives of zoologically distinct types. The physical nature of the groups underlay the degree of civilization they had attained, and determined the kinds of social relations that were possible. Quite apart from the mistaken biological premises, this approach left aside as irrelevant any view of all individuals of whatever physical type as responding in similar ways to social incentives and sanctions; it also ignored the ways in which any person's attitudes towards strangers are an outcome of the social and political relations with other groups and of the individual's position in his own group.

There have been two main hindrances to the establishment of a satisfactory framework for the sociological study of racial relations. One has been associated with understandings of 'racial' difference, the other with the development of sociology itself. In the first place, when groups of racially distinctive people have been brought together, physical appearance has been a marker of group membership. The conflicts that are sometimes associated with interaction between members of racial groups can at times be observed where the groups are identified by religious (or sectarian) markers, as in Northern Ireland or in the disturbances following the partition of India and Pakistan; on occasion there have been linguistic conflicts with similar features. In the early days it was assumed that there was something about 'race' which gave rise to a distinctive kind of group relations; it was physical make-up which determined the social relations so that the emphasis was on the first word in the expression 'race relations'. In the period between the world wars the nature of this mistake came to be more widely appreciated, but it could not be overcome for the lack of an acceptable formulation of the nature of inter-group relations which would explain the consequences for those relations of the use of different kinds of group markers: racial, class, national, religious, and so on. This, the second hindrance, reflected the difficulties in establishing basic sociological principles, and, in particular, the troublesome 'macro–micro problem'. Most of the early sociological theorists, with the notable exception of Simmel, concentrated upon large-scale social phenomena and the explanation of historical trends. They presented social behaviour at the micro level as the product of macro-sociological forces, but they neglected to analyse the nature of nationalism, expecting it to wither away. It is not surprising, therefore, that race should have been introduced to the sociological scene as a possible macro force. Sociologists at this time were also anxious to demonstrate their independence from psychology and to show that they had a subject-matter which could not be reduced to the kind of problematic that was tackled within psychology. So it was also part of a pattern that early writing about race relations took its starting point from the characteristics of groups rather than from case studies analysing how individual members of such groups related to one another within particular social orders.

There is room for dispute about such an interpretation, but certainly there are grounds for contending that it was only in the 1950s that sociologists, led by such diverse figures as Hughes, Blumer, Homans, Goffman and Garfinkel, and stimulated by the analyses of social anthropologists, began to develop techniques for studying sociological factors in inter-personal relations and for showing how macro-sociological trends could be the outcome of changes at the micro level. Peter Rose, discussing the development of teaching in the United States about racial relations, detects changes of emphasis, firstly from the biological aspects of human differences to a frame of reference stressing cultural variation more in the tradition of

Tarde and Durkheim (and best illustrated in the writings of Lester Ward and Albion Small), and then secondly to an approach concerned with the effects of inter-group contact and connecting with the Weberian tradition of interpretive understanding (Rose, 1968: 67–8). He, too, stresses the influence of Robert E. Park as a pivotal figure in moving the emphasis in race-relations teaching from the first word to the second. But it was a slow process, as Rose makes clear. In the early 1940s there was, in the United States, no agreement either about the place of 'race' in sociological theory or about which aspects of the 'race question' were important in teaching. In 1966 most courses were, he found, ethnocentric, in that they concentrated very heavily on United States material and viewed the issues through American eyes. They were infused with an aura of scientific certainty and affected by an undercurrent of moral indignation. Inter-group tensions were presented as a blemish on the fabric of American society which must be understood, and then eradicated. Though many teachers described their courses as theoretical, there was, in truth, precious little theoretical sinew to hold it all together and no genuine link-up with more general sociological theory. So while the teaching displayed a good deal of breadth, it had little depth (Rose, 1968:68, 153–4).

Some sociologists and anthropologists insist that racial relations should be regarded as 'a sub-case of a theory of social stratification'. Indeed, it often seems an unfortunate error that the expression 'race relations' should ever have gained currency since it can prove confusing and there are better alternatives (like, for many purposes, 'minority relations'). Yet, whether justified or not, the expression has obtained general currency. It is used as a subject classification by both the British Library and the United States Library of Congress and is therefore printed on the back of the title page of many books published in those two countries. Such a usage will be taken as authoritative. Whatever its status as an analytical concept, there is therefore now a folk concept of racial relations. English-speaking people now generally believe that these are one kind of group relations; they consider that social scientists ought to be able to explain their special features and to suggest ways of resolving the social problems associated with 'race'.

'Minus one' ethnicity

The use of the adjective 'ethnic' has not changed as much as has 'racial', but an important shift started in the 1930s. Apparently the first author to use the word in the new sense was W. Lloyd Warner in 1941 when he reported on his study of 'Yankee City', a pseudonym for Newburyport, Massachusetts (see Sollors, 1980:648). The picture of the city's status structure which

Warner presented was one he took over from his favourite informants, members of what he called the 'lower upper class'. Warner classified Greek-Americans, Irish-Americans, Italian-Americans, Jewish-Americans and Polish-Americans as ethnics. He said that the immigrants from England, Scotland, Northern Ireland and Anglophone Canada did not form ethnic groups. This was doubtless an accurate observation but he did not pose or answer the question why these people did not form ethnic groups, and what the significance of that might be for his conception of ethnicity.

In one of the concluding sentences of the book on Newburyport's ethnic groups, Warner wrote: 'The future of American ethnic groups seems to be limited; it is likely that they will be quickly absorbed. When this happens one of the great epochs of American history will have ended, and another, that of race, will begin' (Warner and Srole, 1945:295). There is here a conception of a nation divided into races, and races into ethnic groups, which it is helpful to present in diagram form.

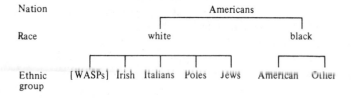

Figure 3 Warner's conception of race and ethnicity

Two things were novel about Warner's conceptualization: the nation–race–ethnic group sequence and the definition of ethnic group. In Europe 'nation', 'race' and 'ethnic group' have until recently been used to denote groups of the same order of magnitude, and not segments one of another. 'Race' was introduced into political discourse in the context of nationalism; it has often been a synonym for nation and the latter word has had a double meaning since it could signify either a community based on common characteristics or a political unit corresponding to a state. Until recently, the adjective 'ethnic' has not been used very often in everyday English since the units to which it might be applied usually had alternative and better-established names, like nation, people or minority. When J. S. Huxley and A. C. Haddon in 1935 criticized mistaken racial doctrines, they proposed the use of 'ethnic group' as a substitute for 'race', implicitly recalling its Greek origin as designating a self-governing political unit, and therefore as resembling a nation. The English, Welsh and Scots are accounted nations comprising the British state, not as ethnic divisions of a British nation or race. In Europe, nation, race and ethnic group have tended to be overlapping and often interchangeable categories, and the overlap can be productive of confusion. For example, British immigration law distinguishes sharply between those who have a connection by descent with the British nation and those who do not. Since this nation has until recently been relatively homogeneous 'racially', the laws can also be seen as discriminating on the basis of race. It is sometimes impossible to separate nation from race.

There have been situations in Europe where ethnic and national boundaries have not coincided, especially if national boundaries are taken to be those of the state (Yugoslavia offers an important illustration); but there is nevertheless a general contrast between European and United States conceptions. In Europe, situations in which ethnic units do not coincide with nations are seen as anomalous, whereas, in the United States, nation, race and ethnic group have been assumed to be different categories altogether.

This arose from the process of nation-building in that country. Those who got there first called the tune: they set blacks apart and expected incoming whites to adopt many of the cultural characteristics of the dominant group. It was an expectation of Anglo-conformity as opposed to the philosophies of the melting pot and cultural pluralism. If white ethnics were to become fully American they were supposed to change so as to resemble the majority, whereas for the blacks to become full citizens the majority had to change so that it no longer disparaged attributes blacks were powerless to alter. Ethnics can be absorbed into racial categories without disturbing the black–white boundary. Hence the sequence: nation–race–ethnic group.

In Warner's presentation White Anglo-Saxon Protestants were not ethnics. No doubt this usage was becoming more common, for shortly afterwards two sociologists remarked 'there is a minor case of change of meaning in the word "ethnic". All human groups used to belong to ethnic groups . . . but now we are beginning to speak of some people as ethnic and others as not' (Hughes and Hughes, 1952:137). The new usage has been called a 'minus one' definition of ethnicity: the dominant group insists upon its power to define; members of that group perceive themselves not as ethnic but as setting the standard by which others are to be judged.

Though the 'minus one' definition of ethnicity may now be in retreat in the United States (because of the change in power relations) its use is still spreading elsewhere. The editor of a newsletter on Ethnic Politics published in Australia recently reported that his use of the word ethnic had provoked responses from the Commissioner for Community Relations and from the National Aboriginal Conference Secretariat. Commending the study of ethnic politics, the Commissioner argued that the word ethnic should 'cover all Australians, whether they were Anglo-Saxons or Assyrians. It was designed to be a unifying word and there is no way in which anyone can arbitrarily decide that any section of the population is not covered by it.' He objected to a 'minus one' definition. Those who spoke for the Aborigines would have been content with a 'minus one' definition provided it was the Aborigines who were left out: 'We, as representatives of Aboriginal people do not identify ourselves as ethnic but rather as the inheritors of the original culture of this country. Our culture, laws, and prior right to this land must be recognized by all who inhabit our land without just treaty arrangements.'

There is a parallel with the word 'native' in English which in the heyday of empire came to mean non-European, as if the English were not natives of their own country. With the passing of empire, the use of the word will probably revert to its earlier meaning. In the United States those who were once so inappropriately called Indians are now often called Native Americans. To call oneself or be called a native of a country may in the future be more of an occasion for pride.

Warner studied a city in which there were few Hispanic-Americans. The question of how they should be incorporated into a classification of groups complicates matters still further. The United States government now prescribes 'If separate race and ethnic categories are used, the minimum designations are:

a. *Race:*
   – American Indian or Alaskan Native
   – Asian or Pacific Islander
   – Black
   – White

b. *Ethnicity:*
   – Hispanic origin
   – Not of Hispanic origin'

i.e. the racial categories Black and White can both be sub-divided by ethnicity: Hispanic and Non-Hispanic (Directive No.15, US Dept. of Commerce, *Statistical Policy Handbook*, 1978:37–8). If this were applied to the diagram of Warner's usage, WASPs, Irish, Italians, Poles and Jews would be sub-divisions of the non-Hispanic ethnic division of the white racial category. There could be a Hispanic division of *either* the white *or* the black racial category: it could be sub-divided: Mexican, Puerto Rican, Cuban, etc.

One implication of this mode of classification can be better appreciated by considering the classification of minorities in Britain. It is illustrated most easily by minorities from countries like India, Pakistan, and Nigeria, though in principle it applies also to minorities from Jamaica, Trinidad, Guyana, etc. If a racial minority is one distinguished by physical characters, and an ethnic minority by cultural characteristics, how are, say, Punjabis in Britain to be classified? As a group they can be distinguished physically from the English though not necessarily from other Asians. They can also be distinguished both from the English and from other Asians in respect of culture, language, religion and geographical origin. As was foreshadowed in Chapter 1, such a group can be classified as both a racial and an ethnic minority (and, of course, as several other kinds of minority as well). The United States practice, as exemplified by both Warner and the official statistics, is to regard majority discrimination as the more important criterion of group character: race, expressing majority prejudice, takes priority over ethnic characters expressing community sentiment. Such a practice may reflect popular consciousness but it is no basis for a scientific classification.

The ethnocentric trap

The creation of a body of knowledge about racial and ethnic relations, and of a battery of concepts for studying them, has been chiefly the work of social scientists from the United States. It is only to be expected that they will, unconsciously, have imported into their work some of the assumptions of their own way of life, so the task of internationalizing the concepts must be in part an attempt to identify these assumptions and make the theoretical structure more nearly culture-free. Chapter 2 addressed this problem by trying to describe forms of New World classification without relying on any particular assumptions about race, but it is not easy, as can be seen by reflecting on the statement made at the end of a long and productive career by Robert E. Park:

> Race relations, as that term is defined in use and wont in the United States, are the relations existing between peoples distinguished by marks of racial descent, particularly when these differences enter into the consciousness of the individuals and groups so distinguished, and by so doing determine in each case the individual's conception of himself as well as his status in the community ... Thus one may say, without doing injustice to the sense in which the word is ordinarily used, that there are, to be sure, races in Brazil – there are, for example, Europeans and Africans – but not race relations because there is in that country no race consciousness, or almost none. One speaks of race relations when there is a race problem (Park, 1950: 81–2).

The difficulty with which Park was wrestling is still troublesome, but his attempted solution is manifestly unsatisfactory. He describes the United States folk conception of race relations; he says that, using this as a definition, there are race relations in Brazil even if Brazilians do not

recognize them as such. Then comes a difficulty: the United States
definition presumes that people will share a consciousness of racial
differences and the Brazilians do not. Park declines to consider whether this
means that the definition is wrong or whether he was in error in concluding
that there were race relations in Brazil. Instead he reverts to the ordinary
United States usage which identifies race relations with a race problem,
without acknowledging that Brazilians do not consider that they have a race
problem. Could confusion be more confounded?

Sociologists can agree that when comparing social relations in two
societies, such as Brazil and the United States, it is wrong to look at Brazil
through American eyes unless the reader is also told how the United States
looks through Brazilian eyes. The anthropologist Marvin Harris (whose
findings were summarized in Chapter 2) has described how he overcame
this kind of ethnocentrism. Two leading United States scholars who failed
to overcome the obstacle are Talcott Parsons and Carl N. Degler. They
have discussed racial discrimination in Brazil on the assumption that there
are black–white relations there; they have concluded that these will come to
resemble black–white relations in the United States and have ignored the
utility of considering whether the trend could be in the opposite direction.
Looking at the Brazilian evidence through the spectacles of their own
culture, they contend that in the long run the polarization of the United
States pattern is 'more favourable to the resolution of the color problem by
means of inclusion and pluralization' (Parsons, 1968:366; 1975:53–83)
and that Brazil may have to follow the route taken by the United States
(Degler, 1971:281).

Degler's conviction is that 'blacks will be recognized as different and
discriminated against whenever non-blacks have the power and an incentive
to do so. So long as men perceive identifying physical differences that can
be used to discriminate against another group, they will do so' (1971:287).
The incentive to discriminate varies from one kind of society to another and,
since competition is increasing in Brazil, antagonism between black and
white can be expected to rise (1971:281).

Parsons' argument is partly derived from general principles (e.g. 'by far
the most important type of process leading either to differentiation or to
segmentation is binary in character') and partly from his interpretation of
emancipatory movements in Western history (with particular reference to
the values embodied in the Protestant Reformation); he does not discuss the
Brazilian evidence, but his argument seems to be that the complex grading
of individuals by shades of pigmentation tends to reinforce the negative
evaluation of blackness and to maintain the pattern of discrimination.

Degler's approach is more closely related to the Brazilian evidence. He
observes that, while the possibility of upward mobility for mulattoes has

made Brazilian discrimination milder, it 'also had the effect of inhibiting the advancement of Negroes as a group' (1971:275). A Brazilian might well emphasize the last three words in this quotation, and ask whether Negroes have to be regarded as a group? Is not the objective of an anti-discrimination campaign to see that all individuals, black and white, are treated on their merits as individuals? In which case might not the creation of a racially based self-conscious group be a retrograde move? That is an argument to be considered later. At this point it is simply necessary to note that, starting from the assumption that Negroes should be seen as a group, Degler refers to changes in the social situation of black Americans, and changes in the attitudes of whites towards them; he believes these changes to be significant, beneficial, and the product of what Parsons called polarization. 'What was once a drawback, under new circumstances, becomes a gain for the Negro in the United States, but just the opposite in Brazil. The historical and deep violence of North American racism has welded Negroes into an effective social force, whereas the ambiguity of the colour-class line in Brazil has left the blacks without cohesion or leaders.' Group mobility, as in the United States, has advantages over individual mobility. The critic might reply that group mobility is advantageous for people who already constitute a group; whether it would be equally helpful to people who do not, is another matter altogether.

Parsons' argument is that the pattern of polarization 'established in the Caribbean and the southern states of the United States by predominantly Protestant English groups . . . became increasingly anomalous and morally untenable with the growth of egalitarian ideas' (1968:366). This raises a number of issues about cause and effect. If Protestantism was as important as Parsons supposes, then similar effects might have been expected in parts of the Caribbean, but H. Hoetink, in the course of a criticism of this thesis, objects that 'nowhere in the Caribbean, Protestant or otherwise, British or not, did or does there exist the rigorous socio-racial dichotomy postulated by Parsons' (1973:140). Degler's argument does not rely upon assumptions about polarization being morally untenable for whites, but assumes that polarization permits an increase in black political power. He contends that for the United States, 'miscegenation offers no "solution" ' (1971:290–1). This makes the same assumption as before about blacks as a group; there is no discussion of any implication that Brazil's prospects would be improved were the society there to become racially pluralistic on the United States pattern. The nature of a pluralistic society is not examined, and there is no consideration of its negative features.

The exposition of the polarization thesis as outlined in the works of Parsons and Degler suggests that any assessment must depend upon the definition of what Parsons calls 'the color problem'. A great deal also depends upon an author's assumptions when he refers to 'blacks' or 'Negroes': are they Americans who happen to have a dark skin? Are they a separate people who should seek political self-expression through an independent state? Or are they something in-between? The future of the Afro-American identity is still a matter of speculation.

Parsons' conception of 'the colour problem' is never made explicit. He is concerned with 'inclusion', which, as he recognizes, 'presupposes some order of common value commitment' (1968:352). Hoetink picks up this point and notes that some black leaders in the United States do not see themselves as Americans with dark skins; they believe that the 'problem' can only be solved by exclusion, by the recognition of a separate black nation. So while polarization may help the development of black pride it does not necessarily lead to inclusion; the growth of a common value system will be greater 'when the line between white and Negro is less rigidly drawn and the system less sharply polarized' (Hoetink, 1973:144).

If the analysis assumes, firstly, that 'blacks' are not necessarily or biologically different from 'whites' and that the differences derive from historical or cultural sources, and, secondly, that individuals will always rank one another in terms of the values inherent in their culture (including differences in complexion), then the 'resolution' of the 'color problem' can be seen to require (i) the reduction of inter-group ranking to the same basis as intra-group ranking; (ii) the reduction of the weight attached to colour differences in the calculation of rank; and (iii) the reduction of the social, political and economic inequalities identified by differences of skin colour. If reduction (i) comes about there will be a trend towards a generally coffee-coloured population in which a pale complexion is preferred to a dark one; reduction (ii) would mean a diminution in the preference for a pale complexion; reduction (iii) concerned with the use of colour as a sign, could be quite independent but would be facilitated by the other two.

Parsons and Degler are, in their discussions, concerned with objective (ii). Adhering to the liberal democratic ethos they do not wish to accept the second assumption (that for the next few generations most people will prefer a pale complexion) believing it to be wrong for anyone to be evaluated in terms of an attribute which bears no relation to his worth as a citizen. Accordingly they express no interest in objective (i) since that accepts the continuation of an undesirable kind of evaluation. They believe that an increase in the power of blacks as a group can cause blackness to be considered as beautiful as whiteness and that the increase in black group power will facilitate the elimination of economic inequalities associated with colour.

Assuming for the moment that Afro-Americans act and continue to act as a group, would such a change promote integration? Though polarization may persuade whites that patterns of white privilege are morally untenable, blacks could well be unimpressed by the moral record of the whites and prefer a solution based upon their self-exclusion from white United States society. An ethnic mobilization movement, unless it declines, is likely to stabilize by the establishment either of a new nation or of a pluralistic social order as envisaged by Degler. Parsons does not consider whether black ethnic mobilization may affect white attitudes or what they find morally tenable, so that claim that polarization will achieve (ii) or (iii) is purely speculative. Since in any foreseeable society there will be some ranking of individuals, there will be some people at the bottom of the ladder. Whether they are content with their position will be more important than whether their low rank is attributed to skin colour or to lack of talent. Therefore objective (iii), of reducing unacceptable differences, is partly independent of the other two objectives. The polarization thesis is surely in part a white liberal reflection of the black movement of the late 1960s in the United States, which was shaped by the black experience in that country. The movement helped many Afro-Americans to an intense feeling of solidarity with peoples of African origin across the world; but the sentiments of these other peoples were different, being moulded by experience in societies with quite other social structures (Jenkins, 1975:127–30). Liberal whites, being sympathetic to black claims, took over many of their definitions even when they ran contrary to the liberal credo (Killian, 1981). Afro-Americans have been unable to maintain group solidarity at the same high pitch, and older differences about the relative merits of different strategies (such as separatism and integration) have re-emerged in new forms. The growing significance of class differences within the black population underlines the unreality of treating Afro-Americans as a single group. Degler's statement might be modified to read that 'miscegenation' offers no solution in the short run, but may do so in the long term; polarization may offer some benefits in the short run but offers no solution in the long term.

A field of study?

By 1950 social scientists in the United States were making less use of the idiom of race, but in Great Britain events took a different course. In that year H. V. Hodson, editor of *The Sunday Times*, delivered an address which resulted in the creation of an Institute of Race Relations and the publication of a quarterly journal *Race* (after the take-over of the Institute by another group in 1972 it was renamed *Race and Class*, see Sivanandan, 1974; Mason, 1983). Hodson, and others with him who were supporters of the Central African Federation (comprising what are now the separate states of Zambia, Zimbabwe and Malawi), stressed the political importance of racial relations. He recognized difficulties over the definition of race, observing: 'some thinkers have reached the conclusion that it is empty of meaning altogether, and that race relations accordingly do not exist, scientifically speaking. This strikes me as being about as valuable as the calculations of the navigator who reckons by trigonometry that his ship must be in mid-ocean when it is evidently in shallow water and about to run ashore' (Hodson, 1950:305; see Hodson, 1956). The metaphor reflected apprehension about the growth of racial conflict, but it was wrongly used. Those who denied that races existed, scientifically speaking, might well have been the first to warn that the ship of state was in shallow water. Their argument was that the threatening shoals were not those of race but would be more accurately entered on the chart as the perils of relative deprivation, anti-imperialist assertion, conflict of interest, or by some name which indicated that their origins were not biological but economic, political and social. In contrast to the Americans, the British at this time saw racial relations as arising from the Western impact upon non-European societies and were not much concerned about group tensions in their own society. All those involved in the new developments, inside and outside the universities, accepted the appropriateness of the label 'race relations'; as Hodson asserted, 'we may not know what race is, but we know what race relations are'.

One argument of this book is that we do not know what race relations are. There are relations in Central America and Brazil which Europeans and North Americans may classify as racial when the people who live there do not. There has been a futile debate as to whether Jews are a race and people will differ about whether the study of race relations should include the study of anti-semitism. This book maintains that there is nothing in the relations between people considered to be of different race that cannot also be found in the relations between people considered to be of the same race. The study of racial relations can be, to some extent, what scholars choose to make it. On the one hand it can be argued that since doctrines of race were an unfortunate mistake, or that their propagation was part of a tacit plot, it is best to study the relations arising between people who are 'racially' classified in terms of more meaningful concepts. On the other hand, it can be urged that since so many believe that there are racial relations it is sensible to take those beliefs as a starting point and go on to explain the complications. On this view, the long-term task of the specialist in racial relations is to work himself out of a job.

Those who believe that racial relations are distinctive may argue that while people can change their religion or language, they cannot change their physical appearance. 'Race' is different in that its implications for social status are transmitted from parent to child with little opportunity for the individual to change other people's perceptions of the kind of person he is. Physical differences of skin colour, hair, and facial features, are particularly noticeable, and, where they are used as signs of group membership, they have been associated with major differences of social privilege. Therefore they carry a heavier emotional load than other forms of group differentiation. But while social differentiation based on 'race' may feel different, or be different, in contemporary America or Britain, that does not make the subject matter of racial relations distinctive when seen in comparative perspective.

To analyse differences in group privilege it is important to get away from assumptions about 'race' and to see the problem in terms of the more general process by which identities or roles are distributed in a population. Some roles are necessarily linked with physical differences: women give birth to babies; young men make the best warriors. In some cultures these links are elaborated in ways that go beyond biological necessity and it is assumed that women are incapable of looking after themselves and that it would be demeaning for a man to care for infant children. Those roles which involve the exercise of power and influence the distribution of resources are seen as attractive; men, or the men of a particular group, may seek to obtain a monopoly over them. Other roles, notably those of menial work, are left over for those who do not succeed in competition for the attractive ones. The same principles apply to the distribution of identities, that is, to culturally defined images about kinds of people.

Sociologists distinguish between ascription and achievement as two ways of distributing roles. Role ascription is seen most clearly when at birth a given individual is born into a family with particular privileges or burdens, as when it is a royal, an aristocratic, a landowning, a labouring or a slave family. The individual is ascribed to the male or female gender on the basis of sexual characteristics. Racial ascription also occurs at birth. It would be possible, though there is no society in which this happens, for roles to be ascribed according to the signs of the zodiac. If that were done and, say, only people born under Leo were selected for leadership positions, the idea would grow that Leos were natural leaders and what was originally an arbitrary method of role ascription would acquire a cultural justification.

In poly-ethnic African societies like Nigeria and Zimbabwe, every African is expected to have an ethnic identity and there is nothing in the nature of that ethnicity which makes it better to be, say, a Hausa than a Tiv, Yoruba, Ibibo or Efik. Certain of these ethnic groups are larger and more powerful than others; for historical reasons a larger proportion of their number may have obtained higher education, so that their groups will be over-represented in high-status positions and it will be advantageous to belong to them rather than to others at the lower end. In this way there grows up a hierarchy of ethnic ranking, and it may be concluded that wherever roles are ascribed to group members they will be so ranked. Role achievement is seen most clearly when an individual, by his own talents and efforts, wins a high place in competition and becomes a university graduate, a manager, administrator or professional performer or, say, a musician or tennis player. In many societies political leadership is attained by a mixture of both processes, the top position being achieved by the most successful member of a limited group of contenders who are all of approved birth or social background.

In Hindu India, occupational roles have traditionally been ascribed on a basis of caste membership. In the rural areas everyone's caste identity is known or can quickly be ascertained; in the cities it may take a little longer but it is no more difficult than discovering whether someone is Protestant or Catholic in Belfast. Not only is there a very rigid system of ascription but it is reinforced by powerful religious beliefs which interpret these distinctions as a basic principle in the constitution of the universe. Contact with people of lower caste may be polluting and anyone affected by it may have to undergo troublesome rituals to rid themselves of the stain. The caste system does not simply divide society into two unequal categories, like whites and blacks, but into thousands of categories. It affects every sphere of life and justifies hierarchical distinction in all of them, thus reducing to a minimum the scope for role achievement. Hindu caste is based on fundamentally different presuppositions from individualistic Western philosophy and cannot be understood if viewed through Western eyes (see Dumont 1966 for a classical exposition). Since there has also been greater material inequality in India than in the capitalist West, those features which in modern America or Britain seem to make racial differentiation more extreme than any other form, can all be seen magnified several times over. The crucial difference is that in the Hindu view of the world role ascription and inequality are taken for granted whereas in the West they run counter to that belief that men are born equal in their basic human rights, including the right to seek their personal advancement. Thus the feeling that inter-racial relations are different from intra-racial relations derives from the ascription of roles and identities on a basis of inherited physical characteristics when other important features of the society are oriented to the achievement of roles and identities by individual choice and effort.

Though it is necessary at times to generalize about the value systems of societies this can also be dangerous, since there is rarely, if ever, complete agreement about these values. Some may dissent and, when their number grows, the overall pattern changes. Thus while race, ethnicity or religion may influence social position a minority may question the legitimacy of their being used in this way. It is probably easiest to illustrate what is involved by considering the significance of religion. The belief in some Western societies that the spheres of church and state should be kept separate is relatively recent and is unacceptable in most other countries. In strongly Islamic and strongly Catholic countries the state is expected to serve the ends which are revealed in religion. The believers may display tolerance to those people who, though not of their own religion, profess another belief which they can recognize as religious, but they will be less sympathetic towards those whom they define as atheists. Those who are so defined may reject the label, claiming that all religion is a delusion and that a neutral classification would be to divide people up according to whether they profess a religion or not, and then, if they do, according to the nature of the religion they profess. Such an approach is unacceptable to the believer; for him religion is truth and it is unbelief which requires explanation. This can be a parallel for examining the use of 'racial' signs to classify people.

Minority members may object to the way in which the majority's beliefs about the significance of race or ethnicity put them at a disadvantage in competing for attractive roles or fasten on them an unwelcome preconception such as a belief that Jews are given to sharp practice, that Anglo-Saxons are inescapably racist or that blacks are dangerous. These can be classed as stigmatized identities. Confronted with such a prejudice, an individual may respond in one of three ways. Firstly, like the atheist in a theocratic society, he may object to the principle of assuming that inherited physical characters have any connection with social ones. Secondly, he may react as members of upwardly mobile Hindu castes have done and object that his group has been wrongly classified without criticizing the criteria by which groups are ranked. Thirdly, he can contend that whether or not it is true that members of his group are tricksters, racists or dangerous, it is wrong to assume that this is true of him. One of the reasons why inter-racial relations seem different is that the presuppositions underlying racial ascription are of a fundamental kind and are effectively challenged only at the first of these three levels.

As a field of study, 'race relations' is defined by its problems and by the traditions of enquiry that have been developed to elucidate them (just as are other subjects within the curriculum). How people react to a stigmatized identity is one such problem. It entails an examination of what people perceive as stigmatization, for in societies in which whites have an advantage there will be some deviant whites who do not wish to be defined as whites; like the atheists in a theocracy they wish to challenge the system by rejecting the principle of classification. Yet since they can, in a sense, resign from their race in a way that members of a disadvantaged race cannot, their reaction may seem no different from that of people who, responding in the third way, are seeking simply an individual exemption.

Where a whole group is dissatisfied with the identity others attribute to them they may organize so as to raise morale, mobilize their power and display a more impressive front. This resembles the second of the three kinds of response but, if successful, it can be a step to a more fundamental challenge. This sort of reaction will be discussed in Chapter 8, in connection with revaluation movements, but the whole question of response to stigmatized identities should illustrate how the problems of racial conflict can be illuminated if they are subsumed as examples of more general problems.

The significance attached to physical differences has facilitated the transmission of inequality from one generation to the next, but the difference between the modes of transmission where racial differences are present and are absent, is one of degree and not of kind. One of the tasks of the sociologist is to find ways of subsuming what appears to be 'racial' phenomena under more general social-science theories.

Conclusion

Brazilian students will view the evidence about black–white relations in the United States within a framework defined by their experience in their own society with its mode of classification. The evidence will puzzle them until they see that it conforms to a different logic. United States students will look at the Brazilian evidence on the assumption that dark-skinned people in Brazil are 'blacks' just as they would be 'blacks' in the United States. Uncritical reliance on such assumptions, and particularly upon the assumption that 'race' relations are a special kind of relations, breeds confusion. Chapter 2 sought to minimize one source of confusion by discussing relations between reds, whites and blacks in the New World in neutral terms without assuming that the ideas about 'race' in any one of the regions was more valid than those of the other two. Chapter 3 set out to alert readers to ways in which changes in the meaning of words like race could affect the interpretation of documents from different historical periods. To assume that a reference to race in 1784 had the same significance as in 1983 is to commit the error of presentism, but that error can take other forms. Racial discrimination has become a very salient issue in the last quarter century. During this period Europeans and North Americans have been much less inclined to regard non-Christians as living in outer darkness than were their ancestors in the eighteenth century. They are also much less inclined to show deference to people of aristocratic birth or to see social relations as based upon inherited status. In earlier centuries racial discrimination was often mixed up with religious discrimination and status discrimination. If the modern student fastens onto the first element and discounts the latter two because it does not seem today as if they could have been so important, that is another example of presentism and it has to be avoided if the analysis of inter-group relations is to be more culture-free.

'Race' relations are distinguished not by the biological significance of phenotypical features but by the social use of these features as signs identifying group membership and the roles people are expected to play. The long-run 'problem' of 'race' relations is that of explaining how groups identified by such signs come to be created, how they are maintained, and how they are often dissolved. This means that the focus must be upon what separates one group from another, that is, upon the boundaries between them. Chapter 5 will discuss some of the theories which have been formulated in the attempt to account for the nature and persistence of these boundaries.

5

Theoretical approaches

The racial theories that were popularized a little before the First World War were a challenge to those who believed that man could write his own history by deciding the course of human affairs. It was at much the same time that the academic study of sociology was beginning to take shape and the major task for the first generation of sociologists – at any rate for those who were interested in racial and ethnic relations – was to establish that the relations that interested them could not be satisfactorily explained in biological terms. This chapter will review the various theories that have been advanced to provide better explanations and will consider them in the order in which they were first published.

The Ecological Theory

The first major sociologist to tackle the question of 'race relations' was an American, Robert E. Park. He took a great deal from the Darwinist approach but answered the selectionists by insisting that 'the individual man is the bearer of a double inheritance. As a member of a race, he transmits by interbreeding a biological inheritance. As a member of society or a social group, on the other hand he transmits by communication a social inheritance' (Park and Burgess, 1921:140. For a fuller discussion of Park's contribution in the field see Banton, 1977:101–11). It is now generally accepted that there is one process of organic or biological evolution and another of superorganic or social and cultural evolution, and that change occurs in different ways in the two processes, but this distinction had to be established by careful argument in the first two decades of the present century.

From Park's writing it is possible to distil a theory which may be stated in four propositions:

1 Migration brings together, in unequal relations, people who are pheno-typically distinct.
2 In relations of competition, individuals become conscious of the features by which their statuses are differentiated.

3 People of superior status are unwilling to compete on equal terms with those of inferior status; they represent the latter as belonging to naturally distinct categories and as therefore suited to a different place in the division of labour.

4 Prejudice is an expression of the group consciousness of the privileged people; it protects their interests and reinforces the structure of categories. Park's starting point was made very clear in one of his latest statements:

> The first movements of mankind seem to have been like the migrations of plants and animals, centrifugal. It was as if they were engaged in a general recognizance and exploration in order to spy out the land and discover the places where the different species might safely settle. It was, presumably, in the security of these widely dispersed niches that man developed, by natural selection and inbreeding, those special physical and cultural traits that characterize the different racial stocks (1950: 85).

In his earlier and more extended discussion, Park presented men as competing for territory, like plants and animals, so that competition was a fundamental process determining the distribution of population. On top of it were two higher levels characterized by other processes. 'The division of labor and all the vast organized economic interdependence of individuals and groups of individuals characteristic of modern life are a product of competition. On the other hand, the moral and political order, which imposes itself upon this competitive organization, is a product of conflict, accommodation and assimilation' (1921:508). (In the later statement Park reformulated this in terms of four levels: ecological, economic, political and one combining the personal and cultural.)

Racial consciousness developed on the second level. It was an acquired trait associated in intensity with the struggle for status; but unrestricted competition could be unwelcome to people on both sides and race relations were often characterized by a relatively stable equilibrium. The superior group might be unwilling to compete on equal terms with those of inferior status and disposed to represent them as suited to a different place in the economic order (Park underplayed this element in his views). The lower group might struggle to acquire a niche in which they would enjoy relative security from competition with members of the more powerful group. Prejudice (which was to be distinguished from animosity) was an attempt to restrain competition so as to establish a monopolistic hold over a niche within the division of labour. Park attached much significance to the development of consciousness on the ecological level, as was evident in his proposition that race relations were the relations between people conscious of the ways in which they were distinguished by marks of racial descent. As has already been seen, this trapped him into viewing Brazil through United States eyes and to neglecting the long chain of factors which intervene between phenotypical traits and cultural meanings.

E. Franklin Frazier, who has been described as Park's most perfect pupil, elaborated the theory in *Race and Culture Contacts in the Modern World*. The book is divided into four parts in parallel with Park's four levels and differs little in conception, though the fourth level is called that of social organization. This is said to be 'created to accommodate peoples with different racial and cultural backgrounds' and to represent 'the heart of the problem'. Where race relations have advanced beyond the regulation of an unequal legal status by the plantation system, there are five alternative ways in which peoples of different race and culture can be made to form part of a cooperating organization: (i) caste, in which inequality is justified in religious terms; (ii) biracialism, as in the United States, in which the principle of caste is interwoven with class distinctions; (iii) cultural pluralism, as in the USSR. In modern industrial societies with increasingly mobile populations, both biracialism and cultural pluralism tend to break down, to be replaced by either (iv) assimilation, as in Brazil; or (v) nationalistic movements, in which the cultural values of the minority are elevated above those of the dominant group (Frazier, 1957·34–5).

The ecological theory was important to the establishment of sociology as an independent discipline; it provided a set of analogies which facilitated the study of racial contacts across the world, but no great claims can be made for it as a general theory because the simple addition of levels was inadequate to expand a theory about the unconscious behaviour of plants and animals to incorporate the conscious behaviour of humans. Park did not succeed in demonstrating that the higher levels were products of the ones beneath them. That the introduction of consciousness into patterns of behaviour brings in a radically new element can be illustrated, firstly, by considering migration. Plant species can colonize new continents when their seeds are carried by the winds or waves, or when they are taken there by birds or men. There is a human analogy, for just as seeds or small birds may regularly be blown to the Antarctic and perish there, so men may continue visiting that continent staying ever longer as their technology enables them to withstand the cold. But this is a poor explanation of human migration. The earlier 'discoverers' of America – both the Norse settlers from Greenland and Christopher Columbus – may have come there by accident, but most human migration is a planned operation drawing upon previous capital and either withdrawing or expanding a colony as advantage dictates.

Secondly, there is an important distinction between the unconscious competition for resources as plants and animals migrate, and the conscious competition of humans; this bears upon the definition of conflict. One sociologist (Coser, 1956:8) has written of conflict as 'a struggle over values and claims to scarce status, power and resources in which the aims of the opponents are to neutralize, injure or eliminate their rivals'. Animals, insects and plants neutralize, injure or eliminate their rivals, but in studying their societies there can be no distinction between competition and conflict. Among humans, any distinction must centre upon the observation that people compete with one another only by observing recognized rules of conduct. Athletics teams compete; if they are caught breaking the rules they may be suspended or eliminated from the competition. Manufacturing companies compete with one another, but are required to observe the law, which may include provisions about fair trading. Members of different racial groups may hate one another, but still feel that it would be wrong to kill their opponents, even though this feeling, and the implicit rule, may be considered suspended in times of riot. The classic example of human conflict is that of warfare, yet there are supposed to be rules of war, and even in wars men retain ideas about fair and unfair ways of fighting. Though there can be no clear general distinction between competition and conflict, the distinction is worth preserving in the study of human societies. Park presented competition as a continuous process which was at work irrespective of whether individuals were conscious of it; that is, he thought of it in the sense in which it is used on the first level, to explain plant and animal ecology. He overlooked the sense in which competition was used on the second level as a way of restraining conflict. Man's ability to regulate competition enables him to achieve the relatively stable equilibrium that can characterize racial relations.

Thirdly, the processes by which humans discover places in which they may settle, and by which they exploit their environment, are so much more complex that the analogy is of little value. When a plant species takes over a new territory this does not of itself change the relation between one plant and another. The new environment may have a special selective effect and bring about a gradual change in the composition of the plant colony. But a human group that settles in a new territory will be already differentiated by status, power and material interest. There will be competition within the group of a kind not found among the plants, and the balance of power within it will be affected by the relative advantage that sections of the group can obtain from exploiting the new opportunities. The ecological approach is of little assistance in the explanation of conflict, or power relations, or the inheritance of inequality in human societies. Far from attempting to demonstrate or strengthen Park's claims about the way in which a change in any one level would inevitably have repercussions upon the others, Frazier passed over this problem, crucial though it was to a genuinely ecological theory. Where the theory proved most useful was in its more modest applications to the differentiation of urban zones and the changes they underwent in the course of a city's economic growth.

The Freudian Theory

The first writer to apply psychoanalytical interpretations to the examination of racial relations in a full length study was John Dollard. He opened his discussion of prejudice with a reference to the view that it was a defensive attitude intended to preserve white prerogatives, acknowledging that this might be one of its functions but objecting that nevertheless such an explanation was unsatisfactory.

> Persons with little need to prop self-esteem through the pain and humiliation of others may participate in formal prejudice patterns, but they will participate without much affect and as a mere convention . . . Race prejudice is an emotional fact and must be connected with the rest of the emotional life of each individual who experiences it (Dollard, 1937:442).

To ask 'why do people need prejudice?' was to ask a new and important question. Dollard's answer was the frustration and aggression hypothesis. When a child is brought up, all sorts of limitations are placed upon its freedom. Social living and human culture require a degree of orderliness and discipline to which children have to be trained. The character of the adult person is therefore a record of frustrations and of reactions to them. According to Freudian theory the basic reaction is the aggressive response designed to reassert mastery, but a child frequently cannot react in this way because the person limiting his freedom is a parent or someone whom he finds it unprofitable to attack. He must either turn the aggression in on himself or store it up, waiting for a suitable opportunity to discharge it. This was Dollard's first key concept, that of a generalized or 'free-floating' aggression held in store. The second one was social permission to attack a particular target group. Society prohibits many kinds of aggression because it can be disruptive, but certain relatively defenceless groups may be made to serve as scapegoats open to legitimate attack. The third key proposition was that scapegoats must be uniformly identifiable so that other persons run no risk of being mistaken for them. This was where Negro 'visibility' came in. The badge of colour was the sign that told the prejudiced person whom to hate and made easy and consistent discrimination possible. 'In our sense' wrote Dollard, 'race prejudice is always irrational' (1937:443–6). In a later article he improved on this formulation by distinguishing two kinds of aggression. When someone attacked the person or group responsible for his frustration, like a striker attacking blackleg labour or an agent of his employer, this was direct aggression. When, however, the person frustrated could not or did not dare attack those responsible but instead took it out on a substitute, he was displacing his aggression. Because there would also be some free-floating aggression seeking an outlet, this would latch on to the expression of direct aggression adding to it an extra and more emotional element which might be responsible for the irrational features often observable in situations of rational conflict (Dollard 1938).

The theory may be outlined in four propositions:

1 Social life causes a build up of frustration in the individual's psychological make-up.
2 The frustration can be eased by being released as aggression.
3 (a) Aggression is more easily released by displacement upon suitable targets.
   (b) For white peoples, blackness is associated with repressed fears and desires.
   (c) The more defenceless a minority, the more suitable it is as a target.
4 Whenever direct aggression is released it is accompanied by displaced aggression, adding an irrational element to the rational attack.

The psychoanalytical approach can contribute more to the study of racial and ethnic relations than just a theory of aggression. In his study of a Mississippi town Dollard was sharply critical of any assumption that custom was powerful enough to maintain the subjection of the Negroes (Banton, 1977:112–22). He held that the social system was maintained by active pressures, social and physical; to identify them it was necessary to lay bare the differential advantages of membership in particular classes and colour-castes and find out how these were translated into personal gratifications. His method was to describe three kinds of gain: economic, sexual and prestige, which middle-class whites derived from their superior position at the expense of blacks and to some extent of lower-class whites. The economic gains derived from their ability to mobilize political power in order to control the economic system to their advantage. Sexual gains could be enjoyed by white men in so far as they had access to black women as well as white women (though Dollard may have conveyed an exaggerated impression of the extent to which they did have or utilize this access). The third gain was what would now be called deference. The white man was accustomed to receiving deference from blacks in advance of demands, it appeared as a submissive affection freely yielded, suggesting that aggressive demands were being passively received, and giving him a gratifying sense of mastery over others. Whites had the satisfaction that went with mastery, superiority, control, maturity and a sense of duty well-fulfilled. They had the pleasure of despising blacks. Negroes were permitted slack work habits, irresponsibility and, within limits, more personal freedom than would have been possible in a competitive, economically progressive society. This helped explain why they did not try harder to change the system. The 'tolerant' attitude of whites towards crime in the Negro quarter and their acceptance of slack work habits further weakened Negro resources for mobilizing pressure against traditional expectations.

The area of overlap between this theory and that of Park is small, and closer examination reveals that they are concerned with different problems. This raises issues that will not be pursued here since this book is primarily concerned with sociological theories, but it should be noted that Freudian explanations can bear upon a central sociological problem: that of how individuals are motivated to maintain or change a social structure.

Structural-functionalism

A new phase in sociological theory, which in retrospect has been identified with the writing of Talcott Parsons, can be discerned in the United States from the late 1930s. Of his contemporaries who tackled questions of racial and ethnic relations the most notable were the social anthropologist W. Lloyd Warner and those associated with him – Kingsley Davis, Wilbert E. Moore and Robin M. Williams – and the considerable group of scholars who contributed to Gunnar Myrdal's massive synthesis, *An American Dilemma.*

These writers applied in their own fields a mode of reasoning that has proven powerful in economics, viewing human behaviour as governed by the efforts of individuals to attain their objectives. To some extent this involved the rational utilization of means which could help them towards their goals (the means–end relation) but it did not exclude considerations which could not be rationally justified (such as the high value placed upon gold, pearls, and diamonds). Each individual sought his own ends but society came about because these ends were fitted into a common pattern (the cooperation associated with the division of labour) and because individuals shared common values (e.g. the beliefs that murder should be punished and that pearls are more valuable than cowrie shells) (see Davis, 1948:143–4). This approach made possible some valuable analyses of basic institutions in United States society and brought to the fore the functional relations between institutions, but it was almost as weak as Park's approach in the treatment of dysfunctions.

The conception of societies as founded upon the sharing of common ultimate ends introduced an element of relativism: social activities had to be interpreted in terms of the value structure of the society in which they occurred. Thus questions of racial discrimination, of assimilation, and of the legitimacy of a minority identity had to be viewed against the background of United States political principles. The leaders of the republic in 1776 had been unable to differentiate their new nation from the English nation by emphasizing differences of race or culture or history: they grounded their distinctiveness in a commitment to a more egalitarian democracy. Successive generations in the United States have been taught that their nationhood derives from loyalty to those principles, so it was not surprising if American sociologists saw their society in similar terms. Gunnar Myrdal's eighteenth-century rationalism fitted in with this outlook almost as if by design. The mistake which he, like others, made with respect to black Americans can be seen from the sub-title with which Myrdal introduced part of his argument, 'The Negro Community as a Pathological Form of an American Community' (1944:927; on Myrdal, see Banton, 1977:125–9). He assumed not only that blacks wanted to be assimilated into United States society like any other minority, but that this outcome was the only one worth serious consideration. Like Warner in his treatment of inter-group relations in Yankee City, Myrdal thought that any attachment of Negroes to separate institutions delayed their assimilation. They could be assimilated only as individuals. Myrdal did not see that the disparagement of blacks was built into the core of the white value structure; that this had to be changed before black citizens could move to an equal footing; and that, by banding together, blacks could exert more pressure upon whites to change those values. To a considerable extent this weakness in the structural-functional approach stemmed from concentration upon a single society and neglect of the comparative perspective.

In so far as the writers of this school examined issues of racial and ethnic relations, they pictured individuals as responding to incentives and as held back by sanctions. To this extent they were implicitly drawing upon a Rational Choice theory, indeed, Myrdal's lengthy consideration of Southern agriculture and the economics of the labour market can be seen as explaining the constraints upon the choices open to those involved. The range of Myrdal's report was so encyclopaedic that it seemed to have said the last word on the subject for a whole generation. Presenting the issue of *The Negro Problem and Modern Democracy* as a moral dilemma for whites, it did not – with some minor qualifications – help the process of refining a sociological theory that could stimulate further research.

The Class Theory

The prevailing orthodoxies were attacked with great vigour in 1948 in a wide-ranging book entitled *Caste, Class and Race*, written by Oliver C.

Cox, a black sociologist from Trinidad who taught in the United States. Two themes run through it. One is the meaning of caste. The second is Cox's conviction that racial problems – and most other social problems – can be satisfactorily explained only in the terms of a political class analysis (see Banton, 1977:129–34 and Miles, 1980, for more detailed discussion).

Cox identified as the crucial fallacy in Park's thinking 'his belief that the beginnings of modern race prejudice may be traced back to the immemorial periods of human associations'; with this went a set of definitions that enabled him to find evidence of 'race problems' among the ancient Greeks, covering up the differences between the ethnocentrism or colour prejudice of ancient and modern times. Cox's thesis was that 'all racial antagonisms can be traced to the policies and attitudes of the leading capitalist people, the white people of Europe and North America, beginning around 1493–4. This was the time when total disregard for the human rights and physical power of the non-Christian peoples of the world, the coloured peoples, was officially assumed by the first two great colonizing European nations.' Capitalism forced employers to treat labour power as an impersonal commodity, an item in the cost of production, like the rent of a building or the rate of interest on a loan, rather than as part of the life of human beings. To make labour power a commodity, the capitalists had to dehumanize it by persuading themselves and others that their workers were sub-human, inferior, or not people like themselves. They began by representing Indians as so barbarous and sinful that they ought 'to serve those of more elevated natures, such as the Spaniards possess'. Then when blacks became available they switched their energies to the development of ideologies which would facilitate their exploitation. Beliefs about racial inferiority were mass psychological instruments serving political and economic ends and were intentionally built up through propaganda. In Brazil, where there was no white ruling class answerable to a foreign white power, there was no use of nationalist ideology to serve the purposes of actual or potential ruling classes, and a favourable attitude towards physical mixing as a means of Christianizing the heathen and exploiting their resources. Such considerations show, according to Cox, that 'race relations . . . are proletarian-bourgeois relations and hence political-class relations'. When, as in northern states, the proletariat advances, black workers are enabled to vote, to acquire a consciousness of their class position, and they suffer less from prejudice and discrimination.

Cox could agree with Park's emphasis upon the importance of the tendency of any group to try to obtain a monopoly upon a valuable niche within an economic structure, but he saw the development of such groups as constrained by a world economic system that limited the available alternatives much more closely than was implied in Park's description of

European expansion. Cox presented racial prejudice as a weapon in the exploitation of others rather than as a defensive reflection of group solidarity. He called upon a theory of ideology which saw the development of ideas as a response to the material interests of powerful classes, but he was careful to maintain that racial groups were a sub-category of ethnic groups, having the same general character except that they could be identified by phenotypical traits.

A view which reinforces Cox's thesis on several important points has been advanced by Marvin Harris, who contends that 'differences in race relations within Latin America are at root a matter of the labor systems in which the respective subordinate and superordinate groups became enmeshed'. Prejudices were developed against Negroes rather than Indians because Negroes could be enslaved and whites needed a rationalization for their ill-treatment of blacks. In Brazil the whites 'were compelled to create an intermediate free group of half-castes to stand between them and the slaves because there were certain essential economic and military functions for which slave labor was useless, and for which no whites were available'. In the United States mulattoes appeared only after a large intermediate class of whites had already secured the positions that freed slaves might otherwise have taken up. This imposed a ceiling upon the mobility of mulattos and set the United States upon quite a different course (Harris, 1964a:65–89).

It will be apparent that both Cox and Harris derive some of their inspiration from the Marxist tradition of social analysis, though neither of them has claimed to be advancing a Marxist interpretation. Leaving the question of Marxism aside for a moment, it should be possible to infer from Cox's book and some similar writing a theory which can be contrasted with the Ecological Theory. To do so it is necessary to attribute to Cox and those who follow him two unstated major premises about the source of class formation. These premises have not been listed as propositions forming part of a theory of racial and ethnic relations since they belong with a more general theory of society. Something which forms part of that theory and can reasonably be called the Class Theory of Racial and Ethnic Relations can then be seen as presupposing (a) that the foundation of social life consists in the material productive forces and the relations of production necessary to the harnessing of them; and (b) that the forms of alignment and conflict which will ultimately prove most important are those based on class interest. The theory then holds that:

1 As European capitalism expanded into territories where natural resources were abundant, there were advantages in securing a source of labour power which, being distinctive, could easily be kept in a servile state.
2 Within this unequal relationship beliefs justifying the inequality were

developed. These have been built into the structure of capitalist societies, dividing white workers from black.

3   Racial categories exist in the social life of capitalist societies because (a) they serve the interests of the ruling classes, and (b) the contradictions in these societies have not yet reached the point at which the true nature of the social system is apparent to the workers.

Any attempt at formulating such a theory in this sort of way will evoke much dispute, but it is incontestable that many sociologists do reason along these lines and if their arguments can be put in propositional form it makes it easier to compare the merits of different theories.

Dispute about whether it is possible to formulate a 'Class theory' in this way is likely to be involved and confusing because class analysis of a Marxist kind derives from the Hegelian tradition in philosophy and draws upon a theory of knowledge very different from that employed in the Kantian tradition from which orthodox Western sociology takes its philosophical directions. A contemporary exponent of the Kantian approach, Sir Karl Popper, expounds a doctrine of what he calls philosophical pluralism, according to which there are three worlds (i) the physical world of matter; (ii) the mental world of subjective states; and (iii) the world of objective knowledge which results from humans' attempts to understand what is around them. This knowledge 'is a product of men just as honey is the product of bees' (Popper, 1972:154). In this tradition, a definition has to be suited to its purpose, depending on the theory to be tested and developed. In Malinowski's splendid phrase, 'without problems there are no facts'. What appears to a research worker as a problem is decided by his training and his interest in following up a line of thought. He uses the theories of his subject to organize and refine his observations. Solving one problem, he discovers more, and from this activity of problem-solving an intellectual tradition emerges.

Those within the Hegelian tradition subscribe to what, by contrast, can be called philosophical monism. The observer is within the world, but there are laws of its development which he can grasp. The world of knowledge is not separate, and what men think they know is determined by their position in societies at particular stages of their development. A man who has grasped the principles according to which his world is developing should use his knowledge to speed that process, serving, in Marx's phrase, as a midwife to history. Definitions must correspond to the nature of the things defined and they can be understood only if they are located in the processes of change. A Marxist would be sceptical of the suggestion that it is possible to select a problem and then compare the power of orthodox sociological and Marxist theories to resolve it; whereas the orthodox sociologist thinks it sensible to concentrate on the sorts of questions that he has some prospect of being able to answer, the Marxist feels bound to concentrate on the politically significant problems. An orthodox sociologist might ask whether racial prejudice (as measured by scores on a particular scale) is associated with downward social mobility (as measured by comparing a male subject's occupational status with that of his father). A Marxist would say that this is not one of the real problems, whereas the existence of racism is such a problem and that it can be accounted for only as an emanation of a particular society located in time and space.

Marxist writers have uncovered many dubious assumptions in conventional sociology. They have been most effective when on the attack. To understand the various kinds of alternative that they have put forward, it is important to bear in mind the changes in the sources of their inspiration.

At the end of the 1940s the image of Marx's work dominant in Western universities was that which Engels had reinforced in his address at his friend's graveside, when he described Marx as a scientist who had done for human history what Darwin had done for the natural history of life. Marx had shown that historical change is ultimately the result of the tools man uses. He had also, by discovering the nature of 'surplus value' placed the study of economics on a sound scientific basis. History and economics had been united. He had explained that when new tools or methods of production were invented their benefits were not equally distributed; one class would be more favourably placed than another to appropriate the surplus value generated by the people who used the tools. Those who could mobilize political power used it to gain or reinforce advantages in the economic structure. Having started upon such a course, they were caught up in the system as much as anyone else and were impelled to compete with one another in the struggle to accumulate capital and discover new markets. Consciously or unconsciously they rewarded those writers who produced philosophies, histories and sociologies which justified the prevailing social order and they saw to it that such works were publicized. In this way the ruling ideas of an age were the ideas of its ruling class. The texts chiefly used in elaborating this view of Marx were *Capital* and the 'Preface to a Critique of Political Economy' with its account of the five stages of historical development and its proclamation that the Marxist could explain 'with the precision of natural science' how in times of crisis the whole superstructure of society was brought into line with changes in its economic basis.

The interpretation of Marxism as the science of history occasioned many problems for its adherents. Most of the difficulties were brought together in the doubts and discussions about determinism. Predictions had been derived from the theory, apparently quite properly, which had not been borne out by events. Where was the evidence of the increasing misery of the proletariat under capitalism? Why had the first socialist revolution occurred in Russia instead of in a more advanced capitalist society? What had Marxism to say about the new class of technocrats in the West who did not share in the ownership of the industries they managed, or about the new class of party officials and bureaucrats in the Soviet Union and the peoples' democracies? Who had predicted them? While Marxists castigated functionalism in sociology they relied upon functionalist arguments to explain such developments (e.g. the nature and extent of racism) as necessary to particular social systems in particular phases of development. The purpose of studying social change was not to understand society but to learn how to change it; but, if the underlying trend was towards the polarization of classes, when was it the midwife's duty to help the proletariat gain greater wages and become more committed to the system? When would it be better to sabotage such gains, increase discontent, and accelerate the revolution?

The debate was transformed in the 1950s by a new generation's discovery – or rediscovery – of the writings of the 'young Marx'. It became apparent from the 'Economic and Philosophic Manuscripts of 1844' that Marx had arrived at his views about the pattern of historical change before he embarked on his study of economic theory. His 'scientific' extrapolations about the future of capitalism came from his encounter with Hegel more than from that with Ricardo. The first reaction to this reinterpretation of Marx was to argue that there had been a major break in his work round about 1845, which enabled the orthodox Marxists to claim that the master's most favoured works were those of the more mature and scientific phase of his career. This defence became untenable with the publication (available in English only from 1972) of a document written some ten years before *Capital* which has become known as the *Grundrisse* (a German word that can be translated as 'foundations'). Even before this, another, and much more flexible, interpretation of Marxism had gained a footing in the West. Marx was seen as offering not a theory but a method or a model that could be used in the study of history and social affairs. As C. Wright Mills (1962:38) wrote:

> A model is a more or less systematic inventory of the elements to which we must pay attention if we are to understand something. It is not true or false; it is useful and adequate to varying degrees. A theory, in contrast, is a statement which can be proved true or false, about the causal weight and relations of the elements of a model. Only in terms of this distinction can we understand why Marx's work is truly great, and also why it contains so much that is erroneous, ambiguous, or inadequate. His model is what is great; that is what is alive in Marxism.

At the centre of the new interpretation, instead of determinism, was a conception of man as possessing talents which no social system had yet enabled him fully to develop. Capitalism was worse than previous systems because it alienated the worker from his product, so it was no use trying to reform society by tinkering with structures built on capitalist principles. The task was to create a social order in which man at last could realize himself. This newer interpretation of Marx did not make such grand claims to constitute a guide to political action. It was ready to see particular sectors or spheres of human activity, such as that of ideology, as enjoying a relative autonomy from the economic base, and it became possible for people to think of themselves as both sociologists and Marxists. For those who insisted upon the primacy of class struggle as an axiom there could be no comfortable compromise: a Marxist must regard 'bourgeois' sociology as a product of class interest intellectually transcended by a more comprehensive structure of explanation. Striving to reconcile such tensions, those sympathetic to Marxism took up many different stances which is why it is so difficult at the present time to characterize a Marxist view of racial and ethnic relations.

The Pluralist Theory

There are fewer writers who call themselves, or are called, pluralists, than there are Marxists, but relative to the numbers involved, the diversity of opinion among the pluralists is every bit as great. The situation is confounded by two different traditions in the use of the word. The first has stemmed from descriptions of the political structure of the United States as pluralistic: power is distributed between the legislature, the executive and the judiciary, between the federal government, the states, and the municipalities; between regional, racial and class interests all represented by a host of pressure groups. The second usage is more sociological: it came into prominence in the early 1960s as a reaction against the inadequacy of the structural-functionalist model for studying societies deeply divided along racial and cultural lines. The most challenging (if at times frustrating) formulation of this new viewpoint came from the Jamaican social anthropologist, M. G. Smith. Smith harked back to the use by J. S. Furnival of the expression 'plural society' to identify the sort of society observable in Southeast Asia where there was a medley of peoples – European, Chinese, Indian and various native groups:

> They mix but do not combine. Each group holds by its own
> religion, its own culture and language, its own ideas and ways.
> As individuals they meet, but only in the market place, in

buying and selling. There is a plural society with different sections of the community living side by side, but separately, within the same political unit. Even in the economic sphere there is division of labour along racial lines (Furnival, 1948:304).

In the pre-independence period, upon which the analysis was based, the plural society consisted of a collection of ethnic communities which shared no common loyalties or feelings of solidarity. During the war they offered little resistance to the invading Japanese. People cooperated because, within the sphere of public order maintained by the imperial power, it was in their interest to do so. 'The typical plural society is a business partnership in which, to many partners, bankruptcy signifies release rather than disaster' (Furnival, 1948:308).

Smith protested that 'unless we choose to ignore one-half of mankind and most of its history, we cannot deny the validity and significance of the distinction Furnival made between those societies which derive their integration from normative consensus, and those which depend for their order or regulation by force' (Smith, 1965:xi–xii). His arguments were the more effective because they echoed the other sense of pluralism as a political theory according to which the state was an association which had distinctive functions but no supremacy over other associations, no monopoly of loyalty, no right to stand as the sole source of morality and no claim to obedience beyond the affairs which were its special charge. Because of its connotations of countervailing power and resistance to centralization, 'pluralism' had positive connotations in the vocabulary of United States social scientists, whereas pluralism in Smith's sense was something for their society to avoid. Hence some of the confusion.

Smith's contention was that if there were societies which continued to exist without a moral consensus 'we need to know the basis on which their present order rests, and their properties as social systems. The key questions here concern the levels and conditions of stability, the degrees of functional coherence, and the structural variety which these societies exhibit' (1965:xi–xiii). His concerns became that of establishing a claim that there is a special class of plural societies and of describing their attributes. His approach cannot by itself offer any explanation of why these societies are plural or of the part played by physical differences in their structure. For this purpose it is better to turn to the work of Smith's collaborator, Leo Kuper, though his standpoint is rather different.

Kuper found both structural-functionalism and Marxism inadequate to account for important features of the racially and ethnically divided societies of Africa. He examined the course taken by the revolutions that occurred in Zanzibar, Rwanda, Burundi and Algeria and found that, although there were class differences in the three black countries after independence, and in Algeria prior to independence, once the revolutions started they developed along racial rather than class lines. From this he concluded that although class conflict might be the source of revolutionary change in many societies, there were some where this was not the case, and he identified plural societies as being built round conflicts of a kind other than class. The conquest of one people by another of different race frequently led to the creation of such societies in which 'it is the political relations which appreciably determine the relationship to the means of production, rather than the reverse, and the catalyst of revolutionary change is to be found in the structure of power, rather than in economic changes which exhaust the possibilities of a particular mode of production' (Kuper, 1974:226).

However fundamental racial differences might be in particular societies, he thought it impossible to develop a general theory based upon racial differentiation since even when that was present it might not be relevant in social relations, and where it was considered relevant its significance was highly variable. Class structures were intrinsic to society but race was not. 'Class societies may be viewed as arising directly out of the interaction of the members of the society', whereas race 'is in some sense extrinsic to that interaction. To be sure, the racial structure is also constituted by the interaction, but the racial differences which are societally elaborated, have preceded that interaction' (1974:61). There are difficulties with such a comparison, even if only because class differences do not necessarily lead straight to class consciousness, and there is anyway room for much dispute as to what people are conscious of when they are class conscious.

From Kuper's views (see especially 1974:203–4) it is possible to deduce a Pluralist Theory as presupposing that the Class Theory explains the nature of racial categorization in societies in which the chief forms of alignment and conflict derive from the relations of groups to the means of production. What Kuper would call his theory of racial relations in plural societies then holds that:

1 Societies composed of status groups or estates that are phenotypically distinguished, have different positions in the economic order, and are differentially incorporated into the political structure, are to be called plural societies and distinguished from class societies. In plural societies political relations influence relations to the means of production more than any influence in the reverse direction.

2 When conflicts develop in plural societies they follow the lines of racial cleavage more closely than those of class.

3 Racial categories in plural societies are historically conditioned; they are shaped by inter-group competition and conflict.

Whereas Kuper's version of a pluralist theory is an extension or qualification of the Class Theory, other writers who favour pluralism as offering an approach to the analysis of racial and ethnic relations make little or no use of class explanations. Nor have they expressed their views in the sort of terms which permit their expression in propositional form. Kuper's theory is directed to societies in which racial and ethnic alignments are no less important than class alignment (like his native South Africa). Central importance attaches to his concept of differential incorporation, which he uses to follow up the way in which particular groups, the ones which are the first to get there in strength, take over positions of power in a changing society and then use those positions to promote their own interests. Because this is the focus of his interests, Kuper tends to take for granted the physical characteristics used to identify groups. He does not investigate variations in their social construction, or the appropriateness of the racial idiom to distinguish the Tutsi and Hutu of Rwanda and Burundi when their physical differences could be so small that in the fighting many were killed by people who thought, wrongly, that they belonged to the opposing group. In this Kuper's work contrasts with that of M. G. Smith who, because he started from societies like that of Jamaica in which there was a continuous gradation of complexion, was at pains to distinguish a variety of ways of analysing variations in what was perceived as 'colour', namely, pheno-typical, genealogical, associational, cultural and structural. Nevertheless, as a proposal for modifying a Marxist approach so as to get a better grip upon the chief features of a certain kind of society, Kuper's theory is a challenge to critics on both his flanks.

The Split Labour Market Theory

An interesting product of the ferment within Marxism is that theory recently advanced by a second sociologist from South Africa who works in the United States. Whereas Oliver Cox minimized the significance of racial prejudice in the white working class, Edna Bonacich (1972) starts from an awareness of the extent to which differential power in the labour market can generate antagonism between white and black workers. Her theory can be stated in the following terms:

1 Some labour markets are split along ethnic lines, so that higher-paid groups of workers are distinguished from cheaper labour by their ethnic characteristics (in which racial features may be included).
2 The three key classes have different interests:
   (a) Members of the business class want as cheap and docile a labour force as possible in order to compete with other businesses.
   (b) Members of the higher-paid labour class are threatened by the introduction of cheaper labour.

(c) The very weakness of the class of cheaper labour makes it threatening to the higher-paid since it can so easily be controlled by the business class.

3 The higher-paid class will seek to defend its position by either,
   (a) pressing for the exclusion of the cheaper class from the territory; or
   (b) resorting to a caste arrangement which restricts the cheaper group to a particular set of jobs paid at lower rates.

4 Ethnic antagonism is produced by the competition that arises from a differential price for labour; it does not necessarily emanate from the dominant group but may be the product of interaction. Ethnic antagonism in large measure expresses class conflict between the higher and lower-paid groups within the labour force.

Cox traced ethnic antagonism to the use of racial ideology by the ruling class to keep separate two sections of the working class who would otherwise unite. By contrast, Bonacich maintains that the business class supports a liberal or *laissez-faire* ideology that would permit all workers to compete freely in an open market; the source of ethnic antagonism is not necessarily found in the business class; in some circumstances it is to be traced to a racial labour aristocracy which seeks to obtain or exploit a monopoly of the better paid jobs. Like Cox, Bonacich locates the origin of ethnic antagonism in the development of capitalism. This produced in Western Europe a white proletariat and a price of labour which is high relative to that in the Third World, so that ultimately it is the international labour market which is split. Also, like Cox, Bonacich employs a strong definition of class in which particular classes are seen as historical entities. She sees her work as falling within the Marxist intellectual tradition but criticizes orthodox Marxists for failing to recognize that the white working class has often been among the more reactionary forces in the modern world. Orthodox Marxists suggest that the white working class has been either duped or bribed, whereas Bonacich's formulation attempts 'to show how the material conditions of white workers produced by imperialism distort the progressive class struggle against capital into a reactionary stance on the race question' (1979:40).

The Split Labour Market Theory can be applied in the study of as many kinds of society as the Class Theory, and many more than the Pluralist Theory; in many respects it marks a significant advance.

Comparison of theories

It is important to the development of their subject that sociologists should seek out situations in which one theory can be confronted with another. Two kinds of confrontation are possible. Sometimes two explanations of the same observation can be compared to see if one is superior to the other. Examining the empirical adequacy of explanations in this way forces people to reformulate and revise the theories themselves. It is a most salutary discipline. In other circumstances it may only be possible to compare theories in the abstract to see if they are logically coherent and consistent; to see whether they rest on the same presuppositions; to ascertain whether they address observations on similar or different levels of reality; and, where possible, to group them so that one can be subsumed under another.

If the theories detailed in Chapter 3 and in this chapter are examined in the second of these two ways, at least three levels of reality can be discerned: the organic level; that of human personality; and that of social action. There is a further possibility, since some writers believe that there are regularities in the development of human societies which transcend those observable on the three lower levels.

Of the theories considered so far, three seek to explain relations on the organic level: the Typological, Selectionist and Ecological Theories; one deals with the level of personality, the Freudian Theory; the level of social action is addressed by the Ecological Theory and by structural functionalism; while the question of a sociological theory of a more historical kind is raised by the Class, Pluralist, and Split Labour Market Theories. Five of these theories propose different explanations of the origin of racial antagonism: the Typological, Selectionist, Freudian, Class and Split Labour Market Theories. Is one explanation superior to the others? On present evidence it would appear that those theories which conceive of racial antagonism as existing on the same level can be confronted with one another whereas those which deal with different levels do not meet up.

The Typological Theory launched the assumption that inter-racial relations were different from intra-racial relations and that therefore some distinctive theory was necessary to account for their special features. It is ironic, in view of its historical significance, that this theory should be the only one of those discussed which has definitely been falsified and superseded. The Selectionist Theory and that part of the Ecological Theory which deals with plants, animals and the behavioural capacity of humans, both explain how, through inheritance and selection, populations with particular genetic characteristics develop in particular environments. Both should be viewed as part of the more general theory of natural selection and evaluated in terms of their ability to account for the observations to which they are addressed.

Humans develop personalities which are more complex than those of other animals and are built round the unconscious drives and inhibitions which the Freudian Theory seeks to interpret. Social and clinical psychologists have formulated a range of more particular theories at the same general level which it is impracticable to review in a book of this kind. There is, of course, an organic basis to behaviour at this level but, since it is more complex, it cannot be adequately explained by the theory of natural selection alone.

In much the same way the level of conscious behaviour is to be distinguished from that of unconscious behaviour. Being born into societies, men and women learn to adopt shared goals and they consciously direct their behaviour to try and attain their ends. Park and Frazier claimed that the study of the conscious behaviour of men and women involved in racial and ethnic relations could be brought within a more general ecological theory, but according to the argument advanced in this chapter the most distinctive features of human ecology are the product of socio-cultural rather than biological evolution and require separate explanations. Most sociological theory is directed to the explanation of social action, but few sociologists have attempted to formulate an explicit comparative theory of racial and ethnic relations.

For several decades now it has been thought useful to distinguish between the realms of macro-sociology and micro-sociology. These expressions have been taken over from economics and they are unsatisfactory in so far as they imply that it is sufficient to carry through an analysis on the macro-level alone or the micro-level alone. Most social scientists would probably agree that macro- and micro- are names for starting points and that any serious analysis will have to cope with the interaction between macro- and micro- phenomena. A better nomenclature has been proposed by Theodor Geiger (1962:147–50) who distinguished between katascopic and anascopic theories. Katascopic theories look downwards, showing how the facts are influenced by macro-sociological relations. Anascopic series look upwards, showing how the facts in question are built up from micro-sociological relations. Both kinds of theory deal with the same level of social reality but differ in their approach to it. If this conception of macro-sociology is accepted then the student of racial and ethnic relations has to take account of just three levels of reality, the biological, the psychological and the sociological.

However, this does not resolve the problem which the Marxist challenge presents to orthodox sociology. Earlier in this chapter reference was made to two interpretations of Marx's work, but there are many schools of thought which are inspired by it in varying degrees. At one end of the spectrum stands Engels' image of Marx as the man who discovered the laws of historical development. Those who today take *Capital* as their main text see the making and transmission of history in the First World of Europe and North America as driven by the necessity of capital to accumulate: this leads to the search for new markets in the Third World and to the attempt to control them so that the capitalists can appropriate the surplus generated by the exploited classes. This is said to explain the origin of racism as a weapon facilitating the exploitation of physically distinguishable peoples. An essential feature of this theory is what may be called a strong definition of class. All recorded history is the history of class struggles. A class is a set of individuals standing in a common relationship to the means of production who will in due course be brought to a consciousness of their position in the process by which capitalism develops. The nature of a class can be understood only if it is located within the historical process.

The other end of the Marxist spectrum shades off into conventional historiography and social science. Orthodox sociologists see the making and transmission of history as an erratic and uncertain process; they are unpersuaded that capitalism is a coherent system or that it increases understanding to state that South Africa, for example, is a capitalist society; they see social and economic relations in the Second World of the Soviet Union and the peoples' democracies as reflecting, in only slightly modified form, the same basic principles as those underlying the economic and social life of the nations in the First World. They note that although Marxism is presented as a comprehensive theory of society it cannot in its own terms deal with the problems presented by population growth; a great deal more of history seems to depend upon chance happenings, upon human personalities, and upon the distribution of natural resources, than upon any regularities in economic development. These sociologists utilize a weak definition of class, often meaning by this word no more than a set of individuals standing in a common relationship to the labour market.

In so far as the Pluralist and Split Labour Market Theories operate with a weak definition of class there is no necessary incompatibility between them and orthodox sociology. They are subject to the same canons of proof as other theories in conventional social science. Kuper's theory of racial relations in plural societies, by its stress upon the differential incorporation of racial and ethnic groups in the power structure, opens the door to conventional narrative history. The Split Labour Market Theory can be used to generate hypotheses which can be put to the test and perhaps substantiated or falsified. If it is developed in this way the parallels between this and the Segmented Labour Market theory in economics will be closer. That theory has been seen as an alternative to Human Capital and other neo-classical theories, but it shares with them similar presuppositions and, with the accumulation of empirical studies, all these approaches may well be brought together within a common theoretical framework. They will be members of a single family of theories.

Those who speak for the Pluralist and Split Labour Market Theories may see things differently. If Kuper's view of the plural society is only a qualification of the Class Theory, and if the Split Labour Market Theory is used with a strong definition of class, then they are to be located in the Hegelian philosophical tradition with its distinctive theory about the nature of human knowledge. The Class, Pluralist and Split Labour Market Theories can then be seen as belonging to a family of theories often identified as historical materialism. The spokesman for this viewpoint claim that all 'bourgeois' social science can be subsumed within their theory and accounted for as ideological distortions of the truth produced by class interest.

Conclusion

This chapter has drawn attention to the way in which successive theories of racial and ethnic relations have been proposed to rectify the weaknesses of their predecessors, and has attempted to demonstrate that the processes of theoretical advance can be better appreciated, and perhaps accelerated, if the theories are stated as sets of propositions, over-simplified though they may be. The discussion of these theories has been compressed because the main purpose of the book is to introduce yet another theory, and to set out a case for it as sociologically more attractive than these others. That cannot be properly done unless the alternative theories have first been described so that the reader can assess their relative merits.

6

How competition affects boundaries

The assumption that there is a distinct kind of social relations to be called 'race relations' stemmed from the Typological Theory and from its confusion between signs and the things they signified. Chapter 2 has shown that the three kinds of classification which developed in the New World – appearance, socio-cultural status, and ancestry – did not result from different combinations of American, European and African genes; but that these were forms of social structure making different use of phenotypical features, like skin colour, in the social placement of individuals. Racial typologists were blind to social processes; they thought that zoological differences determined the character of social groups and their inter-relations. In this they were not wholly wrong, because man's biological constitution does decide what he can and cannot do, but the typologists had seized upon characteristics that turned out not to be very important and, in a pre-Darwinian age, they had no conception of evolution, let alone of the differences between biological and socio-cultural evolution. Nor were the typologists aware of the interaction between psychological processes and social structure. They had no explanation of the ways in which individuals vary in the observance of group norms, or of deviance. No group of any size, be it a nation, a 'race', a class, a congregation or a family, maintains itself automatically. Groups dissolve and change: in so far as they continue over time it is because their members are motivated to maintain characteristic forms of behaviour. When they change, it is because individual motivations have changed.

Group continuity over time is encouraged by tuition. An English schoolboy is given lessons on the history of England. He is taught that there were Englishmen a thousand years ago and that he should identify with these people although in most respects they differ from him more than the contemporary Frenchman or German. He is taught how the English were beaten by William the Conqueror in 1066 and how they defeated the Spanish Armada in 1588, and in this way the idea of the English as a nation is given extra life in the twentieth century. The feeling of belonging to such a group is constantly changing. At one time Englishmen were proud of owning a great Empire; then that declined and the sentiment of belonging with the peoples of Western Europe was strengthened. In the future a European identity may be the most important of all, and Englishness become a subcultural attribute with regional rather than national political significance. Whatever happens, people will read the past in a framework constituted by present-day groupings so that these will appear more permanent than the historical record really allows.

The social framework within which people read the past changes with the social and political structure of their society. The population which in 1776 came together as the United States began by being largely English men and women who, within America, came to differentiate themselves as whites in opposition to the blacks (though it was not inevitable that they should have done so). Later they were joined by people from the Balkans, Italy, Turkey, Armenia and other countries, who were also counted as whites. This again was not inevitable; they might have been considered different races, or the category 'white' might have been changed (as it was in Latin America) had not the black–white opposition been built so deeply into the social, legal and political structure. The recent growth of the 'Hispanic' population has in many places called even further into question the certainty of the classification 'white' and shows that this category is socially as problematic as its opposite. All this is not so much a matter of the categories employed by census-takers as of the relative ease with which a dark-skinned person from, say, Afghanistan, can get himself accepted as white in the circumstances in which social privileges depend upon it, and of the consequences for a local group of accepting people whose membership may change the character or appearance of their group.

To pursue this, it is necessary to examine what determines the character of a group and the relative ease with which people can cross its boundary, as when outsiders are admitted to membership or members forsake the group. These are complicated questions and it is best to approach them by starting with the very simplest kinds of group encounter, gradually taking into account more of the factors that influence the patterns of change which spring from contact.

The beginnings of competition

Perhaps the most elemental form of group contact is that known as 'silent trade' in which exchange occurs without the two groups ever meeting. Silent trade has been reported from all over the world, and as far back in history as the time of Herodotus. The parties to it always find some way of incorporating a pricing mechanism. The Pygmies of the Ituri forest of the Congo have been described as exchanging game and forest products for manufactures and fruit produced by neighbouring Negro settlements of agriculturalists. One group places piles of goods at the trading place and retires. The other group places opposite these piles the goods it offers in exchange. The first group returns; if the terms are acceptable, it picks up the proffered exchange items; if they are not, it takes away its own. The two groups may not be of equal power in respect of physical force but the trading relationship is so limited that the exchange is made on equal terms. Silent trade can occur between groups of very unequal power, as, for example, in Brazil, where the government Indian Service has sought to enter into relations with isolated groups of Indians by leaving piles of presents at the side of paths used by the groups in question. Sometimes the Indians accept them, possibly putting out some of their own products in exchange. Sometimes they upset or spoil the piles of presents to indicate that they wish to have nothing to do with the government's agents.

It is therefore possible to regard silent trade as an economic relationship that has the minimum of social concomitants. It can be seen as a preliminary to the development of forms of trading in which the traders meet and bargain over the exchange or sale of a variety of goods. The social concomitants of trading relations depend on the form and intensity of competition between the partners. Relations may take the form either of individual trade, in which individual members of one group trade with members of the other on the same terms as they trade with members of their own group, or of group trade in which one group as a body exchanges goods or services with the other group. A variation upon these two main forms is that of mixed trade in which members of one group trade with members of the other on an individual basis when exchanging or selling some goods and on a group basis when exchanging others; but, for the purposes of analysis, mixed trade is a combination of the two main forms and does not need separate discussion. There is also middleman trading in which intermediaries buy goods from one group and sell them to the other; this also is only a minor variant since the dealings between the middlemen and the main producers must be on an individual or group basis, or some mixture of the two; it will be further considered in Chapter 8. Individual trade will be used as a model for the analysis of individual competition; this will be presented as the process underlying the creation of the pattern in which people are classified by appearance as this has been described in Chapter 2 in connection with Brazil. Group trade will serve correspondingly as a model for group competition as it existed in the Deep South when whites sought group solidarity in order to obtain maximum advantage from their relations with blacks. This underlay the classification by ancestry in which phenotypical characters were used as signs of category membership.

Relations between trading partners also depend upon the intensity of competition. It can be said that competition begins when two individuals or groups both want the same thing and strive for it within a market. There is ample evidence to indicate that people brought up in some cultures are more competitive than others, and much light has been cast on this by David C. McClelland's studies of the need for achievement as described in *The Achieving Society* (1961). Trade can occur between non-competing groups, as when goods are exchanged on a basis of conventional norms about value rather than supply and demand. People brought up in societies based upon subsistence economies may not be orientated towards competitive trade; unless groups with trading skills move in, as Arabs, Lebanese and Indians moved into parts of Africa, the development of a market economy may be slow. The relatively low level of competitiveness among Indians in Central America is one of the components of the pattern of categorization by socio-cultural status.

The Rational Choice Theory

This theory is an adaptation to racial and ethnic relations of a kind of reasoning which is already familiar, under one name or another, in most of the social sciences. In sociology and social psychology it is known as exchange theory; in social anthropology it is called transactional theory following Fredrik Barth, whose work was inspired by the theory of games; in economics, where it is most highly developed, it is identified as neo-classical micro-economics; in political science, and on the boundaries of politics and economics, it is associated with the work of Anthony Downs and Mancur Olsen, and sometimes with the school of public choice theorists (Barry, 1970). Antecedents of the theory can be found in the works of many social theorists, notably Mauss, Malinowski, Lévi-Strauss, and in the structural-functionalist view of action as the use of scarce means to attain an actor's ends. This makes it difficult to decide just which modes of analysis are to be counted as belonging to this family of theories. It also makes it difficult to find a suitable name. From one standpoint the economic theories are appropriately called theories of rational choice and are to be differentiated from the exchange theories in sociology and social psychology, but these latter theories are as yet less systematic, and more particular. As Anthony Heath (1976:176) explains, the rational choice theories tackle the general domain of choice; exchange is merely one part of that domain. If the exchange theories are to be developed and applied in new fields, like that of racial and ethnic relations, they will need to be related to the more general kind of theory (for a highly elaborate but more limited statement of a rational choice approach to racial relations within social psychology see Blalock and Wilken (1979)). For this reason, it seems best to use the name rational choice theory both for the family of theories and for its proposed new member concerned to explain behaviour in the field of racial and ethnic relations.

The theory that is now proposed shares with rational choice theories in other fields two presuppositions: (a) that individuals act so as to obtain maximum net advantage; and (b) that actions at one moment of time influence and restrict the alternatives between which individuals will have to choose on subsequent occasions. For the sociologist, as for the economic historian, the second presupposition is as important as the first. Anyone who applies this theory must deal with alternatives at least as much as with choices.

The theory holds that:

1 Individuals utilize physical and cultural differences in order to create groups and categories by the processes of inclusion and exclusion.

2 Ethnic groups result from inclusive and racial categories from exclusive processes.

3 When groups interact, processes of change affect their boundaries in ways determined by the form and intensity of competition; and, in particular, when people compete as individuals this tends to dissolve the boundaries that define the groups, whereas when they compete as groups this reinforces those boundaries.

According to the two presuppositions, individuals are pictured as optimizing: they select the alternatives which give them the greatest benefits relative to costs, and their choices have consequences for future actions by them and others. It is assumed that people have wants or goals that cannot all be realized since they live in a world of scarcity.

The first presupposition cannot easily be tested since, if someone fails to exact the maximum material advantage from a situation, this may be because he gets some psychological reward from his restraint that is more important to him than the extra material gain. It is difficult to be sure that individuals optimize, since different people attach different values to, say, leisure relative to additional earnings, and they do not always rank their preferences in a transitive or consistent sequence. If someone forgoes material advantages this may be said, after the event, to display a high revealed preference for leisure. Only if his preferences had been reliably measured before the event would it be possible to check his choice against his stated, or positive, preferences and determine whether he did obtain maximum net advantage. Such difficulties in measuring an individual's preferences constitute a very serious limitation upon the utility of the theory but they do not affect its validity. Since people subjectively attribute value to so many possible outcomes they must continually rank their preferences (although some rankings may not be very stable). Though in the long run they will be drawn towards the optimal solutions, there will be circumstances in which they act on impulse and may come afterwards to feel that they did not identify or select the best alternative. The assumption that people optimize has its problems, but it is very difficult to interpret social behaviour without it, and sociological theories which begin from some other starting point have to incorporate some such proposition when they come to deal with action at the individual level.

The second presupposition encounters other kinds of criticism. Consider, for example, Winthrop D. Jordan's use of the expression 'unthinking decision' to describe how the status of Afro-Americans changed in the seventeenth century. Somehow people who were servants came to be treated as slaves and then later were made slaves by law. White Americans, without realizing what might be the consequences of their actions, set their country upon a course which proved exceedingly difficult to modify. They restricted the alternatives that would be open to their descendants in the future and restricted the alternatives for blacks very much more narrowly. To put it like this is to make a statement that seems obvious and trivial, but it is only by tracing trivialities through to their consequences that it becomes possible to explain why people are later confronted with only a restricted range of alternatives.

The first of the Rational Choice Theory's propositions has already been illustrated by the evidence that physical and cultural differences do not of themselves create groups or categories. It is only when these differences are given cultural significance and used by humans for their own purposes that social forms result. Chapter 2 showed how the same physical differences have been differently used in different parts of the New World, while Chapter 3 explained how, in history, people have come to understand different things by 'race', and the implications of this for the creation of groups and categories. A category is a set of individuals who may have nothing in common except that which the categorizer used to distinguish them. Persons in a particular income band are a category for tax purposes. Members of a category may transform themselves into a group by giving their common characteristic cultural significance and using it as a basis for organization. In the United States, Afro-Americans were initially a collection of individuals from different African peoples having nothing in common except the experience of being categorized and segregated by whites (the exclusive processes referred to in proposition 2).

Chapter 3 explained that in popular speech the idiom of race is used in ways that diverge from scientific practice so that it may be helpful to speak of an Englishman as taking for granted a folk concept of the English race as possessing characters which differentiate it from other races. Equally, there is a folk conception of English nationality which overlaps with that of

English ethnicity. To explain people's behaviour in some circumstances it is necessary to take account of their consciousness of belonging to races, nations and ethnic groups since their beliefs direct their actions. By contrast, analytical concepts (such as inflation) can be used to explain features of people's behaviour of which they are not necessarily conscious. When people are influenced by racial, national and ethnic sentiments they are conscious of a loyalty to a particular group and without this consciousness their behaviour would not be influenced. Yet these sentiments and influences differ from one group and one country to another. In Chapter 4 it was maintained that in the United States ethnicity is a division of race and race of nation, whereas in Europe the three concepts have traditionally related to groups of a similar order. Charles Keyes (1976) has shown that in Thailand ethnic identification, while important, is more fluid than in the United States and can be differentiated at several levels. Anthropologists could doubtless produce further evidence of such variation in the kinds of structures to which ethnic allegiances are tied. To rise above the confusions generated by cultural variation social scientists have to find ways of identifying structures and processes that can be discerned in any kind of society.

The proposal that ethnic groups be seen as resulting from inclusive, and racial categories from exclusive, processes, presents these processes as analytical concepts independent of people's consciousness. Individuals may have very different ideas about the history or culture or sense of a common fate which they share with others and which causes them to come together, but the consequences of these beliefs are similar in that they produce groups maintained voluntarily by the sense of identification. There is an inclusive, group-forming process. Those groups which are characterized as ethnic exemplify the process; so too do groups which form because of identifications based on a sense of common nationality, language, religion, etc. Just as people align themselves with those they see as being like themselves, so they mark off and exclude others whom they define as ineligible to belong to their group. The exclusive process creates a category but those assigned to it may transform it into a group. Afro-Americans did this by developing a shared consciousness of their position in the social structure of the United States.

Discussion of the theory's third proposition, about the form and intensity of competition, will take up much of this chapter. It may be noted, though, that the theory has so far been stated only in general terms and thus further propositions have to be added to it to explain behaviour in particular fields. Figure 4 shows this in the form of a diagram. The first level represents the family of rational choice theories. If theory construction were a tidy business it might then be possible to sort out at the next level particular

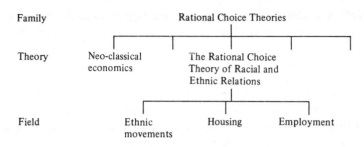

Figure 4   Divisions of Rational Choice Theory

theories applying the same general ideas in particular fields. In practice, however, areas of theoretical work develop which are characterized by both their subject matter and their approach, and the subject matter – as with the theory of games – may not coincide with an empirical area like racial and ethnic relations. The third level is that of fields within empirical areas; the three which are featured in the diagram are those discussed later, ethnic movements (in Chapter 8); discrimination in housing markets (Chapter 12) and in employment (Chapter 13).

The nature of rational choice theories has often been misunderstood, particularly by those who react to the name instead of examining what such theories actually claim. Nevertheless they do have weaknesses which have been highlighted by philosophical analysis (e.g. Hollis, 1978; Elster, 1979). In view of the criticisms it is best to emphasize three features of the theory advanced here: (a) it is a theory of alternatives as well as choices; (b) it is a theory which employs rationality as a criterion; (c) it is a theory of aggregate behaviour.

The claim that this is a theory of alternatives as well as choices may seem to be contradicted by Duesenberry's striking remark that: 'Economics is all about how people make choices. Sociology is all about why they don't have any choices to make' (Heath, 1976:3). The exaggeration is pardonable because it helps to make an important point. Faced by a man with a gun, a person may do what the gunman demands because all the alternatives are so unattractive as not to merit consideration; but they are still there. The black man in the Deep South in the 1930s could decide that he would not play up to white people's expectations of black roles, but he ran great risks if he held to that decision in all circumstances. Rather than bend before injustice some black men did risk their lives, and some lost them, although they could have chosen to play safe. To deny that they acted from choice is to deny them their human dignity. Moreover, political structures are probably most secure when people are kept unaware of potential alternatives and, in a situation such as that which existed in the Deep South, it was whites as well as blacks who had to be persuaded that the prevailing order could not be changed. So sociology is also about choices, but it has to explain why people are presented with particular alternatives when there are other less visible ones in the background, and how, with different modes of social organization, yet further alternatives could be created.

It is impossible to specify in the theory the nature of the alternatives that will be open to people because these come into focus only in the examination of particular societies. The theory recognizes that the alternatives are part of structures inherited from the past which generate as well as regulate conflict. In applying the theory it may be more important to account for the particular range of alternatives available to individuals than to analyse choices between them. When minority members are excluded from certain positions or do not perceive them as being among the possible options, the political issue will probably be that of enlarging the range of alternatives. The intellectual issues, however, will be those of accounting for the refusal of individuals to enter into exchange relations in certain fields (e.g. marriage, extension of the franchise) and of explaining how the privileged group is able to create and maintain its monopolistic position.

The theory is not an attempt to explain only rational choices; nor is it silent about irrational or habitual behaviour. It is an approach which judges all kinds of behaviour in terms of the criterion of rationality, i.e. whether the actor is maximizing his or her net advantages (see Farmer, 1982). Not every shopper makes the 'best buy' but he or she tries to learn from mistakes and is drawn, consciously and unconsciously, towards the best use of scarce resources. When someone fails to make that optimum choice the theory can, in principle, measure the costs he or she incurs. There is no assumption that people have all the information necessary to know what is the optimal decision. The weakness lies rather in the observer's lack of reliable information about the actor's various preferences, particularly about idiosyncratic preferences, making it difficult to know how far he or she succeeded in maximizing the net advantages. Limits to the power of rational choice explanations have been demonstrated in the theory of games by the discovery of problems which players cannot solve without cooperating, but nevertheless this kind of theory can be developed in some very sophisticated ways and can, for example, take account of differences in the considerations which bear upon risky choices as opposed to riskless choices (Heath, 1976:75–90).

The claim that this is a theory of aggregate behaviour is a defence against the argument for free will, summed up in Martin Hollis' judgement that 'rational man cannot choose his preferences'. Given that a particular person likes to smoke cigarettes, that he will allocate a particular proportion of his income to the satisfaction of this taste, and that he prefers some brands to others, it will be possible to predict how his purchases of cigarettes will respond to either a change in his income or a change in brand prices. What cannot be predicted, on this information, is a decision to stop smoking altogether. To furnish a complete explanation of an individual's change of preferences is beyond the power of rational choice theory, or indeed of any social science theory. But changes in aggregate behaviour, such as the number and social characteristics of people who stop smoking after a publicity campaign of a given intensity, is another matter altogether. This is the theoretical ground covered by Durkheim's famous study of suicide, which demonstrated that though every single suicide results from an autonomous decision there are nevertheless patterns of suicide which can be explained sociologically. .

One of the weaknesses of sociological theories of racial and ethnic relations has lain in their attempts to explain variations of attitudes within groups. They have often assumed that all members of a given group felt similarly and had difficulty accounting for the behaviour of members who were seen as deviant. The Rational Choice Theory assumes that different people have different tastes or preferences, just as they display different tastes when they go shopping; and that aggregate behaviour is an outcome of individual variation within market structures. Unlike some kinds of structural-functionalism it is not committed to a conception of society as based upon the sharing of ultimate goals and values, recognizing instead that individuals' interests will often conflict.

Individual competition

The theory assumes that when members of two groups encounter one another each individual will identify with his own group, since he will obtain important material and psychological rewards from membership. If the encounter is maintained, it will be because members of the two groups are exchanging goods or services of some kind and relations between them can be likened to relations of trade. In order to identify the principles of exchange, let it be imagined that some cattle-herders, Group A, encounter some sheep-herders, Group B, and that nothing differentiates the groups other than their two products. Members of each group will welcome a change in their diet and will exchange beef or mutton. The beef producers would regard mutton as a delicacy and might be willing to give 5 kg beef in exchange for 1 kg mutton. If members of the two groups encountered one another as individuals it is possible that in one exchange 4 kg beef might be traded for 2 kg mutton, in another 5 kg for 5 kg, in a third 2 kg beef for 7 kg mutton, and so on. When the traders of each group conferred with one another round the fire in the evening they would discover that they had traded at different rates and from this could deduce the relative values placed upon the two products by people in the other group. If there was an even distribution of initial rates, and the members of the two groups were all equally adept in bargaining so that no one was able to take advantage of any one else, the rate of exchange between beef and mutton could settle at one for one and the people on both sides would benefit equally since they would each have been willing to give five for one.

If the two groups are to continue to trade they will find it advantageous to learn to speak to one another. Still assuming that neither group takes advantage of the other, there will be situations in which one individual is willing to offer another so much beef now in return for a promise to deliver a larger quantity of mutton at a future date. This introduces an element of credit and the payment of interest in return for credit; it is based upon a contract between the parties and in the long run will depend upon measures for enforcing that contract if one party defaults (as Thomas Hobbes put it, 'there are no covenants without the sword'). There will be a market regulated by political institutions. Even if members of the two groups are equally skilled in bargaining they will differ among themselves. In each group some will identify more strongly with the group than others. Those of high status may feel that they have more freedom to be unconventional, as by striking up friendships with members of the other group. Those of low status may either feel the more obliged to conform or they may feel that they have little to lose if they attract more disapproval; these potential deviants may take a greater interest in the other group and gain psychological rewards from associating with them. Having begun by learning how to talk with members of the other group, and perhaps learning their recipes for cooking their kind of meat, people will begin to exchange other features of their culture leading eventually to intermarriage. This is the essence of the process of assimilation.

It is probable that, at the point of initial contact, Groups A and B could differ in more than the production of beef and mutton. The herding of cattle requires different techniques and has different implications for social organization than the herding of sheep. Cattle can graze on poorer pasture and move or be moved more readily when the pasture is exhausted, so cattle-herding peoples are often more mobile than sheep-herders. In such societies people base much of their culture on their animals and look down upon people who make a living in some other way. Yet in the course of trade they may come to appreciate the use or beauty of things which form part of the culture of the other group. The parents of a child in Group A might, to start with, consider it unthinkable that their child should marry anyone but another member of their own group, but, if after a while they found that they could make only a disadvantageous match within the group while a marriage on attractive terms could be arranged with someone in Group B, there would come a point at which the latter match became more attractive. Gradually members of the two groups would come to share the same values in all respects except those directly associated with their mode of animal husbandry. It is in this way that individual competition can explain the development of a social pattern by which people are classified according to appearance.

The simplest example is that of marriage, and it is appropriate because the principles by which colour differences are evaluated are no different from those which can be discovered in circumstances in which colour is not a factor at all. It illustrates how the first of the two modes of appraisal mentioned in Chapter 2 could have become established. A study in Aberdeen (Illsley, 1955) found that tall girls were more likely to marry men of high social status; this suggests that men put a higher value on relative height among brides, though girls who were exceptionally tall may have been at a disadvantage. Just as bridegrooms may prefer taller brides, so may they prefer women with a particular skin colour, or women of intelligence, pedigree or wealth. Romantic love may sometimes bring together partners of very different social status, but usually it is subject to a social conditioning of which the parties are not conscious and aggregate behaviour reveals clear patterns. Men find it easier to fall in love with women who are rich, but not too rich, or with women whose poverty is compensated by beauty or intelligence. As Kingsley Davis remarked, 'culturally defined patterns of selection always involve a trade, a reciprocity which ensures a certain kind of equality by balancing between the two mates all the qualities which enter into the calculation of marital advantage' (1941:386). The cultural pattern in Brazil has put a positive value on lightness of complexion in relatives by marriage and associates generally, so that men have tended to prefer lighter-skinned brides. Instead of a sharp distinction between 'white' and 'black', a continuous gradation has developed; a fair complexion is associated with high social status and a dark with low social status. If the cultural definition remains unchanged, so will the status connotation, for socially successful dark men and their descendants will tend to marry fair women, and socially unsuccessful fair men will tend to marry darker women. Over the course of time the process of exchange should then produce a population with a uniformly light-brown complexion.

The significance of competition in such a process can be illustrated from Cuba where, as in the rest of Spanish America, successive governments attempted to keep distinctions of ancestry, socio-cultural status, and appearance in line with one another. The pressure was the stronger because of the emphasis in Spain on the varying degrees of prestige attaching to levels in a highly developed social hierarchy and to legislation prescribing the kinds of occupation fit for people of different status. These laws were eventually repealed in Spain, but in 1807 a proposal for similar changes in Spanish America was rejected because of the presence there of 'a multitude of *pardos, zambos, mulattos, zambaigos, mestizos, curarterones, octavones.* All of these are vitiated at their very roots and are corrupt . . . if the decree were to be made applicable to those countries, disorder and consequences detrimental to the State would result, for it would be thought that it dispensed the vice they bear in the very origin' (Martinez-Allier, 1974:85). The Crown had enacted a law to prevent 'unequal' marriages, making parental consent necessary for the marriage of anyone under twenty-five years. When consent was withheld appeal could be made to the civil authorities who had power to issue a licence permitting the marriage. In the eyes of the Church all Catholics enjoyed absolute freedom of marriage and it was better that men and women should live together in matrimony than live in sin. In the eyes of the authorities political considerations came first. The conflict between these views is well expressed in the 1855 report of a provincial governor about the inadvisability of granting a licence to a mixed couple:

> From the purely religious point of view this marriage imperiously demands government cooperation; but there is little doubt that the dissemination of ideas of equality of the white class with the coloured race puts in jeopardy the tranquility of the Island, the largest proportion of whose population consists of the said race; it is no less true that by authorizing marriages between one and the other race the links of subordination of the coloured people to the white will tend to be subverted and weakened and . . . the day would come when those encouraged by the example of unequal marriages which favour them, will aspire impetuously to achieve a rank which society denies them and as a consequence public order would be upset; it is therefore the Government's duty to prevent such a situation at all costs (Martinez-Allier, 1974:46).

This may have sounded persuasive in an official report, but in other ways it was unrealistic, as some of the bishops tried to point out. In the first place the image of Cuban society as consisting of a series of distinct layers was already out of date. There were rich coloureds and poor whites, while some coloured people were more fair of complexion than some whites, even, on occasion, whites from Spain. Whether someone born in Cuba counted as white depended upon the register in which his baptism had been recorded; this gave rise to a further set of problems. Describing the registration of baptism of his children, one parent explained 'some are in the book for whites and others in that for *pardos*, according to the judgement of the different priests who baptized them'. The white fathers of illegitimate children born to coloured mothers could conceal the status of the mother when having the child baptized, so that legal status was often a poor guide to appearance.

In the second place, there were groups like the Amerindians and Chinese who did not fit anywhere in the three-tier scheme of whites, coloureds and blacks. Consistent with their own notions of ancestry, the Spaniards had recognized that most Indians were of pure descent and had their own hierarchy of rank. There was therefore no bar upon marriage between a Spaniard and an Indian, so Indians counted as whites. When Chinese indentured labourers were introduced in the early 1850s as a result of the growing labour shortage in Cuba, they posed a problem because 'although they are considered as white, public opinion and custom places them in a condition inferior to whites'. Their skin colour might be lighter than that of many Spaniards but they were very poor. Had they followed their rules, the authorities should have insisted that a Chinese wishing to marry a coloured woman first petition for a licence; that they did not do so, betrays their doubts about the true status of the Chinese and therefore about the rationale of the existing rules.

In the third place, it was only the most zealous priests who did much to dissuade people from living in concubinage, especially when they were of different status. The official casuistry was that if a Spanish aristocrat seduced a mulatto girl he did her an injury if he refused to marry her, but if he did marry her he did a greater injury to his relatives by staining an entire noble lineage, and this was contrary to the interests of the state. For a coloured woman to live in concubinage with a white man might be a better match, in her eyes and those of her family, than marrying a coloured man. For a white man it was very convenient, since his having lived in such a relationship would not necessarily hinder a subsequent marriage to a white woman; for a white woman to live with a coloured man was a different story. So it was the hypergamous union in which the man took a partner of lower status which was tolerated. From such unions came many children of intermediate appearance; the growth of this section of the population made it the more difficult to preserve the distinction between white and coloured (Martinez-Allier, 1974:46, 74, 76, 101).

When the civil authorities considered appeals against parental refusal to permit a marriage, they weighed the arguments of morality and policy, of ancestry and merit, with great seriousness. In 1791 a woman who was the 'sacrilegious' daughter of a priest wanted to marry a *pardo*. Her sister objected, and the Cuban authorities upheld her objection. The woman appealed to the King who overturned the refusal on the grounds that the couple already had children and the girl's illegitimate origin offset her suitor's inferior colour. When people sought permission to marry, the local authorities and the parish priest had to submit reports on the social and moral standing of the suitor and the bride. The documents regularly recognized that there could be a 'trade off' between the whiteness of a suitor of lowly occupation and the high community standing of the family of a bride of fair complexion. Thus one young man, a discharged soldier and by occupation a shoemaker, petitioned to marry a freeborn *parda* who was a legitimate daughter of a captain of the *pardo* militia and, moreover, a wealthy man owning property. The authorities reported that the marriage 'cannot do any harm' while cautiously adding, 'it is not known for certain whether the suitor is of pure blood; besides he has no distinction whatsoever'. This marriage was permitted though some comparable petitions were rejected. When the suitor held a more elevated rank than that of shoemaker the obstacles were greater but they could occasionally be surmounted. Of one would-be bride it was said 'in the class of the coloured she is held to be among the most respectable on account of her distance from the black colour and from slavery and on account of the good manners of her ancestors which is what bestows distinction in the classes of colour'. Moreover 'her father was a *hacendado* and her brother has been decorated by His Majesty . . . for his services rendered to the country in the persecution of fugitive slaves'. These special merits in terms of social status and complexion appear to have made her worthy in the eyes of the authorities of a match as outstanding as that with a white man who 'belongs to the class of distinction both on account of his birth as well as of his social status for he has been a Lieutenant of the 2nd Battalion of the Infantry Regiment of Havana' (Martinez-Allier, 1974:11–12, 24–6).

This study presents a picture of mid-nineteenth-century Cuba as a competitive society in which individuals were continually pressing against the modes of division established in an earlier age. The mulattos were as committed to the system of rank as the whites, being acutely conscious of the distinctions which lifted them above the people lower down. By the time slavery was finally abolished in 1880, a pattern of classification by status had been established in which colour was an element which could be counterbalanced by other kinds of claim to precedence and was moving in the direction that has been described for northeastern Brazil in the twentieth century.

In its analysis of the choice of marriage partners in circumstances of racial and ethnic contact, the Rational Choice Theory assumes that the groups which come together already have different attributes of some kind and that these are evaluated. People on the one side will be attracted to, or repelled by, characteristics of the other, but they will not all be equally attracted or repelled. Because of these interactions the values placed upon the attributes of the strangers will change. The Rational Choice Theory cannot explain the initial values which the groups bring to the encounter but it can help explain why they change in particular directions and at varying speeds.

Since this exposition of the theory has so far concentrated on a discussion of the kinds of exchange involved in marriage, it may be helpful to mention an example of quite a different kind. In Malaysia the government has sought to increase Malay participation in the business sector and reduce the near monopoly previously enjoyed by the Chinese. To this end it gives favourable consideration when granting licences to 'joint ventures'; these are companies with both Malays and Chinese as directors. A Chinese entrepreneur looking for partners to form a company will therefore place a higher value on the services of an influential Malay as a co-director than those of a Chinese businessman with rather more experience in the particular line of business. The encouragement of joint ventures has the same sort of effect as inter-group marriage in mixing group attributes on the basis of a common scale of value.

In Brazil and parts of the Caribbean, categorization by appearance was established because members of different groups were brought into individual competition. Since there were fewer Portuguese women there was more inter-group mating. Because there was no continuing European immigration mulattoes established themselves in an intermediate status. Even where there were no Indians, there were usually four groups to be considered (the metropolitan government, the white settlers, the free coloured and the black slaves) and varied alliances were possible. For example, when the American Revolution raised the spectre of a successful revolution among the white planters of Saint Domingue, the French government tried to cultivate the loyalty of the coloured group. They pressed for the reduction of discrimination against this group, telling the planters that this class constituted the greatest barrier against troubles from the slaves (G. Hall, 1972:191). One of the critical factors in Caribbean history was the price that the whites had to pay to inhibit an alliance between the coloured group and the slaves; to the twentieth-century student, that price often seems to have been very low.

Markets

In the previous section it quickly became apparent that it was impossible to discuss even the simplest kinds of exchange without making assumptions about non-economic relations between the parties and non-economic rules about bargaining processes. Markets are essential to social life and yet there is always a tension between the principles which underlie the structure of a society and those which are the foundation of a market. The men who signed the United States Declaration of Independence asserted that humans are endowed with an unalienable right to pursue happiness; yet if they are to succeed in the pursuit they need as children to grow up in a social group in which parents of some kind provide an atmosphere of love and emotional support. Any attempt to organize family life on market principles, with would-be parents paying other women to bear children or buying children from those willing to produce them in anticipation of a sale, would be doomed to failure. The free market releases forces of the greatest value to social progress but these forces have to be restrained if they are not to damage the society itself. The market exists because it enables people more effectively to realize their objectives, but these objectives spring from the social organization and not from the market, which can operate only so long as the society provides people able and willing to make use of it.

In the technologically simple forms of society, such as were found on the islands of the Pacific, market principles governed only certain kinds of exchange. A Polynesian might exchange one kind of food for another, one kind of tool for another, but there was no way of exchanging food for tools. Some of these societies used shell coins in different series as a kind of money: each series facilitated a particular kind of transaction but there was no certain way of expressing the value of a coin belonging to one series in the values of another. It was once thought that such societies had primitive economies and primitive money because their inhabitants were primitive in the sense that they were unable to grasp the connections necessary to calculate prices or rates of interest on loans. This, it is now understood, was quite wrong. Money is used to assist the working of an economy and to enable demand and supply to be brought into relation by the price mechanism. The economy of a Pacific island has to provide for more serious problems than this. If there is a natural disaster, and half the staple crop is destroyed by a hurricane or an insect pest, an increase in price would not bring onto the market any more of that crop if, being a perishable commodity, it has been impossible to store any of the previous years' harvest, and if the island has no trading relations with some other island from which it could be imported. On such an island the most efficient way of feeding the population is to organize production on a family basis. Some goods may be exchanged against others but if every kind of good could be exchanged against every other kind at a price, this could upset the pattern of social obligations upon which the family structure depended. Primitive money in some respects resembles the ration tickets or coupons which governments have issued in times of war or crisis to see that every citizen can obtain an allowance of food, clothing or petrol at a stable price lest the shortage of goods should cause demand to push the price up in an inflationary fashion and create new problems (Douglas, 1967). The way in which primitive money, or partial substitutes for money like coupons and licences, are used, opens a special insight into the inter-relations of the social structure and the market.

In small, technologically simple societies only certain things are counted as exchangeable goods. With economic growth, the size of the market increases, more things are treated as commodities, goods are brought from a greater distance and the opportunities for profit multiply. The expansion of the market, which is often identified as the growth of capitalism, permits the total population to grow and enables most people to benefit from dramatic improvements in the standard of material living. It also has undesired consequences in that divisions deepen between people who stand in different relations to the market, and the pursuit of profit leads man to damage his natural environment. If manufacturers are allowed to release gases into the atmosphere, or effluents into the rivers, they create costs for other people; if they lay the land waste they destroy an amenity that could have been of benefit to future generations. Ideally the market should be organized so that all costs are entered into a social balance sheet and the beneficial features of individual profit-seeking are utilized while the unwanted consequences are avoided. How to achieve this is one of the master-problems of the present age.

Industrial societies treat a great variety of things and services as commodities, but they limit the operation of the market in many fields. Men may not lawfully sell themselves into slavery, nor enter into contracts which impose burdens upon their children. In many countries people can sell their own blood, but only under medical regulations; women sometimes sell their hair, but adoption of children and the acquisition by hospitals of bodies for dissection are carefully regulated to prevent the growth of markets in babies or cadavers comparable to that in used cars. Not surprisingly, therefore, the use of market principles to set the terms on which one man works for another raises more fundamental social issues than the use of those same principles to facilitate the transfer of rights over things; it generates more tensions and restrictions upon the market.

This chapter illustrates some elementary connections by suggesting how contact between two groups could give rise to a market in beef and mutton, but here and in subsequent chapters it goes on to take account of the complications which arise in real life. Groups and individuals who derive particular benefits from exchange acquire power which they can use to influence the terms of future exchanges. Markets have to be managed, usually by governments, and these may seek to promote fair competition or may permit particular groups to enforce terms which are to their own advantage.

At the beginning of this book there is a quotation from James E. Meade, winner of the Nobel prize for Economics in 1977, claiming that in the ideal society each citizen would act selfishly in the market place and altruistically at the ballot box. By altruistic political action there can, for example, be an alleviation of poverty that could not be effected in the market. Meade (1973:52–3) goes on to contend that 'for the Good Society we need a combination of economics, ethics and politics: first an *economically* efficient selfishness *à la* Adam Smith in the market place; second, an ethical search for justice to guide the formation of individual's preferences as between different governmental policies, and third, some humdrum political rules of voting to choose between any resulting conflicting views about such policies'. This states concisely some of the main features of the relationship between choice on the one hand and alternatives on the other that is implicit in the theory set out in this chapter. It is timely to emphasize it at this point since the way in which markets are managed is crucial to the analysis of group competition.

Group competition

In discussing individual competition the reader was asked to imagine a situation in which members of Group A were willing to offer 5 kg of beef for 1 kg of mutton, while members of Group B would give 5 kg of mutton for 1 kg of beef. It was said that if people on either side bargained as individuals, and were equally good at bargaining, the rate of exchange might settle at one for one. But what if the cattle herders were better at bargaining? They might combine and arrange for one of their number to trade on behalf of the group. He would seek to conceal from the sheep-herders the information that members of Group A would be willing to give up to 5 kg of beef for 1 kg of mutton and would bargain with different members of Group B (either individually or collectively) until he discovered that they would take 1 kg beef for 5 kg of mutton. Members of Group A would be doing twenty-five times better than their minimum terms of exchange. Having secured such an advantageous position, it would be in their interest to maintain it.

However, there could well be conflicts of interest within Group A. Some members might have more beef they wanted to exchange, or a greater desire for mutton, whereas their representative was supplying no more than 100 kg beef in exchange for 500 kg mutton. If the two groups produced the same amount of meat this would mean that members of Group A were holding 400 kg they had been unable to exchange because at a rate of five for one Group B's demand for beef had been satisfied. Members of Group B might trade further if they could get better terms. So members of Group A would be tempted to go behind the back of their representative and offer, say, a further 50 kg beef in exchange for, say, 200 kg mutton. The beef producer who broke away from his group in this way would benefit at the expense of other members of it. They would wish to punish him for this and force him to comply with group policy. The central problem of monopolistic organization as a social form is that of manipulating producers to follow a policy which brings them higher returns than they could get from individual competition, but lower returns than they could get if they traded individually while the other producers were trading as a group. This is sometimes called the problem of the 'free rider' (see Olson, 1965:76).

In their analysis of monopoly, economists have mostly been concerned with its effects upon pricing (but see Kirzner, 1973:88–134), whereas a rational choice theory of racial and ethnic relations must concern itself more with the establishment and maintenance of monopoly as a social form. Members of a category with a potential monopoly may come together and create a cartel because each person individually calculates that it would be in his interest to do so. Once created, some members may have greater interests in the maintenance of the cartel than others and the former may use whatever means they have available to force the others into line and keep them there. A monopoly pattern in racial relations can be maintained only when members of the privileged group can be persuaded that their individual interests point in the same direction as that in which they believe their collective interests to lie. To repeat the previous argument in more familiar terms, white employers might be required by law or group pressure to reserve one kind of job for white workers and to pay them £2 per hour, and to pay black workers £1 per hour for slightly less skilled work. Some black workers would be more skilled or more productive than some white workers, so it would be in the interest of the employer to breach the requirement (as by creating an intermediate job category or introducing a bonus scheme). He could be prevented from doing so only by the threat of punishment or by being persuaded that evasion was against his long-term interests because of the other consequences likely to flow from it. A racial ideology may be more important as a way of keeping in line members of the privileged group than of trying to justify their privileges to outsiders or of trying to weaken the self-confidence of those whose abilities are disparaged.

It is customary to define monopoly as the position of a seller who controls the entire supply of a particular product, but in practice there is usually competition between close substitutes. When the price of petroleum was increased by OPEC (the Organization of Petroleum Exporting Countries) some people changed their home heating from oil to gas or solar, and more resources were invested in the development of new sources of energy. Usually product substitution is easier than in this case. Monopoly is therefore better seen as the position of a producer who is immune from the threat of other entrepreneurs doing what he does (Kirzner, 1973:106). To secure or maintain such a position the would-be monopolist has to prevent competing products or competing entrepreneurs obtaining entry to the market. In some circumstances he has also to watch out for the demonstration effect whereby one attempt to control the market stimulates others. Those who can control the supply of labour in relatively unattractive occupations have been able substantially to increase their rewards. Work on the docks or collecting garbage was initially of low status and poorly rewarded, but where the workers have by unionization established a monopoly position they have been able to obtain much higher wages.

The privileged group in a racial monopoly situation continually reinforces its position, ensuring that one criterion, such as ancestry, over-rides all other modes of categorization, and anomalies are relegated to the lower category. It seeks to prevent the operation of those forces which would reduce the differences between the groups and promote their assimilation. Nevertheless its privilege is the more difficult to maintain because members of the new generation of the group are inclined to believe that their long-term interest favours greater flexibility. Pressure comes from those areas which are less easily subject to regulation; education, mass communications and easier travel spread knowledge of alternatives. Changes in technology and world trade increase business interests in de-segregation. Outside groups motivated by moral outrage or hope of political advantage try to upset the structure. Such changes result in the use of increased threat by the privileged group, withdrawal or rebellion by the unprivileged, or a variation in the rate of exchange between the two sectors.

In this way it is possible to see that the special factors which, in the Deep South, brought about the selection of ancestry as the prime criterion of group ascription, are features of the more general pattern of establishing and maintaining monopolies. Like the other models, it shows the micro-sociological forces underlying larger-scale changes. It shows how, in a bargaining relationship, a position of strength has associated weaknesses, and draws attention to the points of stress and of likely change. The status of the higher groups in the Central American pattern of categorization by socio-cultural status is also based to some extent upon monopoly power.

The most extreme form of group competition is that of physical attack. It counts as competition only in the ecological sense of struggle for resources and in sociological terms is more properly considered as conflict. In ecological theories this was represented as contact on the ecological or biological level in which there were no social relations between the parties and no shared moral order (Frazier, 1957:92). In the United States it suited the whites to make treaties with the Indians and then later it suited them to break those treaties. In Australia the Aborigines were insufficiently powerful to oblige the whites to make treaties; they wanted the land and were unwilling to take any step that might imply that it was owned by the Aborigines. In the middle years of the nineteenth century there were whites who poisoned Aboriginal waterholes and left out meat, flour or liquor that contained arsenic or strychnine so that those who drank the liquid or ate the food died horrible deaths. Since all the land in the sub-continent was claimed by some tribe, and the tribes were often hostile towards each other, those Aborigines who were displaced from their own territory might have nowhere to go. In the United States as the frontier was pushed westwards, and in Australia likewise, there were whites who formed hunting parties to go shooting the native peoples for sport. In Brazil, where matters were no better, they collected clothes from hospital patients who had died of smallpox in order to distribute them among Indians and spread the disease. The weaker the native peoples were, the more brutal their treatment at the hands of those who considered themselves civilized.

Sociological questions arose at a later stage when the Europeans were forced to enter into relations with the remnants of native peoples no longer able to make their own living, and with the children of native women by European fathers, but at the initial stage the question is that of explaining how the Europeans brought themselves to treat human beings as if they were not human. The simplest answer is that when men are subject to little social restraint they will pursue what they consider their interest without scruple, and will later seek to justify it in whatever way they can, as by arguing that the others attacked them first, or that their action was necessary to ensure their own survival. In the first half of the nineteenth century they asserted that the native peoples were savages and cannibals beyond the reach of reason; in the latter half of that century they made increasing use of ideas of racial inferiority. A critical phase in the process was that of stereotyping: for example, Aborigines were 'myalls' or 'niggers'; they might be 'boys', but never 'men'; their women were 'gins' and their children 'picaninnies'. Murdering an Aborigine might be 'shooting a snipe'. In 1883 the British High Commissioner wrote candidly and privately to his friend the British Prime Minister:

> The habit of regarding natives as vermin, to be cleared off the face of the earth, has given to the average Queenslander a tone of brutality and cruelty in dealing with 'blacks' which it is very difficult for anyone who does not *know* it, as I do, to realize. I have heard men of culture and refinement, of the greatest humanity and kindness to their fellow whites, and who when you meet them here at home you would pronounce to be incapable of such deeds, talk, not only of the *wholesale* butchery (for the iniquity of *that* may sometimes be disguised

from themselves) but of the *individual* murder of natives, exactly as they would talk of a day's sport, or of having to kill some troublesome animal (Evans, Saunders and Cronin, 1975:78).

Since such conduct was sometimes justified by reference to Darwinian ideas about the struggle for life, it is perhaps worth observing that when in the animal and insect worlds one species invades the territory of another it is unusual for it to kill off its competitors. In the natural order, *Homo sapiens* is distinguished by his readiness to destroy other species and to slaughter his own.

Relations between native peoples and invaders will more readily result in misunderstanding and conflict when members of the two groups have different attitudes towards competition. The whites who entered the territory of the native Australians were strongly oriented towards maximizing their incomes, both by competing with one another and by uniting to take over the natural resources commanded by the Aborigines. In the cultures of the Aborigines there was little if any private ownership and each member of a group was expected to share food with the others. Consequently Aborigines expected whites to share their wealth and appear to have thought they were entitled to a share of the crops the Europeans cultivated in their land. They could not understand the differences of rank in white society; nor did they see the need to continue working once immediate needs had been met. Some young Aboriginal men, motivated perhaps by curiosity about the newcomers or perhaps by a desire to escape troubles in their own groups, were willing to work for Europeans. Those who dived for shells could sometimes dictate the terms on which they would work, but on land it was more difficult. That they were unwilling to accept the restraints placed on white labourers was possibly less surprising than the unreadiness of the white workers to accept them. Those Aborigines who persevered most to come to terms with white society found that white workers would not allow them to undertake the same work for the same pay and treated them with contempt. So, in general, they opted for Aboriginal values, settlement patterns, family life, and rhythms of work even when that choice brought them only a miserable level of material comfort (Reynolds, 1981:116–27).

Another possibility when an incoming group is more powerful is for its members to enslave the indigenous people or confine them to reservations. It forces them to provide services on terms to which they would not have agreed had they been able to bargain equally. The dominant group then organizes to defend its monopoly. Its members compete with one another on an individual basis, but combine to force down the prices they are willing to pay for the other group's products and to force up the prices they demand for their own.

The essence of group competition is monopoly and the obtaining of greater returns than would be forthcoming in a more equal exchange. It can be seen as an exploitation of a position of power. To analyse imperfect or monopolistic competition, or to calculate the rate of exploitation, it is necessary to have a conception of perfect competition. To measure transactions against this notional standard is not to assume that there ever has been a market in which competition has been perfect, any more than there has ever been a frictionless pendulum. But in mechanics it is often useful to study observations about motion by reference to a model of a frictionless pendulum, and likewise in economics it can be helpful to analyse situations in terms of deviation from perfect competition.

It is only consumers who actually want perfect competition. Private individuals, corporations, trade unions and governments continually seek to control markets for their own ends, so it is not out of place to recall some famous words of Adam Smith in *The Wealth of Nations*: 'to expect that freedom of trade should ever be entirely restored in Great Britain . . . is absurd . . . not only the prejudices of the public, but what is much more unconquerable, the private interests of many individuals, irresistibly oppose it'. He warned that those who speak in favour of competition cannot be protected from either insults or real danger, 'arising from the insolent outrage of furious and disappointed monopolists'. Individuals and companies regularly seek monopolies; governments may create them or oppose them or pass laws against discrimination to reduce market imperfections. Just as it is useful to examine each kind of imperfection to determine where it originates, what maintains it, and what effect it has upon the market, so it is useful to examine the ways in which relations between members of different ethnic groups are affected by factors which, for example, influence the values placed upon skin colour, or limit the kinds of choices open to minority members.

The model of perfect competition has to be modified if it is to recognize that some buyers and sellers have extra advantages. They may have power, perhaps, through membership in employers' associations or trade unions, to influence the terms on which exchanges occur. Some people qualify for better-paid posts because of the capital that has been invested in their education or their health, or in giving them valued characteristics. Buyers and sellers are socialized into their societies, so that they have particular tastes. They identify more readily with people who possess socially valued characteristics and may therefore be said to have a taste for association with such people which may affect their behaviour in housing and other markets. These tastes may be related to mechanisms which advance or maintain private interests (e.g. in residential segregation). The phenomenon which is identified as racial prejudice has psychological and other components, but in some circumstances it can properly be seen as a kind of consumer behaviour, for the rejection of a minority member as a neighbour may be no more than the obverse of a preference for a majority member. The values which people place upon social characteristics derive from their own socialization and the structure of power in earlier generations. Indeed, some economic theorists, following Ricardo and Marx, have maintained that a theory of distribution must be prior to any theory of value, since price-relations or exchange values could only be arrived at after the principle affecting distribution of the total product had been postulated (Dobb, 1973:169). Many of the advantages which some people enjoy over their competitors in present-day markets derive from events in the previous generation; while these advantages may be reduced, other kinds of inequality will be transmitted to the next generation. Market situations in the real world will always be characterized by imperfect competition and will always need to be placed in their historical and political context, but the model of perfect competition provides a base-line enabling the social scientist to attempt an assessment of the extent to which exchange relations are affected by factors like monopoly power.

It can be shown by close philosophical analysis that a system of relations based upon economic rationality alone cannot resolve contradictions that can arise within it. The notion of perfect competition must depend upon sociological assumptions about the competitors who maintain the system. Economists who study international trade have to allow for the possibility of retaliation (e.g. by raising tariffs) on the part of a state affected by changes in the terms of trade. Once the wider issues are considered it becomes obvious that markets are always embedded in political processes. It is ultimately a political decision as to what things may be bought and sold, in what circumstances, and subject to what sanctions. No one would find it worthwhile striking a bargain if the deal could not be enforced, and that leads straight to the courts and the kinds of laws by which they settle cases. The actions of invading whites who in Australia and North America drove the native people from their land were motivated by the whites' intention to establish their own markets and dictate the terms on which Aborigines and Indians might participate in them. Similar principles also apply in the analysis of the relative positions of ethnic groups in industrial cities, though they are less easily perceived. If young blacks riot in Brixton or Baltimore this can be seen as the acting out of the belief that they cannot get a return from the market proportionate to the contribution they are willing to make. They threaten to disrupt the market unless changes are made which will allow them to get better terms. In so doing they may both put pressure on middle-class blacks and increase the bargaining power of black representatives. The white press, on the other hand, by stressing the possible consequences of a white backlash can reinforce the power of those who negotiate from the other side.

In group competition it is not only goals and services but threats which are traded, and one threat is the possibility of so damaging the economy that everyone is worse off. Group power is increased when all members are persuaded that their individual interests are best served by collective action, but it can also be enhanced when a less-respectable section of a group resorts to forms of violence of which the respectable section cannot approve. When a minority is relatively small it will not be seen as threatening unless its members compete for a particular range of jobs. The smaller the proportion, the more minority members will be perceived as individuals and the less tension there will be.

Inclusive and exclusive boundaries

Since the effect of consumer demand is to promote exchanges between groups and reduce cultural differences, the study of inter-group relations must look to the points at which groups remain distinct, that is to their boundaries. Decisions important to the character of any group will be taken at the centres of power but groups grow or diminish by actions at the periphery as individuals cross the boundary to become new members or to leave the group. Racial and ethnic groups can be differentiated along two dimensions reflecting the hardness of their boundaries and the relative privileges of membership. A hard boundary is one that is difficult to cross; usually it will be a question of someone's wanting to cross the boundary in order to become a member, but groups that are hard to join are often hard to leave. The significance of race is that it can be used to draw a very hard boundary and it is usually difficult for a person of inappropriate characteristics either to join or leave a racial category. The greater the privileges of membership, the more incentive there will be for people to seek to join (see Trosper, 1976, for an illustration). Figure 5 represents this classification in

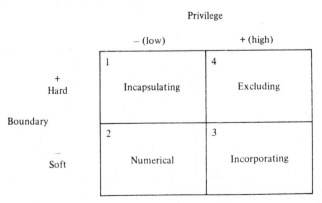

Figure 5 Groups defined by boundary and privilege

diagram form. The horizontal axis measures the degree of privilege, the vertical one the hardness of the boundary, and the diagram is divided into four quadrants, or boxes, for convenience in use. Note that it classifies groups in isolation, although it is often possible to appreciate the characteristics of a group only in relation to some other group, e.g. an excluding group exists only in relation to an excluded group.

In the long run, the degree of hardness of a society's or a group's boundary is likely to depend on that society's or group's relation to its environment. It may be in the group's interest to make entrance to membership easy or difficult. Studies of traditional African societies show that they vary in their ability to incorporate foreigners; only if their political system is characterized by a conception of citizenship can they cope satisfactorily with an influx of strangers (Cohen and Middleton, 1970:17). Yet, once a particular strategy for dealing with strangers has become institutionalized, it may be maintained although it no longer suits the group's interest. The Afrikaans-speaking white minority in South Africa has been exclusive and introverted, rewarding members for being preoccupied with the group's distinctiveness, and consequently it has assisted to high political office men with little experience of the world outside. (The great exception to this was the career of Field Marshall Smuts, but the political and academic distinctions he won overseas were liabilities to him among his own people.)

For a group to have a hard boundary, is for it to present an exclusive front to others. It shuts itself off. If no one else wants to join the group, perhaps because it does not control any valued resources, then its exclusiveness will have few consequences for outsiders. Yet if a group is in a privileged position the nature of the boundary has important consequences for non-members. If, seeking to defend their privileges, the group members deny entry to would-be recruits, then they are likely to develop images of themselves and of outsiders that will justify such policies. People who feel themselves excluded are likely to fight back, organizing to pursue their objectives, and developing an image of themselves which counterbalances the implication that they are unworthy of belonging to the privileged group. In doing so they will develop a group consciousness (or heighten that sense if they already have such a consciousness), and this will define a boundary around their group which will not be quite the same as the boundary round the privileged group even if there are only two groups in the society. Applying these terms to the case of black and white relations in the Deep South of the United States as they were in the 1930s, it can be said that the whites drew a boundary round their group which excluded blacks from valued positions. The blacks were not simply an excluded category of individuals; they too formed a group to which individuals were conscious of belonging.

That there is a relation between the character of the group and its boundary can be seen from a consideration of what constitutes deviance. A purely religious group may show no concern with the political opinions of its members but is likely to expel any who start to advance unorthodox religious doctrines. If it is a sect committed to a particular inspiration or a painstaking observance of scripture, its tolerance of deviance will be low, and the group will be both small and subject to schism. A purely political group, on the other hand, will not be concerned with the religious beliefs of its members and will be agitated only by political deviance; if the group is committed to a specific theory of political action it too will be small and prone to schism. While the character of the group decides whom it will admit and retain, the availability of a clear demarcating line, like the highly visible criterion of skin colour, enables a group to form more easily.

If members of a privileged group do not try to restrict their privileges but are willing to admit acceptable individuals from other groups, then the exclusive boundary will be soft and probably indistinct. Instead of a sharp distinction between members and non-members there will be a continuous gradation. Where there is an undisputed geographical boundary or an obvious physical difference between populations it is much easier to make a social boundary hard. Where there is a high level of personal acquaintance, individuals' claims to social status will be easily ascertained and evaluated. In most parts of Northern Ireland a clear distinction can be made between Protestants and Catholics because it is easy for two people who have previously been strangers to pick up clues about one another's background from information about where they live, their acquaintances and so on. This sort of distinction would scarcely be possible in a larger social system or one in which there was more social mobility. In that sort of system, a distinction would have to be based upon some visible difference to be effective in such a wide range of circumstances.

The speed with which members of an excluded category or an incoming population come to feel themselves a group and to draw an inclusive boundary around themselves will depend upon the hardness of the exclusive boundary that confronts them. How hard it is will depend upon the nature of the criteria of membership as well as upon the forces which motivate members of the established group to maintain a separate organization. In some countries ethnic organization is legitimate and expected, whereas in others it is regarded with disapproval as detracting from citizenship. A country like Nigeria is made up of people belonging to ethnic groups with distinctive language, culture and territory. Irrespective of the motives for maintaining ethnic distinctiveness, such a pattern of social differentiation is bound to change less slowly than one based upon individual socio-economic status. When people of, say, Yoruba or Ibo background act on the assumption of their ethnic distinctiveness, they are implicitly acknowledging the legitimacy of ethnic distinction and are encouraging other groups to organize on an ethnic basis. If each person belongs to one particular ethnic group and is excluded from all others, each boundary will be equally inclusive and exclusive unless some groups are more privileged than others. In a society in which differences of origin are supposed to be irrelevant to political and economic activity, common ethnicity will be a legitimate basis for organization only in the private sphere, touching upon leisure-time activities.

New groups may form within a society because of changing social attitudes. A striking example is provided by the recent appearance of 'gay' associations and campaigns. There is reason to believe that in every society there is a proportion of homosexual males and females, but in many of them this has been regarded as an illegitimate condition requiring punishment or treatment. If a society does become more tolerant of homosexuality, the process is one by which exclusive boundaries against homosexuals are softened and they are allowed to form a legitimate group with its inclusive boundary.

There are some situations in which a group can be said to maintain a hard boundary but to enjoy no particular privileges (box 1 in Figure 5). Religious minorities, like the Amish, Hutterites and Dukhobors in North America, provide striking examples. The Amish have been relatively successful farmers, but not outstandingly so, since they have been reluctant to adopt machines and other new techniques, so they have not excited the envy of their non-Amish neighbours. Their exclusiveness has therefore not had serious implications for the attitudes and conduct towards them of others. Immigrant minorities also sometimes seek to incapsulate themselves and maintain their traditional ways undisturbed by the life of other groups around them. The Welsh settlements in Patagonia, the Gypsies in California, and first-generation Chinese settlers in a great variety of cities, all provide good illustrations of this process. Other examples can be found in circumstances in which distinctive groups control an ecological niche of no very great value, like, say, the coastal fishing, the laundry business, or restaurants with an ethnic style of cooking. The desire to preserve ethnic distinctiveness may therefore be associated with an interest in defending a monopoly. It should also be noted that most incapsulating minorities are small ones and that the inclusive boundary which they build around themselves is not necessarily opposed by any exclusive boundary.

Sometimes individuals with common characteristics do not show any group consciousness or develop group activity: they constitute a numerical minority (box 2). The Maltese in London in the 1950s and 1960s are a possible example: because some individuals convicted for organizing vice rackets were believed to be Maltese and had attracted persistent and extensive press publicity, many Maltese in London did not like to identify themselves or to congregate with other Maltese (Dench 1975). When individuals are hindered in their desire to join the majority, they too may be a numerical minority; only if they abandon their desire will they have any incentive to form a group, in which case they will harden their boundary and move into box 1, though they will not move so far up the vertical axis as some of the other groups mentioned. For example, to be born to Old Order Amish parents is virtually the only way in which a person can become a member of that group.

When a relatively privileged group has a soft boundary, outsiders are fairly readily admitted to membership and the group extends its influence by absorbing other peoples round about it (box 3). As Chapter 2 has explained, in Guatemala, as in many other parts of Central America, the population is divided into two categories, *ladinos* and Indians. The *ladinos* are ready to recognize their partially Indian descent because that strengthens their claim to historical roots on the American continent, but they also want the Indians to give up their 'backward' ways and live as they do. So if an Indian has learned to speak Spanish and dresses like one of them, he does not have great difficulty in getting himself accepted as a *ladino*. The privileged group is amorphous because it is no longer tied to an imperial country. Its members can look after their own interests by making distinctions of status within their ethnic group and by manipulating the ethnic boundary so as to catch as many outsiders as possible with the net. The process is reminiscent of the explanation given by some of the Tiv people of Nigeria who have been busy expanding their territory for some generations: 'We do not have a boundary, we have an argument' they say. Where the Tiv dispute with their neighbours as they push outwards, and maintain their ethnic distinctiveness, the *ladinos* deal with outsiders and individuals and manipulate a soft boundary to suit their advantage.

The situation that has attracted most attention arises when a privileged group maintains a hard boundary, shutting out others who may, initially, have no group organization of their own (box 4). The outsiders knock for admission but the door is never opened to them. Initially, therefore, the excluded individuals form an involuntary minority and are a social category rather than a self-conscious group. They deny the legitimacy of the arguments used by the privileged group in excluding them. The best described example of this situation is that of the American Deep South, first in the era of slavery, and then in the era in which black subordination rested on the manner in which the laws were enforced (especially with regard to voting) rather than in the content of the laws themselves. Admission to the privileged group was in most places dependent upon qualifications of skin colour, 'racial' appearance and ancestry, though the group was itself stratified along socio-economic lines. The subordinate group did not maintain a hard boundary. For example, Chinese immigrants in Mississippi were able to take black consorts and a very few were absorbed into the black population. Elsewhere persons of partially Indian descent were likewise absorbed. John Dollard, who undertook research in a relatively small Mississippi town in the 1930s, remarks (1937:242) that he was invited to preach in a Negro church, whereas it would have been extraordinary for a Negro to preach in a white church.

Political legitimations of inequality are manifold. One set of circumstances in which their nature is often made very clear is in imperial rule, and in the changes that come about when a colony obtains independence. In these circumstances it is often easier to see that how and where a group boundary is drawn is not just the expression of group sentiment but something subject to calculated political regulation. In the Roman Empire, Roman citizenship was held out as a privilege that could be earned by the worthy. In more recent times, French colonial administrators in Africa followed a policy of incorporation summarized in the exhortation *instruire la masse et dégager l'élite*. In French and Portuguese colonies *évolués* and *assimiladoes* were admitted to positions of privilege and a line drawn between them and the mass. The old Spanish rule which reserved to Spanish-born people the important positions in the colonies drew a boundary which became increasingly difficult to maintain as the population of creoles (persons of European or part-European descent born in the colonies) grew in size and power.

Figure 5 refers to groups but, as the discussion has shown, persons allocated to box 2 do not constitute a group and are better referred to as a minority. This concept has caused some confusion since many sociologists have followed Louis Wirth (1945:347) in defining minorities as collectivities subjected to unfavourable treatment irrespective of their relative size, so that black Africans in South Africa are counted as a minority even though they are a majority of the population. The difficulties inherent in such a definition appear when a situation such as that in Northern Ireland is examined. If, contrary to Wirth's recommendation, by minority is meant no more than a category consisting of less than half the numbers of some named population, it becomes possible to say that Protestants are a religious or denominational majority in Northern Ireland but a religious minority within Ireland as a whole. A Belfast Protestant belongs to a political majority within the Province but in relation to the United Kingdom he can be seen as a member of an ethnic minority since all Northern Ireland people share some common characteristics distinguishing them from English and Scottish people. A Belfast Catholic may belong to the same ethnic minority *vis à vis* the United Kingdom, and, if he is a Republican, simultaneously belong to a national minority in respect of both the United Kingdom and the Province of Northern Ireland. A Catholic who is a Unionist is a member of the political majority in Northern Ireland but of the religious minority. These numerical entities vary in the extent to which they form the basis for self-conscious groups, whether of the majority or minority. Wirth's definition can lead the student to overlook the minorities within the minorities, and the varying extent to which political, religious and other boundaries coincide, whereas it is the divisions within groups and the cross-cutting ties between groups which usually keep conflicts within bounds and often open up possibilities of their resolution (see Banton, 1977:146–50 for a more extended discussion).

The classification of groups and minorities by boundary and privilege does not assume that group relations remain constant. Since changes in a group's boundary are usually associated with changes in relations with other groups, it is not easy to conceptualize them in a diagram like that of Figure 5, which serves to classify single groups by themselves. Another kind of diagram that provides a better means for representing group changes is discussed in Chapter 7 but some illustration is possible utilizing Figure 5. Consider the case of the Polish Jews, who in the later years of the nineteenth century were the politically unprivileged group in a box 1 situation, confronted by a Gentile majority that would be located in box 4. The Jewish community was enclosed by a hard inclusive ethnic boundary maintaining a distinct identity; this boundary was the harder because the Gentile majority persecuted them, making it exceedingly difficult for any Jew to join this politically privileged group. But those Polish Jews who emigrated to New York found themselves confronted by an incorporating majority of a kind that belongs in box 3; the exclusive boundary was weak and minority members could more easily pass into the majority. This weakened the cohesion of their own group so that only those committed to religious orthodoxy remained an incapsulating group. The others were tending to slip down the vertical scale into a box 2 situation. Assimilation came to be seen as a much greater threat to their group identity than it had been in Poland, and the group had to develop new institutions, like day schools, to reinforce their distinctiveness.

Holding the line

The position in small town Mississippi in the 1930s offers a classic example of a privileged group maintaining a hard boundary, but even so not all interaction between blacks and whites took the form of group competition. When blacks bought stamps at the post office or gasoline at the filling station they paid the same price as whites. There were black landowners and entrepreneurs who employed white workers and upper-class blacks who out-ranked many whites in terms of social status. It was a pattern of mixed competition which banned certain kinds of transaction or exchange, permitted others on the white man's terms, and allowed yet others to take place on free market principles.

The areas in which the whites guarded their boundaries most fiercely were those of black access to white women and black access to political power. These conformed with the second mode of appraisal outlined in Chapter 2: any degree of black ancestry was likely to be an absolute bar. Both whites and blacks might value wealth, education and social position in a prospective marriage partner but there was no way in which a high score on one of these criteria could be traded against a small measure of black ancestry. This is the more striking in that there is evidence that black Americans (at least until recently) have also placed a high valuation upon a light skin colour in a prospective spouse. In the 1920s Melville J. Herskovits (1930:241) asked 380 Negro students at Howard University (in Washington, D.C.) to compare the complexion of their parents: 30.3 per cent of the students said their father was lighter-skinned, but 56.5 per cent that their mother was lighter; 13.2 per cent replied that they were about the same. Similar results were obtained with Negro students in New York. The figures suggest that Negro men preferred to obtain fair-skinned brides and the more successful men were in a better position to fulfil this preference. The author remarks that Negro men who are themselves of a fair complexion will find it more difficult to obtain Negro spouses of lighter complexion than themselves, so this weighs against the general tendency for the men to seek fairer-skinned wives (compare also Hill, 1944). This observation draws attention to the boundary which has defined the Afro-American group; had it not been maintained by forces which have their origin in other, ultimately political values, the tendency Herskovits describes would have been working to dissolve the distinction between blacks and whites.

Much has changed since then and there may now be more Afro-American men who prefer dark-skinned wives, seeing darkness as a way of reinforcing their ethnic identity. If that is the case, it is because the subjective valuation they place upon different shades of skin colour has changed, and whatever the present pattern may be it will also depend upon the attitudes of their prospective brides.

To maintain their privileges, whites in the Deep South drew a sharp line between themselves and the blacks in everything which they saw as bearing upon the possibility of social equality. They justified this on the grounds that social equality might lead to intermarriage. They gave ceremonial significance to signs which differentiated whites and blacks, such as the reservation of the titles 'Mr' and 'Mrs' to white people. Toilets might be labelled 'white ladies' and 'coloured women'. Black men were called 'boy' or, if elderly, they might be 'uncle'. This was carried to great lengths. Local post-office staff might cross out the 'Mr' on a letter before delivering it to a black man; a telephonist might refuse to put through a telephone call to 'Mr Brown' if she knew Mr Brown to be a black man. And, of course, an unsubstantiated accusation that a black man had made an improper advance to a white woman could (but did not necessarily) lead to a lynching and to psychopathological behaviour by whites.

Just where the line was to be drawn was a question the whites considered with great seriousness. Discussing forms of address, Charles S. Johnson (1943:140) wrote:

> middle- and upper-class Negro women never permit their first names to be known . . . The wife of a well-to-do Negro business man went into a department store in Atlanta to enquire about an account. The clerk asked her first name and she said 'Mrs William Jones'. The clerk insisted on her first name, and when she refused to give it, declared that the business could not be completed without it. It was a large account; and the manager, to whom appeal was made, decided that 'Mrs' was simply good business and not 'social equality'.

A contemporary study of Natchez, Mississippi (Davis, Gardner and Gardner, 1941:16) reported a comparable incident:

> a Negro customer returned a coat which she had bought from a white clothing merchant. The clerk was unwilling to accept the coat and when the assistant manager accepted it, the clerk said to another clerk: 'This is perfectly terrible. I think it is awful. We can't put that coat back in stock.' The latter said 'I know it. Who wants a nigger coat? I don't feel like showing that coat to anyone; nobody wants to buy a nigger coat. Some little white girl will probably come in and buy it and not know it is a nigger coat.' She hung it up very gingerly and didn't touch it any more than necessary. The assistant manager then said: 'I think that is awful. We certainly couldn't make a practice of doing that, it would ruin our business if anyone knew about it. No one would come here to buy their clothes.'

In the first of these stories the manager is described as being free to choose either way. The possibility of losing a large account seems to have helped him decide that addressing the customer in the way she expected was good business. In the second story the assistant manager decided likewise that it was good business to allow the customer to return the coat, but nothing is said about what happened to the coat afterwards. In a small store the owner would probably have put it back in stock. It is said that 'every man has his price' and a store-owner who would pay out of his own pocket if a coat tried on by a little black girl could not subsequently be sold to a white customer, would probably not have put a very high price upon his prejudice. As the Latin phrase had it, *pecunia non olet*, money has no smell, and a black customer's money is worth the same as a white customer's. In a free market the regulation of exchange by money will dissolve qualitative distinctions between the goods sold and reduce them to quantitative differences, expressed in money, and reflecting the tastes or preferences of the customers. Qualitative distinctions, like that which may have prevented the coat being sold to a white purchaser, can be maintained only if there are exceedingly powerful supporting devices. In this story the supporting device is the belief that any white person who put on the coat tried on by the black girl would be polluted by the contact. Such a belief arose in the Deep South from the desire of the whites to prevent association with blacks on terms of social equality. The taboo upon certain kinds of contact was fashioned to make possibly deviant whites toe the line. (The analysis of gender roles and ethnic relations is developed in Banton, 1979.)

If every man has his price, the price mechanism and the notion of 'good business' pose the greatest of threats to a social system such as that of the Deep South. The most effective defence is to arrange the society so that, as far as possible, people whose price might be low are never put in the position in which they can discover just what their price is. Whites must be brought up to believe that their privileges are part of the natural order and outside the reach of the market. Though in reality blacks and whites are in competition with one another, the division of benefits must be presented as the outcome of more fundamental differences. It was suggested earlier that there is a relation between the character of a group and its boundary. A white-supremacy society like that of Mississippi will regard breach of the racial taboos by whites as the greatest of treachery because it makes it more difficult to hold the line; whites will regard as 'real crime' on the part of the blacks anything which damages shared white interests or challenges the line; assaults or robberies between blacks will worry them little. To hold the line it is also necessary to have ways of dealing with possible anomalies, like the illegitimate children of white fathers and black mothers who testify by their very existence to the injustice which such a social order breeds. The Deep South did not find that too difficult a problem.

There is a second threat inherent in such a system. Whites can compete with one another in the enthusiasm they show for identifying ever more forms of black–white association that they consider should be prohibited or regulated by law. In 1909 Mobile passed a curfew law applying exclusively to Negroes and requiring them to be off the streets by 10 p.m. In 1930 Birmingham, Alabama, legislated to prevent whites and Negroes playing at dominoes or checkers together. In 1935, Oklahoma separated the races while fishing or boating. When the blacks are excluded from power, a process can start – as it did in the Deep South from the 1890s and in Rhodesia after 1923 – by which the white political scene grows ever more hostile to any relaxation of the boundary between the groups. The cost of maintaining inequality within the society rises while at the same time the ruling group has more difficulty responding to external pressure. The system becomes incapable of managing gradual change.

Conclusion: theory and history

Racial and ethnic relations have wrongly been seen as special kinds of social relations, distinct from one another and distinct from other kinds of social relations. The error has arisen from a failure to appreciate that differences in peoples' physical appearance and history do not of themselves create groups. Only when they are given cultural significance do they become a basis for social organization. The kinds of differences which in European languages have been called racial and ethnic, have been used to create distinctive roles, allocating people to them in accordance with their appearance and affiliations. In this way these differences have become markers of group identity; it has been easy to assume that the groups were distinctive because of physical and historical differences and to overlook the social processes by which the groups have been created and are maintained.

No modern approach to these matters can take the existence of groups for granted. Individuals have to be motivated to maintain groups and what serves to motivate one individual may not be effective with another. Though groups have their core values, change occurs at their boundaries as some members leave and others try to join. Beliefs about race have been used to exclude some who would join, and to create categories of individuals who are ineligible or entitled to fewer privileges. Ethnic groups, at least in industrial societies, are by contrast founded upon voluntary identification; an ethnic-minority member can leave to join the majority in a way that someone assigned to a racial minority cannot. Since those who are excluded often band together and form a group, the same collection of individuals can be both a racial and an ethnic minority. They may also be a religious, linguistic and political minority, for the same principles govern the formation of minorities and majorities of all kinds; racial and ethnic relations are not special.

To understand the complex processes of group maintenance and change it is necessary to simplify and analyse what might happen in encounters between people belonging to previously separate groups. An earlier chapter has shown that 'race' can be defined in different ways for different purposes. How should it be defined for the purpose of studying 'racial' relations? This chapter has argued that the prime criterion for defining such relations must be the use of beliefs about the significance of race in order to draw social boundaries. A theory of racial relations must therefore, in the first place, be a theory about the creation, maintenance and change of such boundaries. This is to express the matter in very abstract terms. To apply the theory to the analysis of particular situations it is essential to take account of the resources possessed or controlled by groups. Boundaries are important because they can be used to deny others access to such resources. To study the effects of such exclusion upon the life of a group, such as the ways in which it makes for inequality, it is then necessary to call upon other branches of the family of rational choice theories, such as, for example, that which is concerned with human capital.

This chapter has not reached so far; it has simply contended that the social processes resulting from encounters can be illuminated if they are analysed in terms of the Rational Choice Theory according to which group members exchange goods and services, seeking their own advantage. If they compete with one another on an individual basis this will tend to dissolve group boundaries. If they compete as groups, their shared interests will lead them to reinforce those boundaries; the whole life and culture of the privileged group will be oriented to defending their exclusive boundary, while the life of the subordinated group will be directed towards the cultivation of their inclusive bonds so as to mobilize strength for the attack upon the practices which exclude them from privilege.

Can the Rational Choice Theory be confronted with the theories set out in Chapter 5? According to the argument in that chapter it is desirable to compare theories, preferably in terms of their power to predict or to explain events, or, when this cannot be done, in terms of their conceptual coherence and consistency. The contrast between these two modes of comparison is the contrast between scientific explanation and historical interpretation or between strong and weak forms of explanation; it parallels the use of a set of propositions as a theory and as a model, as the two were distinguished by C. Wright Mills.

Scientific explanations are deductive. If a heavy object falls to the ground it is possible to explain the event by reference to the law of gravity, according to which unsupported objects move towards the centre of the earth. By specifying that the object in question was no longer supported its fall is explained; the fall of similar objects in similar circumstances can be predicted. It is a strong explanation. The impossibility of accounting for historical events, or of predicting their occurrence, in this fashion becomes apparent to anyone who tries to answer a question like: 'Why did the United States withdraw from Vietnam in 1973?' There are many plausible answers, none of which can be as secure as explanations of the speed and direction in which heavy objects fall. If there can be no unequivocal answer to a question about an event to which there was a lead-up of only a few years, there can be much less chance of finding a single best explanation of a longer historical sequence (for an elaboration of this view applied to the dissolution of the Campaign Against Racial Discrimination in Britain, see Banton, 1972).

Though deductive explanations appealing to universal laws are, in the writing of history, either impossible or so trivial as to be of no value, history is always written from a point of view. Every historian must work with some philosophy which directs his attention to particular questions and underlies his assumptions as to how it is that one kind of event follows another. The Christian may see history as the unfolding of God's purpose for mankind. Edward Gibbon, the historian of the decline and fall of the Roman Empire, said that he could find no such meaning in history; for him it was but 'the register of the crimes, follies and misfortunes of mankind'. Of late it has been common to oppose idealist and materialist philosophies of history; these are based upon contrasting models of society, the one stressing the importance of shared values in the various patterns of social living, and the other the importance of shared material interests. Addressing the question posed by Chapter 2, as to why relations between reds, whites and blacks gave rise to different modes of classification in three regions of the New World, writers attribute varying significance to the factors from which an answer can be constructed. Towards the idealist end of the scale are those who look first to the religious beliefs and cultural patterns originating in Europe which the whites brought with them to Brazil, Mexico and the United States, in order to account for the differences between the social patterns in these countries. Towards the materialist end are the writers who start from the assumption that relations between masters and servants in the processes of production fashioned the ways in which the parties came to perceive one another. When sociologists turn to historical studies they inevitably rely upon philosophical assumptions of some such kind and the distinction between sociological theory and the philosophy of history sometimes becomes blurred.

The eight theories of racial and ethnic relations discussed in this book can be seen both as philosophies of history and as possible social scientific theories. The history of contacts between reds, whites and blacks in the New World, could, for example, be written from a Typological viewpoint attributing the greater economic advances made in the United States, and the lesser mingling of racial stocks in that country, to the superior racial qualitites of the whites who settled there. Such an interpretation might not persuade many people, but, if it was skilfully presented, it could not be disproven. The same history could equally well be written from Selectionist, Ecological, Class, Split Labour Market and Rational Choice viewpoints; each would concentrate upon particular aspects of the sequence of events and each could claim to interpret those aspects better than the alternative modes of interpretation. Since each interpretation would be adjusted to take account of the known facts, none could be falsified.

Most of the writing about racial relations has been at least in part historical, seeking to explain how present-day problems have come about. So many factors are relevant to the understanding of these problems that it is difficult to allow for them all without discussing the history of particular countries. Yet if theories are to be developed which can at least move towards the kind of deductive explanation which characterizes science, it is necessary to narrow the focus. The more closely an *explanandum* can be specified, the better the chance of finding an explanation. To work for the advancement of knowledge about racial relations it is therefore necessary to move forward on two fronts simultaneously, improving both historical interpretations and theoretical frameworks. It is necessary to resemble the writing of economic history on the one hand and the development of economic theory on the other.

A concept like inflation, as has been refined in economic theory, can be used to illuminate economic relations (say, a change in price levels) in historical periods before the concept existed, and it can be used in the study of societies that do not have any proper form of money. Economic theories can be refined by trying them out on historical material to see whether, on the face of things, there is a plausible case for them, but it is improbable that any such theory could be properly tested on historical data since it is too difficult to control all the variables. There are general concepts in social science such as, for example, relative deprivation and reference groups, which are as culture-free as the concept of inflation and can be distinguished from conceptions of race and caste which are tied to particular cultures. Such general concepts, drawn from social anthropology, provided the framework for the study of inter-racial unions in early-nineteenth-century Cuba referred to in this chapter. It should be possible to develop theories and concepts of inter-group relations which can, on the one hand, be used in historical interpretation as the concept of inflation is used, and, on the other hand, be subjected to more rigorous testing whenever it is possible to control the relevant variables.

The remainder of this book therefore falls into three main sections. Chapters 7 and 8 elaborate upon the presentation of the Rational Choice

Theory in this chapter by showing what is entailed in the processes of individual and group competition. They are followed by chapters about the history of three countries likely to be of particular interest to the reader, written from the standpoint of the Rational Choice Theory. The third section then consists of two chapters about the ways in which Rational Choice Theory can be developed to account for the differential position of minority members in the housing and employment markets. Though these chapters do not reach the point at which the theories can be said to have been tested, they suggest that the time may not be far off when fairly rigorous testing will be possible. They are followed by a concluding chapter about the inferences that can be drawn by those concerned with public policies in this field.

7

Individual competition and boundary change

This chapter discusses the sort of situation in which, by immigration, a minority group is established in a more powerful receiving society. Minority members have to respond to the pressure of expectations from the receiving society which generate the forces of assimilation mentioned in the previous chapter. There are also forces within the minority which resist those pressures and the struggle between the two can best be shown by looking more closely at changes within the immigrant family. For this purpose it is convenient to begin with a reconsideration of the analysis advanced by W. Lloyd Warner in his study of 'Yankee City', not because it was a model of its kind, but because its clarity enables the critic to uncover its presuppositions and ascertain where it went wrong.

The Warner model: family and assimilation

The recognized ethnic groups in Newburyport ('Yankee City') in the mid 1930s were the Irish, French Canadians, Jews, Italians, Armenians, Greeks, Poles and a few Russians. In their homelands, the family structure of all these groups had been of a type which Warner called patriarchal, taking its form in every case except that of the Jews from the functions of the family in a relatively simple agrarian economy. By the standards of an industrial society the traditional family was large; sons, even after marriage, might continue to live under the parental roof and so form a three-generation unit. All its members were dependent upon the family land and what this could produce; there were no state benefits for the sick or unemployed. The other members were subject to the authority of the father because he controlled the land; he and his wife could decide when they would retire and hand it over to the next generation, and how the patrimony would then be divided. Until that time the other members had to rely upon his skill as a manager in trying to get the maximum yield from the land and the stock. The father organized the production and his wife the household. The younger generations were subject to their authority because all were dependent upon the group and its success both in producing for the market and in competing with similar groups for status in the local community. Though these patterns of authority had their sources in the economy they were elaborated and maintained by customary practice, and supported by community opinion, so that young people who deferred to their parents would enjoy honour when in due course they joined the senior generation. The fifth commandment instructed them: 'honour thy father and thy mother that thy days may be long upon the land which the Lord thy God giveth thee'.

In Massachusetts this pattern was shattered. The immigrants lived in smaller family groups which were no longer self-sufficient, cooperative producing units. Previously both husband and wife had worked, often together, in the fields and around the home, but in an industrial city the man alone was a producer so that his wife became more dependent and subordinate to him. The children no longer worked with their parents: they went off to school where they were taught in a new language how they should behave in the United States. Not only were they removed from their father's authority and sphere of expertise, but they were taught, by their peer groups if not by their teachers, norms of conduct contrary to those cherished by their parents. Indeed, their parents might have to consult them about the meaning of documents written in English and about the American way of doing things. The authority structure of the family was turned upside-down. Much of the pain of the immigrant experience was concentrated in the relations between the first two generations. Parents who might have looked forward to being honoured in their old age found themselves scorned and contradicted. The children were under tremendous pressure to conform to the expectations of their peer-groups; they had to engage in individual competition with their class-mates at school and their families could not stand behind them in their dealings with the children of other families to the extent that would have happened in the Old World. The children felt guilty about what was happening to their parents and tried to resolve their conflicts by super-patriotism; as the principal of one of the local schools remarked 'they seem to become more American than the Americans'.

The structure of relations in a family pattern is never static; if, in the traditional farming family, some new tool became available that the son knew how to use but not the father, authority would tip over towards the son in this sphere. In the Massachusetts setting, this sort of change occurred in almost every sphere within the space of a few years. The father lost his claims to expertise, the support of a wider group, and much of his ability to reward and punish. The conflicts were greatest with adolescent children. Many ethnic fathers expected their children to surrender their wage packets to be given pocket money in return. Speaking of girls who had to do this, one Greek boy said 'that isn't right because it makes them hold out money on him – about twenty-five or thirty cents at a time. They save it up until they get money to buy a dress'. Many ethnic parents expected to be able to prevent their children marrying someone they thought unsuitable and to control their courtship, which ran counter to American patterns of 'dating' and caused their children to 'hold out' on their parents in this sphere also.

In Newburyport, Jews originated from the petty-bourgeois class in Russia; they were already adjusted to urban living so the transition did not involve so great a shock to their family's internal structure of roles. Yet it was a Jewish father who was quoted as saying, in bitterness: 'Children are not worthwhile, what do you get out of them? Once you used to get respect and honour at least. Here they throw you away. You become a back number. My daughter had a birthday party last Sunday and she had some friends up. You know where we stayed? In the kitchen . . .' One of his children said of him: 'Oh, he gets me sick. Everytime I have some friends up to the house, he wants to sit with my mother in the parlor. You know what that does to a crowd of young people. What have we in common with them? Nothing, so then they sit in the kitchen, with the door open, so they can hear everything that goes on. Peeking on us! . . . he's always telling me how they used to do things in Russia, but this happens to be the United States of America, not Russia, and the twentieth century, not the nineteenth . . . He thinks I don't respect him. Well he's right, and you can see my reasons'. In the Old World a marriage was a union of families as well as individuals, and it was important to the parents to have a say in who should be their son- or daughter-in-law. Because of their position in the economic structure, as farmers or small businessmen, they could apply sanctions to a disobedient child. In Massachusetts, a Polish man said he had talked with his son about a career and had received the reply: 'Don't worry, father, when I graduate from high school, we'll see how much money you have saved up to see whether I can go to college'. Here the son was applying a sanction on his father, who was unemployed and apparently could not even understand that he was being upbraided (Warner and Srole, 1945:103–55).

If an ethnic group is to maintain its character, it is essential that young people marry others of the same ethnic group (a crucial consideration when, as in the case of the Jews, a special set of religious beliefs is at the core of ethnicity). In New England at the time of the Yankee City research a tendency was developing for those Catholic Irish who did not marry fellow Irish to marry other Catholics, be they Italian, French Canadian or Polish; for Protestants to marry Protestants, even if of different ethnic background; and for Jews to marry other Jews who might well have originated in a different part of Europe. There was said to be a triple rather than a single melting pot. What intermarriage can mean for ethnic communities is illustrated more vividly by the case of the Japanese in Hawaii. Up to 1945 almost every Japanese bride there married a Japanese bridegroom, but, by 1980, 59 per cent of Japanese were marrying spouses from other groups. The Japanese girls had stayed on longer in the educational system; they had met boys of other groups and were better informed about the expectations of marriage that prevailed elsewhere. Many were not attracted to the prospect of playing the traditional role of the Japanese wife; the non-Japanese bridegroom obtained a bride who was more deferential and solicitous than the brides of his own group. Thus, when the Japanese girls married out, both of the partners got a better deal, in that she did not have to be so subservient and he had a more deferential bride. This put the pressure on the Japanese men and the non-Japanese women to be less demanding in their expectations of the marital relationship. It resembled the position at the end of the Second World War when women in the United States complained that so many G.I.s stationed in Germany were coming home with German brides because German women conceded men more authority in the home.*

Warner's assumptions

Warner set out to tell part of what he called 'the magnificent history of the adjustment of the ethnic groups to American life'. The motive power was the immigrant's response to new opportunities: 'He is drawn by the attractions of the Yankee City residential and occupational hierarchies and begins his upward climb in both.' The magnetic power of 'American equalitarianism, which attempts to make all men American and alike' drew the immigrants into a system of individual competition which gave them finely graded places in the order of stratification so that 'our class system functions for a large proportion of ethnics to destroy the ethnic subsystems and to increase assimilation'. Ethnic groups were ranked in what he called a 'scale of subordination and assimilation' whereby those whose physical and cultural traits were most like those of the original Yankee stock were most acceptable socially and most nearly assimilated (Warner and Srole, 1945:2, 79, 285, 295).

Some of the implicit features of this conception become explicit if it is represented by a diagram of the kind suggested in Figure 6. It shows two groups, A (the majority) and B (the ethnic minority), with a cultural difference that is scored as 10 points along the horizontal axis. After one hundred years group B has been completely absorbed by A, which has continued along precisely the course it would have followed had B not

---

* Hawaii may seem a special case because Asian groups are a substantial proportion of the total population. In 1980, 22 per cent of Japanese marriages were to a white partner. Yet the same trend has been even more marked in Los Angeles where, by 1979, 50 per cent of Japanese marriages were to non-Asians (Kitano *et al.*, 1982).

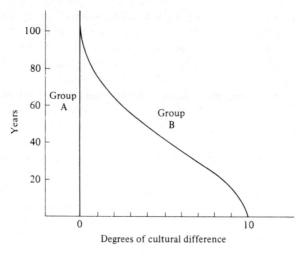

Figure 6   The Warner model of assimilation

appeared upon the scene. The zero point from which Group A starts is put a little distance to the right of the vertical axis, so that the line representing its course is not confused with the axis showing the passing of time. This diagram brings out three features of the Warner conception. Firstly, time: some groups are assimilated more quickly than others; secondly, that the difference between the two groups is that of their culture; and, thirdly, that the process of assimilation operates upon the totality of the minority's culture.

But it is a matter of common observation that cultural change among immigrants proceeds more rapidly in respect of behaviour that helps them earn a living, like learning a language, than in their private domestic lives. The implication of a uniform process of change is misleading, as is the failure to acknowledge that the receiving group undergoes change in absorbing the other. A more helpful diagram would be of the kind provided in Figure 7. This preserves the time dimension, the broken lines representing the courses that groups A and B would follow if there were no cultural change whatsoever, but it separates the speed and direction of change. The lines running up to points C, D and E might, for example, represent change in respect of language, cuisine, and a particular sporting activity. Taking first C, this indicates that the minority has found it convenient to adopt the language of the majority, but at the same time has contributed some words and expressions to the common speech, so that A has come one-tenth of the way towards meeting B, while after sixty years the two groups can no longer be distinguished linguistically. In respect of cuisine, D, change is more

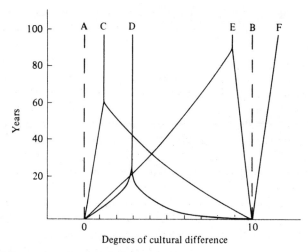

Figure 7 Processes of cultural change

evenly balanced and more rapid, each group adopting some of the dishes favoured by the other, but because the foodstuffs of the native group are cheaper, B adopts more from A than A does from B. It is easier to try a new dish than to try a language, and people rarely lose status by trying new foodstuffs, so assimilation proceeds more rapidly in this field than in some others, and after 25 years the groups are no longer distinguishable. In both these instances the minority changes in the direction of the majority, but sometimes it is the other way round. This may happen when the minority brings a cultural feature particularly suited to the receiving country, as Swedish settlers brought techniques for constructing the log cabin to the United States. Majority changes in the direction of the minority are, however, more likely in the expressive than the instrumental realm. Minorities bring dances, costumes and sports, which, like football, may soon lose their ethnic identification, or, like judo and karate, may become both ethnic and international. The line leading to E represents a situation in which after 90 years a minority sport has been generally adopted in a slightly modified form.

The weaknesses of the Warner model are well known. It is now widely accepted that a conception of assimilation as a unitary process is misleading. The B group moves towards A at different speeds in different areas of life and the A group usually moves itself. Stages in processes of change have occasionally been discerned but they are restricted to particular circumstances. The adoption by immigrants of majority practices may give an appearance of change but underlying values may not have altered. Moreover, the majority itself is divided by socio-economic status, regions, life-styles and perhaps by ethnicity. Social life in the different sectors, of work, schooling, home and religion, may be compartmentalized so that it becomes difficult to identify the group or practices in the majority society to which the minority may be expected to assimilate. It is customary to ask to what extent a minority is assimilated, but the question can also be asked of the majority.

This brings out the questionable assumptions lying behind Warner's apparently simple proposal to write about 'the adjustment of the immigrant groups to American life' as if others did not have also to adjust to them. Warner's analysis might have been better had he paused to consider what he meant by assimilation. On this point the entry in the *Dictionary of the Social Sciences* may say more than it intends, when under the heading 'assimilation' it begins 'the term literally means the process of becoming "alike" or "more alike" '; but then continues (italics added) '*as used in sociology,* it denotes (a) the process whereby a group, generally a minority or an immigrant group, is through contact absorbed into the culture of another group or groups; (b) the result of such absorption'. Why should usage in sociology have become different, and is this justified? At the beginning of the century sociologists used the word to denote the process of becoming alike or more alike (Simons, 1901). What happened was that shortly afterwards many articulate people of Old American stock began to worry about the possible implications of the immigration of so many people from the Mediterranean countries who were thought to be of inferior racial stock and unable or unwilling to become model citizens of the United States. It was seen as a problem of Americanization and the word assimilation came to be used in this sense in popular writing. Many sociologists followed the crowd, and Warner was among them because, in this as in other fields (see Thernstrom, 1964:230, 239), he quite explicitly used the folk concepts of some of his subjects in order to analyse their society. He states that in Yankee City the Canadians, Scots, English and Northern Irish had not formed ethnic groups; they were not 'ethnic people'. Without realizing what he was doing, he took over the Yankees' assumption that they had no ethnicity since ethnicity characterized the people who had not yet been fully Americanized. The American social system was not a melting pot, Warner wrote, but one which transmuted diverse ethnic elements into elements almost homogeneous with its own. With justice, he has been criticized for equating assimilation with a process of Anglo-conformity whereby the immigrants have to adopt the values as well as the language of the group who got there first and assumed control of the levers of power.

The facility with which Warner adopted the folk concepts of the people he studied may help explain some of the limitations of his discussion of the place of religion in connection with assimilation. The immigrant was expected to change much but he was never expected to change his faith. Catholics and Jews were not to be assimilated to Protestants because the constitution of the United States was founded on the separation of church and state. The legitimation of religious difference provided a vehicle for cultivating cultural characteristics and social ties based in the sending societies.

One of Warner's most interesting critics, Milton Gordon (1964), compared three models of the processes of ethnic change in immigrant minorities. One was that of Anglo-conformity, which has been represented in Figure 6. A second was that of the Melting Pot, in which all groups pool their characteristics. This is represented in the lines leading to positions C, D and E in Figure 7; the extent to which the members of one group move in the direction of another will reflect the relative power of the groups, but after a while it will be difficult to distinguish one group from another. The third model comprised two versions of pluralism: cultural and structural, according to whether the minority retained elements of distinctive culture or was distinctive because its members continued to associate with one another rather than with members of the majority. These processes could also be represented by the lines leading to positions C, D and E in Figure 7, with the minority moving towards the majority in some respects (position C), remaining distinctive in others (position E), or meeting the majority nearer the middle (position D).

Many of these conceptual lacunae exist because assimilation has been discussed almost exclusively with reference to situations of immigration. Yet minorities are not necessarily immigrants, nor are majorities necessarily indigenous. Minorities may be subjected to a pressure to change that is implicit in the political and economic superiority of an expanding group – as white influence has spread in Amerindian regions in the United States, or English influence in other parts of the United Kingdom. Assimilation can be said to have occurred in Brazil, where a clear division between Europeans and Africans (and to some extent between them and Amerindians) has given way to a continuous gradation without one group having absorbed another. This is a reminder that while there may initially be just two groups (as in Figures 6 and 7), an intermediary group may appear such that others are pressed to change in its direction, constituting a process which is sometimes called creolization. Moreover, ethnic change at the local level may in the short term, and in certain features of behaviour, run in a direction opposite to that of change at the national level. A group which is a numerical minority in the state may be in a majority locally, so that people belonging to the national majority may be under pressure to change towards the group which is the local majority even if it is a national minority. For example, in parts of British cities where there are substantial numbers of black children it is not uncommon for white and Asian children to interest themselves in black music and adopt black speech patterns.

Among the weaknesses in Warner's analysis was his failure to acknowledge that the process he studied was but one variety of assimilation among many, and that change could follow a different course when the power relations between the groups were less unbalanced. Another over-simplification was his representation of assimilation as a process occurring on the group level. From the illustrations he gave, it is clear that he saw individual actions as building up to create the process, but because his focus was on the group he took account only of those individual actions which could be fitted into his model and ignored those which could have pointed to the limitations stemming from his assumptions.

To measure cultural changes it is necessary to specify quite closely which feature of culture is being examined and to delimit the populations (groups A and B) precisely. Any reduction in cultural difference, regardless of which group moves most, and for what reasons, is seen as part of the process of assimilation. A movement in the contrary direction (to position F in Figure 7) is regarded as a process of differentiation. A group that is assimilating to the minority in certain respects may increase its differentiation in others. For example, a recent study of a Sikh community in England reports that an increasing proportion of young men are wearing the turban. This is the result in part of growing pressure for conformity within the ethnic colony and in part of a reassertion of ethnic pride in the face of white rejection (Ballard and Ballard, 1977:47). Other groups differentiate themselves on account of shared beliefs (as Black Muslims in the United States have laid a particular stress on the avoidance of pork), so that the increase in cultural difference is an unintended consequence of their actions. These processes are not limited to ethnic groupings. The history of social stratification is replete with examples of upwardly mobile groups trying to assimilate to groups higher in the scale, and of these groups trying to prevent this by sumptuary legislation or by adopting new social styles. There is no fundamental sociological difference between the two kinds of change, but it is convenient to distinguish ethnic change as cultural change identified with ethnic groups.

Group orientation

Warner described a situation in which the rewards offered by the majority (or receiving society) for conforming behaviour by members of the immigrant group, were so great relative to the rewards an immigrant could

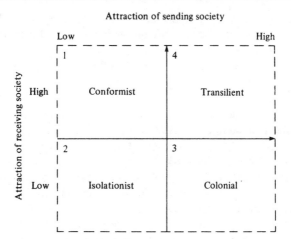

Figure 8 The orientation of immigrant groups

receive for loyalty to his traditional culture that cultural change was overwhelmingly on the part of the minority moving towards the majority's expectations. Change is rarely that simple and, though it is not possible to attempt a classification here of all the various kinds of relation between majority and minority, it is desirable to identify, as one of the most relevant dimensions, the relative attractiveness to the immigrant of the cultures of the sending and receiving societies.

The disposition on the part of an immigrant group to maintain or reduce cultural differences, i.e. its group orientation, will be affected by the extent to which members of the group are disposed to adopt the values of the receiving society, or hold to those of the society from which they have come. This is represented in Figure 8. The vertical axis measures the attractive power of the receiving society, the horizontal axis that of the sending society. The intersection creates four quadrants or 'boxes'. The circumstances defined by the boxes below the line (2 and 3) result in minority groups with relatively strong boundaries; those defined by the boxes above the line (1 and 4) result in groups with very weak boundaries because the members of them respond as individuals to the relative attractions of the two societies.

Box 1, the upper-left-hand quadrant, is the place for immigrants strongly attracted to the receiving society and willing or eager to conform to its expectations. The Yankee City groups described by Warner belong in box 1, beginning towards the bottom left-hand corner of the box and moving up towards the upper left as the disposition to conform to the New England pattern of life increases with the passage of time. Box 2 contains immigrant groups who have left their original country not in order to join another, but in order to be on their own. Many religious communities, like the Hutterites, the Amish and the Dukhobors, have left Europe for North America in order to live a separate existence, conceding only the minimum to the demands which their new state makes upon those who would be its citizens. Box 3 includes migrant workers who are in the receiving society but not of it. Their group life may be maintained by the rotation of personnel, usually male, with new migrants coming to take the place of 'target workers' who have saved the capital they want and are returning to their home country. A special category of migrant workers, which could well be called migrant rulers, has been made up of European administrators employed by imperial countries to administer the affairs of countries they have conquered or taken into protection. Being richer, the administrators can afford to bring out their families and to send their children back to the sending society for schooling. They are also groups who go out to settle new territory intending to create an outpost of their home country, and these, like the British in New Zealand, may eventually become independent societies. Since the original sense of the word 'colony' is that of a settlement of people residing in a foreign country, and there is no convenient alternative word, the adjective colonial is the most suitable designation for the outlook of a group oriented towards the society of its origin. (Since the Second World War the critics of imperialism have often referred to it as 'colonialism'; they have been concerned about circumstances in which colonization has been accompanied by the subordination of the local population, but this is more truly a characteristic of imperialism.) The groups in boxes 2 and 3 seek to resist the attractions of the receiving society by strengthening group boundaries and employ a strategy known as incapsulation. Box 4 encloses migrants equally attracted by both societies. Some Europeans who settle in North America decide after a while that they would be happier in the countries of their birth but when they return there they compare them unfavourably with North America. They have difficulty settling in either society because they have become so conscious of the attractions of the other and they end up feeling as if their personal centre of gravity is somewhere in the mid-Atlantic. Anthony H. Richmond (1967:252) has revived the use of the name 'transilient' for migrants who move around benefitting from the international market for their occupational skills, and the word can appropriately be applied to those people who come to feel attracted to both a sending and a receiving society.

A comparison of Figure 8 and Figure 5 will show that isolationist and colonial groups draw hard boundaries around themselves. The former tend to be unprivileged and therefore incapsulating groups; the latter may well be privileged (since otherwise they would be less anxious to retain their homeland ties) and they will then be excluding groups. Conformist groups are likely to be numerical minorities gradually losing their distinctive characteristics. Transilients are not a group at all but a category of individuals, so they are not represented in Figure 5.

Comparison of the two figures can also remind the reader that the United States has been unusual in its constitutional separation of church and state. Immigrants can retain their faith and still be loyal citizens. In many Muslim and Catholic countries the position is quite different. It is as if the people believe that there is one true religion and that therefore the institutions of the state should express the faith and facilitate its extension. By definition, unbelievers cannot then be good citizens. The implications for minorities of such a situation have been shown in a study which compares the position of Jews in Tunisia and Morocco and Arabs in Israel. Because of the official tie between religion and politics in all three countries, members of a group following a minority religion can share only marginally in the state's political identity and mission. They may be attracted by the receiving society and be willing to conform to many of its expectations (box 1 in Figure 8) but be met by exclusion on account of their religion (box 4 in Figure 5). Their political assimilation is prevented. Caught in a cleft stick, members of such a group may emigrate, weakening the community that remains so that its religious attachment may decline, or they may identify with their co-religionists elsewhere (Tessler, 1981). The complexity of such situations demonstrates – if demonstration be needed – that it is impossible to capture in a single diagram more than a few of the dimensions on which patterns of ethnic relations can differ. That this is so only underlines the need to be clear for what purpose situations are being classified and what theory is being utilized.

The social processes which bear upon members of groups may lead them to change their orientation and cause the group to move from one 'box' to another. For example, the history of native Americans in the southern states shows that in the late eighteenth and early nineteenth centuries some groups were adopting many elements of white culture, but with the establishment of the slave regime the rewards of participation in the new states were outweighed by the costs to the Indians of being forced into a servile status, so they withdrew from interaction with whites so far as possible, only returning to closer relations when the balance of rewards shifted (J. H. Peterson, 1971). In Figure 8, if the sending society is replaced by traditional Indian society and the receiving society by white American society, this would mean that in the eighteenth and early nineteenth centuries the Choctaw, for example, could be located on the right-hand side of box 1, moving under the slavery period to the left side of box 3 and then back again in more recent times. These changes have been largely in

Table 1: *Immigration to the United States, 1899–1952, by major categories*

	Total arrivals	Percentage departures
Italian	4,068,700	55.1
Hebrew	2,082,136	4.8
German	1,892,151	18.2
Polish	1,694,891	36.3
English	1,544,733	25.1
Irish	1,151,826	11.6
Scandinavian	1,119,561	23.5
Mexican	789,336	28.1
Scottish	676,335	14.9
French	621,390	17.8
Slovak	560,496	55.0
Greek	551,893	49.3

Note: 'Hebrew' ceased to be used as a category in 1944; subsequent arrivals were listed by national origin.
This table is based on figures presented by Charles A. Price in *Harvard Encyclopedia of Ethnic Groups*, 1980, pp. 1036–7.

response to the sort of rewards they were offered for participating in the majority culture, but a diagram like Figure 8 is unable to reflect the changes which two cultures have undergone over time.

The rewards which are offered to minorities if they will conform to majority expectations can be increased if the minority bargains successfully. This is discussed in the next chapter in connection with revaluation movements.

Return migration

Isolationist and colonial groups try to present a group front to the receiving society. Where immigrants are conformist or transilient they are more inclined to confront the receiving society as individuals. The reactions of people in the conformist category have been discussed in connection with Warner's study of assimilation, but more needs to be said about the migrants who do not remain in the receiving society.

It is not always appreciated how many migrants return to their homelands. Table 1 is based on successive Annual Reports of the US

Commissioner General of Immigration. Using the categories employed by his department, it selects the twelve for which the largest total numbers of arrivals in the United States during the period 1899–1952 were recorded, and the percentages of persons in the same categories who left the country during the same period. The full table from which it is extracted records very high percentage departure figures for some smaller groups, including 91.9 per cent for Bulgarians and 87 per cent for Turks. The total of departures of Chinese is greater than that for arrivals, indicating the diminution after 1899 of a population of immigrants who entered before that year. Not everyone is attracted by the prospect of settling in a country which can offer a higher standard of living to their descendants, but cannot match the emotional rewards of the homeland for those who have grown up in it.

The worst persecution may not for everyone counterbalance the attractions of the homeland. Between March 1938 and November 1941 some 126,500 Jews succeeded in fleeing from Austria; it seems probable that at least 6 per cent returned. The interpretation of the available statistics is particularly difficult, but it would seem that the availability of compensation (which was far from generous for Austrians) cannot have been a major motivation. Those who did return were very conscious that they were returning to 'cursed soil', to areas where the worst atrocities against European Judaism originated, and that their action was condemned by fellow Jews. Yet still some returned, a significant number even from Israel, and to judge from the answers they gave to interviewers, many of them did so because of a homesickness for the city they had known before the holocaust (Wilder-Okladek, 1969).

Resisting assimilation

Members of immigrant groups are often willing to conform to the expectations of the majority society in matters that pertain to the obligations of citizenship but wish to retain their ethnic identity in their private domain. They may accept that everyone should speak the language of the receiving society but want their children to learn also that of their sending society and believe that the retention of minority languages should be encouraged by the state as an element of enrichment. Above all, they oppose any tendency to disparage the culture of their sending society.

Minority members who adopt such a stance face two main problems; firstly, that of generation differences. Members of the first generation have been brought up in the values of the sending society and are more attracted to it than are their children; it is much easier for them to return to the sending society should they wish. The second generation, as has been shown, is under great pressure to conform. In the third generation there is a slight reaction, giving rise to what has been called Hansen's law: 'the almost universal phenomenon that what the son wishes to forget the grandson wishes to remember' (Hansen, 1938:9). Yet by this stage fundamental changes have already occurred. Secondly, it is not easy for an immigrant group on its own to draw a line between the domain of citizenship in which its members conform and the private domain in which they do not. The minority may seek to resist assimilation but it is unlikely to succeed unless the majority joins in and tries to prevent assimilation (minority resistance may be either a consequence of majority exclusion or a cause of it). It is possible to argue that a minority must resist assimilation in everything or in nothing, and that there is no half-way house. Certainly, only a handful of cases can be cited of minority groups which have been able to retain their identity for more than three generations, especially in an industrial society. To do so, the group must, above all, be able to retain the loyalty of its children, and to this end it must be able either to offer them emotional and material satisfactions greater than the apparent satisfactions held out by the environing society or to prevent them going to places in which they might hear those siren voices. The Jewish rabbis said that 'the world is poised on the breath of school children' and this reflects the importance to any minority group of securing the commitment of the young people with whom the future of the group rests. To explore such issues it is helpful to examine the circumstances in which minority members have been motivated to maintain an isolationist group identity as pictured in Figure 8. In terms of Figure 5, it means analysing processes characteristic of an incapsulating group which maintains a hard inclusive boundary, either in response to a hard excluding boundary on the part of the majority or evoking such a boundary.

Among the groups which have been successful in maintaining an isolationist identity, one of the most outstanding is the Old Order Amish of Pennsylvania. They descend directly from religious reformers in Europe who wished to make a sharper break with the Catholic tradition than Martin Luther's. A group whom others called Anabaptists (because they believed in a second baptism) wanted complete freedom of religion and a voluntary church in close conformity with the early vision of Christianity displayed in the New Testament. They criticized Luther not because he 'tore down the old House, but that he built no new one in its place'. To build a new one they took literally the Sermon on the Mount, renounced oaths and revelling, the use of the sword whether in war or civil government, economic rewards and personal adornment. The true church should depend not on baptism administered in infancy, but on regeneration and change of character. Instead of embracing the whole of humanity, the church was to be a voluntary adult fellowship of disciplined and committed people. The

Anabaptist groups sometimes identify themselves as 'non-resistant' because of their renunciation of all violence and their belief that a man should turn the other cheek to anyone who smites him. Their movement, which started in 1525, divided into three sections: the Anabaptists of Holland called Mennonites after their pastor–leader Menno Simons, the Swiss Brethren, and the Hutterian Brethren of Austria, who, after a remarkable history of persecution and flight from Switzerland to Hungary, Roumania and then Russia, have now established collective farms in many parts of Canada, the United States and South America. The first group of Amish, about 500 in number, settled in Pennsylvania in the eighteenth century.

The Amish broke from the Swiss Brethren in 1693–7, following Jakob Amman, a preacher who took with particular seriousness New Testament injunctions like 'if any man that is called a railer or a drunkard, or an extortioner, with such a one do not eat' (1 Corinthians 5:11); 'if he neglect to hear the church, let him be unto thee as a heathen man' (Matthew 18:17); 'be not conformed to this world, but be ye transformed by the renewing of your mind' (Romans 12:2) and 'be ye not unequally yoked together with unbelievers' (2 Corinthians 6:14). To him and his followers such passages were instructions to withdraw from the world and concentrate upon a life of purity. If any member of the congregation left the church, married outside the brotherhood, or broke its rules, he was to be shunned. Unlike the Mennonites, the Amish do not seek to convert others to their faith; with few exceptions, only the children of members of the Amish church, through instruction and baptism, become members themselves. They interpret 'be not conformed' as an injunction not to dress and behave like those outside the brotherhood. Amman argued for uniformity in dress and maintained that it was wrong for men to trim their beards. Any kind of ostentation in the costume of adults was so much deplored that each community developed its rules about the number of buttons a man might have on a workaday shirt or the width of the brim of his hat, and at one time the Amish were distinguished from the Mennonites by the willingness of the latter to permit the use of buttons whereas the Amish allowed only hook-and-eyes on men's Sunday coats and women's dresses. The stress that is placed upon the distinctive costume; the minute regulation of material possessions (no cars, no electricity, no telephone, and only certain kinds of bottle-gas kitchen stoves which do not encourage vanity); and the home-centred pattern of organization (religious services are held in turn at the homes of members of the congregation); the use of the German language for worship and their own dialect (called Pennsylvania Dutch) for ordinary conversation; all these serve to bind together the members and help them preserve their separate way of living.

Most young American boys want to drive cars; most girls want to visit the cinema and to utilize labour-saving devices in the home, so the Amish achievement is sociologically remarkable. In the past they suffered cruel persecution, and every Amish generation is taught from *The Bloody Theatre or Martyrs Mirror* of their ancestors' faithfulness under torture. Amish hymns tell of 'the present terrible last days' in which so many false prophets and tyrants destroy unity among men and persecute the righteous, yet there is not much persecution to which their bishops can point nowadays. The crucial institution in contending for the loyalty of the new generation is therefore the school. As Anabaptists, the Amish have always held that the task of training children belongs to the church-community and not the state. They fear the possibility of their children leaving the faith since, as parents, they are personally accountable to God for their upbringing, while if they lose their children to the world they lose their hope of salvation and of their spending eternity together in heaven.

Officials in some localities have taken Amish parents to court, seeking to force them to send their children to ordinary schools or make them stay longer in school, and one of these cases went as far as the US Supreme Court. The Amish saw threats to their communities in the consolidation of elementary schools, the extension of compulsory schooling, in conscription, and in federal old-age insurance programmes. In every instance some Amish suffered the consequences by paying fines, serving prison sentences or moving to other localities.

Despite the community's strenuous efforts to promote a sense of shared identity and dependence on the group, there are young Amish who desert their communities. It comes as a surprise to the reader of John A. Hostetler's admirable book about the Amish to learn that of the two principal kinds of deviance, they are less worried about young people who 'turn wild' than about those who show too much interest in religion. One instance is described of a seventeen-year-old going off to a secret Bible study group and his mother protesting: 'We know that it cannot be the Lord's will for the young folks to come together like that' (Hostetler, 1968:230). The pressure to conform is very great. A young man reported: 'My chums got suspicious and were afraid I had a "strange belief" when I refused to smoke'. The boys drink, tell obscene stories, smoke, behave in a rowdy manner, purchase automobiles, and so on, but this does not threaten the group so long as they give up these characteristics of immaturity when they are baptised and assume adult status. Since the Amish constitute a religious society, defection takes the form of religious deviance. The greatest threat is posed by the Mennonites with their stress upon faith rather than social conformity, but a community may split or decide to join one of the other groups of Amish congregations that are less strict than the Old Order, like, for example, the Beachy Amish who allow their members to own automobiles.

Not all Amish children do give up worldly ways at the age when they are due for baptism. There is an overall drop-out rate of approximately 25 per cent, usually the children of family heads who only marginally conform to the rules, or of parents who do not farm or cannot help set up their children with farms. Amish families are usually large (seven or eight children are typical) and married couples devote much time to the care of their children. The young are given rewarding and responsible roles in family and farm work. Families cooperate with others in major tasks, such as barn-raising. Since their way of life depends upon family farming, the Amish man must work hard to keep his sons and daughters on the land. An annual population increase of 3 per cent (which means a doubling of the population every 23 years) has so far counterbalanced the drop-out rate. The area of Amish settlement has expanded and, since the maximum size of a congregation is limited to the number who can meet in one house at one farm (30 to 40 households), new church districts have had to be established.

There are now about 80,000 Amish settled in twenty states of the United States and one province of Canada (Hostetler, 1980). Their history shows that a group can resist assimilation when it organizes the central features of its life so as to strengthen both its inclusive and exclusive boundaries, making it difficult for those born into the community to leave it, and even more difficult for outsiders to join. They accept changes that do not threaten the social bond and see no inconsistency in using felt-tipped pens for writing but driving a horse and buggy, in using a pay telephone but refusing to have a telephone in the home, in riding in automobiles but not owning them. At the same time they have created foci of concern within the group (like watching that the orders about buttons are observed) and have differentiated their way of life from the outside society in most of the major ways except food taboos. Though they seem to be a model community in their display of an ideally peaceable way of life, they can maintain it only because they oppose their life to that of 'the world'. If 'the world' tried to be Amish the scheme would collapse. Equally, Amish belief falls into a conforming routine that can be hostile to spiritual renewal and its groups continually divide. It is religion which most threatens the maintenance of their culture although it is religion which provides the basis of their way of life.

The Amish have a distinctive religion and a special set of supportive institutions. The Gypsies have neither of these, and are more dependent upon the majority society, so their survival over an even longer period is a yet more remarkable story. They may well have originated from India in the fifth century. The earliest groups entered Europe in the fourteenth century and had reached Scotland by 1505. Initially they were often welcomed but their way of life soon alienated them from the rest of the population and they were subjected to a harsh persecution which subsided in the nineteenth century only to be revived more brutally in Nazi Germany when over a quarter of a million Gypsies were murdered. Most of the European nations, Britain, France, Portugal, Spain, the Netherlands and Germany, deported groups of Gypsies to various parts of the New World and there are now probably more than half-a-million Gypsies living in the United States and Canada, mostly from Rom, Romnichal and Boyash sections of the Gypsy people. The Rom are divided into four main *natsiyi* or 'nations', the Machwaya (who are considered an elite), the Kalderasha, Churara, and Lowara. Each nation is divided into clans (which appear previously to have been matrilineal) and families though families may come together and form a *kumpania* which is a cooperating economic group (Hancock, 1980).

The relationship between the Gypsies and the majority society does not fit well into any of the categories used in sociology for inter-group relations. Non-Gypsies are called *gazhé* or *gajé* in the United States, and *gawjas* or *gorgios* in Britain (where Romnichals predominate). The quality of this relationship is well illustrated by the difficulty of identifying any Gypsy. Introducing her study of a Rom *kumpania* in California, Anne Sutherland (1975:26) writes that 'anonymity and invisibility combined with intense secretiveness are keys to the ability of the Rom to adapt and survive in an alien culture. Most are not registered at birth, in school, in a census, or with draft boards. Outside police records and welfare departments they do not exist.' She might have added that neither are they registered with the tax authorities. Even when they do have a name officially registered, it is usually not their own, and they may claim to be Mexican, Indian, or anything else besides Gypsy if it is to their advantage. All Rom have at least two names, one for use among gypsies and one or more for use with *gajé*. Within the same *kumpania* several Gypsies might use the same *gajé* name in order to increase their anonymity and compound the possibilities for confusion should some outsider wish to identify them.

In certain respects the relationship of Gypsies to *gajé* seems to be one of parasitism: 'the only truly acceptable relations with *gajé* are situations of economic exploitation or political manipulation' (Sutherland, 1975:13). Yet there is more to it than that. The Gypsies have survived because they have been able to provide distinctive services, traditionally as coppersmiths, fortune-tellers, musicians, horse-traders, seasonal workers (e.g. berry-picking), and more recently as dealers in scrap metal and repairing damage to the metal panels of motor cars. In most British cities private householders find it inconvenient and expensive to arrange for the removal of old domestic machines and bulky objects. Many old cars are simply left near the roadside. Gypsies have found ways of making a profit as urban scavengers, separating the different kinds of metal and selling them to specialist purchasers. Some have specialized in laying tarmac for house-holders on their paths and driveways, filling a niche in between the big companies and the 'do-it-yourself' operation. These occupations appeal to them because of their independence, their mobility and the opportunity to make a profit from small bargaining (for a fuller account of Gypsy occupations in Britain see Adams *et al.*, 1975:113–54).

Gajé accustomed to buying most of their goods in shops where the price is clearly displayed, are rarely very good at bargaining, and certainly no match for the skills of the Gypsy. Perhaps the best name in English for their technique is 'hustling'. Anne Sutherland (1975:21) wrote that 'they delight in deceiving the *gajó*, mostly for a good reason, but sometimes just for the fun of it or to keep in practice'. Acquiring welfare benefits comes into the same category. Such a payment is not considered to be a hand-out, but money that they persuade the *gajé* to give them; it is seen as 'an incredible stroke of luck, yet further proof of the gullibility of the *gajé*'. Since the Rom have large families and are adept in securing extra allowances for old, dependent, disabled and blind members of their households, they qualify for substantial payments. Though they manipulate any such scheme to their own advantage they do not attempt systematic frauds. In California they may be accused of traffic and garbage offences and of stealing from shops, but they are not involved in felonies or offences of serious violence.

To see the Gypsy–*gajé* relationship as one of parasitism would also be to overlook the ways in which the majority make it difficult for Gypsies to continue their own way of living. Whether Gypsies are legally entitled to enter the United States as immigrants is uncertain. In Maryland, state law requires Gypsies to pay a licensing fee of $1,000 before establishing homes or engaging in any business. In New Hampshire in 1977 two families were legally evicted from the state without being charged with any crime, solely because of their ethnic identity (Hancock, 1980). In Britain, local authorities have been very reluctant to provide sites at which Gypsies can stay; they have dug ditches and erected barriers to keep them off possible stopping places, and have done a great deal to make them feel unwelcome. It is only the settled population who vote and are represented in local government bodies. Often it is the well-meaning people who are the greatest threat, particularly those who want to place Gypsy children in *gajé* schools and persuade them to abandon the way of life of their ancestors. Gypsies have reason to perceive the outside world as hostile to their culture.

Gajé hostility and condescension, and the mutual incomprehension of the two groups, have helped the Gypsies remain distinct, but even more important have been Gypsy beliefs about pollution. Surveying the refuse left on a recently occupied roadside site, non-Gypsies not surprisingly conclude that Gypsies are dirty. But Gypsies want to keep their distance from *gajé* because they believe them to be dangerously unclean. If the Rom, when travelling in the United States, have to go to a restaurant, they avoid using the plates, glasses and cutlery washed in the establishment. They ask for plastic cups to drink from, and food wrapped in paper. Amid outraged stares from other customers and waiters, they eat with their fingers and worry constantly about catching some disease from the *gajé* around them. Some, if they have to go to a public toilet, will use paper towels to open doors and turn faucets. If Gypsies occupy a house previously inhabited by *gajé*, they first fumigate it, scrubbing the floors with astringents and repainting the walls. Chairs are particularly suspect unless they can be scrubbed. At the root of these attitudes are the Gypsy distinctions between things that are clean (*wuzho*), that are temporarily or honestly dirty (*melalo*), and that are defiled and defiling (*marimé*, in Rommichal, *mokadi*) (Miller, 1975). Sutherland (1975:263–4) contends that this set of concepts and their related beliefs, called *romaniya* and translated as 'religion' by the Rom, is the clue to their unusual ability to maintain their ethnic continuity while making major changes in their way of life.

For the Rom, the body is divided at the waist, the upper half being *wuzho* and the lower half *marimé*. A woman may expose her breasts to anyone, but the sight of her legs is shameful and disrespectful. If she were to throw her skirts over a man's head this would, in theory, make him *marimé* for ever after. *Marimé* is also the word used for banishment; when Gypsy courts have been convened to hear allegations of immorality or crime, a not uncommon punishment is for an offender and his family to be declared *marimé* for a period of thirty days; during that period they are unclean and other Gypsies will not eat or associate with them. The distinctions between things that are *wuzho, melalo* and *marimé* are elaborated to create six different categories of food and of items of clothing which have to be washed separately. Women are not supposed to wash clothes in the laundromat but to do it at home with separate wash tubs or basins. In Britain similar distinctions are found. Gypsies will use one bowl for personal washing, one for washing up, one for laundry (excluding the tea towel which is washed with the utensils) and one for vegetables. If a utensil bowl is used for personal washing it is permanently contaminated, as are items of china with cracks or chips or ones that have been touched by certain animals. A stray dog was seen to run into a trailer and snatch some meat off a Crown Derby dish; the dish was immediately destroyed. The belief that *gajé* are unclean reinforces the assumption that – whatever they may say to non-Gypsies about wanting schooling for their children – anything that characterizes the outside society is not for them. Thus a fourteen-year-old Gypsy girl was seen to tear up a magazine, remarking: 'Only Gorgios read'. In such ways opposing stereotypes are reinforced. In the very week that a county councillor asserted that every warden of a Gypsy site should be armed with a gun, a woman anthropologist moved onto such a site in the capacity of warden. The Gypsies were equally concerned with her well-being, but whereas the councillor saw the threat as coming from inside the site, the Gypsies feared outsiders might attack a woman living alone: 'If anyone comes here at night and tries to get into your trailer, young lady, don't open the door, just keep hollering and we'll come. You'll be alright with us around to look after you' (Adams *et al.* 1975:49–51).

The boundary between Gypsies and *gajé* is not so hard that people cannot cross it. There is a steady trickle of Gypsies who abandon their communities for the wider society, but there are also *gajé* who marry in and become accepted. The boundary is maintained by a series of inclusive forces. Firstly, just as cattle-herding people constantly talk about their cattle, so the Rom constantly talk about themselves. Sutherland – who taught in a Gypsy community school – says that she had to be careful not to take sides during a crisis – and that there were, on average, three crises a week. Gypsy life is self-centred because it is very conscious of status differences; families struggle to improve their status and to disparage that of others. Secondly, Gypsies have a symbolic system and set of rules which are inculcated early. People in any culture find it difficult to eliminate ideas about uncleanliness and profanity which they have learned as small children, but since there is always a pressure to relax the rules at the margin or in new circumstances, so Gypsies watch one another to see how orthodox they are. Thirdly, the life of the Gypsy community is enclosed; almost everything that a member should want can be found within it, and, if it should become necessary for someone to go, say, to hospital, senior members of the group make the arrangements. Social contact with *gajé* is limited to specific relationships. Gypsies have their own procedures for dealing with disputes and deviation; punishments often fall on the family as well as the individual offender. These inclusive processes evoke hostility from *gajé*, creating an exclusive boundary which reinforces the first one. As Sutherland (1975:290) observes, other ethnic groups in the United States are integrated into American culture to the extent that an important part of their identity includes being American, and they are caught up in the system of social stratification. The Gypsies are not involved with the wider society in either of these ways. Consequently, the value problems they pose are far more troublesome; is their history a justification for allowing them to continue to live as they please? Can *gajé* teachers and welfare workers insist on Gypsy children attending school and being drawn into majority culture, without presupposing that the majority's way of life is morally superior? And is this justified?

The achievement of the Amish and the Gypsies in preserving their identity can be compared with the story of a group which tried to do likewise, with a reasonable prospect of success, but failed. It is that of a colonization movement in mid-nineteenth-century Wales which was motivated by economic and nationalistic ideals. This was a time when the population of Wales had increased substantially and the desire of many Welsh people to better themselves was running ahead of the opportunities provided in their own country's economy. It was a time when new territories were being developed overseas and there was a shortage of competent farmers relative to the amount of land available for settlement. The Welsh colonizers decided to establish their settlement in Patagonia, and the Argentine government held out to them the promise of provincial self-government. After initial success the colony was seriously affected by flooding and doubts arose about the wisdom of their location. There was also conflict with the authorities over a requirement that they should participate in military drill on Sundays. So the colonists considered relocating in the Transvaal. Hearing of their situation the Australian government sent an agent to try to persuade them to move to Australia. The Argentine government wanted them to stay, and that is what they did.

The settlers hoped to govern themselves as an independent nation practising the religion of their choice in their own language. They aimed to populate a substantial area by attracting more emigrants from the homeland (a hope that was finally dashed by the outbreak of war in 1914). By this time there were two settlements, of 4,000 and 3,500 people, fairly large by comparison with the Amish but possibly insufficient for the Welsh venture, although they had many of the attributes that served the Amish so well. For example, they displayed a 'strong sense of mutual obligation within the framework of family and friendship, the cooperative work group, the village and the chapel, a general preference for small-group identification, and a willingness publicly to criticize anyone who deviated greatly' (Williams, 1975:187). Attendance at chapel and the reading of the Bible gave a central meaning to their collective life. They believed that they were succeeding and considered themselves superior to their non-Welsh neighbours, disapproving of the sale to non-Welsh of land which they could not cultivate themselves but which might one day be needed for members of their community.

After a while, Welsh farmers started to hire non-Welsh farm labourers, but as the language of farm work remained Welsh this probably occasioned less change than the government's insistence that from 1896 schooling had to be conducted in Spanish. Three years later the minutes of the municipal council were also being kept in that language. Though Welsh remained the language of the home, and marriages to non-Welsh were restricted, a fundamental shift was under way. By the 1960s most community members spoke only Spanish. There were many households in which parents addressed their children in Welsh but were answered in Spanish; there were others in which the children attended religious services in Welsh out of a feeling for family solidarity but they did not understand what was said. Out of a desire to retain the interest of the young people, some chapels had started to conduct part of their services in Spanish. The attempt to create a new Wales on the other side of the world had failed because the communities could not offer the younger generation prospects as attractive to them as those held out by Argentinian urban life. They had not been as effective as the Amish in building barriers high enough to shut out the outside world, quite probably because they put a higher valuation upon education and were less inclined to see it as a threat to the chances of being re-united in the next world.

Comparison of the groups which have resisted assimilation and tried to stay separate – and there are many more than have been mentioned in this chapter – suggests that their relative success depends upon their ability to bind their children to the group as tightly as they are bound themselves, and that this depends upon both inclusive and exclusive processes. Strong inclusive bonds require an internal social structure which can match the services available in the majority society and is given psychological significance either by beliefs built deep into personality structure (as with Gypsy ideas of pollution) or by the promise of a better life in another world as a reward for conformity. It helps if individualism is devalued and punishments fall on the family as well as the offender. The inclusive bond also rests on the group's ability to give its children a better start in life as by providing capital to purchase a farm or to set them up in business (possibly by furnishing dowries for their daughters).

The development of the welfare state with its provisions for helping society's casualties means that those who break away from their groups need not fear destitution, while in the eye of the would-be isolationists, the scholarships for further education are Greek gifts tempting the brightest youngsters away from their groups and setting a standard with which parents can rarely compete. Such temptations will be fewer when there is an exclusive process throwing minority members back upon their groups. The Amish have experienced martyrdom for their faith. The Gypsy way of life stimulates majority rejection. The Jewish beliefs that they are the chosen people and that the Messiah is still to come, together with an intricate set of ritual obligations and ideas of pollution, have bound them together; they have the longest and most continuous experience of persecution; yet whenever the threat is lifted they have difficulty in maintaining religious observances and preventing out-marriage. In New York the out-marriage rate hovered around 6.5 per cent in the years 1940–60, but rose to 17.5 per cent five years later. Of every 100 Jews who married in the years between 1966 and 1972, 32 married non-Jews. Approximately one-fourth of the intermarrying non-Jewish females converted to Judaism, but few non-Jewish males did so (Goren, 1980). In the United States the proportion of Jews opposed to intermarriage has dropped so that it may now be below 50 per cent. The social nature of the Jewish minority seems to be changing and the political identification with Israel becoming more central.

Nearly 26 per cent of the United States population are white Catholics and 57 per cent white Protestants, but only 15 and 27 per cent identify themselves as having an ethnic as well as a religious identity. Because of intermarriage an increasing proportion can claim more than one kind of ethnic identity and many of them, it seems, prefer to claim none at all. Surveys reveal that, of all white Catholics born since 1945 who had attained adulthood by the mid 1970s, 41 per cent were of multiple ethnic ancestry and 44 per cent had married non-Catholics. Noting the speed of change, the author of a recent discussion of these trends (Alba, 1981) entitled his essay 'The Twilight of Ethnicity Among American Catholics of European Ancestry'.

The two ethnicities

'What does he know of England who only England knows?' asked Kipling. When people travel overseas they become aware of all sorts of ways in which their home country is distinctive that previously they had taken for granted. Their attachment to their fellow nationals changes. A Canadian in Paris may greet with enthusiasm another Canadian for whom he would not have crossed the street back home in Toronto. Their sharing of a common citizenship would scarcely ever have been important in the home town but away in a foreign country it becomes a possible foundation for important social relationships. This change in the significance of an ethnic tie from one situation to another has been noted in many contexts. In the 1950s it was often discussed in connection with tribal identities in Africa. People in positions of importance were accused of favouring those who belonged to their own tribes, but was that because they possessed a common homeland culture or because of the significance of that common possession in a new situation?

Those who viewed developments in Africa from the standpoint of European history expected tribal sentiments to lose significance as the smaller African groups were merged in larger units. It was thought that Africans living in towns and labour compounds would become 'detribalized', but, to the contrary, it seemed as if in such circumstances tribal affiliations became more important. J. Clyde Mitchell (1956:30) maintained that the word 'tribalism' was being used in at least two different senses; he sought to distinguish between membership in a distinctive social and political system in the rural areas, which he called 'tribal structure', and the significance of that link for interactions in a new situation, which was the tribalism of the city. Immanuel Wallerstein (1960:130) proposed almost the opposite solution to the same problem when he wrote 'we shall use the word tribe for the group in the rural areas, and ethnic group for the one in town'. The same distinction has to be drawn for modern industrial societies, but some other names are needed for the two kinds of ethnicity when the immigrants' original identities are not tribal.

These names may not commend themselves to everyone, but a preliminary solution is to distinguish between what may be called majority ethnicity and minority ethnicity. This distinction has not been drawn previously because there are other names for majority ethnicity in regular use. A large social group that possesses a distinctive culture shows ethnic characteristics, but when the group's boundaries coincide with political boundaries it will usually be identified in political terms rather than by its ethnic characteristics, and called a nation. People from such a group living as a minority in a different nation or a cosmopolitan city may use their distinctive characteristics as a basis for organizing mutual aid and for pressing their shared interests. If they accept the political order in which they find themselves, they are likely to be defined as ethnic groups (in contra-distinction to national minorities which see themselves as belonging to a different nation and wish in some way to change their political situation).

Minority ethnicity is dependent, firstly, on the desire of minority members to utilize their common ethnic characteristics, and, secondly, on the readiness of the majority society to regard ethnicity as a legitimate basis for the formation of minority groups. The United States and Canada have both been tolerant of the tendency of immigrants to retain loyalties towards the countries from which they came. Since most of the inhabitants of both American countries have been either immigrants themselves, or the descendants of immigrants, it has been legitimate for people to claim identities associated with their countries of origin while claiming to be loyal citizens of the countries in which they live. Indeed, in parts of the United States and Canada, men and women have been expected to have the attribute of ethnicity as well as that of citizenship, so that it used to be said (by those who did not subscribe to a 'minus one' definition of ethnicity) that there were no unhyphenated Americans. Everyone was an Afro-, Anglo-, Greek-, Irish-, Italian-, Jewish-, or some kind of American. No one was just an American.

British, German and Scandinavian immigrants had resources and skills that enabled them to spread out over the United States. Most of the other groups were less well prepared and their members tended to settle in slum areas of the cities where they developed political 'machines' that provided them with a variety of services in return for their votes. In their native lands most of them had not been entitled to vote: they had experienced governments as tax collectors and punishers, and thought that the further away they kept themselves the better. In these circumstances there arose the local political 'boss' who helped people obtain jobs and services, advised them about their problems and arranged charitable events. There was strictly speaking no politics within these 'machines', which were more like informally structured businesses dominated by a leader who owed allegiance in an almost feudal fashion to the boss of the larger area in which his precinct was situated. Tammany Hall in New York was the centre of the best known of these organizations; one of its stalwarts, Edward J. Flynn, put it this way: 'The immigrants, . . . being human, wanted friends, jobs, the chance to become citizens. Tammany was smart enough to offer them all three, in return for a life-time and often second-, third-, and fourth-generation fealty to the [Democratic] party. It was as simple and obvious as that' (Gerson, 1964:11). Because minority ethnicity served important functions for these latter groups, their common links with their sending society acquired new significance. By 1914 they had become strongly interested in their native countries: many who had not experienced the intoxication of nationalism in their homelands discovered it in the United States. The loneliness, poverty, and prejudice of the slum areas coupled with the scorn of the better-established groups created the conditions in which such immigrants could find a new dignity by committing themselves to the political causes of their native lands.

During the First World War the Office of Public Information set out to inculcate Americanism. Loyalty Days were organized to give different ethnic Americans an opportunity to express their love for their new home. They were so successful that they were still being arranged when Louis L. Gerson (1964) wrote his book *The Hyphenate in Recent American Politics and Diplomacy*; he thought them a boon to politicians who sought to cultivate the ethnic vote. Yet these activities were two-edged: one of their organizers could regret that they 'did more for the Europeanization of the immigrant than his Americanization. The old country was glorified and its national anthem was sung.' The politicians wanted the votes of the ethnic groups: they sought to have a 'balanced ticket' reflecting the ethnic composition of the locality, and they were prepared to tailor their views about foreign policy to secure support. It has long been customary for the platform committees of the major parties immediately before the quadrennial sessions of their national conventions to hear at length the proposals of ethnic representatives in order to formulate policy statements in electorally advantageous terms. Such groups, as Jewish-Americans and Polish-Americans have recently demonstrated, continue to be influential, and, in the careful words of a senator, 'sometimes press courses that derogate from the national interest' (Mathias, 1981:977).

Politicians are anxious not to become the prisoners of these groups. Their chief weapon of defence has been their power to define what the interests of the United States require. Thus when, in 1916, an Irish-American representative rudely criticized the President for failing to meet the hopes of Irish Catholic electors, Woodrow Wilson replied by inviting this man and all 'disloyal Americans' to vote against him. Circumstances also arise in which a common ethnicity is no longer a legitimate basis for political organization. In the same year, 1916, there were many people who considered themselves both Germans and Americans, with two loyalties; but when the two countries went to war they had to choose. In the United States German-language newspapers ceased publishing and German-American societies found new names.

Early settlers from Britain in North America possessed a majority ethnicity to which they made no reference since it was contained in other identities such as, initially, English nationality and the profession of Christianity. As settlers they, with others, started to create a new United States ethnicity. Because it looked like a transplanted English ethnicity there was little awareness of any distinction between the new majority ethnicity and the minority ethnicity of the English immigrants. In the United States, as in Australia, powerful groups attempted to keep the majority ethnicity close to the minority ethnicity of that section of the population which had English origins. They were the most successful because United States interests in international politics did not clash with those of the British and raise problems of loyalty. So when settlers arrived from Germany and Poland they were not seen as acquiring a United States majority ethnicity. The use they made of their minority ethnicity differed. Groups like the Swedes, who maintained high rates of in-marriage but had relatively high levels of literacy and occupational skills, escaped the urban slums and were very ready to adopt the culture of their new country; since they encountered few barriers, they changed relatively quickly and were regarded as having assimilated faster than most other groups. The minority ethnicity which they retained was largely personal and sentimental. Groups which were caught in the slums utilized their minority ethnicity in the attempt to overcome the obstacles they faced on the route to full participation. They would have discarded their minority ethnicity more rapidly had not politicians found it convenient that voters should form ethnic constituencies. While the 'minus one' definition reflects the outlook of dominant groups inclined to identify their ethnicity by other names, it is not necessary to use the word in this way. Like the word 'culture', ethnicity can be attached both to a group at the national level and to groups within a nation.

The organization of ethnicity at levels below the nation-state takes different forms in different countries and stages of assimilation. Where there are only a few people from a particular locality or country they have to combine with others who are relatively close culturally or to attach themselves to another group. Danes, Norwegians, Icelanders, Swedes and Finns in the United States could be Scandinavians. Other conglomerations may be given misleading names. Thus in a Northwestern Ontario town the category Ukrainian comprehends Polish, Rumanian, Russian and Yugoslavian apparently because the Ukrainians are the most numerous representatives of what appears to others to be a single ethnic unit. The anthropologist heard someone called 'Uke' and enquired if he were a Ukrainian. The answer was 'yes', but when asked from what part of the Ukraine his family came, the man replied: 'They didn't. They came from Poland. I'm a Polack.' He chose to present himself as a Ukrainian because in the receiving society ethnic identities had been redefined (see Figure 9). Immigrants are absorbed into a receiving society by a process in which the smaller groups are first incorporated into larger ones before they in turn are absorbed in a national unit. Because of intermarriage, many people will be able to claim membership of more than one ethnic minority, and they are more likely to align themselves with the one that is larger or of higher status in the area in which they live.

To distinguish in this way between majority and minority ethnicity is the simplest solution for analysing ethnic sentiments in connection with immigration but the nomenclature is not so appropriate for the study of polyethnic societies. In countries like Malaysia, Guyana and Fiji, the numerically largest group may organize as an ethnic group rather than as representatives of the nation. The expression 'minority ethnicity' implies that this is the ethnicity of a smaller group opposed to a larger one, whereas the distinction to be drawn relates to the social and political use made of ethnic characteristics and to the mobilization of ethnic sentiment. Once people engage in vigorous competition on an ethnic-group basis even members of the larger group may display the characteristics of what was earlier called minority ethnicity. So it is perhaps better named as mobilized ethnicity in contrast to latent ethnicity.

In a recent volume Glazer and Moynihan (1975:19–20) contrasted the conceptions of ethnicity implicit in the approaches of those whom they called 'primordialists' and 'circumstantialists'. According to the primordialists: 'Men are divided thus and so, the reasons for this division are deep in history and experience, and they must in some way be taken into account by those who govern society.' This is a view of majority or latent ethnicity and it tends to be viewed most sympathetically by anthropologists. The circumstantialists dissent from it: 'We are doubtful of any such basic

(after Stymeist, 1975:50)

Figure 9 Ethnic categorization in a northwestern Ontario town

division and look to specific and immediate circumstances to explain why groups maintain their identity, why ethnicity becomes a basis for mobilization, why some situations are peaceful and others filled with conflict.' This is a view of minority or mobilized ethnicity, and it appeals most to sociologists and to urban anthropologists.

Conclusion

Two American authors have proclaimed that 'the point about the melting pot is that it did not happen' (Glazer and Moynihan, 1963:xcvii). Writing about Negroes, Puerto Ricans, Jews, Italians and Irish of New York City, they contended that 'The ethnic group in American society became not a survival from the age of mass immigration but a new social form' founded in shared interest. It is important to emphasize this distinction between the old and the new social forms: the survival of the sending society's majority culture is the old form; and its transformation into a minority ethnicity given meaning by the receiving society, and serving as a basis for the organization of an interest group, is the new one. It is equally important to appreciate that outside New York and some other cities the receiving society gave less encouragement to this new social form and the pattern of change was closer to that suggested by the image of a melting pot. Other new social forms were taking shape as well, and among these must be counted a deeper sense of nationhood as the United States learned, in Hungary in 1955, in Vietnam, the Middle East and in Iran, the limits to her power to mould international affairs, and as the media of mass communications involved the whole body of citizens in a greater consciousness of national issues than had ever previously been possible.

Processes of ethnic change in an industrial society are too varied for more than a few of them to be captured by a single model however useful it may be in providing an overall characterization. So many variables can be important that the social scientist needs to identify very precisely just what problem is to be pursued and to examine the background factors, local, national and international, only in so far as they bear upon that problem.

8

Group competition and market management

The previous chapter, contending that individual competition dissolves group boundaries, was concerned with situations in which new groups entered established societies. The incomers were less powerful; they might either seek their individual ends or organize as groups in order to stay separate, but in the latter event they did not use their group organization to compete with the majority for the same ends as those sought by majority members. The present chapter begins by considering situations in which the incoming group is of greater power and uses that power to regulate competition to its members' collective advantage. Such regulation is clearly seen in what have earlier been introduced as plural societies. Their characteristic feature is that they derive from a stronger group taking charge of territory occupied by one or more native groups engaged in traditional modes of production. The stronger group, usually an imperial power, secures those sections of the economy which are of interest to its members and does not interfere in the lives of other groups if their ways do not touch upon its interests. A numerically small group can in this way rule a much larger population if the latter is ethnically and politically divided, for it is often easy to play off one section against another. This is the plural society described by Furnival.

In the course of time, competition between the subordinate groups develops, and competition between one or more subordinate groups and the ruling group. That group, pursuing its political and economic interests, tries to control the market within which this competition occurs. It has to encourage the native peoples to sell produce if it is to raise revenue by taxation and if its commercial interests are to make profits. If the native peoples are not very competitive, another ethnic group may be allowed to come in and develop trade, thus increasing the plural element in the social order. Since the unrestricted growth of the market could threaten the governing group's monopolies, it may reinforce ethnic boundaries, seeking to confine each group to a particular section of the market; the best-known example of this is the South African policy of *apartheid* discussed in the next chapter. Once a fully fledged plural society has taken shape, the maintenance of order depends upon the restraint of competition between groups. Since circumstances change, governments are never able for long to confine groups to those activities which suit other peoples' interests. The subordinate groups learn to mobilize their political power and force out the intruder, installing an independent government which usually reflects the interests of the largest section of the electorate. The new government may find it no easier to regulate the competition and may become more authoritarian. Sometimes it fails, as in the case of Uganda discussed below; the social order breaks down, and one or more of the ethnic minorities is expelled or slaughtered. In such circumstances competition has given way to conflict. Seen from this standpoint, it is unwise to regard plural societies as a permanently distinct class of societies; the features which characterize them appear at a certain stage in a sequence of conquest and rule by an invading group.

The legitimation of racial roles in Uganda

In 1890 the British and the Germans agreed between themselves that the country west of what is now Kenya north of latitude 1°S should fall within the British sphere of influence. The Imperial British East Africa Company agreed to administer the region on behalf of the British Government. They declared a protectorate over the area four years later and in 1900 concluded a special agreement with the Kabaka, or King, of Buganda whereby he was recognized as its ruler so long as he remained faithful to the protecting authority. By 1914 Uganda's boundaries had been fixed and British administration had reached most areas. Railways were built to open up the interior and facilitate the export of cotton and coffee to the East African coast. To help in the construction of the railways, Asian workers were brought over from India, and, while they were later repatriated, this connection helped the growth of an Asian population and traders. Since the government had forbidden the alienation of land, those Europeans who did not hold government posts, or work in the Christian missions, were, like the Asians, mainly businessmen dealing with the commercial and processing side of agricultural production. The British were under less pressure from African political movements than in other parts of the continent at that time because the native population was divided, particularly over Baganda claims to hegemony, and the character of the likely successor government was uncertain. The British withdrew as part of their general policy of decolonization and not because their position was becoming untenable inside the country. Uganda became independent in 1962. The population numbered six and a half million and was 98.7 per cent African. The Africans were divided into a variety of ethnic groups and there were tensions between the economically more advanced southern peoples, organized in four major kingdoms, and the less advanced and less hierarchially organized peoples of the north. The 87,000 non-Africans included 63,100 Indians, 6,000 Pakistanis, 2,800 Goans, 10,900 Europeans, 1,900 Arabs.

A good example of how ethnic and racial distinctions were reflected in economic organization is provided by Cyril Sofer's (1954) account of relations in Jinja; this is a town originally built up by Asians as a trading centre, which from 1949 enjoyed a construction boom when work began there on a dam across the Nile to generate hydro-electric power. Two years later, the town's population was 14,900 Africans, 5,100 Asians, and 800 Europeans. Europeans were recruited to fill the managerial posts, Asians as supervisors and Africans as unskilled workers. People of these three categories brought to the employment situation their distinctive cultural expectations of work behaviour and different degrees of industrial skill. To each group, the expectations of members of other groups appeared unreasonable. Asked whether they preferred to work under a European or an Asian, Africans indicated a clear preference for the European who seemed to be more interested in keeping Africans at a distance than in keeping them subordinate. The European owed his racial community an obligation to behave in a dignified and restrained manner, and had a prestige which induced the African to respond more easily to his orders. An African was bound by an elaborately deferential etiquette in his interaction with a European; the latter did not make a reciprocal deference return, but had implicit obligations towards the African to afford him leadership, protection, and behavioural models. These obligations provided the justification for his presence in the country and were surrounded by a complex set of official and unofficial sanctions within the European community. The Africans believed that the Europeans did not have African interests at heart, and they were most suspicious of any change proposed by them. Greatest friction arose between Africans and Asians. As the Asian had less prestige than the European, the African was slower to respond to his orders and it was therefore necessary for the Asian to be more vehement to achieve the same result. Squeezed between temporarily immigrant Europeans and the rising African mass, the Asian was anxious to show the European that he was superior to Africans and to dissociate himself from them. The African, on the other hand, knew that the power of an Asian supervisor was closely circumscribed by that of the European. He could challenge any order of an Asian's in the security that the European would adjudicate between them. Furthermore, the Asian group readily became a scapegoat for African discontents.

In the course of his analysis, Cyril Sofer argued that instances of friction in the case under study do not arise only or mainly from cultural differences between the racial groups, but that 'they stem also, and perhaps more importantly, from the structure of characteristic social relationships which exist between the groups' (1954:72). Men were recruited to perform particular roles which brought them into defined relationships with members of other groups, so that they saw only certain aspects of these other groups' cultures. Thus their roles and relationships influenced the attitudes they developed. Closer examination showed that each group's position in the social system was reflected in, and supported by, its view of the society as a whole, of the other groups, and of itself. The European viewed the system as harnessing European leadership to help Africans to attain higher living standards and a greater measure of political autonomy. He thought of the Asian as hard-working and clever at business, but crafty and devoted exclusively to the pursuit of material wealth. The African he perceived as ignorant, childlike, suspicious, and uncooperative. The Asian considered the chief purposes of the prevailing policy to be the preservation of the power of the British and the defence of British and African interests against economic development under Asian leadership. Asians saw Europeans as hypocritical but shared their view of the African. To the African it seemed that the whole organization of the society was based upon foreign exploitation of himself and his country. He perceived the European as rich, powerful, and clever, but haughty and insincere in his protestations of benevolence. The Asian appeared to the African as dishonest, unscrupulous, and resentful of African progress because it spelled his eventual expulsion from the country. This influence of roles upon attitudes provided reinforcement for a social system that might otherwise have been too unstable.

The same study also showed that changes initiated within an industrial concern can influence roles and relations in the community outside. In the Jinja instance, a number of European artisans were introduced for construction work. Being in a low rank compared with other Europeans, they tended at first to behave in the same way as the Asians in trying to demonstrate their superiority to those below them. As their numbers grew, however, these Europeans felt a greater security within their own group and began to behave in a more relaxed and tolerant way in their relations with others.

Thus industrial changes created a European sub-category inferior in many respects to a considerable number of Asians and to a growing elite of Africans educated in Europe. The pattern of colour differentiation became less distinct. Events in the wider community had effects in industry and developments in industry had repercussions in the community because both plant and community relations were involved in a wider system. The consequences of changes had cumulative effects. As African political power increased, so the overall system became more integrated and the cumulative tendencies became stronger.

The Sofers' research showed members of the two socially superior groups resisting the appointment of members of the inferior groups to the posts they thought themselves better able to fill. It showed the growth of ideas which, not altogether satisfactorily, tended to legitimate the prevailing order in the eyes of members of these groups so that competition between ethnic groups was suppressed and the British could rule with relatively little opposition. It also demonstrated that members of each group needed the support of their fellows and were therefore restricted in the social alternatives between which they could choose. With reference to one set of Europeans this is well brought out in a study from the neighbouring territory of Tanganyika (as it then was), dealing with small and isolated communities of white government officials and showing how pressures internal to the groups prevented their adaptation to the changing political environment. European wives were involved in their husbands' work without being able to participate in it. As they were continually meeting the same group of neighbours, the women's social worlds were very restricted and unrewarding; in-group gossip became the substance of their lives. Officials low in the government hierarchy were, with their wives, usually in the majority. They tended to be aceptical of imperial policy, hostile to African advancement, and influential with regard to the tone of community affairs.

When senior African civil servants were appointed to these stations, new problems arose. The senior European, usually the District Commissioner, was expected to be the social leader of the community as well as its chief official. In the new situation he could follow one of three strategies in attempting to combine his social and official roles. Firstly, he could align himself with the Africans; secondly, he could attempt to promote social contact between Africans and Europeans; thirdly, he could align himself with the majority party among the Europeans and limit his contacts with the Africans to official business. The first strategy never succeeded because the Africans were less well paid; they were dependent upon the European official who wrote annual confidential reports upon their work, but often sympathized with the nationalist movement; the African wives were often uneducated and socially uncomfortable in a European setting, whereas the European wives were uncomfortable in any other. The African civil servants therefore did not welcome the first strategy and in any case could not repay with social approval a District Commissioner who sacrificed the approval of the majority of his own group. The second alternative also usually failed, primarily because the government did nothing to encourage it. For example, liquor licences could have been refused to clubs and hotels known to practise racial discrimination; yet, despite the significance of discrimination in the eyes of educated Africans, the colonial government would not endorse such a policy. When European officials tried to mix socially with Africans they usually caused new tensions as much as they eased old tensions, and the District Commissioner who tried to bridge the gap lost his informal leadership of the European community. If he made no such attempt, ignoring the government's declared policies of multi-racialism and an integrated civil service, and adopted the third strategy, he had a much easier life. Tanner writes: 'This was a much more satisfying role, insuring, as it did, that the official would always be among Europeans who shared his political and social opinions. All the more satisfying, as it assisted the official to make up his mind to retire as soon as possible, and to receive group approbation for his wise choice' (1965:301). Although choice of the third alternative might have evoked short-term African hostility there is little evidence of its doing so. Africans expected Europeans to segregate themselves while still functioning as government servants in what was seen as a transitional phase. Thus the choices of people on both sides of the colour line can be seen as responding to the rewards available.

There is more information about the choices made in situations of this kind by Europeans than by Africans so it is easier to use such examples, but in the East African case the same principles must apply to any group, including relations between Africans of different ethnicity. Uganda was emphatically a plural society after as well as before independence, in that there were major tensions between African groups and these groups were differentially incorporated into the political structure. The split between the northern and southern peoples was complicated by the special position of the Baganda, the main southern ethnic group. The British had never conquered the Baganda, who had indeed invited them into the country and shared their victories and reverses. The British had entered into a treaty with the Baganda as partners, though of unequal strength, and, as this gave the Baganda a privileged position in the protectorate, they held together to defend that position. At the pre-independence election the Baganda party (Kabaka Yekka) obtained 22 seats in the National Assembly; Milton Obote's Uganda People's Congress won 43 and the Democratic Party 25. The UPC entered into a coalition with the KY and the Kabaka became head of state. Groups which had supported the DP (including a southern ethnic group with a grievance against the Baganda) transferred support to the UPC permitting Obote to contemplate forming a one-party state. But there was a further significant division in that the Nubis, a relatively newly formed ethnic group and marginal to Uganda as a geographical unit, held a central position in the Army. Obote relied on them in his struggle with the Baganda, and particularly upon Idi Amin, an officer of the Kakwa group who are the most numerous and centrally placed of the larger Nubi group. When Obote moved against his over-mighty subject, Amin staged a coup (Southall, 1975).

The Amin regime, though initially popular, lacked any broad base of support and was soon in trouble. It would be convenient to have a scapegoat, and a suitable one was to hand in the shape of the Asian minority. Amin despoiled them and ordered their expulsion. His regime came to be based upon the support of the Army combined with the appeal which the President had among the common people in the rural areas. It was eventually overthrown by Ugandan rebels supported by the Tanzanian army, and when the government fell the remains of the state apparatus collapsed with it. In such circumstances a state can break up into the constituent elements of what was a plural order, or, as has happened in Burma, the central government can lose most of its authority and different regions revert to being governed by regionally powerful individuals or groups much as was the situation before the formation of a nation-state.

The main problems of plural societies stem from the way that the constituent groups differ from one another on so many dimensions: ethnic, linguistic, religious, political and often territorial. There are relatively few instances in which members of two groups share common interests and are influenced by what Max Gluckman called cross-cutting ties. That two people compete vigorously and are strongly opposed to one another in one relationship does not weaken the social order so long as there are other relationships in which they share interests or cooperate in a struggle with yet other people. A prescription for an economically progressive yet well-integrated society would be for every member to have multiple allegiances so that he or she would have different allies and different opponents in successive struggles. Gluckman drew attention to the action of those British steel workers who, at the time of the 1926 general strike, were responsible for the maintenance of the furnaces. They kept them fired, because if the furnaces had gone out they would have taken months to repair and there would have been no work for anyone else. In the strikes on the Zambian Copperbelt in 1935 essential services were maintained. During a strike five years later these workers were threatened. Gluckman observed that at this time not all African miners appreciated the consequences of neglecting the smelting furnaces and there was dispute over the course of action that best suited their long-term interests (1969:386–7). In Europe, trade union leaders, and their members, are aware of their employers' market position and are more likely to take industrial action when that position is strong. When it is weak they act on the basis of interests shared with the people who at other times are seen as opponents. Capitalist production can give employers and employees shared interests as well as dividing them from each other. Where there is opposition between ethnic groups, in either a developing or an industrial society, it is usually less easily overcome because all the lines of social division are congruent. Many people live most of their lives within ethnic communities and have few ties which cross the boundaries so that the ethnic opposition cannot be counterbalanced by the cross-cutting ties deriving from other forms of opposition.

Sequences similar to that of Uganda can be observed in the histories of other recent African revolutions, as has been shown by Leo Kuper in his book *The Pity of it All* (1977) about events in Algeria, Zanzibar, Rwanda and Burundi. In each of these countries there were socio-economic as well as ethnic differences, and more ties derived from interests shared between members of different ethnic groups than there are in contemporary South Africa. Though the revolutions were initially concerned to secure political and economic equality, they all changed into conflicts in which the major groups were polarized on ethnic or racial lines. The path to independence in Algeria was signposted by a series of massacres leading to casual slaughter on the streets and bombings by the French *Organisation Armée Secrète*. In Zanzibar there were riots prior to independence, and then in 1964 an African revolution in which several thousand people of Arab descent were killed. In Rwanda, 10–12,000 members of the ruling Tutsi ethnic minority were slain in a revolution of the previously subordinate Hutu. Some of the Tutsi fled to neighbouring Burundi, a country with a comparable ethnic composition. There, possibly fearing a similar revolt, the Tutsi struck first, massacring some 200,000 Hutu. The men who had spoken for Tutsi–Hutu conciliation were the first to be slain. Nor could group membership always be determined at sight. Some of those hacked to pieces with machetes were Tutsi mistaken for Hutu. If the fateful processes of polarization can start under circumstances such as those of Rwanda and Burundi, then what Kuper (1977:268) calls a Gresham's Law of Conflict by which 'the harmful and dangerous elements drive out those which would keep the conflict within bounds' can apply wherever the polarizers are not opposed by powerful groups determined to thwart them.

Power and community in Northern Ireland

Northern Ireland provides an illustration of a plural society in which 'harmful and dangerous elements' have been prevented by state power from driving out those who 'would keep the conflict within bounds'. Territorially, Northern Ireland is an area where the nation-states of Great Britain and the Republic of Ireland overlap. In the seventeenth century the British rulers of Ireland offered grants of land to Britons who were prepared to maintain forces to keep down the surrounding rebels, and thousands of Scots and English took up the offer, settling for the most part in the northeastern counties. Their descendants are committed to the Union of Great Britain and Northern Ireland dating back to 1801, and their political views are most strongly expressed through the medium of the Protestant religion. Of a population of one and a half million, nearly two-thirds are Protestant and just over one-third Catholic. Seen in the wider context of Ireland as a whole, the Northern Protestants are not a majority but a minority, for ninety-five per cent of the Republic's three million population is Catholic. The Unionists are opposed by those who believe that the six counties are naturally part of the Irish state and that the creation of an independent province in 1920 was an illegitimate action in which republicans had reluctantly to acquiesce. There are some Protestants who support the Republican cause and some Catholics who wish the Union maintained, and probably many more Unionists who deplore the style of fundamentalist Protestantism, but in general the two religious persuasions are firmly identified with opposing positions concerning the overriding issue of Ulster politics – that of the Border. Everyone is expected to be either a Protestant or a Catholic; there is no third possibility. Every Protestant is expected to be a Unionist, every Catholic a Republican, and vice versa; it is made very difficult for any individual to avoid these identifications.

Had the Union of Northern Ireland and Great Britain been carried through according to a strictly constitutional logic, there would have been no separate assembly in the province, any more than there was in Scotland. Northern Ireland would have had as many seats relative to electors in the Westminster parliament as did England. However, the British government followed another political logic. Recognising that the position in Northern Ireland was different from that on the mainland, it established a separate legislative assembly in Stormont Castle and gave the province less representation at Westminster. This structure was established to suit the interests of the Protestants and is a classic example of the differential incorporation about which Leo Kuper writes. The lengths to which the Protestants would go in using their power was illustrated by the position in Londonderry before its political control was vested in an independent commission. For local government purposes electoral boundaries were so drawn that the Protestant third of the population elected twelve members of the city council while the Catholic two-thirds could elect only eight councillors. The political system of Northern Ireland was stultified by the absence of any floating vote. The parties sought the support of their faithful and it was useless to try to obtain converts from 'the other side'. The politicians were the captives of the party committees since they had to be re-adopted each year. Change could come about only by change in the population; the Protestants expected an increase in Catholic strength because their higher birth-rate was not fully compensated by their higher rate of emigration. Fear of the Catholic birth-rate was a major factor in the Protestants' belief that their way of life was threatened by an imminent Catholic takeover which would result in the province being absorbed into what they saw as the economically backward intolerant theocracy of the Republic.

Writers familiar with ethnic and racial conflicts elsewhere have been tempted to see the Catholics as 'blacks who happen to have white skins' but, as Elliott Leyton shows in his study (1974, 1975) of the two sections of a rural community, this is fundamentally misleading. There are two distinct ethnic communities in Northern Ireland which share some important cultural characteristics, but are opposed to each other on so many dimensions that there are few cross-cutting ties, while the effect of IRA (Irish Republican Army) action has been to diminish such ties as remain. If an English youth organization holds a summer camp at which Protestant and Catholic school children from Belfast make friends with one another, they are prevented by other children from maintaining those friendships after their return. Yet though the cleavage between Protestant and Catholic runs deep, there must be other factors holding it in check, for otherwise there would by now have been civil war. Instead, the incidence of homicides in which one civilian kills another of the opposed group is low by comparison with the murder rates accepted as normal in many cities of the United States.

One of the most widespread patterns in the building of communities is the expectation that a person should assist his or her kinsmen. Anthropological studies indicate that in some parts of Ireland kinship is weak and that a farmer is more likely to call upon a neighbour for assistance than a kinsman. It seems as if the strength of kinship depends upon the extent to which valuable resources, like land, are controlled by groups of relatives of roughly equal social status. Many of the studies of Northern Ireland stress the importance of social networks originating in kinship ties for determining an individual's access to employment and to other resources. Leyton reports of the area he studied: 'It is almost impossible to obtain an apprenticeship in a good trade, and difficult to find well-paid jobs without a strong supportive network' (1975:85). Men help their own, which means in the first place their kin, and in the second their co-religionists. This pattern is taken for granted among both Protestants and Catholics. In a study of another locality Rosemary Harris (1972) stressed that while Protestants and Catholics have much in common they are largely unaware of this since, even where they live alongside one another, their patterns of friendship and social activity are so separate. In the country districts people know one another personally and they interpret people's behaviour as a response to personal ties and interests. They carry much of this pattern with them into the towns where Protestant and Catholic neighbourhoods are territorially distinct, so that Belfast has been called an assemblage of urban villages. A critical factor in the maintenance of separation has been the insistence of the Catholic hierarchy that their parishioners' children should be taught in Catholic schools; so, from the age of five, the two groups of children are taught different interpretations of their common history, are exposed to different influences, and are kept apart. It might be thought that since Protestants and Catholics are not physically distinguishable, there would be many occasions in the cities in which someone would not know whether a new acquaintance was a member of his own group or not and that a different social style, of more impersonal behaviour, would grow up. This is not the case. Nuances of speech, complexion and behaviour often provide clues, but if they fail it is usually sufficient to ascertain what school the other attended (Easthope, 1976:433).

In a short but convincing analysis of the character of conflict in Ulster, Harold Jackson contends that virtually everyone feels himself under threat and reacts accordingly. Because of the lack of contact, people on either side are quite unable to recognize good intentions held by people on the other (1972:192–3). In the village studied by Leyton (1975:13) the Protestants regard their Catholic neighbours as equally and fully human but as misguided and perverted by heretical doctrines and evil institutions. This recognition of the essential humanity of the other side – 'we're all the one blood if you go back far enough' – is reflected even in times of extreme political tension. In the cities such feelings are swamped by the sense of threat, and among the working class there is a general preference for living with fellow members of the same group. Any suggestion that the Catholic population in Belfast should have been dispersed would have been regarded with horror by them, as threatening their desire to maintain their own tradition, and, in more recent times, their physical security. Where, in the past, the segregation of Catholics has been weakened and Catholics have moved into a new area, Protestants have perceived the area as declining in social status.

The most striking outward manifestation of the social division into two mutually exclusive groups is the celebration of sectional festivities by public parades and demonstrations. The Protestants celebrate the Battle of the Boyne and the heroism of the Apprentice Boys of Derry: the Catholics commemorate the Easter Rising and the Feast of the Assumption. If an individual fails to affiliate himself openly with his own side on such occasions, he is liable to lose their support. Thus the moderates are forced to identify with the extremes and are trapped within the social system, for emigration is almost the only alternative open to them. Rosemary Harris (1972:187–97) concluded that the basic political problem of the poorer

Protestant was that to secure his independence from the Irish Republic he had to support politically those whom he neither liked nor trusted. He had to vote for incorporation in the United Kingdom although he disliked the English. He had to vote for Unionist leaders whom he distrusted, sometimes because they seemed too English, sometimes because they were identified with other localities or were of higher social status. Accusing them of insufficient loyalty to the Protestant cause seems to have been a vehicle by which the ordinary man could express his resentments in criticising leaders otherwise out of his reach. In so doing he only stepped up the polarization and stretched group competition over economic and political resources to cover other aspects of social life, including the symbols people used to represent the nature of their society.

Yet still there is no civil war. People on the two sides regard themselves as responding defensively rather than offensively. Comparing her research findings in 'Ballybeg' with those of a Dutch social anthropologist who studied a town ('Patricksville') in the South in which there was a political but not a religious division, Rosemary Harris (1979:48) remarks that the Southern town is every bit as sectarian and partisan in relation to sport and recreational organization as the Northern locality. In Patricksville, the townspeople are predominantly poor and they support Fianna Fail, while the more prosperous people in the surrounding rural area favour Fine Gael. The former party is historically identified as placing a higher priority upon the unification of Ireland than the latter, and memories of the struggles with the IRA over the independence of the Republic are kept alive in contemporary party opposition. Thus despite the lack of religious division, the apparent ideological similarity of the two parties, the greater opportunity for people to change their party allegiance, and the general acceptance of the state's legitimacy, the population of Patricksville is fundamentally divided, perhaps even more so than in Ballybeg. This suggests that the segregation of social networks can have a cumulative effect without either physical or religious identifications.

In the community he studied, Leyton discerned a reality transcending the relations of exploiter and exploited, and contended that its relative stability in the midst of violent rhetoric and action was maintained through important sets of shared values and integrating structures. Protestants and Catholics believed themselves to be of one blood. Violence between them tended to be directed towards symbolic objects or, if personal, to have been kept at the level of fists and clubs rather than guns and firebombs. It was only against foreigners that violence could be taken to the point of murder. The sense of belonging together was shown at funerals when people of both sides would share the grief, join the wake, and take part in the long procession to the cemetery. People on both sides saw themselves as belonging to one superior race, as sharing a regional identity, and as being morally superior to the despised English. When in Toronto or New York, emigrants from either side would help each other in finding jobs and housing. They shared similar values about obligations towards kin and neighbours; they agreed upon the criteria by which one man was ranked as more worthy, or of a higher status than another; they subscribed to the same view of the nature of politics; they understood that in certain contexts, like international sport, and at times in employment, the opposition between Protestant and Catholic, Orange and Green, was overlaid by other priorities (Leyton, 1974:193–7). In other words, there were some situations, outside their homeland, in which Protestants and Catholics used their common ethnicity as a basis for a friendly relationship.

The relations and values which can enable a rural community to transcend its oppositions may be weaker in the city where the extremists can more easily put pressure on the moderates. Because in the city people of one side can in their daily lives be more independent of those on the other, a greater measure of polarization can result. Had the British government not been willing to deploy military force and Irish government given substantial support to this policy, the 'harmful and dangerous elements' might well have changed a situation of polarized competition into one of open and bloody conflict. This is not to suggest, however, that the continuation of this kind of policy will resolve the political issue. 'Power-sharing' between Protestants and Catholics could work only so long as both sides accepted the legitimacy of a political structure which separated Northern Ireland from the Republic. There is little reason to believe that the bulk of the Catholic population of the province can accept such an arrangement as anything other than a temporary provision.

The international labour market

In plural societies of the kind with which Furnival and Kuper were concerned, there was no shortage of labour in the territory, though the Europeans might have difficulty getting the native people to sell their labour power in the market. In some other circumstances the landowners had an opportunity to sell plantation products on a booming world market (notably that for sugar in the middle of the nineteenth century) but could not get enough local people to undertake the work for the kind of wages that would enable them to make a profit. Work contracts were almost invariably drawn in terms highly favourable to the employer and were enforced by legislatures and officials whose sympathies were equally one-sided. The inequality of power permitted gross economic exploitation, indeed the story of economic growth in many places is the story of struggles to control and exploit labour.

Thus after the ending of slavery there was in many parts of the Caribbean an excess demand for labour that was met by the importation of indentured workers from China and India. The indentured workers were in many respects in a less favourable position than the former slaves; they entered stratified societies at the bottom of the social order. Because the societies were strongly stratified, and the newcomers' presence was desired by the ruling class, there was less scope for opposition from any workers just above them in the scale who viewed them as a threatening form of competition.

It was very different in Queensland. An important source of labour in Australia had been the transportation of convicts instead of their being sentenced to serve terms in British prisons. Australian farmers had convict labour assigned to them and gaols were built on farm properties in which the men were to be confined when not at work. 'Time-expired' men who had completed their sentences were available for work. In 1839 Britain ceased the practice of transportation and the demand for labour ran ahead of supply; by 1848 the annual wage rates were £30 for a single man and £25 for a single woman. In that year one colonist wrote home: 'all we want to be the most prosperous colony in the world is labour,' and his brother added, 'I do not at present see how we are to obtain labour and I do not care, so long as we get it'. Consequently when later that year 56 Chinese contract labourers disembarked in Brisbane, they were welcomed as the saviours of the sheep farmers. Queensland was a 'big man's frontier' where it was possible to make substantial profits from sugar-cane cultivation, provided capital, labour and other resources could be mobilized on the large scale that plantation farming required. One planter who proposed importing 400 contract labourers from southern Italy exclaimed wistfully, 'if we could only induce some European farmers – men of our own colour – to accept these terms . . .' while a group of planters later petitioned the Colonial Secretary (in vain) to supply 5,000 European indentured labourers. Another group complained that of 550 positions reserved for Europeans only 10 had been filled. White workers were neither cheap, reliable, nor amenable to discipline, so employers looked elsewhere. Peru seemed one possible source, and India another, but as to the latter the Permanent Under-Secretary for the Colonies in Whitehall replied:

> I have read with very great and painful interest the accounts of the Colonists' dealings with the Aborigines . . . I am confident that the Indian Government will not permit those for whose welfare they hold themselves responsible . . . to leave India with the intention of locating themselves in districts where they are exposed to casualties of this kind.

It was in such circumstances that the first 67 indentured servants from Melanesia were brought to Brisbane in 1863, starting a traffic that continued until 1891, when it was brought to an end by the collapse in the sugar market at the end of the 1880s and by mounting white hostility (see Evans, Saunders and Cronin 1975 as the source for statements about Queensland).

The colonist who did not care how the labour was obtained spoke for most of his fellows. Many of the Chinese labourers were kidnapped, tricked or misled by unscrupulous agents. In China their trade was called that of 'buying men' and the only difference between the procuring of an African slave and a Chinese labourer was that the latter had signed a contract. Perhaps a third of the Melanesian labourers were procured by illegal or nefarious means; in 1885 a Royal Commission described the sequence as 'one long record of deceit, cruel treachery, deliberate kidnapping and cold-blooded murder. The number of human beings whose lives were sacrificed during the "recruiting" can never accurately be known.' In Queensland the Chinese were better treated than the Melanesians, but in both cases there was considerable variation from one employer to another and some Melanesian contract labourers must have been satisfied or they would not have signed on for second and third periods. One Chinese when brought before a court for absconding asked to be given another term in gaol rather than be sent back to his employer, and, on the evidence, many others must have felt similarly. When sugar was booming, the plantations were substantial enterprises. One estate harvested 12,500 tons of sugar in 1889. In another the work force consisted of 175 Europeans, 50 Chinese, 50 others (Malays and Javanese amongst them), 325 Melanesians and 70 Aborigines. Wages were quoted as £52 per annum for Europeans, £30 for Chinese, £12 for Melanesians, while Aborigines were usually given only their rations.

There were those who contended that the Kanaka (as the Melanesian was called) was worse off than he would have been as a slave, certainly in the United States. It was argued that in the West Indies the slave had a market value and the owner wished to make best use of his investment whereas the Melanesian was under contract for three years and his employer had no interest in keeping him fit for any longer than this. Some were driven inland to work as shepherds, without footwear (despite the infestations to which barefoot people were exposed), guarded by armed men on horseback with stock-whips. They were forced to work excessively long hours on heavy work, were poorly fed, and got no protection from the courts. In the years 1882–4 the European death rate ranged between 15 and 17 per thousand; the Melanesian death rate was seven times higher, between 75 and 148 per thousand. That there were no revolts among the Melanesian workers on the worst estates can be explained by the short period of indenture, the strength of inter-tribal hostility, and the willingness of masters to allow palliatives in the form of alcohol, gambling, and visits to prostitutes.

Queensland also differed from the Caribbean in the size and power of the white working class. It was a democracy for whites, in which there was 'no bowing and scraping and bubbing and curtsying to the Squire'. The introduction of a politically weak labouring class which could be exploited by the wealthy was seen as opening up divisions among the whites and damaging their relative equality. The big sheep farmers and the owners of sugar and cotton plantations attempted to placate the white workers by proposing to employ contract labourers on the islands of Moreton Bay or in non-white occupations so that there would be no racial competition. The Melanesians were to work as domestic servants, shepherds or agricultural labourers, but in 1884 legislation was enacted further restricting their employment.

After 1852 large numbers of free Chinese immigrants entered Australia to seek their fortunes in the goldfields; they were not in direct competition with whites but their very presence evoked many fears. In 1861 an Aliens Act was introduced to prevent Asians becoming naturalized unless they had been residing in the colony for three years and were living there with their wives. Then they were subjected to discriminatory taxation; even naturalized Chinese were prevented from being candidates for either house of parliament; Chinese were prohibited from leasing land in any type of mining district even if they had obtained licences to mine in that area; they were limited by law to the least rewarding kind of mining; they were subjected to physical attack and police harassment; they were accused of introducing disease. In William Lane, Australia had her own Jack London. Both of them were socialist journalists and novelists influenced by the works of Herbert Spencer, and men who sought to glorify the 'race instinct'. Lane depicted white womanhood as threatened by the sexually depraved and sensuous Chinese, and as betrayed by upper-class whites who conspired against their own race by employing or trading with 'the yellows'. The pressure upon them was such that in 1886 a group of Chinese petitioned the Queensland Parliament:

> [We] . . . feel certain that the antipathy now held by Europeans against . . . [us] will become still greater as public meetings continue to be called . . . for the purpose of exciting the population to rise . . . [the Chinese will] solicit at the hands of your Honourable Government a free passage back to their own country and a refund of the price paid by them for admission into this Colony.

Other Chinese persevered. They managed to lease land and develop the growing of fruit. One sub-inspector of police reported: '. . . the Chinese farmers who employ Aborigines treat them very much better than most of the white people who employ them. The Chinese offer better wages and what is more pay the Aboriginals their wages when due; they also house and feed them well.' The Chinese paid higher wages to the Melanesian workers and occasionally gave them a share in the profits from their farms. But the Chinese were also blamed for introducing Aborigines to the smoking of opium, and under the *Aborigines Protection and Restriction of the Sale of Opium Act* of 1898 they were prevented from employing any coloured labour. The shipping of the fruit was undertaken by an Australian company with a monopoly on the coastal trade and 'there was a tendency to feel that too much trouble need not be taken over the Chinaman's produce'. Finally, in 1920 the Returned Soldiers' Association petitioned to have Asiatics excluded from the banana industry and their farms were taken over for soldier resettlement schemes. Nor was it any easier for Chinese craftsmen. As a result of pressure from the Furniture Manufacturers' Union a law was enacted in 1888 that all furniture made by Asiatic labour was to be stamped accordingly; the stamp was to be applied in 'any place in which one Chinese is employed'.

Despite its demand for cheap labour, Queensland in 1901 went along with the other states in adopting a 'white Australia' policy. Their reasons for doing without Melanesians are summarized (Evans, Saunders and Cronin, 1975:222) thus:

> The masters and their conservative supporters viewed them as a containable source of cheap labour to be exploited; the urban liberal described the Melanesians as posing a social threat to a democratic community and demanded their total exclusion from Queensland, while the white worker regarded the Islanders as a cause of racial pollution.

The pattern of anti-Chinese attitudes was fundamentally similar. These conclusions fit closely with what might have been expected from either the Split Labour Market theory or the Rational Choice theory. The position in Queensland between 1848 and 1901 is well described by proposition two of the former theory. Group oppositions were stronger than in New South Wales and Victoria because the Queensland climate was less temperate and the colony was closer to the Asian and Pacific territories from which non-white immigration might be expected. The planters contended that the contract workers could be confined to fixed economic and social positions, obviating any competition with white workers; this would be the 'caste arrangement' referred to in proposition 3(b) of the Split Labour Market

Theory, and which gave way after the decline of the sugar plantations to exclusion as described by proposition 3(a).

The contract workers introduced into Queensland were individuals from many different places. Up to the 1880s they were not often subject to racial stereotyping, nor were their characteristics discussed in the same context as those of the Aborigines. The Chinese were seen as a civilized people, not, as in California, as non-whites. Contemporary Australian attitudes towards non-European workers have to be seen in the context of attempts to control the labour market. Representatives of male workers complained about competition from female workers, from pensioners, from the inhabitants of the Blind Asylum and the prisons, and from workers who had migrated from other parts of Australia. They objected to assisted immigration from Britain, describing the British pauper as congenitally unfit for Australia (e.g. *The Barrier Miner* asserted that 'the British beggar is a beggar by hereditary instinct, and a debilitated wreck on manhood through the transmitted blood of weakness and disease'). As Andrew Markus (1979: 255–6) comments, 'when the focus is on men who perceived Chinese competition to be a direct threat to their livelihood it is not necessary to invoke notions of racial superiority and exclusiveness to explain their actions ... Fear produced a hatred whose expression was facilitated by, but was not a product of, the idiom of the day.' That idiom started to change in the 1880s, particularly with the use of Social Darwinist ideas to explain the rapid decline in the Aboriginal population. A quantitative analysis of the Queensland newspaper *The Worker* has found that in 1890–1, 92 per cent of the references to non-European workers were specific (e.g. they were identified by their nationalities) whereas by 1899–1901 over 30 per cent of references were generalized (e.g. employing racial categories) (Markus, 1979:259). By categorizing and stereotyping people as representatives of racial types the white population was able to increase its group solidarity at the same time as it excluded non-whites. The white working class had most contact with the newcomers and were the most conscious of them as competitors; they mobilized their political power to eliminate the competition and in this process the use of racial ideology was crucial, both to the organization of demonstrations and to the formation of an alliance with the urban liberals.

Similarities in the approaches from the Split Labour Market and Rational Choice Theories can also be seen from a comparison of the experience of Japanese immigrant workers in Brazil and British Columbia (Makabe, 1981). When the Japanese came to Brazil in the early part of the twentieth century there was a labour shortage. The immigrants started as farm workers but, being thrifty, achievement-orientated and skilful, they were able to set up as independent farmers and prospered from the sale of coffee.

They faced no competition from Brazilians in this field. Having migrated as family units they readily established a self-contained community which did little to attract either attention or antagonism. It was a very different story in Canada. The Japanese who migrated there were young males who went to a part of British Columbia in which there was a ready supply of white immigrant workers; they were employed in industries like fishing, boat-building and forestry which were already very competitive. The Japanese were used by employers as cheap labour so white ethnic workers saw themselves as engaged in competition with the Japanese as a group. There were riots, violence, and successful moves to exclude Japanese from the labour market. Those Japanese who remained were able to establish themselves first as soft-fruit farmers and then in commerce, only because these sectors were established on such a secure basis of individual competition that it was exceedingly difficult for the government to devise regulations that would discriminate against them. This comparison underlines the importance in generating ethnic conflict of the intensity and form of competition, together with the ability of employers and those workers who have strong unions or the vote, to control the terms on which workers are hired.

Rapid economic growth in the nineteenth century gave rise to a high demand for labour in territories that were being developed to produce for the world market. A century later with a more advanced technology, the world situation has changed. The main problem is now seen as one of over-population and of a greater supply of labour than is necessary to maintain present living standards. Countries all round the world have tightened their restrictions upon immigration and it has become difficult to find governments willing to take more than a few thousand refugees from Uganda, Vietnam or Cambodia, not to mention Somalia. Some indication of the problem for inter-group relations of this new situation can be seen in small island economies which have grown rich from tourism, such as Bermuda and the Seychelles. They must limit immigration because the islands are small and if the population grew too greatly this would diminish the attractiveness of the territory to tourists. To take advantage of their economic opportunities they may need skilled labour and be able to get it relatively cheaply on the international market. This nevertheless occasions resentment on the part of native workers who argue that the island is theirs, and are resentful that highly skilled immigrant workers should be so well paid. On the other hand, no increase in wages or in the incentives for training held out to local workers would produce a supply of qualified local people for these posts quickly enough to take advantage of the market opportunities.

Relations in Bermuda also illustrate the proposition advanced in Chapter 6 that when groups compete with one another they trade threats as well as goods. The effectiveness of threats depends upon vulnerability, and small countries dependent upon tourism as a money-earner are very vulnerable to any threat of public disorder. In the early 1950s Bermuda was as sharply segregated as North Carolina (to which it nearly corresponds in latitude). Black people, who constituted 61 per cent of a population of 37,400, were barred from the best hotels and from other public facilities. They were required to sit downstairs in the cinemas; if they attended a Church of England service they had to sit at the back; they were expected to know their place and be thankful for favours. From 1959 this pattern was forcefully challenged. Segregation was terminated and two main political parties established: one a business-oriented party supported by whites and well-to-do blacks, the other a trade-union-oriented party that had very few white supporters. In the following years there was a sequence of civil disorders, all but two of which would in most countries have been reported in only the local press. In 1977 a week-long emergency was called on account of riots and firebombing that resulted in property damage exceeding nine million dollars in value; three people lost their lives in one of the fires, but there was no looting.

The Royal Commission appointed to investigate these events quoted in its report witnesses who testified, *inter alia*,

> 'each riot I as a young man could identify with . . . 1965, '68, '70, '77, and I can almost say that there will be another';
> 'the only thing the businessmen know is dollars and cents . . . so for that reason I sat back and cheered';
> 'the establishment hears only the sound of breaking glass';
> 'we need riots to shake up the Government'; and
> 'we need a riot every few years to get things done in this country'.

The Commission concluded that there was a feeling widespread among black Bermudians that rioting, though regrettable, could be a legitimate mode of protest. In that respect there was a parallel with the civil disorders in London in the 1820s and 1830s when England enjoyed a form of rule that had been described as 'aristocracy tempered by riot'. The Commission also feared that many Bermudians had come to believe their country's position to be strong enough for it quickly to recover from temporary setbacks when in reality the balance was quite delicate (Bermuda, 1978). Threats had been successful in making the government listen to people who felt neglected, and they played an important part in regulating the inequalities associated with race.

It would be very misleading to look at black–white relations in Bermuda as resembling black–white relations in Detroit or Washington. Bermuda has a free-enterprise economy which in most sectors promotes individual competition, while distinctions of skin colour are more easily forgotten in a small-scale society with a high level of personal acquaintance. It is much more difficult in such circumstances to define what constitutes ethnic antagonism, especially since much of the black resentment was directed less towards the Bermudian-born whites than towards the English-born whites who had obtained the right to work and vote in the country and were benefiting so much from its prosperity. Seen from one standpoint, Bermuda might appear a good testing ground for theories of racial and ethnic relations. Seen from another, it would be very unsuitable because the sorts of measure that are acceptable in Detroit or Washington are too simple to comprehend the complexities that obtrude when the scale of the social relations is reduced.

Middlemen minorities

In Chapter 6 it was held that the character of the boundaries between two interacting groups depends upon the form and intensity of competition between them. Mention was made of the possibility that a third group might serve as an intermediary and modify the effects of competition. The characteristics of such groups have been listed in the discussion of what are called 'middlemen minorities'. These have been described (Turner and Bonacich, 1980) as likely (i) to occupy middle-rank positions, and (ii) to be economic middlemen involved in the movement of goods and services. Amongst the explanations as to why such minorities should appear and persist, three variables are often mentioned: (a) cultural variables, representing characteristics the minorities have brought with them from the sending society; (b) contextual variables, particularly the availability of a niche within the receiving society's social and economic structure which the minority can capture; and (c) situational or historical variables, which sometimes boil down to being in the right place at the right time. The defining characteristics of middlemen minorities are said to be (a) social, for they are, among other things, self-segregating; (b) interactive, since they are influenced by the tension that permeates their relations with the majority; and (c) economic, in their market activities which, as Bonacich (1973:583) remarked earlier, show a preference for capital liquidity since they want to be able to pull out of the market quickly if there is any indication that they may otherwise be driven out.

The theory advanced by Turner and Bonacich includes nine propositions intended to explain why such minorities should form and persist. The first is as follows:

> The more an ethnic group (a) constitutes a numerical minority;
> (b) is located in a culturally homogeneous society from which
> it is culturally distinctive; and (c) has emigrated from a society
> of declining peasant agriculture, where there is some hope of
> return and where kin are left behind, then the greater the
> probability that the group will form large numbers of intra-
> ethnic organizations and develop a high degree of intra-group
> solidarity.

The remaining eight propositions are of a similar form, and reflect the variables and defining characteristics mentioned above. This theory is quite compatible with the Rational Choice Theory and can be seen as an application of it to a particular problem area. It presents the members of a typical immigrant minority as sojourners who come to the receiving society intending to earn, save, and go back, but in the receiving society they acquire new goals and put off the day of return. Their organization is the outcome of a series of calculations as to the best way of attaining their changing goals in changing circumstances. They may miscalculate. The Asian groups resident in Uganda which were described earlier in this chapter underestimated the risks of attack and expulsion under an independent African government. They hoped, wrongly, that the economic contribution they were making to the country would outweigh the jealousy evoked by their relative prosperity. The Chinese who took part in the Australian and Californian gold rushes underestimated the hostility that would be displayed towards them and the political power of their competitors. In the long run it seemed better to withdraw than to persevere.

The value of analysing developments among middlemen minorities in this way is brought out powerfully by Orlando Patterson's (1975) comparison of the Chinese minorities in Jamaica and Guyana. After the ending of slavery in the West Indies the planters wanted labour but the ex-slaves were unwilling to work for the wages offered, so indentured labourers were imported from the East. The employers were disappointed with their Chinese workers and the Chinese no less disappointed by their working conditions. In Jamaica, as elsewhere, they escaped from agricultural employment and sought other ways of making a living. At this stage they were not so much a group as a collection of individuals whose main problem was simply that of surviving (the census of 1891 recorded 373 Chinese males and 108 females, about 0.1 per cent of the total population). Jamaican society offered them just one economic niche – that of retail trade. As workers had moved out of the plantations they needed to obtain goods from some independent source. The coloured and white middle and upper classes (including the Jewish minority) were not interested in opening village stores because this would have gone against their aspirations to social respectability. As Patterson writes 'a white man serving a black ex-slave was unthinkable to everyone. A coloured gentleman serving an ex-slave was quite thinkable to the whites, and to the blacks; but to the coloured that such things were thinkable was a source of humiliation, outrage, and utter disgust, and its realization was to be avoided at all costs.' The Chinese seized this opportunity, and, having done so, transformed themselves from a collection of individuals into an ethnic group. They did not organize on any basis of 'racial purity' since, because of the imbalance of sexes, many Chinese men took black concubines to mother their children and these became socially and culturally Chinese, the more effectively because many were sent to live for a while with kinsfolk in China.

The period from 1900 to 1940 was one of ethnic consolidation. At the beginning of it the Chinese began to convert to Roman Catholicism, which in Jamaica was very much of a minority religion, so that while conversion entailed a compromise with Western culture it helped the Chinese to remain socially exclusive. After 1940, however, tensions developed within the minority because the younger generation were unwilling to be deprived of a Western education and in this way to suffer a disadvantage compared with their fellow Jamaicans. The Chinese had to decide between continued ethnic solidarity on the basis of cultural exclusiveness or continued prosperity based upon a greater measure of integration. Mainland China became Communist and Jamaica moved towards political independence. The younger generation of Jamaican Chinese determined to be Chinese Jamaicans instead, and they were able to pull their elders with them, so that the minority became an integral section of the island's bourgeoisie. They had taken the decision that was in their best class interests. They did so without ceasing to be an ethnic group, for, seeking to conserve their wealth, many parents would marry their daughters only to men who were members of the group; this meant that a Chinese ancestry, plus Chinese physical traits, came to distinguish an ethnic subdivision of a class. Some Chinese Jamaicans, particularly those in the professions who wanted as wide a clientele as possible, have been inclined to leave the group and marry non-Chinese, so the group will probably become smaller and, because of its distinctiveness, could well find itself politically vulnerable.

The persuasiveness of Patterson's analysis of the changes in Jamaica is strengthened by his comparison with what happened in Guyana. Though the importation of Chinese indentured workers into that country followed a very similar course, they were much less successful when they moved into retail trade because the Portuguese had got there before them. The Chinese had too little share of the retail market for this to be a foundation on which to create an ethnic group, so they followed the course which best suited their economic and social interests: that of diversifying and seeking employment in a wide range of occupations. They could not succeed in this if they were exclusive so they chose to 'creolize' themselves, adopting the new culture that was evolving from the interaction of Europeans, Africans and Indians. They became Christians earlier than the Chinese in Jamaica and, unlike them, joined the majority denominations, first the Church of England and then the Pentecostal sects of the blacks. As tensions grew between the Indians and the blacks, people of Chinese origin were seen as mediators between the opposed groups. Though the Chinese Guyanans are less than one per cent of the population one of their number was chosen as first president of the newly independent nation. No similar appointment would ever be considered in Jamaica. The man who became Prime Minister there in 1981, Edward Seaga, is of partly Lebanese origin but his ethnic background has not been a political asset since Jamaican society is relatively homogeneous in respect of colour and ethnicity.

Helping people to compete

In the plural societies of the colonial period the imperial power had little difficulty regulating competition. Different groups found their own niches in the economic order and brought up their children to follow in their footsteps. Tension often came to centre upon access to positions in official organizations, like the civil service, rather than upon the areas of society dominated by the market economy. Where, as in Malaysia, the majority group attained political power it was faced with the task of developing competitiveness amongst its own people if market mechanisms were to function as a means of allocating social and economic rewards.

From early in the sixteenth century, European trading nations attempted to control trade through the Strait of Malacca between Malay and Sumatra. In the nineteenth century, the Portuguese and the Dutch were succeeded as the dominant power by the British. The peoples of the peninsula were at this time far from homogeneous but the experience of alien rule stimulated a common identification which was greatly enhanced by the growth of the non-Malay population. Shielded by the colonial power, Chinese and Indians settled in Malaya, and, being used to a competitive money-based economy, they prospered so well that the Malays soon felt that the country would before long be no longer theirs. Gradually a Malay political and ethnic consciousness developed and found electoral expression, but the leaders could not press too rapidly for independence lest, in the new state, power fell to the immigrant Chinese and Indian groups. They opposed the British plan for a Malayan Union since it would have created a state based on individual citizenship, eliminating the traditional privileges of the

Malays which in their earlier negotiations with the British had been accepted as part of the constitution.

A new party, the United Malays National Organization (UMNO), joined with the Malayan Chinese Association (MCA) and the Malayan Indian Congress (MIC) to form the Alliance Party which contested the 1955 elections and won 51 out of 52 elective seats in the Legislative Council. The prospect of stable government assured, the British agreed to independence which took effect in 1957. The Malays were the largest single group, comprising half the population of just over six million, the Chinese accounted for 37 per cent, the Indians and Pakistanis over 10 per cent, while Aborigines, Eurasians, Europeans and smaller groups made up the balance. Malay political leadership was ensured by legislation in 1962 permitting the mainly Malay rural constituencies to contain as few as one half the number of electors in the urban constituencies where the Chinese were concentrated.

The Malay party made great demands upon their coalition partners but the concessions thus obtained (over the proportion of government scholarships, civil service posts, trading licences, etc.) were insufficient to satisfy Malay voters who believed that as the country was theirs so should be the fruits of economic activity. So in the 1969 election the UMNO lost support to the more extreme Pan-Malayan Islamic Party (PMIP) while the MCA lost more than half its seats to more extreme communal parties. The MCA announced that it would have to leave the coalition. After the results were announced on 13 May Malays and Chinese started to fight one another in the streets of Kuala Lumpur. The government declared a state of emergency and suspended parliament.

Its main problem was Malay dissatisfaction over the economic disparity between Chinese and Malays, coupled with the evidence that, if economic development proceeded on the existing basis, this disparity would not be reduced. The Malay political elite increased its demands upon the Chinese and Indian leaders insisting that if a multi-racial society was to be maintained, drastic steps would be necessary to facilitate Malay advance. Government power would be used to favour 'joint' ventures between Chinese and Malays in the business sphere. It was announced that in future it would be unlawful for anyone to raise publicly the question of Malay privileges. These are stated in article 153 of the constitution as follows: (1) four-fifths of appointments in the Malayan Civil Service are reserved for Malays; (2) three-fifths of university scholarships are reserved for Malays; (3) the King may issue new permits or licences to Malays in whatever proportion he deems reasonable. In addition large tracts of land liable to lower rates of taxation are reserved for Malay owners. Especially since 1969 these policies have been formulated in terms of favouring not Malays but the *bumiputra* or 'sons of the soil', an expression which includes aborigines as well as Malays.

The implicit theory is that once the *bumiputra* have reached a position of equality the government will dispense with the programmes that have been needed to help the Malays 'catch up'. Up to the time, in March 1981, when the fourth Malaysian economic plan was presented, progress had been very encouraging, largely because of Malaysia's strong position in world trade. Her traditional exports of tin and rubber had been surpassed in value by oil and substantial deposits had been found of natural gas. By transferring state assets to a *bumiputra* unit trust it would be possible to attain the objective that, by 1990, 30 per cent of the nation's wealth should be in Malay ownership (other Malaysians are to own 40 per cent and foreigners 30 per cent). Malays were moving to the cities so that what previously had been Chinese constituencies were becoming mixed. Economic growth was generating a new demand for labour and the Prime Minister said it would be necessary to import thousands of workers soon and hundreds of thousands later. The ethnic allegiance of those workers could be very important.

When peoples' incomes rise they discover new appetites, and targets which seemed reasonable in 1969 may soon seem irrelevant. Members of the other groups cannot be confident that once the Malays have caught up they will abandon any of their special privileges. Differential treatment generates beliefs by which those who are favoured come to consider their privileges justified. Some power outside the system might change the rules to keep the competition on equal terms but no group within such a system is likely to favour a change of rules to its own disadvantage. If one Malay party were to propose this, it could easily be outflanked by a party that made a sectional appeal to the electors. At this level the analogy that sees ethnic relations as market relations breaks down, for it cannot explain the political processes that determine the terms on which individuals compete. It is for such reasons that Alvin Rabushka and Kenneth A. Shepsle (1972:217) conclude that democratic institutions are unable to resolve the intense but conflicting preferences that characterize the plural society.

Revaluation movements

Another aspect of group competition remains to be discussed. This chapter has so far been concerned with the use of power by a dominant group, but a subordinate group can also act so as to increase its power in an exchange relationship. To go back to the example of the cattle and sheep herders, it could be that Group A utilizes monopoly power to establish an exchange rate of 1 kg beef for 2 kg mutton. After a while, members of Group B become dissatisfied and decline to purchase any more at this rate, holding out for better terms. Since it is still advantageous to members of Group A to trade on any terms up to 5 kg beef for 1 kg mutton, they agree to a different rate. The market rate will reflect the relative ability of the members of the two groups to mobilize their resources, psychological as well as material, and take advantage of the differences in the groups' relative preferences for beef and mutton. A new movement in either group which demonstrates that its ʾmembers are willing to make sacrifices may enable the group to get better terms from its trading partners.

The outstanding characteristic of ethnic mobilization movements is that, when successful, they induce the members to set a higher value upon their common ethnic characteristics. They have been discussed, in a limited way, by A. F. C. Wallace (1956) who proposed the name 'revitalization movements', defining such a movement as 'a deliberate, organized, conscious effort by members of a society to construct a more satisfying culture'. Such movements, he wrote, had been known under a variety of names including nativistic, revivalistic, millenarian and messianic movements; they included cargo cults and the religious movements which led to the foundation of Christianity, Islam and Sikhism, as well as to revivalistic movements within these religions. For a movement to qualify as one of revitalization, the persons involved in it 'must perceive their culture, or some major areas of it, as a system (whether accurately or not), they must feel that this cultural system is unsatisfactory; and they must innovate not merely discrete items, but a new cultural system, specifying new relationships as well as, in some cases, new traits'. Wallace was concerned primarily with the psychological processes in the prophets or innovators, and the effects of the movements they started upon the internal life of the groups. The concern of the present analysis is with the inter-relations between changes internal to these groups and their external relations. For this reason, and because Wallace's definition is very exigent, it seems better not to employ it in the present context but to coin a slightly different name that can be used to designate movements of a similar kind. All movements which influence the values which members of a group place upon their self-identification in exchanges with others can be called revaluation movements. For example, if members of a group are commonly servants to members of another, they pay a price in terms of personal dignity and self-respect in entering a servile relationship. Sometimes they come to believe that the price is too high and grow more reluctant to enter such relationships. This may be because they have new alternatives open to them or because, as a result of group mobilization, they have come to place a higher subjective value upon their dignity and self-respect.

Some people are more proud than others of the nations (or ethnic groups) to which they belong. National pride varies from one nation, and one period of time, to another. Crucial to these variations are processes of comparison. An individual is free to choose between the relative importance of various group identifications. He can identify himself as a Canadian, a Catholic, a trade unionist, a member of a local community, a cosmopolitan, or as someone whose main task is simply to survive. He will invest time and emotional energy in different identities according to the material and psychic reward he can expect to obtain from them. When fellow Canadians win gold medals in international sporting tournaments he will obtain more satisfaction from his national identity than when they do not. When national identity brings little satisfaction, a religious or cosmopolitan one may become relatively more important. But comparison processes cannot alone offer a sufficient explanation of changes. Children are brought up to believe that certain identities are important and these are reinforced by collective ceremonials like, in Britain, a coronation or a Royal wedding, or, in the United States, a presidential inauguration or the daily oath in the classroom.

The problem of ethnic mobilization is this: the value people place upon their ethnic membership may change because circumstances change, making that membership seem more or less valuable. Yet a leader can persuade others to set a higher valuation on their ethnic membership when there has been no such change in their circumstances. More important still, when circumstances change the extent to which groups change depends upon leadership and persuasion; there is no automatic response. The leader has to persuade his or her fellows to put less time and energy into non-ethnic memberships and activities, and transfer it to their ethnic membership; the leader exhorts them to invest in that membership in the expectation of a future return in material or emotional satisfaction greater than can be expected from other activities.

A simple example of an ethnic revaluation movement can be found in a study (Banton, 1957:162–83) of the relations between ethnic groups in a West African city. In the mid-1940s ethnic identities were so ranked that members of the more orthodox Islamic groups from the far interior were accorded more prestige than those from the coastal groups. The city of Freetown was founded on land which had traditionally formed part of Temne territory but the Temne were accorded very little prestige and some of their young men chose to try and pass as members of other groups. A young Temne schoolmaster (who after independence rose to become Deputy Prime Minister of Sierra Leone) set out to rectify the situation by organizing the kinds of activity that would appeal to the young men. He was successful in this. The young men's societies became so popular that they attracted members from other tribal groups. The Temne moved up the ethnic hierarchy and they took more pride in being Temne. To understand the schoolmaster's success it is necessary to appreciate three dimensions of rank: land, religion and culture. The Temne claim to a degree of precedence as owners of the land was discounted because they ranked low on the scale of religious status. One of the groups above them in the scale had attractive recreational societies and the Temne had none. The schoolmaster organized such societies by appealing to Temne notions of the status which land-ownership should confer. They then used these societies to further their political claims in elections; with better organization they were able to collect money for mosque-building and activities which lifted their claims to respect on the religious dimension.

For a more complicated example it is instructive to compare the revaluation movements of two Hindu castes, one of which is described as unsuccessful. The older sociology textbooks used to describe Indian society as consisting of a series of castes ranked in terms of their ritual status and grouped in the four *varna* categories. Recent research shows that the units of the system are the many thousand *jatis* which organize life at the local level. Each *jati* has monopoly control over one or more occupations. But as circumstances change some occupations provide opportunities for ac-cumulating greater wealth while others die away. The claims of *jatis* to precedence are ranked along several different social and cultural dimensions; economic power can enable a group to purchase ritual status. In south Indian villages it is common to find some six to fifteen castes in the middle reaches of the hierarchy whose relative rank is disputed, while studies elsewhere report extensive disagreements about rank. Historical evidence also makes clear that some castes have risen in rank and others fallen.

The first of these caste-mobility movements is that of Holerus, a landless untouchable caste in south India who have traditionally lived by working and performing services for Havik Brahmans (Harper, 1968). Earlier in the present century a Holeru man would enter a lifelong indentureship to a Havik who would finance the Holeru's marriage. The Havik provided the money and the Holeru worked to repay him; the indenture system was the Havik's guarantee that he would be recompensed. In the attempt to raise their status the Holerus have stopped eating beef and have given up disposing of dead cattle for other castes, although the beef was used to supplement an otherwise very meagre diet. The Holerus will no longer supply wood for Havik funeral pyres; some refuse to clean Havik cattle sheds; their caste council forbids them, on pain of out-casting, to accept the drink of milk at marriage which used to symbolise their lifelong allegiance to a Havik; and they avoid other signs of low ritual status. They carry their resistance to the point at which an increasing number are not marrying. They work as wage labourers but do not seek any alternative and less expensive way of celebrating marriage, though exchange marriages are becoming more frequent. Their struggle to enhance their status has been conducted according to the principles of Hindu culture, reinforcing their commitment to it; believing that a caste's rank is in part based upon the elaborateness of its marriage rites, to adopt a simpler rite would seem to devalue their previous struggles.

The Holerus have been faced with two alternatives. The older course offered them a proper marriage with an expensive and elaborate ceremony which brought them ritual satisfaction and the economic security offered by a master who would give them steady work and help in sickness and old age. The newer course was to work as a wage labourer with a higher daily wage but no security; with greater self-respect and the esteem of others for being independent; but with little prospect of marriage. Many Holerus tried to resolve the dilemma by appearing to choose the former course, undertaking an indenture, but breaking the contract soon after receiving the benefits. This suited their individual interests but had the predictable consequence that Haviks stopped trusting Holeru promises so that the older course is no longer open to Holeru workers. There is little question that the collective action of the Holerus qualified as mobilization: their group has achieved much greater unity and has acted in pursuit of common interests. Yet it has been unable to move above any other caste in the hierarchy. They argue, in effect, that caste rank should be based on the strictness with which a caste observes ritual requirements, but they have been unable to persuade other castes to adopt this criterion since it is not in their interest to do so.

The second caste mobility movement is that of the new Cauhāns of North India. They used to be known as Noniyās and were traditionally makers of salt and saltpetre. Where there was little scope for these activities they took new ones, and many acquired considerable wealth by contracting for earth work, brick-making and similar services for the British government. Following this occupational breakthrough others became schoolteachers and postmasters as well as contractors. In 1898 a Noniyā formed the Rajput Advancement Society to press the claim that the Noniyās were really Cauhān Rajputs of the Kshatriya *varna*. They claimed to descend from the last Hindu king of Delhi whose caste had been almost destroyed by the Muslim invaders of the twelfth century. In 1936 they adopted the sacred thread distinctive of the rank they claimed. Kshatriya landlords first opposed this but they then gave way. Brahmans may scoff at their claims, but will officiate at Noniyā weddings and ceremonies designed to enhance their prestige by conspicuous consumption. The leaders of all castes point to the Noniyās as having risen in the hierarchy, so in this sense the movement has succeeded; but the anthropologist who studied it (Rowe, 1968) remarks that many, and particularly the urban elite, are having second thoughts. Sophisticated Cauhān lawyers and teachers have become more secular and committed to the doctrines of political equality. They feel at home in situations in which class is the crucial measure of social rank, and many are active in anti-caste movements. Some point to the scholarships available to the children of Depressed or Scheduled Castes, and other privileges, concluding that their new rank is a disability in modern circumstances.

Comparison suggests that both Holerus and Noniyās succeeded in organizing so as to place a higher valuation upon their group identity. The Holerus' movement was an autonomous cultural change, not a response to circumstantial change; it failed because it was confined to a limited locality and there were no major changes in the economic structure. The Noniyās succeeded because they benefited from economic change and possibilities for geographical mobility; they did not need to displace a competing group so much as secure a better position in a changed structure.

Some religious movements can be seen as responses to stigmatized ethnic identities. One such is that of the Nation of Islam or Black Muslims, as found in cities of the United States. It would be wrong to present this movement as a reaction to the low status of blacks in the eyes of whites since there is good reason to believe that blacks were dissatisfied with the pattern of relations in their own group irrespective of what the whites thought. Many of them were uncertain about the place of blacks in United States society: were they Americans, when those who spoke for American society did not accept blacks for what they were? Or were they Africans who, if they could not return to that continent, had to secure a territory in which they could build their own society? The Muslim reply was that the United States had offered blacks only a slave identity. Blacks should realize that their true identity was that of Muslims. They should cast off their slave names and live according to the Koran. The Muslims emphasized discipline in the congregation and in the family. Wives must defer to their husbands; Muslim men must protect and care for their women-folk; no-one might drink alcohol, eat pork, or behave in an unseemly manner (Essien-Udom, 1962). They restricted the range of social relationships with whites that they were prepared to enter. They increased the cultural distance between their group and the white majority in a way that can be represented by saying that they had moved to position F in Figure 7.

This movement can be interpreted as asserting that blacks had allowed themselves to be given a false identity. Being a Muslim became a charter for a new way of life which reversed many of the behaviour patterns that inhibited working-class black economic advance and led to disorganized family living. A collection of people who had previously belonged only to a category were formed into a group with a very hard boundary towards the whites. The members invested heavily in the group, for it made many demands upon them, and it brought them rewards of pride and dignity as well as the consolations of religion. Though it was not ostensibly concerned with the position of blacks in a white-dominated society, it had the unintended effect of lifting its members in the black stratification system. The English Puritans described by Max Weber were concerned for their future in the next world, but their religious beliefs had the unintended consequence of making them richer in this world. In similar fashion members of the Nation of Islam have pursued a religious objective that has given them a greater stake in a society they disparage.

Many young black males of West Indian origin in Britain today similarly doubt whether there is any satisfactory place for them in the society in which they find themselves. Some are attracted to the Rastafarian belief, according to which they are the people of Ras Tafari, the (former) Emperor of Ethiopia. This religion has the potential to provide an ideology for blacks in Britain which could give them a new sense of dignity and self-worth. Yet whereas the Nation of Islam incorporated a work ethic that brought Black Muslims the reputation of dependable workers and occupational success, Rastafarian beliefs celebrate withdrawal from the world of work. These beliefs will have to change before they could be the basis for a successful revaluation movement (Cashmore, 1981).

Comparison of the two caste-mobility movements and the two religious/ethnic movements suggests that it is of limited use to study mobilization or revaluation movements apart from their structural context. The Holeru movement could not attain its objectives, though individual Holeru may prefer their present situation to that of life-long indenture. The Cauhān movement attained the objectives of its initiator but his successors question whether the investment was worthwhile. The Nation of Islam and Rastafarian movements demand an investment on religious or ideological grounds; the former provides a social as well as a religious return but the latter is unlikely to repeat this. Attempted revaluation movements frequently fail. For example, in the cargo cults reported from so many parts of the Pacific, leaders enjoin their followers to destroy their most prized possessions; by such an act of faith on the part of the whole community, so it is believed, the spirits will be moved to send cargo more valuable than the goods which have been destroyed (Burridge, 1969). In effect, the followers transfer their investments from material possessions to spiritual merit, but they are misled by a false prospectus and receive no return on the reinvestment. When a group attempts such a movement and fails, it is likely to become more demoralized, uncompetitive, and vulnerable to aggressive action on the part of others. A revaluation movement which succeeded, was the political movement of Afro-Americans in the mid and late 1960s which followed a strategy resembling that of the Nation of Islam at several points.

It could best appeal to young blacks by excluding white sympathizers and adopting a threatening posture towards white society. It declared, in effect, that blacks had to be more proud of being black and that they had to attain a position of political and economic equality before they could weaken the group's inclusive boundary and start to compete with whites on a more individual basis. By mobilizing, Afro-Americans improved their bargaining power as a group.

If the Rational Choice Theory is utilized for the study of revaluation movements it should be possible to develop A. F. C. Wallace's analysis to formulate propositions about the factors favouring mobilization, such as the personalities of leaders, their ability to communicate with followers and the availability of sanctions to hold members in line. Such factors will govern the movements both of minorities and of majority members who mobilize in order to resist minority demands. It may then be possible to formulate further propositions about the exchange of threats: how far a minority can sustain a present sacrifice in hope of a future gain; how majorities can respond when only a section of their membership will have to bear this burden of concessions to the minority, and so on (see Hechter *et al.*, 1982). Yet it will be difficult to develop these modes of reasoning to the point at which predictions can be made about the success of attempted revaluation movements, too much depends upon the circumstances of individual cases, as that of the Holerus has demonstrated.

Changes in the valuation of shared characteristics other than those of ethnicity can also be analysed using this approach, though it does not always contribute any very new understanding. For example, reference was made in Chapter 6 to the way that in Western societies homosexuals have changed from being a category to a group. It would seem, after the event, as if the costs to many individuals of 'coming out' and identifying themselves publicly used to be greater than any emotional benefits they expected to obtain from doing so. In more recent times this has changed: there is less social disapproval of those who take this step and they gain greater peace of mind. The women's movement also invites comparison because it has employed tactics of consciousness-raising similar to those employed by Afro-Americans, in this case to change women from being a social category and make them more of a self-conscious group. They have been exhorted to bear the heavy costs of struggling against what they consider demeaning treatment in order that those who come after may be treated better. The women's movement has fought not so much for better treatment relative to men as for the abandonment of gender as a criterion for differentiating roles in inappropriate situations (*cf.* the discussion of responses to stigmatized identities in Chapter 4). In this respect it can be seen as one step ahead of the black movement as this took shape in the United States in the late 1960s.

Conclusion

The study of group competition is the study of monopoly in a wider sense than that which is conventional in economics. Group competition may be a matter of one group using its political power to force members of another group to provide goods or services on terms highly favourable to members of the dominant group. But groups also compete for status. In Chapter 4 it was maintained that whenever group membership is ascribed there will be a hierarchy in which some groups are ranked above others, although there will often be disagreement about the relative rank of particular groups. Membership of ethnic groups, or 'tribal' groups in African cities, and of caste groups in Hindu India, provide examples. Those individuals who are assigned to membership of such a group will have that membership in common; it will be a matter of pride to them if their rank is high, and of shame or anxiety if it is lower than they think it should be.

Hierarchies of this kind develop only where members of different groups are in regular contact. In the early years of European penetration into East Africa the indigenous ethnic groups were, for the most part, in contact with their various neighbours on a one-to-one basis and were not conscious of having a rank in a wider system. With the extension of British influence that changed. Those who came to the towns were more conscious than others that a new social order had been created with Europeans at the top, followed by relatively wealthy Asian traders, and other Africans, perhaps belonging to one of the more powerful tribes, who were able to look down upon them as uncivilized. As nationalist politics took hold, the native people became less willing to accept rule by Europeans; the psychological costs to their pride of being subordinated by others steadily increased. A similar process was at work in Malaysia where the Malays considered themselves, as owners of the territory, to have prior rights to its produce, but found the Chinese were gaining the upper hand in the cities; it wounded their self-esteem and their sense of propriety. When groups like the Malays have had the political power to lay down rules governing group competition they have regularly done so in ways that are to their own economic benefit, but it is insufficient to see their actions as motivated by economic considerations alone. The discussion of revaluation movements should have demonstrated that groups differ in the values they put upon their pride and upon their willingness to forgo other gratifications in order to mobilize with the intention of improving their status.

Examples of the use of political power to manage market relations are easily found. In the Ugandan case the British were unwilling to admit European artisans into the country because they wanted to preserve the image of the European as someone of professional status. There were practical reasons for this, as the authority of British administrators could have been undermined by the presence of whites who had to compete with Asians and Africans. Only the equally practical arguments for importing artisans who could carry out the skilled work involved in building the dam, installing the generators, and so on, led to a change in policy. In Northern Ireland, the Protestants used their political power to ensure that Protestants got more than a proportionate share of the good jobs, houses, and so on. In Queensland, the whites used their power in the most obvious way to confine Chinese, Melanesians and Aborigines to the jobs they did not want for themselves, and to see that they were paid less well than whites would have been paid.

An immigrant minority is confronted by an already existing economic structure. Its members look around to see what are the best opportunities open to them to pursue the objectives that have brought them to the country, and the character of their group changes as they choose between successive sets of alternatives. The comparison of the Japanese in Brazil and Canada shows how the opportunity structure is influenced by the form of competition, while the example of the Chinese in Jamaica and Guyana suggests that the choices can reflect an accurate calculation of the strategy which will bring the greatest financial return. Some groups, like the Asians in Uganda, fail to predict future developments; the history of that country, indeed, shows how policies of short-run aggrandizement can bring desolation if they destroy the political framework essential to market relations. When people cannot predict whether they will be able to harvest what they have sown, there will be little production for sale. When no one can be sure of being able to enjoy the fruits of his labours there will be less work done.

When plural societies move from colonial rule to independence, competition increases. Because the old government regulated the market fairly closely, the supporters of the new government looked to it to meet their aspirations. In the course of his comparison of politics in the ethnically bipolar states of Guyana, Malaysia and Fiji, R. S. Milne (1981:140, 155) remarks that 'what needs to be stressed about ethnic demands on the government is not so much their concentration on collectively provided goods as their extremely competitive nature, almost resembling the demonstration effect in the consumption habits of individuals'. He says that the relaxation of import duties on mandarins and other oranges during the Chinese New Year produced requests that the duty on imported dates be lifted on the ground that they had religious significance for Muslims. Whatever was given to one group was seen as some kind of deprivation by the other groups. The power of governments to regulate markets may be limited by international economic relations but with an expanding economy, like that of Malaysia, its power can be considerable. So simple a rule as the declaration that, to conduct a business, a person must hold a licence, gives the government power to introduce quotas stipulating what proportion of licences will be given to various kinds of applicants, and what proportions of employees of different ethnicity they may engage. The Malaysian government has used such powers to increase the proportion of Malays in the commercial sector but it has not contemplated their use to increase the proportion of Chinese in the army or the police. After the 1969 riots the then Prime Minister agreed that when the Malays had improved their position in the economic structure they would no longer need special privileges under the constitution, but he added 'it is not for the others to demand this': a clear statement that the rights of citizenship could be subordinated to ethnic politics.

In discussing the cases of Uganda, Northern Ireland and Malaysia it has not been necessary to expatiate upon the exchange of threats, because their relevance has been all too obvious. President Amin issued threats to the Asian minority, saying, for example, that they should not refuse to let their daughters marry Africans, but he did not attempt to set any price for lifting his threats. In Northern Ireland the IRA have threatened to disrupt the economic life of the province unless their demands are met. In Malaysia the riots of 1969 were a warning to the Chinese that, unless they made concessions, their security, and that of their businesses, was in peril. The only answer to such threats, as has been seen, is for the government to use its power of coercion, and this is scarcely a remedy when the threats themselves come from government forces.

The purpose of this chapter has been to show the character and implications of group competition, not to try to prove any theory. Most of the observations in it can be made consonant with the main competing theories, but they surely also show that important features of racial and ethnic relations are bound up with attempts to manage markets.

*　　*

Entr'acte: a note on historical comparisons

The reader who is unacquainted with the histories of racial relations in South Africa, the United States and Britain should bear in mind, throughout the next three chapters, this last conclusion about the connections between racial relations and the management of labour markets. It is impossible to compare one country's experience of racial differentiation with another's without making use of some simple model of society. As useful a model as any is that suggested by the events in Queensland discussed in this chapter (pp. 183–7).

The Queensland case is of a territory isolated from the world market which was invaded by whites who dispossessed the native peoples. The whites were profit-maximizers. To make a profit from the resources they had seized, they needed more labour than they could get from their own country, so they imported labour from countries where people were of different appearance. Such differences made it easier for the new workers to be treated as a separate category, confined to particular kinds of work and paid less than the market value of their economic contribution. This treatment of them was then ideologically justified by reference to their racial characteristics. The exploitation of the imported labour generated tensions between classes within the white population: the upper class drew most profit from it; the middle class disliked this as a threat to democracy within the white group; the working class saw the imported workers as competitors and were the most committed to the racial ideology.

The history of group relations in South Africa departs from this model in many respects. For two centuries the whites there had little opportunity to make much profit from the country's natural resources, and some of them took up a cattle-herding way of life like that of the native peoples; they were very little profit-oriented. With the discovery of mineral wealth and the creation of an economy that was part of an international market, all the various ethnic groups were brought into relations of interdependence. Industrialization brought both black and white country-dwellers onto the urban labour market. The whites were poor and unskilled Afrikaners who in an unregulated market would have earned no more than the blacks. To protect them from such competition the government divided the labour market by enforcing a colour bar, laying the foundations for apartheid. The dominant Afrikaner group used its political power to create a structure in which, from the moment of birth, all whites had massive advantages over members of the other groups. Class divisions within the white population were minimized; indeed it is possible (though not necessarily illuminating) to argue that the whites as a whole constitute the South African upper class. Having established the clearest example of group competition anywhere in the modern world, the whites now feel sufficiently secure in the economic domain for the government to relax the rules a little and permit a measure of individual competition and association within a legal framework designed to preserve group differences.

The history of group relations in the southern region of the United States is closer to the Queensland model; the blacks and whites were interdependent from the outset but in a very unequal relationship that was justified by a racial ideology. In the south, white workers saw blacks as competitors and utilized the ideology to advance their interests. However, the south was part of a large political unit in which the principles of individual competition were more firmly established, and mass immigration from Europe continued throughout the period of acute inter-regional tension; it was halted only in the 1920s. The major advance towards black political, economic and social equality came one generation after the ending of white mass immigration when most of the whites had secured their positions.

The Queensland model would be of no use for comparing minority relations in Britain with those elsewhere, did it not contain another element, that of migrant labour. Melanesians were imported to work for a period and return to Melanesia. Chinese, who might have settled in Australia, were subjected to so many handicaps that they returned to their homelands. Only whites were wanted as settlers. In South Africa the whites attempted to establish the cities and industrial centres as white territory to which blacks would come only as migrant workers. They were unable to maintain this policy because the black reserves could not sustain the burden of supplying labour on the whites' terms while the labour demands in the cities and industrial centres could not all be satisfied by a constantly changing workforce. In the United States a migrant labour force has been supplied primarily by workers from Mexico, who, so long as they remained migrants, lacking political patronage and trade union power, have been treated in ways that bear comparison with the Queenslanders' treatment of Melanesians.

Migrant workers came to Britain from the West Indies and the Indian subcontinent in the 1950s and 1960s, at the same time as the so-called 'guest workers' were streaming to work in the factories of Germany (and, indeed, to those of most countries in continental Europe and Scandinavia). Those who came to Britain had to contend with the handicaps that beset migrant workers everywhere, but they suffered the extra disadvantage of being physically distinguishable. It is not easy to determine the extent to which some of their difficulties are to be attributed to their being migrants rather than to their being racially distinguished. They entered a social and economic structure which had been built on conceptions of individual competition and provided no legitimate basis for treating members of an overseas minority as a distinctive group. They were also, especially by comparison with South Africa and the southern United States, only a tiny and very heterogeneous minority. The forms of discrimination which they encountered therefore tended to be more individual: to get the same kind of job as their white competitors they needed to be better qualified; to rent the same kind of housing they might have to pay more.

In the United States Afro-Americans had a common identity thrust upon them, giving rise over a period of two to three centuries to one of the classic examples of ethnogenesis: the creation of a people. In South Africa the corresponding process has been slower. Though the growth of 'black consciousness' has lately been significant, especially in the cities, the black people are members of culturally distinctive nations with historic claims to large portions of the states' territory. The heightening of black consciousness affected minority sentiment in Britain as well, but the migrant background of the minorities there suggests that comparisons with the Hispanic minorities in the United States may often be more rewarding than comparisons with Afro-Americans.

In so far as it is possible to see racial relations in terms of the encounter between groups, with group competition yielding place to individual competition, South Africa today presents more features than the other two countries of the earlier phases of contact, and Britain is furthest removed from them.

9

Boundary maintenance in South Africa

The history of any country can be written from many different standpoints, but the contrasts in South African historical writing are particularly vivid. For some writers the foremost perspective is the response of the southern African peoples to an unparalleled political, cultural and economic onslaught. Others set out to describe the creation of a new state from the perspective of one of the European groups, though much can also be learned about that process by examining the vicissitudes of the numerically smaller communities, particularly the Indians and the Cape Coloured people. In recent years, however, the most salient contrast has been that between the liberal interpretation, focusing on the interrelations between the main racial groups, and the radical interpretation which sees cultural differences as changing more rapidly in the search for economic advantage within a capitalist framework (Wright, 1977, 1980). Anyone coming afresh to a new field of study is grateful for an intellectual map which explains who are the main contributors, their general approach and the kind of evidence they have put forward. Since historical writing is selective in a different way from natural science, it is inevitable that even the most useful map will be misleading in some respects. Those who approach the historical record from different philosophical standpoints cannot agree on the relative importance of different elements in it, and when they compile their maps they will use different coordinates. Each contributor moves on, responding to criticism, and to the way he or she is located in other people's maps. Thus any attempt to characterize the vigorous debate in recent historical writing about South Africa becomes out-of-date as soon as it is published.

This chapter looks at the growth of competition in South Africa and its implications for the drawing of boundaries between groups. It pays particular attention to the Afrikaners, since they have been the pace-making group which has done most to influence those boundaries during the past one hundred years. By the eighteenth century the Afrikaners could be recognized as a group distinguished from the Africans in appearance, socio-cultural status and ancestry, though their way of life was not much more advanced technologically. They could be distinguished from the rest of the white population by language, and to some extent by religion, and had differentiated themselves from the people of the Netherlands from whom they were mostly descended. To resist the pressure that came from the English-speaking population they needed to be economically independent; to resist the pressures that would arise from mating with people of African, or part-African descent, they needed to emphasize the physical signs of difference and to keep distinctions of appearance, socio-cultural status and ancestry in line so far as possible.

Prior to the Great Trek (which started in 1835) the intensity of competition was relatively low and the relations between the people of different groups reflected their characteristics as individuals. The growing opposition between Briton and Boer led the Afrikaners into sharper conflict with the African peoples and powerfully reinforced the Afrikaner sense of group identity. Then they were caught up in the long chain of events that stemmed from the discovery of valuable minerals; their desire to benefit from these new opportunities for wealth led them to exploit their political strength to the disadvantage of the non-European groups. In so doing they established one of the clearest patterns of group competition and built up group boundaries in a manner without equal in the rest of the world.

Non-competing groups

When in 1652 the Dutch East India Company established a permanent settlement at the Cape of Good Hope, it was to be a station assisting trade with the East. The company wished to keep to a minimum any contact with the local peoples. This proved increasingly difficult, despite official threats such as the proclamation of 1774 that anyone bartering with the Kaffirs was a violator of the public peace, liable to the confiscation of property, corporal punishment, or even a sentence of death. The difficulty was that, once settlers moved away from the harbour and sought to make a living by farming and stock-rearing, they wanted Africans to work for them. Land appeared to be plentiful, even if it was often of poor quality, but labour was scarce. From this sprang various forms of servile labour, whereby workers were bound to an employer, such as 'apprenticeship' and the importation of slaves (Robertson, 1934–5). Predictably, a conflict of interest developed, with the settlers struggling for liberty, protesting against corruption in the company (which did not administer its affairs well enough to avoid bankruptcy) and demanding some voice in the government of the colony. It is part of this pattern that the first recorded use of the name 'Afrikaner' should date from an incident in 1707 when a settler was arguing with a magistrate and objecting: 'I am an Afrikaner . . . I will not be silent'.

The settler population did not start as a homogeneous group. The Company had difficulty attracting desirable people of sound Protestantism and of Dutch or German extraction willing to settle; but, after 1688, 200 Huguenots made the journey and were distributed among the Dutch farmers. A variety of circumstances combined slowly to bring this collection of individuals to a consciousness of shared interests and a common way of life. The historian de Kiewiet declared 'in the long quietude of the eighteenth century the Boer race was formed' but the process of ethnogenesis, that of creating a people, took longer than this. To start with, some Netherlanders married Bengali women who were freed slaves; indeed, two famous Afrikaner leaders, Paul Kruger and Louis Botha, were descended in part from a West African black woman married to an Indian slave. During the first twenty years of the settlement three-quarters of the children born to the Company's slaves had white fathers, and in the eighteenth century at least ten per cent of all marriages in one of the oldest churches in the Cape were clearly mixed.A study of the parentage and marriages of the Afrikaans-speaking group indicates that in 1807 at least a quarter (and, if unions outside marriage be included, up to a third) of that population had a black or brown grandparent. Very recently it was calculated that on average seven per cent of the Afrikaners' genetic inheritance is from black Africans (Fredrickson, 1981:112, 114; Freund, 1976; *Sunday Times*, 15 February 1981 quoting Professor Leon Hattingh). In succeeding generations a mixed ancestry might provide grounds to disparage a person's claims to status but the relationship would be between people personally acquainted and there is little evidence of sharp group distinctions based upon colour being drawn before the 1840s. It has also to be remembered that most of the genetic mixture originated from unions with non-Europeans brought into the Colony rather than from unions with the Africans native to the locality.

In the early years of the nineteenth century settlers living in the interior, and herding sheep and goats, dressed themselves in skins from their own animals. Apart from their ox-waggons they brought no technological innovations and, since there were no proper markets, they could not produce goods for exchange. The subsistence economy dominated almost everywhere until the start of mining, and it was a common thing up to the middle of the century for the Boers to be clad in skins (*Boer* is the Dutch word for farmer and it became a synonym for the white Afrikaans-speaking population). Thus the settlers had adapted to their environment, to the slow African rhythm of movement, and to the semi-nomadic pastoralism dictated by a soil that was rarely suitable for agriculture. The Boer was attached, not to any particular farm or any spot, so much as to his cattle. On the open frontier, wealth was reckoned in cattle and in sons. Sheila Patterson (1957:19) describes the frontier Boers as independent, self-reliant, unimaginative, tenacious, enduring, roughly courteous, hospitable, devout. The Boer lived, writes the historian G. M. Theal, 'under skies such as those under which Abraham lived. His occupation was the same, he understood the imagery of the Hebrew writers more perfectly than anyone in Europe would understand it, for it spoke to him of his daily life.' The open frontier was the territory which had not been brought securely within the scope of white power. In this zone the colonists had to attract indigenous labour with positive incentives, and alliances crossed the lines of colour. Whites were not all masters; non-whites were not all servants. There was less prejudice in these circumstances than within the closed frontier that marked the zone of white control and the reduction of non-white workers to a servile status (Adam and Giliomee, 1979:92–3).

A common way of life is only one element in the creation of a people. Equally important is the consciousness of interests shared in opposition to some other group. This was reinforced, after the reestablishment of British rule over the colony in 1806, by the setting up of circuit courts which punished whites for maltreating Khoikhoi ('Hottentot') servants, by the introduction of a rule making English the compulsory language in the Civil Service, and by the planting of some 5,000 British settlers amongst the Boers. Dissatisfaction with these measures led groups of Afrikaners to trek inland and take over land which, at that time, was not being fully used by the African pastoral peoples. A series of natural scourges including drought, floods, and African attacks, coupled with the insecurity of frontier life and the shortage of both land and labour, led to further migrations, and, in particular, to the Great Trek of 1835. This migration towards the north east brought them into conflict with African peoples who, from a military standpoint, were more powerful than those they had previously encountered.

Between 1816 and 1828 the Zulu chief Shaka brought together the Nguni peoples into a single Zulu state making himself master of 80,000 square miles of land, lord over 100,000 people, and commander of a much-feared army. The British had, in 1824, established a small settlement at Port Natal (Durban) to trade in ivory and skins. Though the Zulu were the more powerful they could see that the whites possessed weapons and equipment far superior to their own and the result was an uneasy balance of power. Though there was no common economic or political order, they engaged in economic and political relations that began, slowly and in a small way, to provide a basis for closer inter-connection. Small Natal tribes that had been scattered by the Zulu regrouped under British protection and Zulu refugees fled to the settlement. Alarmed that this might incite the Zulu King to attack them, the British sent him an envoy in 1835 to negotiate a treaty endorsing the King's power over refugees. This can be seen as an acknowledgement of Zulu overlordship. The British contributed trade goods and medicines, started farming, and introduced missionaries, all in return for a relatively unmolested existence.

The balance was upset by the arrival, in 1838, of a large party of Boer trekkers. They had started their migration at a time when much of Natal was unoccupied because of the devastation occasioned by Shaka's conquests and the difficulty experienced by his successor, Dingane, in his attempts to hold together his political inheritance. About 12,000 Voortrekkers journeyed into what became the Orange Free State and on towards the Transvaal, spreading a thin layer of settlement over the most desirable part of an interior already settled by a virile Bantu population. The trekkers had to fight. In 1838 Dingane put his mark to a document granting land to a Voortrekker advance party, summoned them all to a celebration and then put them to death, while a small English group looked on helpless. Dingane almost annihilated other groups on the eastern side, but to the west the trekkers held him off and in the end were victorious. The first trekker republic was founded in the Transvaal in 1837 and others followed; the trekking movement can be said to have ended in 1852. These republics were exclusive bodies. Some prescribed that no English and no Catholics could be members and that admission could be accorded only to people who were members of churches subscribing to the Heidelberg catechism. The Transvaal constitution of 1856 was also explicit in stating: 'The Volk desires to permit of no equality between coloured and white inhabitants in Church or State.'

The Trek has given rise to a potent series of legends, for the Afrikaners see their past in terms more romantic even than those cultivated by Hollywood's films of life on the American frontier. Their male ancestors are seen as god-fearing frontiersmen who had to contend, on the one hand, with the hostility, treacherousness and savagery of the African, and, on the other, with the unwarranted interference and dog-in-the-manger attitudes of the British. They were sustained by the piety and endurance of their women who had to carry a tremendous burden if they were to run a household and bring up children in primitive circumstances. The children too were obedient and conscious of the need for them to contribute in any way they could. This way of life was vitally concerned with local democracy, the establishment of law and order, and profoundly contemptuous of urban frivolities. These attitudes have not been abandoned and are vitally important over a century and more later, for the Afrikaner view of their own history influences their conception of other peoples' (see van Jaaresveldt, 1964). They say, in effect, that 'we became a nation in the face of British and African hostility. If neither of these much larger groups could crush our sense of nationhood, how little chance there is of our being able to prevent the growth of a similar sentiment among African peoples as the twentieth century draws to a close! Politicians can only guide such massive popular movements; they cannot dictate.' As Prime Minister Hendrick Verwoerd was later to answer a question from the Leader of the Opposition, concerning the possible independence of the Bantustans: 'If it is within the power of the Bantu, and if the territories in which he now lives can develop to full independence, it will develop in that way. Neither he nor I will be able to stop it.'

But this is to run ahead of events. The British had not been fond of the Boers, who had appeared to General Dundas at the very end of the eighteenth century as a 'troublesome and disaffected race . . . the strongest compound of cowardice and cruelty, of treachery and cunning, and of most of the bad qualities with few, very few, good ones of mind'; yet the British abandoned their good relations with the Zulus as the Boers continued their expansion. Before the year 1838 had ended the Zulu army had been defeated at the battle of Blood River and the Boers had taken possession of Natal. This battle is regarded by the Afrikaners as a turning point in their history. Many believe that God responded to their ancestors' prayers on the eve of the battle by giving them divine assistance, and this is commemorated annually by the Day of the Covenant ('I will establish my covenant between me and thee and thy seed after thee . . .' Genesis 17:7–8). The Dutch Reformed Church in South Africa has developed Calvin's doctrine of election, to conceive of a corporate election whereby God has elected the Afrikaner nation and given it a special mission to spread Christianity in Africa while preserving the distinctions between peoples which are part of God's design.

In 1879 there were further hostilities when the British, aided by a dissident Zulu faction, defeated the then King Cetshwayo and divided his people into thirteen independent units. Eight years later the British decided to occupy Zulu territory and exercise direct control. Struggles between Zulu factions increased the power of the relatively small British administration to govern the entire region. With the introduction of taxes and cash trading, with evangelization and the opening of schools, with increased migration by younger Zulu to work for European employers at the age when they would earlier have entered a Zulu regiment, and because of other changes, the Zulu became more and more dependent upon the whites. In his analysis of these events, Max Gluckman (1940) argued that it was money rather than the maxim gun or the telephone, that established a measure of social cohesion by creating common, if dissimilar, interests in what could after a time be regarded as a single economic and political system. The desires of the Boers for land, of the British for trade, and of the Natal colonists for labour, had brought them to absorb Zululand into the expanding industrial and agricultural organization of South Africa. That organization created situations in which some blacks and some whites had shared interests in opposition to other blacks and whites; for example, a chief and an administrative official would both wish to discourage activities which disturbed the established order; a missionary and an African Christian would combine in resisting the evangelism of a different denomination; a trader was interested in profit as well as in pigmentation. Thus the form of the new organization could blur the distinctions between black and white unless barriers were created to direct the new economic forces into segregated channels.

In the old Cape Colony the spirit of economic competitiveness burned only feebly throughout the nineteenth century. Local life, says Macmillan (1949:306), who was there as a child, was without the fundamentals even of organized agricultural industry: home-produced butter, cheese, bacon and biscuits were in short supply and of poor quality; like canned fish and bully beef, these were among the staple imports. The greatest export trade in fruit had not begun. No-one dreamed of manufacturing boots or shoes or blankets, let alone steel or heavy arms; the mines were far away and the Cape politicians were concerned with them only as contributors to railway and customs revenues. In the Cape non-whites could qualify as electors and there was a tradition of the formal equality of all men before the law. Maurice S. Evans, writing in 1911, thought that a visitor from Natal would be surprised by the mixing of people of different colour in the streets, on the tramcars, in the railway stations, and in the cinema – all to an extent that would be impossible in an Eastern town like Durban and unthinkable in Johannesburg. Cape Town was unique, but its lower level of concern about distinctions of colour raises interesting questions as to the factors which lay behind the drive towards segregation.

Group competition

The transformation of relations between black and white, and between Boer and Briton, can conveniently be dated from the often-quoted words of the Colonial Secretary in 1867 when he placed upon the table of the House of Assembly one of the first lumps of gold to be discovered, and said: 'Gentlemen, this is the rock on which the future success of South Africa will be built.' To start with, the mining of diamonds was more lucrative, over £1,600,000 worth being exported annually, while during the following century no less than £700,000,000 worth of diamonds was recovered. The mining boom on the Witwatersrand, deep in the Transvaal, attracted a huge influx of foreigners and foreign capital (mostly British). The Transvaalers saw these *uitlanders*, their industry, and their commerce, as threatening the Boers' newly regained independence and the way of life for which they had undertaken the Great Trek. They welcomed friendly advances from Holland and Germany as possibly opening up ways of resisting British influence; they withheld voting rights from most of the *uitlanders* and declined to change their administrative arrangements to suit the mining companies. The *uitlanders* organized to press their claims and then, in 1895, the so-called Jameson Raid set in train the events which led to the war of 1899–1902.

The British called it the Boer War. The Afrikaners, remembering the hostilities of 1880–1, called it The Second War of Independence. The British put nearly 450,000 men into the field, whereas the Afrikaners had 88,000 under arms. The fighting foreshadowed that which devastated Vietnam two generations later. It was possibly the first guerilla campaign, a struggle in which Boer marksmen inflicted disproportionate casualties upon British troops dressed in uniforms better suited to a ceremonial parade and trained for quite a different sort of combat. To deprive the Boer commandos of support the British rounded up Afrikaner women, children and farm servants, confining them in concentration camps which were struck by typhoid, enteric fever and measles; 26,000 prisoners died. Discussing the way these events are represented in the Afrikaner version of their history, Sheila Patterson (1957:37, 46, 240–2) quotes the ironically entitled poem by 'Totius' (D. J. duToit) *Forgive and Forget*, which tells of the little thorn tree over whose face has rolled a wagon's heavy wheels. The thorn-tree's 'loveliness was shattered, its young back broken through':

> But slowly, surely upright,
> The stricken tree has come,
> And healed its wounds by dropping
> The balm of its own gum . . .
>
> The wounds grew healed and healthy
> With years that come and go,
> But that one scar grew greater,
> And does not cease to grow.

This may serve to remind the reader that one group's conception of and attitudes towards other groups is influenced by the first group's conception of itself, and that conception is fashioned by poets, songwriters and historians as well as by politicians.

The union and the labour market

Leonard Thompson, writing in the Oxford History of South Africa, underlined the hostility of British governments in the 1860s, towards any proposals for territorial expansion, particularly in South Africa since it had consumed too much of the taxpayer's money without providing any appreciable return. Two policy options were recognizable; there was the

Indian model, of despotism tempered by paternalism; and the Canadian model, of delegating to the settler community control of their local affairs. South Africa did not correspond well to either of these situations but the British tended, hesitatingly and with many compromises and afterthoughts, to base policy on the Canadian model. The British colonies and the Afrikaner republics were to be joined in a self-governing, white-controlled, federal Dominion under the British crown, following the precedent of the Canadian federation of 1867 (Wilson and Thompson, 1971ii:248–50, 291). The war of 1899–1902 was a dramatic setback to hopes of incorporating the Afrikaners in such a political unit. There was a good reason to believe that the gold-mining industry would stimulate the economic development and modernization of the country, but this could not occur in a setting in which different ethnic groups led separate lives. The mining companies wanted supplies of cheap labour. The rewards to be obtained from mining were bound to attract a motley variety of individuals and many of them would acknowledge no obligations to South Africa. A political framework had to be created within which the many divergent interests could be regulated.

Sir Alfred Milner, the energetic High Commissioner for South Africa, wanted 'a self-governing white Community, supported by well-treated and justly-governed black labour, from Cape Town to Zambesi'. To ensure that this community was loyal to the Empire he advocated mass immigration from Britain and the denationalization of the Afrikaners by modern education and economic development. But, as Thompson says, far from destroying Afrikaner nationalism, Milner and Chamberlain were the greatest recruiting agents it ever had. Many British people, too, felt that their country had behaved in a foolish and bullying fashion, and the political situation was transformed by the Liberal election victory of 1905. Thus it was that in 1907, only five years after the conquest of the Afrikaner republics at a cost of twenty-two thousand men, two hundred million pounds, and universal obloquy, Britain allowed them responsible government. By the same action, of course, it also allowed them power over Africans living within their frontiers. The task of Milner's successor, Lord Selborne, was made easier by the influence of two Afrikaners, Louis Botha and Jan Smuts, who had been esteemed commando leaders during the war. They spoke for reconciliation. Firstly, within the Afrikaner minority *bittereinders* (Bitter-enders) were to make peace with *hensoppers* (hands-uppers). Secondly, Afrikaners were to be reconciled with British Trans-vaalers, by insisting that the war had been instigated not by them but by mining magnates and British officials. Thirdly, the four colonies (Cape, Natal, Orange Free State and Transvaal) were to unite. Fourthly, South Africa was to find a place for itself within a liberalized British Empire. It was this that was achieved in 1910 with the creation of the Union of South Africa and the swearing in of Louis Botha as its first Prime Minister.

At one time it seemed as if the movement towards unity would be thwarted by the commitment of the leaders of both political parties in the Cape to retain the principle of 'equal rights for all civilized men' under which a small proportion of non-whites were allowed to vote. The solution adopted allowed the Cape to keep its franchise but stipulated that every Member of Parliament was to be of 'European descent'. The African People's Organization (representing the Coloured community) and the Native Convention organized a deputation to London which was led by a former Prime Minister of the Cape Colony; though it gained significant support in England it could not affect the outcome. The British government was primarily concerned to see the new dominion established, although a minority of parliamentarians contended in vain that the goal should not be attained by sacrificing the political rights of Africans, Asians and Coloured People.

The Union's main economic problem was the supply of labour. Its ultimate significance was graphically described by C.W. de Kiewiet (1941:96):

> Of the resources that permitted South Africa at long last to take its place beside the Australian colonies, New Zealand, and Canada in the economy of the world, native labour was one of the most important. What an abundance of rain and grass was to New Zealand mutton, what plenty of cheap grazing land was to Australian wool, what the fertile prairie acres were to Canadian wheat, cheap native labour was to South African mining and industrial enterprise.

But, to start with, Africans were reluctant to sell their labour power to European employers. Nor was there anything about their labour that made it naturally 'cheap'; it was cheap relative to the cost of importing labour from elsewhere, and it was cheap because Africans were unable to bargain with employers and push up the level of wages to the point that would have been reached in a perfectly competitive labour market.

In the late nineteenth century, Africans and other non-white farm workers were bound to the service of particular employers; they were not free to move from one employer to another in search for better conditions or higher wages. When diamond prospecting started near the Orange River in the 1870s, black prospectors attempted to stake out claims but white miners persuaded the Cape government to declare that only white men could be granted diggers' licences (Fredrickson, 1981:216–17). After the Anglo-Boer War, when the mine-owners drastically reduced wage levels, there was a virtual strike by African workers so that the supply of workers dried up (Schlemmer and Webster, 1978:16). Since the mine-owners were desperate for labour, the British High Commissioner arranged, in 1904, for the importation of Chinese labourers on contract, and over 50,000 were introduced to work in the mines. To mitigate protest from white workers a schedule was compiled of skilled occupations from which the Chinese would be barred and this list subsequently became the basis for the claim that these jobs belonged exclusively to white workers. Criticism of the scheme was nevertheless bitter and, with the approach of Union, the British government had it terminated. The repatriation of the Chinese meant that the mining companies were forced, as the President of the Chamber of Mines said in 1912, into 'scouring' the Union for African labour and that this 'had led to unseemly competition amongst all employers of labour for the services of the natives'. Employers were bidding against one another for African labour, and, as minework was unpopular, this was forcing up African wages. To stop this, the companies agreed that all recruiting be placed under the management of the Native Recruiting Corporation. This reduced the costs of recruitment and kept wages down. Had it not been for the Corporation, the more productive mines would have outbid the less productive, but if the same companies owned both more- and less-productive mines they had less interest in making the best use of scarce labour resources.

Useful to them as it was, the mining employers' monopsony position (i.e., as the sole buyers) was insufficient to provide a supply of cheap labour. They had to recruit from all over southern Africa and every year imported over 60,000 workers from Portuguese East Africa. Governments imposed taxes to force men to work for wages. Recruiters encouraged Africans to acquire debts which could only be discharged by entering employment. All employers benefited from legislation restricting the contractual rights of non-white workers, like the Master and Servant laws and the pass system which made it easier to identify and apprehend absconding workers. Thus government collaboration was invoked to bind Africans to contracts into which they might have entered without understanding their full implications. The mining employers benefited further from agreements among themselves and from the control they obtained over their workers by housing them in compounds that resembled prisons. Mine workers were under contract to work a set number of shifts, but the wage system introduced by the Recruiting Corporation provided that, if in any shift a miner failed to shovel sufficiently to clear the face, or to drill a sufficient depth, that shift did not count and he had to work another. The Corporation also stipulated that the average wage paid to African piece-workers might not exceed 2s. 3d. per shift, and that any company which allowed the average to exceed this minimum would have to pay a fine to the Corporation (Johnstone, 1976:30–45). This was the maximum-permissible-average wage agreement, and it further reduced competition between companies.

The mining employers had also to compete for labour with the agricultural sector. In the early years of the twentieth century there was a common practice known as 'farming on the half' whereby Africans who owned their own ploughs and oxen entered into partnership with white land-owners. They worked the land, sowed their own seed, harvested the crop, and then handed over half of it to the land-owner in return for being allowed to cultivate, raise stock, and live on his land. This enabled whites (who often thought manual labour beneath their dignity) to farm with a minimum of effort and permitted the blacks to reap the rewards of their work in a way they could never do as hired hands. Many white farmers, like the Prime Minister and the Minister of Native Affairs, disapproved of an arrangement which offered Africans returns much greater than the wages most whites were prepared to pay. Another arrangement was 'Kaffir farming' whereby white farmers rented to Africans land they could not farm themselves. When there were a large number of rent-paying tenants the Africans lived together on a 'location'. Living in a village or location they could change jobs, bid up wages competitively, or even refuse to work and exact more favourable terms. Disapproval of these practices contributed to the formulation and enactment of the Natives Land Act of 1913, though the primary reasons for this measure seem to have been the general shortage of men wishing to work for wages and the fear (apparently without foundation) that many Africans were buying farms. The 1913 Act can therefore be seen as part of the white drive towards a situation of monopsomy by which the buyers of labour colluded to prevent anyone paying wages above the minimum. As Francis Wilson observes, for farmers the Land Act was what the maximum-permissible-average wage agreement was for the mining magnates (Wilson and Thompson, 1971ii:127–30).

The effect of the Act was to uproot hundreds of black South Africans. Hardest hit were the black *bywoners*, wealthier Africans who had built up teams of oxen and farming capital. Unaware that it had become illegal for any farmer to offer them the terms to which they had become accustomed, and unwilling to become servants, they chose to try their luck elsewhere, but found only disappointment; many ended up in the towns. The Act was a major step in the process of reducing the opportunity for black farmers to compete with whites, even in relatively unattractive circumstances; but it did little to prevent white farmers from allowing blacks to squat on land that would otherwise not be used. Nor did it stop blacks taking the place of whites on the land as tractor-drivers and managers so that the *beswarting* (blackening) of white country districts became as much a bogey as the *beswarting* of the cities. As early as 1832 there was evidence of land-owners replacing unsatisfactory white managers with Africans and the process continued steadily. As workers were attracted to the cities, rural employers had to increase wages (Wilson and Thompson, 1971ii:131, 145–6).

Another response to what was seen as a shortage of labour was importation. Indentured Indians were brought to Natal from the 1860s and many remained on completion of their terms of service. By 1887 whites there were objecting to the presence of the free Indian as a competitor either in agricultural or commercial pursuits. Their hostility was increased by the immigration into Natal of 'passenger' Indians. Once the colony was given responsible government, its legislature passed laws to prevent any more Indians obtaining the vote, in order to restrict immigration, and to reduce their ability to compete economically with whites. The Indians, under Gandhi's leadership, pioneered militant forms of constitutional struggle and at meetings of the Prime Ministers of the British Empire the Indian government pressed for recognition of the political rights of Indians in South Africa, but to little avail. The Union of South Africa was to be governed in the interests of the whites.

That is not to say that all whites had similar interests. With the growth of manufacturing industry the demand for African labour had been increasing, but the outbreak of war in 1914 further aggravated the labour shortage and intensified the conflicts of interest. Many of the English-speaking skilled workers enlisted in the armed forces and their places were taken by unskilled Afrikaner workers from the country areas who often had to be taught how to do underground work by the African workers they were supposed to supervise. These were the white workers most threatened by the competence of experienced African miners, so it is not surprising that they were also the most anxious about the enforcement of a colour bar preventing the appointment of Africans to semi-skilled positions. The labour shortage weakened the employers' bargaining power and they conceded to demands of the white miners for higher wages, shorter hours and a 'Status Quo' Agreement prohibiting the displacement of white by non-white workers. The concessions on shorter hours for whites reduced the hours worked by the Africans also, so that on average they were working five or six hours per shift instead of eight. Despite rising unemployment after the war, the white miners obtained further wage increases with the result that by 1921 white labour costs were 60 per cent higher than in 1914. In 1921, 21,455 white miners earned £10,640,521 and 179,987 African miners earned £5,964,528.

In the same year the price of gold started to fall. The Chamber of Mines informed the Mine Workers' Union that there was no alternative to a reduction in the wages of the white workers and it was eventually agreed that they would be implemented in August. Then the Chamber wrote to say that the regulations would be amended to make less use of white workers in supervising safety provisions underground, to which the union objected. Smuts, the Prime Minister, convened a meeting at which the representative of the Chamber agreed to fix a ratio of white employees to black while the union agreed to changes in inspection which would reduce the length of time African workers were kept waiting. Smuts was insistent on the need to preserve the so-called statutory colour bar embodied in the regulations under the 1911 Mines and Works Act which protected the jobs of some 7,000 white workers. He did not take the same view of the conventional colour bar guaranteed only by the private Status Quo Agreement, which protected some 14,600 white jobs. Frightened by the continuing slide in the price of gold, the Chamber acted precipitately, by-passing the conciliation procedure and declaring that they would terminate the Status Quo Agreement from 1 February 1922. The South African Industrial Federation, representing the Witwatersrand unions, was under great pressure because of disputes in coal-mining and the electricity-generating industries as well; it called a strike in all three from 10 January. Smuts told them that striking was profitless and that if they submitted their case to the Board of Conciliation there would be no change until the Board had reported. But, as often happens in situations of this kind, the two parties became more intransigent and some opposition politicians inflamed the situation. So on 11 February Smuts appealed to the employers to reopen the mines, to the workers to return, and promised police protection wherever it was possible to restart production.

In the next two weeks about 5 per cent of the workers returned to work and many more were ready to follow them. On 2 March the unions asked the Chamber of Mines to agree to a conference without conditions that would have the sole purpose of ending the strike. Two days later, the Chamber returned an arrogant and insulting reply which infuriated Smuts, who thought a peaceful settlement was within his grasp. The moderate trade unionists formed a new representative body which they hoped the Chamber would recognize, but at this stage union militants seized control and a general strike was declared. Among the militants was the Council of Action, some of whom were members of the Third International and committed Communists; they must have felt ill at ease when some strikers refurbished an old May Day banner to read 'Workers of the World Unite and fight for a White South Africa'. Only one Communist wanted to speak against the hostility towards Africans that the strike was generating, and he was never permitted to speak from a working-class platform. The militants were chiefly concerned to gain control of the Afrikaner strike commandos. They seem to have failed; murderous attacks were launched on the African miners' compounds (apparently in the attempt to provoke African retaliation and then a white backlash in the Afrikaner rural areas). There was a general assault on the police and the situation became one of armed revolt. On 9 March Smuts mobilized the citizen reserve and brought in infantry, artillery and aircraft. According to the official records 72 members of the police and military were killed and 81 civilians (though there may have been more of the latter). In subsequent court proceedings eighteeen men were sentenced to death for murder and the sentence was carried out on four of them (Hancock, 1968:62–88).

At the polls in 1924 Smuts' government fell to an alliance of the Labour and Nationalist parties who then formed what is sometimes called the 'Pact' government. This then implemented its 'civilized labour policy' by which many Africans were dismissed from government employment to make room for whites. One product of this policy was the 1926 Mines and Works (Amendment) Act, which provided legal support for the white miners' claim to all jobs classed as skilled. The Act can be seen as a further step in a process of reconciliation between whites, whereby white employers accepted that, if they were to maintain the prevailing political order, they had to purchase the support of the white working class at the expense, in the long run of economic growth, but in any event, at the expense of the non-whites.

Interpretations

In the brief discussion of 'theory and history' which concluded Chapter 6, it was argued that every historian must work with some underlying philosophy. Differences of philosophy explain why it is that historians with access to the same information advance different interpretations of the same events. Whereas scientific theory concentrates the student's attention upon sharply defined problems, the historian can control the multiplicity of variables that enter into his problems only by exercising a personal selectivity. In so doing he will be guided by a model of society that is either implicit or explicit.

Such considerations are very relevant to the debate about approaches to the history of South Africa that has been initiated by writers who find inspiration in the analyses of Karl Marx. Among them the historian who has most closely studied the white gold miners' strike of 1922 is Fredrick A. Johnstone (1976). It can be useful to consider his claims in some detail because they parallel other arguments about the merits of Marxist analyses in the field of racial and ethnic relations. The claims in question are scarcely modest. At the outset it is not difficult to agree that in South Africa a system of extreme social inequality has developed in which a relatively small group of whites has increasingly subordinated a large population of non-whites. But when Johnstone says that the past development and present nature of this system present difficult problems of explanation, it is well to pause and ask what kind of explanation is possible of *explananda* that are as general as these. For most scholars, explanations are deductive; something is explained when it is shown to conform to general laws. The process whereby understanding of historical sequences is deepened might be better called one of interpretation. For Johnstone, understanding and explanation are synonymous; this may not be of importance, but it makes a difference to the assessment of his claims. For this author is confident that most writing on his chosen subject reflects 'deficiences of approach'. Instead, he puts forward 'a Marxist structuralist approach, which sees and explains the system of racial domination as a product of the system of production of which it formed a part . . . its general thesis is that this racial system may most adequately be explained as a class system'. 'Explanation' is a reiterated theme.

The model of society which underlies this approach resembles that which C. Wright Mills had in mind when he described it as what was alive in Marxism. But to show that one model is more useful than another there has to be some means of deciding which one casts more light on a problem of interest to both contending parties. If the dispute remains on the level of the philosophy of history, readers will line up behind the historians whose philosophy they share and it will be impossible to compare the merits of different approaches. To make progress it is necessary to examine the explanation (or interpretation) of observations which can be accepted by those who utilize different models. For example, Johnstone (1976:201) summarizes part of his thesis by writing: 'We saw how . . . each group sought to maximise the benefits and minimise the costs which it derived from the racial system, by extending the scope of operation of its own class colour bar and reducing the scope of operation of the other group's. And we observed how and why this led to conflict.' Even those who are most firmly committed to a Marxist analysis have great difficulty deciding just what kind of class the white workers constitute. But, apart from this use of a contentious word, it is difficult to imagine the grounds on which any historian or social scientist might object to such a statement. It is surely common ground among all students that individuals who share interests within social systems, on whatever lines they are structured, try to utilize or modify those systems to promote their interests. To call those groups classes does not give the reader any additional understanding about the manner in which they struggle. It may well be that the leaders of a group are able to mobilize their fellows by appealing to the belief that they belong together as a class (just as other leaders can mobilize their fellows by appealing to shared religious identities). The non-Marxist sociologist has no difficulty recognizing that people are sometimes motivated by beliefs about class. It may be important to one historian to describe a colour bar as a class rather than a group colour bar because that connects up the description with a philosophy of history, but explanation requires more than that.

It might be better to take a yet more specific question like: 'Why was a general strike declared in March 1922?' This should surely illuminate the deficiences in previous histories and the superior explanatory power of the new approach. Yet Johnstone will not go so far; he does not suggest that a strike was inevitable; if the Chamber had been more conciliatory on 2 March, or if the union representatives had outwitted the militants by holding their meeting in a secret location, things might have turned out differently. Johnstone's account of what happened reads much as conventional 'liberal' history would do, though it makes use of an additional and sometimes turgid vocabulary. He also leaves on one side the question of whether a Marxist understanding of the nature of the system would have helped the trade-union leaders who had to decide what strategy to follow as events unfolded around them. This aspect may have been left out because it was considered in an earlier study which paid careful attention to the role of the Communist Party. It is an important question for those who believe that Marxism offers more than a philosophy of history. If it is a science it must provide a guide to action.

One of the leading communists at that time, Ivan Jones, argued that the abolition of the colour bar would benefit the mine-owners and, by depriving the white worker of his privileged status, lay the basis for workers' unity. The mine-owners represented the forces of progress precisely because they clamoured for 'cheap labour'. If this was the case, Marxists would be in error if they supported the strike. The contrary argument was that while the strike was reactionary in content it was progressive in form since it stimulated the growth of class consciousness among white workers. Their consciousness might be at fault in that they could not perceive their long-term identity of interest with the black workers, but having once achieved some form of class action it might be possible, under communist leadership, for the white workers to move to a more true class consciousness. Subsequent events have shown that, on its own terms, this was an optimistic view, since in most industries the gap between white and black workers has increased; thus H. J. and R. E. Simons (1969:276–7) in their history show sympathy for Jones' view, suggesting that a closer analysis might have persuaded the communists that the interests of the white and black workers were contradictory. There was little basis for a shared class consciousness since white underground workers acted as contractors who in effect hired African members of work teams and this made them exploiters as well as exploited. Whether this difference between the positions of blacks and some whites in the system of production was so important when the white workers had the vote and the blacks did not, would be questioned by those less committed to this kind of Marxist orthodoxy. In any event, Marxism seems to have been useless as a guide to action for the miners in 1922.

Johnstone's discussion of group relations in the gold mines in the period leading up to and immediately following the strike, apart from its substantial contribution to conventional history, demonstrates how that history can be organized in the categories of class analysis and criticizes attempts to organize it in alternative categories. A writer who seeks to show that his explanation is superior to that offered by members of another school, must first understand the explanation he wishes to supersede, and in this Johnstone has signally failed. He states that the predominant school of thought 'proceeds initially within the analytical framework of neo-classical economics'; it pictures South African society as consisting of two parts, the capitalist economic system – which is seen as harmonious, just, and functional – and the system of racial domination – which is seen as a dysfunctional intrusion from somewhere outside. Johnstone believes that neo-classical economics assumes that capitalist society is the normal form of human society and that it is a 'harmonious and consensual system of group relations, in which all individuals are equal beneficiaries from the existence and operation of the market economy'. Not surprisingly, he concludes that those who employ such an approach have been unable to explain the fundamentally conflictual, coercive, and non-consensual system of group relations in South Africa (Johnstone, 1976:204–7). But this is a travesty of the views of those against whom he argues. It would be equally possible to portray neo-classical economics as centrally concerned with the study of market imperfections and taking monopoly as one of its main objects of study. An economist who regards the process of competition as harmonious is a signally bad economist.

The nub of the contest can be found in the statement that the 'pluralist type of explanation . . . does not in fact provide an explanation at all, but merely amounts to a tautological redescription of the phenomenon to be explained' (Johnstone, 1976:209). It is a fair criticism, but it can be applied with equal justice to Johnstone's own redescription in his preferred terms, or to one which, like the present chapter, presents the same events in terms of a model of the forms of competition. The basic difficulty is that, while sociological theories can be useful in the writing of history, it is impossible to subject those theories to any rigorous test within the framework constituted by the analysis of particular societies. The unique features of such histories dictate the form of the analysis, and the impossibility of comparing alternative outcomes means that an interpretation can be only more or less persuasive to those who read it. Talk of explanation in any strong sense is out of place.

Group competition intensified

The Pact government which came to power in 1924 was led by General J. B. M. Hertzog, a conservative Afrikaner who had split from Botha and Smuts in 1913. According to Howard Brotz (1977:6), Hertzog to start with saw South Africa as basically an agricultural country, but soon recognized that the only satisfactory future for the rural poor whites was for them to obtain paid employment in the cities. In government he took over Labour policies designed to strengthen the privileges of white workers at the expense of blacks, while implementing Afrikaner desires for greater independence from Britain (as in the bitter tussle that led to the adoption of a distinctive South African flag). Afrikaans became an official language. Hertzog extended the vote to all white men and women. He founded a state-controlled iron and steel corporation. The character of his 'civilized labour policy' can be seen from figures showing that on the state railways, for example, the proportion of unskilled white workers employed increased from 9.5 to 39.3 per cent, and that of black workers decreased by a corresponding amount. After the election of 1929 Hertzog would have been able to form a government without Labour support but he retained Labour ministers in the cabinet and, as his problems increased because of the deepening world depression, he broadened the coalition by bringing Smuts and his party into the government.

South Africa's abandonment of the gold standard sent up the price of gold by nearly 50 per cent and the economy recovered. One of the main problems of the government was that the same forces that drove the poor whites into the cities also drove the blacks there. The *Report of the Native Economic Commission 1930–32* accepted the general white view that 'it is undesirable to encourage the urbanization of the Native population' (although that was just what a colour-blind policy of economic growth would have favoured). It stated:

> It is perfectly clear that a considerable number of Natives have become permanent town dwellers ... In the interests of the efficiency of urban industries it is better to have a fixed urban Native population to the extent to which such a policy is necessary than the present casual drifting population ... To continue employing Natives in urban areas, but to treat them as if they should not be there, is both illogical and short-sighted.

It would seem as if most of the whites preferred to be illogical and shortsighted. They wanted black labour but did not want the labourers, and certainly not their wives and children; they wanted to believe that the problem could be solved by developing the reserves and making these the basis for such political rights as the blacks should be allowed.

One of the obstacles to the formation of the Union in 1910 had been Afrikaner objection to the provision in the Cape province whereby members of the Coloured group could qualify as voters. The Cape Coloured people are of mixed origin. One study of blood grouping in Cape Town has concluded that they were constituted by approximately equal proportions of European, Asian and Southern African genes. In the United States they might be called blacks, but then it would be more difficult to distinguish them from the section of the southern African population which descends from those who occupied the territory before the European invasion – the Zulu, Khosa, Sotho, Tswana, Khoikhoi, and so on – who are now conventionally identified as blacks. George M. Fredrickson (1981:255–7) observes that indeed the Cape Coloured resemble the black Americans in their social situation and historical experience more closely than do the black South Africans; the latter retain distinctive languages and cultures that, in the United States context, parallel those of North American Indians Both black Americans and Cape Coloured make up similar proportions of the total population of the countries in which they live – about ten per cent or slightly more in recent decades. The proportion of Coloureds relative to whites in South Africa resembles the proportion of blacks to whites in the southern United States during the segregation era, and the position of the Coloured in the western Cape in recent times can be compared with that of blacks in the cotton belt before the great migration to the cities. Both groups were given equal rights under the law, including the opportunity to qualify for the vote, and then lost most of these rights when the whites turned upon them. Fredrickson contends that what happened to Afro-Americans in the period 1890–1910 was not fully experienced by the Cape Coloureds until the 1940s and 1950s, but in both instances there was a prior history of partial or customary segregation and an erosion of political and civil rights that anticipated formal and complete disfranchisement. Where the parallel is weakest is that one strand in white South African thought, supported among the Afrikaners by Hertzog, favoured the economic and political (but not social) integration of the Coloured with the whites, in order to strengthen the white section of the population in opposition to the 'natives'. Coloureds were expressly exempted from Hertzog's 'colour bar' legislation and they have always enjoyed privileges denied to the blacks.

The partnership of Hertzog and Smuts in government brought about the fusion of their two parties to create the United Party, but Dr D. F. Malan would not follow Hertzog, he and his associates remained separate as the Purified National Party. When the Second World War broke out Hertzog wanted the Union to stay neutral but he lost the vote in the House of Assembly and, as the Governor-General refused to call a new election, Smuts took over as Prime Minister. Nationalist Afrikaners saw South Africa's participation in the war as an action serving Britain's interests rather than their own. Economically, however, South Africa's position had been improving steadily during the 1930s and the wartime restriction of imports assisted domestic manufacturing industry. The discovery of new gold fields and the beginning of uranium mining were to stimulate an influx of capital and immigrants, both black and white, once the war ended. In 1948 Smuts' government, contrary to all expectations, was defeated at the polls and power went to a coalition of Malan's nationalists and the small Afrikaner Party led by N. C. Havenga, Hertzog's political successor.

Though the coalition had only a narrow majority it sufficed for them to enact a sequence of measures forming the basis for their programme of apartheid (separateness). They began by abolishing the Indian franchise granted two years earlier, and followed up with the Population Registration Act (establishing a register to record the group to which each individual belonged), the Group Areas Act (dividing towns as well as villages and allocating each zone to a population group), the Suppression of Communism Act, the Separate Representation of Voters Act (removing Cape Coloureds from the common electoral roll) and the Bantu Education Act (placing all Native education under government control). They made marriages and sexual relations between whites and non-whites unlawful. They segregated the universities and schools. It is important to note that the Suppression of Communism Act enabled the Minister to name as a communist anyone who had ever 'advocated, advised, defended or encouraged the achievements of any of the objects of communism' either actively or by any 'omission which is calculated to further the achievement of any such object', etc. The wording is so comprehensive that it gave him power to name as communists people who would not be so considered in any of the countries of Europe. Since at this time one of the main threats to the implementation of apartheid was the influence, at home and abroad, of white liberals and radicals, the government had to suppress dissent among the whites before it could impose its policies upon the non-whites.

The economic policy of apartheid can be seen as an attempt to prevent any competition between whites and non-whites, and, to a lesser extent, to reduce competition between non-white groups. It increased the opportunities for the privileged groups to use the power of the state to further their own interests. For many Afrikaners, ideological objectives were paramount, but they used their political power to build up the economic strength of their group so as to buttress these ends. The Nationalists have aimed to create a corporate state in which the interests of capital and labour are coordinated by state bodies directed by members of the Afrikaner political elite. The economic policy of successive South African governments since 1910 can also be seen, especially in its relation to the reserves or Bantu homelands, as one of extracting the maximum labour power from Africans at the minimum cost, indeed at one stage below the cost of labour reproduction. As the African subsistence economy declined, so employers had to increase wages in order to bear the full labour costs (Wolpe, 1972). This policy was facilitated by preventing Africans from organizing industrially to compete with the employers and, in so far as the competition was imperfect, they were exploited.

In March 1960 a crowd of Africans who had converged upon the police station at Sharpeville in the Transvaal, as part of a peaceful protest against the pass laws, were fired on by the police. On the same day there was a similar scene at Langa, in Cape Province. Altogether that day 72 Africans were reported killed and 180 wounded (many of them shot in the back). Later that year there was a referendum to decide whether the country should become a republic. Fifty-two per cent of those who voted supported the proposal, so the following year Prime Minister Verwoerd presented the Commonwealth Conference with a formal application for South Africa's continued membership as a republic. He encountered so much criticism that he decided to withdraw the application and returned home to establish a republic outside the Commonwealth. A resolution of the World Council of Churches in 1960 to the effect that 'no man who believes in Christ may be excluded from any church on the grounds of his race or colour' was explicitly rejected at all five synods of the Dutch Reformed Church in 1961, and the Church left the World Council at the same time as the state left the Commonwealth. In these two years South Africa's international isolation increased dramatically and there was a flight of capital as overseas investors wondered whether their capital was safe in a country that seemed to be heading towards revolution.

It is sometimes suggested that the course of South African history was fore-ordained. The Afrikaner population was growing more rapidly than that of the English-speaking whites. Few non-whites could vote. The main opposition to government policies was bound to come from the black population and, as their strength increased, the political parties would have to compete by proposing yet more extreme measures to reinforce white privilege. As Howard Brotz (1977:3–4) has observed, there seems to be a cyclical pattern in South African history. In 1910 the centre groups united on a policy of reconciliation between the English- and Afrikaans-speaking whites; three years later Hertzog split off to form the National Party and spent eleven years in the political wilderness before coming to power. In 1934 the centre groups united again but Malan stayed aloof for fourteen years until he, too, became Prime Minister. In 1969 after Prime Minister H. F. Verwoerd appointed two English-speakers to his cabinet and began to woo the English vote, Albert Hertzog (son of the earlier premier) broke away to form the Herstigte (Re-established) Nasionale Party; though the HNP increased its share of the vote from 3 per cent in 1977 to 14 per cent in 1981 it still won no seats. One in five electors voted for some form of power-sharing with blacks. One in five Afrikaner electors voted for the HNP, but so far this party has been no more than a brake upon a government seeking to reduce the chances of overt conflict. Although these sequences have produced what appears to be a steady progression, Brotz maintains that there have nevertheless been occasions when wise statesmanship could have strengthened or restored the centre: Smuts could have brought Havenga into his government in 1944 or could have broken Malan's coalition by agreeing to serve under Havenga in the period after 1948. Whether such a move would have been sufficient to preserve the Indian franchise and permit a liberalization of the regime is doubtful, but it tells against any assumption that the more extreme brand of Afrikaner nationalism was bound to prevail.

A state without a nation

In European history the sentiment of nationalism has often led to the creation of a state or the revision of the boundaries of states. Because the two have gone together in this way, Europeans have been inclined to interpret developments in other continents in the light of European preconceptions. When movements opposed to imperial rule arose in black African countries, Europeans readily called them nationalist although they were not based upon the desire of an ethnic group to acquire the constitution of a state as the expression of their nationalism; indeed, the boundaries of these colonial territories had often been drawn without any understanding of the territorial limits of ethnic groups. One of the problems of many of the new African states has been to create a feeling of belonging together amongst peoples who had little in common with one another prior to their experience of imperialism. Seen from the narrow perspective, therefore, there has been only one genuine nationalism in South Africa, that of the Afrikaners. They wanted to make the structure of the state suit their desires as a national group, whereas the African National Congress and most African political movements, at least until recent times, have wanted to foster a national sentiment amongst all the inhabitants of the country as a way of improving the existing state.

What was the character of Afrikaner nationalism and what its driving force? In the second chapter it was suggested that reds, whites and blacks in the New World were initially differentiated in terms of ancestry, appearance and socio-cultural status. The whites attempted to maintain a pattern in which ethnic differences of ancestry were congruent with differences of appearance and socio-cultural status, but had in the end to abandon this venture and allow one criterion to dominate. The policy in South Africa shows a determined attempt to maintain a pattern of congruent differentiation on all three dimensions. Whites, Indians, Coloureds and the various African ethnic groups were all to be kept separate even at the expense of economic efficiency and the growth of the consumer market. Such a policy looks to a West European or North American as if it were motivated by the sentiments they think of as racial or racist, but this is not altogether accurate. The Afrikaners, especially in reaction to Milner's policy of denationalization, were anxious to preserve their language and culture from anglicization. They saw themselves as a *nasie* (nation), or a *volk*, rather than as a race. Their culture could be maintained and transmitted only by people born into it and of an appearance acceptable to other Afrikaners, so ancestry, appearance and socio-cultural characteristics became signs of membership in the Afrikaner group. The arguments they use to defend their policies depend upon assumptions about the distinctiveness of peoples and the essential quality of nationhood (reflected most poignantly in the idea of a covenant between God and the Afrikaner people) and not upon typological or selectionist theories of racial inequality.

The Afrikaners' sense of a shared identity grew from their feelings of weakness in the face of English military and economic might. They were the little thorn-tree crushed under the wheels of the wagon that was thrusting its way in where it did not belong. Threatened by successive dangers, they had survived by being true to themselves. When, after the formation of the Union, poor Afrikaners moved to the cities there was little other than their complexions to distinguish them from the blacks, and Afrikaners saw in this a peril as great as any of those that had tested them earlier. Between 1921 and 1933 the number of poor whites trebled, making a total equal to about a quarter of the Afrikaner population. To Hertzog they were a sad reflection on the group he considered to be the pioneers of civilization in southern Africa, and a constant reminder of his people's social inferiority by comparison with the English. There was always the danger, too, that unemployed whites might make common cause with the blacks and form a militant non-racial workers' movement. A central element in the Afrikaner's outlook was the fear that the Afrikaner language and culture would be swamped by the strength and richness of English culture so that one of the themes of nationalist politics was the need to protect their language. The manner in which their country was brought into the war in 1939 strengthened their feeling that true equality with the English group would never be possible until they were their equals in power (Adam and Giliomee, 1979:104–60).

Middle-class Afrikaners, particularly educators and clergy, played key parts in persuading their fellows that they could attain individual dignity only through group identification and assertion. They were brought to believe that 'die party is die volk end die volk is die party' (the party is the nation and the nation is the party) or, as Dr Verwoerd was to assert almost without challenge during his premiership, 'The National Party was never and is not an ordinary party. It is a nation on the move.' This identification was perhaps the chief magnet which finally drew and kept the overwhelming majority of Afrikaners together after generations of schism and squabble (Wilson and Thompson, 1971ii:370) but it was supported by a clutch of economic institutions and cultural associations within which Afrikaners could cooperate with one another. As was noted earlier, the Afrikaner notion of their own identity has governed their conceptions of other peoples. As one spokesman insisted, the Bantu is neither a backward black Englishman, nor a backward black Afrikaner, nor even a backward black Bantu. He is a Zulu, or a Xhosa, or a Sotho, or a member of some other African nation. Government policy must be based on the Bantu authorities in the Bantu areas, not upon the denationalized Africans of the towns. So, 'once this idea is grasped that the South African Government is handling this issue not upon the basis of westernizing individuals but on the basis of civilizing nations, a great many things and a great many laws that must from the outside at first blush seem to be not only incomprehensible but also reprehensible, fall into pattern' (Pienaar and Sampson, 1960:9, 11, 21).

The logical development of this outlook was the Promotion of Black Self-Government Act of 1959 which recognized the various black ethnic groups as national units and introduced constitutional provisions permitting them to progress from being national states within the Republic to becoming independent states. The Transkei was declared independent in 1976, Bophuthatswana in 1977, Venda in 1979 and Ciskei in 1981. The population of these various territories can be seen from Table 2. The government of the Republic regards Transkei, Bophuthatswana, Venda and Ciskei as independent sovereign states able to send out their own diplomatic, sporting and other representatives, just like any other state. The governments of every other country in the world have refused to recognize these 'Bantustans' as independent, regarding them as puppets created to serve the political and economic convenience of the whites. Pretoria's policy is seen as a cover under which the government plans to push many of its human problems into regions with few natural resources, and, by declaring them independent, to disclaim responsibility for them. Afrikaner ideologists, on

Table 2: *The population of South Africa, 1980*

	Total	White	Coloured	Asian	Black
White areas					
Cape	4,907,867	1,211,720	2,191,325	27,695	1,477,127
Natal	2,535,234	558,044	87,753	648,768	1,240,669
Transvaal	7,884,223	2,274,239	217,215	111,966	5,280,803
Orange Free State	1,833,216	311,374	51,748		1,470,094
Sub Total	17,160,540	4,355,377	2,548,041	788,429	9,468,693
National states					
KwaZulu	3,187,981	2,370	1,888	6,154	3,177,569
Gazankulu	477,901	960	246	1	476,694
Lebowa	1,661,634	3,207	271	31	1,658,125
Qwaqwa	155,077	207	81		154,789
KaNgwane	160,044	92	67	3	159,882
KwaNdebele	166,543	48	6	12	166,477
Sub Total	5,809,180	6,884	2,559	6,201	5,793,536
Total, Republic of South Africa	22,969,720	4,362,261	2,550,600	794,630	15,262,229
Transkei (1970)	1,783,203	9,146	7,526	11	1,766,520
Bophuthatswana (1970)	903,883	1,929	1,229	32	900,693
Venda (1970)	272,452	540	38	3	271,871
Ciskei	635,631	1,798	3,471	9	630,353
Total, South Africa	26,564,889	4,375,674	2,562,864	794,685	18,831,666

the other hand, believe that just as it was impracticable for Afrikaners to live as an unequal part of a Union under the British crown, so would it be for black nations to be unequal parts of a white state. They seem to see no possibility of ever eliminating the racial inequality within a unitary state.

Much of the recent debate about South Africa has been directed to the examination of two alternative propositions. On the one hand it is asserted that capitalists have to utilize the available resources in the most rational way possible and that there is no place in such a system for decisions based upon racial prejudice. On the other hand it is averred that the legal restrictions upon the power of blacks to compete with whites are based upon group interest, not prejudice, and that if capitalism has any rationalizing tendency it is towards the rationalization of domination. Much evidence can be cited in support of each of these claims. A difficulty with both of them, as with any functionalist explanation, is that systems vary in their degree of integration. In complex industrial societies those who take decisions rarely have to live with all their consequences: very often some of the costs have to be paid by the next generation. When capitalists are in a position to take a profit they may not take the maximum possible if that would oblige them to change an operating structure with which they are familiar and to which they have grown accustomed. A lesser profit with less inconvenience may seem more attractive. The natural wealth of South Africa since the 1930s has been so great that her economy could tolerate substantial inefficiency and still operate effectively in international competition. The controls upon black labour created employment for an army of white bureaucrats; their wage bill was a public cost and their vested interest a political liability; the policies they implemented were dysfunctional from the standpoint of maximizing national income while bringing very real benefits to particular sections of white society.

The same evidence will also permit of a third interpretation, one which sees the structural transformation of South Africa as the outcome of an ethnic revolution (Adam and Giliomee, 1979:160–95). This emphasizes the ways in which the economy has been fashioned in the service of Afrikaner group interests. In 1948 the average income of Afrikaners in the cities was around half that of the English group. Though 59 per cent of the white population had Afrikaans as their mother tongue, in 1954 the Afrikaner share of the national income was one quarter. In mining, the Afrikaner share was 0.5 per cent and in retail trade but 6 per cent of the annual turnover. The new government in 1948 set out to help those who had voted for it and in the first five years the index of real white wages rose by over 10 per cent while that of blacks fell by 5 per cent. The government used the public or semi-state corporations to promote Afrikaner economic progress to spectacular effect. Afrikaners already dominated the public services, including the police, holding posts from top to bottom. Most of the English group were not perturbed about the anti-democratic aims and methods of the nationalists so long as business prospered, and an increasing proportion started to vote nationalist, but they have since come to resent the way in which the public sector of the economy has been built up and state power used to favour nationalist private industry. By the end of the 1950s the poor whites had disappeared. By 1976 those Afrikaners who were in employment were earning on average the same as members of the English group; they still had some way to go if they were to catch up in respect of income *per caput*, but, given the power they enjoyed in so many settings, it could be said that they had attained equality.

In the view of Heribert Adam, this sequence shows that an ethnic oligarchy underestimates the rising costs of maintaining its rule, so that the chief task of the state becomes that of crisis management. Having attained its main objectives the oligarchy is anxious not to lose the rewards, and its ideology changes. Howard Brotz (1977:79–108) found that in business contexts the Nationalist government behaved much like any other business though their labour-relations policies still reflect the Nationalist-Labour pact. In upgrading black labour an employer has been left to do what he wants – provided there is no protest from white workers. In commercial employment, black professionals directing other blacks may earn the same as their white equivalents. In industry, jobs are being reclassified so that, for example, on the railways black 'marshallers' do the same work in one yard as white 'shunters' do in another (but for a lower wage). Whites are gradually moved out of the jobs that are reclassified. In the regulation of labour relations a key element has been the exclusion of blacks (but not Coloureds or Indians) from the status of employees; they have counted instead as operatives. Blacks could form unions, but because they were not 'employees' these unions could not represent them in bargaining over wages or conditions. The employer bargained with the white union over matters concerning both whites and blacks. In 1973 there was a wave of 'strikes' in Natal when the blacks simply stayed away from work; they had no representatives with whom the employers could negotiate, but wages were increased. The government subsequently appointed a Commission of Enquiry into Labour Legislation and, in line with its recommendations, has extended the definition of 'employee' to cover all blacks continuously employed in the Republic; it has relaxed the restrictions on 'mixed' unions, and it has abolished the provisions for 'job reservation'. The Commission recommended that the regulations requiring separate facilities in factories and offices for persons of different races be repealed and these matters left for employers and employees to sort out together; this principle was accepted. Unions remain subject to financial inspection, may not affiliate to political parties, and may not sponsor candidates in elections, but the changes in labour relations over the last twenty years have undoubtedly been substantial.

Conclusion

It has been the easier for South African governments to reinforce the boundaries between the white, Indian and black African populations because those groups had distinctive cultures. It has been more difficult for them to maintain the boundary between the whites and the Coloured population, especially when there is personal contact and people can share interests which cross the colour line. Some 45 per cent of a sample of Afrikaners interviewed in 1972 indicated that they would call an Afrikaans-speaking Coloured an Afrikaner; by 1977 this figure had risen to 52 per cent. In 1975 47 per cent of a sample of Afrikaners thought that Coloureds should be allowed to represent Coloureds in Parliament (Adam and Giliomee, 1979:125). Despite the government's efforts to enforce segregation, inter-racial mating still occurs; how the consequences of previous unions generate present pressures towards assimilation is illustrated by a book about a school in Cape Town with a poor academic record. The sociologist did not intend to undertake a study of racial relations; without expecting such a conclusion, he discovered that the main problems of the school derived from the incompatibility between the government's notion of a clear distinction between blacks and whites, and the actual state of affairs in a locality where considerable physical assimilation had occurred. In some households some of the children appeared 'white' and others 'coloured'. Some parents and some children were 'pass whites'. The school needed to admit 'pass whites' to keep up its enrolment. The Principal, the School Board, and other parties had an interest in maintaining an institution which could deal with the anomalies of the racial classification system while any other solution to the local problem could well have been more troublesome (Watson, 1970). Because the officials were dealing with the anomalous children and parents as individuals, so, although they were classifying them as white or coloured, they were in a sense weakening the colour line. They were recognizing that whites and Coloureds were not really two distinct groups.

Boundaries can be reinforced in ways that ensure the social separation of population groups, but when these groups are economically dependent upon one another something more than force is necessary to ensure cooperation. As the Oxford History makes clear:

> The dominant facts of South African society are its interracial composition and development. There are large numbers of whites, Coloureds, and Indians, who have all contributed to the growth of the country, and are bound together by innumerable ties of interdependence in its industrialized economy. Few sectors or groups could be detached without serious disruption of the society. Moreover, the urban forms, the industrial skills, the educational system, and many of the religious beliefs were largely introduced from Western Europe, so that the contribution of whites is deeply embedded, together with the contributions of other racial groups, in the foundations of the society. The present cohesion of the different racial and ethnic groups derives in part from this interweaving of roles, interests, and contributions. It is not simply the result of the exercise of naked force (Wilson and Thompson, 1971 ii:470–1).

This interdependence will grow. The pressures upon the boundaries which the government of the 1950s hoped to make secure for all time will increase, from both within and without. The westernization of the black African population and the growing social stratification of their group and the Afrikaner group will create more ties that unite their interests across group boundaries. The whites are conscious of their international vulnerability and anxious for the future, while Afrikaner solidarity may be weakening. The government may retreat from areas where its predecessors imposed segregation and leave it to the parties to act in accordance with their own wishes. For example, the Theron Commission in 1976 explicitly recommended that scientific, professional, industrial, business and similar interest organizations 'themselves (and without official directives and conditions)' be left to decide whether or not they will admit Coloured as well as white members. Once the principle is established for one group it will be extended to others.

To assess the chances of significant constitutional change occurring peacefully in South Africa is virtually impossible, given the uncertainties of international politics, but in any such evaluation two considerations merit particular attention. The first is the country's rapidly increasing wealth. In 1980 the real Gross National Product increased by 8 per cent. With so much extra wealth in the economy it would not be difficult to eliminate wage differentials, to purchase the cooperation of elites that can claim to represent minorities, and to make the Bantustan policy more attractive. The second is that the South African system for reducing racial and ethnic competition has been highly bureaucratic, formalized, and dependent upon detailed legal formulations. The authority of 'the law' has been so used as to induce people to comply with restrictions that they otherwise would not have accepted. Because they see the necessity for law and they regard certain laws as desirable, so they are the less likely to object to others which do not command their consent. This system has moulded the expectations of many people so that they do not perceive all the alternatives that could be open to them and they acquiesce in practices which outsiders would consider intolerable. If the system were rapidly to lose legitimacy in the eyes of large numbers the pace of change could accelerate dramatically.

10

Changing boundaries in the United States

It is appropriate that a chapter on racial boundaries in the United States should come after a discussion of such boundaries in South Africa, since South Africa shows many features of the earlier stages in the sequence of interaction set out in Chapter 6. Racial and ethnic relations in South Africa centre upon groups which originally were distinct along many dimensions and sought to remain that way. In the United States the European culture and economy dominated those of the other groups to a relatively greater extent than occurred in South Africa. This created conditions such that the Native Americans, Afro-Americans, Mexican-Americans, Puerto Ricans, and other physically distinguishable groups could have been incorporated into the majority society in much the same way as the nineteenth- and twentieth-century immigrants from Europe were incorporated. From an early stage blacks in North America used the same language, professed the same religion, and participated in the same culture and economy as the whites. They did not have reasons for wanting to remain separate comparable to those of blacks in South Africa and they were better prepared to compete with whites. Without slavery there would still have been prejudice against people with dark skins but had slavery been brought to an end in a different way, or had the free blacks been able to secure a better niche in the economic structure, the boundary between black and white could have started to blur from the end of the eighteenth century as it did in Brazil. Whereas the history of South Africa is characterized by group competition, the history of the United States offers a more diversified picture in which group and individual competition often exist side by side.

Land

In 1491, on the eve of the European invasion of South America, the native population of the territory north of the Rio Grande was between 10 and 12 million (Dobyns, 1966). For three centuries the native tribes were powerful forces whom the Europeans had to treat with circumspection, but their position was progressively weakened by the spread of new diseases introduced by the Europeans, smallpox, cholera, and measles in particular. In the nineteenth century they were made to feel the full force of white demands, and by the 1930s their population had fallen to less than half a million; the immigrants had over the same period grown to number some 122 million in the United States and over 10 million in Canada.

The Europeans wanted the land. What they had to offer in return may not today seem of comparable value: gifts and annuities in money and trade goods, sometimes, but not always, including guns and ammunition. But the tribes were weakened by epidemics and could not expect to defend effectively the full extent of the territory that was theirs. If they would enter into treaties conveying land to the invaders, the British were willing to acknowledge the prior sovereignty of the Indian nations, conceding their title to the remainder of the land and guaranteeing them occupation of it 'as long as the waters flow and as long as the grasses grow' – to quote a phrase routinely inserted into the treaties (Dorris, 1981:48). Before them, the Spaniards, though they did not negotiate treaties, had also recognized that the Indians were self-governing and had insisted that there could be no legal transfer of land to settlers unless the Spanish government had approved the terms of the transaction. The British and United States governments later enacted similar laws.

In the late twentieth century, it seems incongruous to refer to an Indian tribe as a 'nation', but that was indeed the basis of the treaty-making, and it is fundamental to an understanding of the position of Native Americans as a minority in the present time. Whereas the minorities seek rights *from* the United States, the Indian nations initially granted rights *to* the United States; this implies that they control everything they did not expressly sign away. Their spokesmen insist that the United States should honour the promises its representatives made one or two centuries earlier (Dorris, 1981:62). Nor was the designation of native tribes as nations at all strange in the south east when British, French and Spanish forces were struggling for control and Indian support could be critical. Their leaders were given European titles and often commissions within the military hierarchies of the colonial powers (Peterson, John H., 1971:121). Where the settlers felt confident of their power it was another story. From the beginnings of the colony in South Carolina in 1670, the colonists made a practice of capturing and selling Indians into slavery. They took advantage of the Indians in many ways, allowing them to build up vast debts for the purchase of rum, and they brought upon themselves the Yamasee War of 1715 which almost extinguished the colony. Thereafter they were more careful. The colonists were ready to promote hostilities between tribes and between Indians and blacks, employing Indians to track down runaway slaves and to help crush slave insurrections, such as the Stono Rebellion of 1739.

Circumstances varied from one locality to another, but in general the colonists did not encourage Native Americans to participate in the economic structure they were creating. The only place for the Indian, as for the African, was as a subordinate prevented from competing equally with whites. The Indians, for their part, did not greatly desire most European goods; they did not wish to produce for the market or seek wage-earning employment. If they competed with fellow Indians it was for status within their own society. Consequently they did not press upon the boundaries of others' groups and the congruence of appearance, ancestry and socio-cultural status was maintained by inclusive processes particular to each tribe.

Labour

On the South Atlantic seaboard, in the region around Washington, a social pattern was established in the late seventeenth century whereby people were classified as either white or black; their classification determined their political rights and their status in every sphere of life. The pattern was an outgrowth of a form of chattel slavery new to world history. North America was an almost virgin continent, and land was readily available. The Europeans started farming on a basis of indentured labour: in return for a free passage to Virginia or Maryland, men in England agreed to work for a colonist on arrival. Most wanted to make farms for themselves as soon as possible rather than work as hired hands on another man's account. Land-owners had to look elsewhere for a supply of labour. They wanted men who would be obliged to work for them for a substantial period, and since most men found the prospect of setting up on their own so attractive, that meant a form of labour that was bound to a particular employer, in slavery or in a servile status. After the mass importation of Africans started about 1640, they found that source of labour in the slave trade. The early settlers were allotted land on the basis of so many acres to each head of household according to the number of people he brought with him (the headright system). Someone who owned a large number of slaves could claim a correspondingly large allocation of land. Chattel slavery grew from a desire to profit from the ready availability of land; since African labourers were more easily exploited and physically distinguishable, blackness and slavery became confounded. Then in 1776, when the whites declared that they had a natural right to life, liberty and the pursuit of happiness, they made it possible for the blacks to make the same claims of them as they made of King George III.

The Africans came from societies in which, apart from a very limited use of Arabic, writing was unknown; houses were built of wood, dried mud and foliage, and the transportation of goods or persons was on men's shoulders. Those Europeans who in the late eighteenth century pondered the reasons for Africans' technological backwardness almost invariably, certainly in Europe and even more in America, attributed it to environmental factors. They perceived the West African environment as harsh and hostile to cultural growth. They assumed that as Africans moved to a more temperate climate and benefited from the examples offered by white civilization, they would in due course catch up. How long this would take no one tried to calculate. At this time only a handful of men speculated about whether African backwardness could spring from some biological difference and be permanent. One of the main reasons for the unpopularity of such ideas was that people looked to the Bible as the authority on man's history. That seemed quite clearly to declare that all men were the descendants of Adam and Eve so any suggestion that different races descended from different ancestors was branded as impious.

It can be fairly easy to force people to work for a period of weeks or months, but to force them to work for years without hope of reward is much more problematic. As the supply of labour improved, slavery began to appear less necessary and for a time it appeared as if it might be quietly abolished. Then, unexpectedly, a great new market for cotton was created: slaves became more valuable and a consistent, self-confident social system was built upon slavery in the Southern states. The assumptions of white superiority and freedom, and of black inferiority and slavery, were fateful, for they spread across the United States and then to other parts of the world. A new kind of boundary between blacks and whites was constructed and embedded so deeply into the social structure that it took more than a century, and more outside pressure, to bring about fundamental change.

In most societies to call a man black has been to make a statement about his complexion. It can have that significance in the United States, but this use of the word has been overshadowed by another. The social vocabulary of colour there (with some exceptions where Asian, Native American or Spanish-speaking populations are concerned) presupposes that people are divided into two categories, white and black, and that everyone belongs in one category and one alone. To call a man black is therefore to say that he is 'a' black, someone identified with similar others who share a history, sentiments of solidarity, and the experience of second-class citizenship because of their category membership. Only in the United States has so clear a two-category system based upon ancestry been developed, so it is important to try and account for its special features.

An explanation must begin with the distinctive features of American Negro slavery. As Thomas Sowell (1975:3) observes, earlier in history dominant classes owned slaves but the source of their domination lay elsewhere; slave-owning was made possible by their wealth rather than being the cause of it. The United States, especially once the plantation cultivation of cotton started, was different. Slave labour is suited only to those kinds of production in which the worker can be forced to labour, for men will not work so hard for a master as they will for themselves. In an ideally functioning economy, selling a slave to the highest bidder would mean selling him to himself – even if he had no desire for freedom as such, but bid only on the basis of his anticipated future returns. Once, therefore, the ratio of the availability of labour relative to land had evened out, a time was bound to come when slavery would be uneconomic and the political system would have to confront the problems of its abolition. Had the economic and territorial growth of the United States after 1776 not been so rapid that time might have come sooner and the trauma of abolition been less severe, but emancipation was delayed by the introduction of cotton cultivation and the boom conditions which that product enjoyed on the world market. For the cultivation of cotton favoured the plantation, on which relatively large work groups could be closely supervised by a few overseers.

The plantation belt in the South stretched in an arc from Virginia down through Mississippi into Texas. In North Carolina it was relatively narrow; in South Carolina it was much broader, covering most of the land of the state; how big this belt was relative to the rest proved of the greatest significance for a state's politics and for white attitudes on every topic upon which slavery had any bearing. Where slave-holding was less prevalent and where slaves were held in smaller units there was less bigotry and less repression than in the cotton belt. But the pressure to subjugate the plantation slaves psychologically and physically was so over-riding a consideration for the white ruling class that they made this the dominant theme of all white–black relations, encompassing non-plantation slaves and free blacks as well.

If the boundary between black and white were to be relaxed then the restrictions upon the free blacks would probably have been eased first. The 'free persons of colour' came closest to being truly free during the seventeenth and early eighteenth centuries. There were already some prosperous black plantation owners in the seventeenth century and they exercised most of the rights of white men of property, some of them owning slaves. Well into the nineteenth century free Negroes legally voted in North Carolina, Tennessee and Maryland among the slave states, but during the 1820s those three states plus New York, New Jersey and Connecticut, either prohibited Negro suffrage altogether or narrowed it severely by comparison with that of white men. Moreover, every one of the new states of the West, as they entered the union after 1820, resolutely excluded the

244 *Racial and ethnic competition*

Negro from the vote even as they proclaimed their democratic virtue by enacting universal white manhood suffrage. The advance of democracy for whites meant less freedom for blacks. In the South the position of free blacks became more and more precarious: between 1829 and 1836, for example, six states in the South enacted laws requiring newly freed Negroes to leave the state (Degler, 1971:257–8). The free black population had to find homes in the somewhat less repressive states of the upper South and in the North, but even in the North new obstacles were being raised against them. As white working men obtained the chance from the 1830s to form trade unions, they, too, excluded blacks from belonging.

There is much evidence to indicate that in the South decisions about using free wage labour as an alternative to slave labour were influenced by careful economic calculation. If it cost $500 to buy a slave, it might be unwise to have him working on the waterfront where he could easily fall victim of an accident. When Frederick Law Olmstead saw that on the Alabama River slaves were working at the top of the chute while Irish deckhands below had to capture and stow the wildly bounding bales, he had his own surmise confirmed when the captain explained 'the niggers are worth too much to be risked here; if the Paddies are knocked overboard or get their backs broke, nobody loses anything' (Phillips, 1918:302, 384). Nor was it thought sensible to use slaves for draining malarial swamps or building levees that might collapse on the workmen. Slave-owners calculated the likely gains and losses from hiring out slaves as artisans and moved them between urban and rural employment as profitability indicated. Since there were fewer substitutes for slave labour in the countryside, demand was inelastic by comparison with the cities, where free immigrant labour was more readily available. Consequently the cities shifted towards the relatively cheaper form of labour and the urban slave population declined (Fogel and Engerman, 1974:102). When conditions were right, urban slavery was sufficiently profitable for it to expand despite increasingly restrictive laws and the risk of losing capital if the slave were to run away. Moreover, profit-seeking slave-owners were quite willing to modify the nature of the master–slave relationship when it suited them. Slaves in lumbering – which, unlike cotton cultivation, required both dispersion and initiative – or employed as drivers in the Carolina swamps, had to be given greater freedom and financial incentive. So did slaves hired out as urban artisans. Theoretically, as Sowell (1981b:97–8) observes, the slave-owners could have made most profit by allowing their slaves to purchase their freedom, but this was rarely allowed because the manumission of such slaves would have made it so much more difficult to retain the remainder in slavery.

There were many Southerners who believed that slavery was a major reason for the economic backwardness of the South by comparison with the

North. Cassius M. Clay, the Kentucky editor, condemned slavery because it degraded labour. It encouraged whites to see physical labour as degrading, while those whites who did work had to face the competition of slave labour so that their wages could not exceed the subsistence level which was the pay accorded to slaves. Slavery tied up capital, for the employer had to buy his workforce; either he had to pay interest on the money he had borrowed for this purpose or he had to put so much into the purchase of slaves that he had less over for the fertilizer or tools that would have lifted production. No factory owner in the North would think of buying his workforce; he wanted to be free to hire and fire. Moreover, slavery hindered the development of a home market for local industry because it restricted consumption. The economic arguments about American slavery are very complex, but there is good reason to believe that while whites may have made a profit from slave-holding they might have been able to make greater profits in an economic system that was not based upon slavery. Their long-term interests spoke for abolition, though most could not appreciate this while there were short-term gains to be made. More important still, there was no easy way of ending slavery, for how could slave owners be compensated for the loss of the capital they had invested?

At the beginning of the nineteenth century Southern slave-owners were not under very much pressure to defend the institution of slavery. The Quakers had decided that it was wrong and had released their slaves (though without admitting them to their own congregations) and the debate about the morality of slave-owning was stretching out to involve a wide section of the public. In previous centuries the whites had pointed to Biblical references justifying the enslavement of captives taken in just wars; some maintained that persons who were already slaves when purchased could be held in that condition; and they pointed to Saint Paul's action in returning the slave Onesimus to his owner (Philemon 12–16). But there were arguments on the other side and the opposition of moral claims was swept up into the political tensions between Northern and Southern states. White Southern slave-owners were increasingly put on the defensive; support for abolition in the South withered (though a motion for gradual emancipation brought to the Virginia legislature in 1831 only narrowly failed); the whites for the first time could benefit from an intellectual argument with which to reply to their critics. Previously they had defended slavery as a necessary evil, but in 1837 John C. Calhoun made a famous speech in the United States Senate in which he turned this around. He combined two theses. Firstly, 'there never has existed a wealthy and civilized society in which one portion of the community did not live on the labor of the other' (not for nothing has he been called the Marx of the master class!). Secondly, when these two portions of the community were distinguished by physical and intellectual differences, the disorders and dangers resulting from the conflict between labour and capital were reduced. The eager pursuit of gain should be restrained. Therefore, 'the relation now existing in the slave-holding States ... is, instead of an evil, a good – a positive good'. Some subsequent commentaries have misrepresented the positive-good doctrine by implying that the racial thesis stood alone.

After the first decade of the century, environmental explanations of racial differences were losing their force, but up to the 1830s open assertions that Afro-Americans were permanently inferior because of biological differences were exceedingly rare. This then started to change, though not all the defences of slavery were racial. George M. Fredrickson (1971:43–70) has pictured the slaveholders' conception of their society as caught upon a dilemma: was the African a dependant or child who might one day grow up? or was he an inferior species? Both possibilities posed problems for the aristocratic view of the social order. One variant of the view of the African as a child was the revival of Aristotle's assertion that some men are slaves by nature. The organization of society should take account of natural differences for it is cruel to force people to be free if they do not have the capacity to behave like freemen. Whites as well as blacks could be natural slaves. George Fitzhugh, the most articulate spokesman for this view, attacked Northern pretensions, maintaining that the patriarchal slavery of the South was less dehumanizing than the wage slavery of the capitalist North. The earliest significant statement of the case that Africans were members of a species inferior to whites appeared in a book published in New York in 1830. This second view was given more authoritative expression in the mid 1840s and began to gain ground in the following years.

There is little reason to believe that the non-slaveholding whites, the 'plain folk' of the South, would have sympathized with the aristocratic social philosophy that lay behind the doctrine of slavery as a positive good. Nor was such a philosophy likely to commend itself to the Southern white workers who found themselves competing with slave labour, and, as has just been noted, were sometimes employed to undertake the more dangerous work. Another aspect of the competition for work between white wage labour and black slave labour can be seen from the calculations of a Louisiana state senate committee in 1853 dealing with the construction of canals, levees, and plank roads. They discovered that the state could save $79,140 a year if three hundred slave carpenters and mechanics were used instead of three hundred white labourers (see Wilson, 1978:42–3, or Shugg, 1939:89 for details). With the extension of the suffrage to white males irrespective of property-owning qualifications in the 1830s, the white workers obtained the political leverage to ensure that their demands were noticed. They wished to reduce the threat of black competition by claiming that certain jobs should be reserved for whites; so they contended that blacks were inferior. This growing political pressure worked to create a more favourable climate for a racial defence as this took shape in the typological theory of the 1850s. George Fitzhugh deplored the doctrine of *Types of Mankind* not just because it was at variance with scripture, but because 'it encourages and incites brutal masters to treat negroes, not as weak, ignorant and dependent brethren, but as wicked beasts without the pale of humanity.' The political tide, however, was flowing in the opposite direction. The white ruling class, wanting the support of the white working class, came increasingly to adopt their views about racial differences and by the late 1860s Fitzhugh was describing blacks as an inferior race.

The maintenance of slavery was facilitated by the attitudes of working-class whites not only in the South, but in the North, where they feared that abolition might send a flood of blacks north to compete with them in their labour market. Such attitudes had indeed been an important element in the ending of slavery in the North. As John Adams wrote: 'Labouring white people . . . would no longer suffer the rich to employ these sable rivals so much to their injury'. If this was equally true of the South, then the objections of white workers should have been to competition from slaves rather than from blacks. But most poor Southern whites opposed the competition of blacks whether they were free or slave. Throughout the *ante-bellum* years, as members of labour organizations and as voters, white workers objected to the teaching of skills to slaves and to the self-hiring of slave artisans (they were able to get laws against the latter passed in most Southern states but they were not always well enforced). The simplest interpretation is that the white workers wished to minimize all forms of competition, and the rationalizations for objecting to competition from blacks were more readily available than those for objecting to slaves. If they could base a case on racial grounds it stretched more widely and was more enduring.

The importance of the socio-economic dimension in the development of racial definitions can be seen from a comparison with the British West Indian islands where English social attitudes had to interact with a demographic structure more like that of Brazil, since whites were far less numerous, and there were fewer white women relative to white men. As a result a special place for the mulatto was worked out in the law of Jamaica in the eighteenth century whereas in Barbados, where the demography was more like that of the United States, this possibility was rejected.

In the United States, the free blacks (who amounted to more than 11 per cent of the total Negro population before the Civil War) had to find homes and work in the Upper South and the North because, unlike Brazil, there was no niche in the Southern economy that they could make their own.

Competition from immigrant whites was too strong. Carl N. Degler (1971:241–4) cites some cases from Southern courts which suggest that in other circumstances mulattos might have been accorded a different status from blacks. Louisiana came nearest to this, but by the middle of the nineteenth century it was under pressure to conform to the general Southern pattern. In one case (Catterall, 1926iii:601) a white man appealed against conviction because a free mulatto had been allowed to testify at his trial. The appeal was unsuccessful. In the court of appeals the judge acknowledged that practice in Louisiana was different, remarking that from the beginning of the state 'free persons of colour constituted a numerous class. In some districts they are respectable from their intelligence, industry, and habits of good order . . . such persons as courts and juries would not hesitate to believe under oath.' This suggests that even without a distinctive economic position, when mulattos were sufficiently numerous and 'respectable' they could be accorded a distinctive status. In other parts the free blacks became the social elite of a separate Negro community, though the educational and social gulf between them and the mass of the black population was very large. Almost half the Negro population of the major *ante-bellum* Southern cities were officially listed as 'mulatto', so the social gap was marked by physical differences. In New Orleans, which was untypical, the mulattos formed a separate group having nothing to do with the blacks. In several Lower South states there were slave-owning mulatto planters who played patriarchal roles after the manner of the upper-class whites with whom they identified (Berlin, 1974). Elsewhere, the unwillingness to be identified with the ordinary blacks entailed, in Sowell's words, an unwillingness to engage in the kinds of community service work and charitable organizations that characterized other American ethnic groups in their periods of poverty, while colour differences made it easy for the black bourgeoisie to believe that ancestry in a genetic sense was the real reason for their higher socio-economic status (1975:41–2).

The position of free blacks was made very difficult, particularly in those states, and regions within states, where plantation slavery was concentrated. Sometimes they were forbidden even to send their children to private schools at their own expense; sometimes they were obliged by law to step aside or get off the sidewalk when they met white pedestrians. Their very presence was an indication to other blacks that they did not have to be slaves, and was therefore a challenge to the system whites had constructed, in which a black or brown skin was supposed to be the sign of a slave. The psychological strategy of the slave-owners was not to starve or maltreat slaves, for then they would have done less work, but to make them feel dependent on their masters. Olmstead concluded that the planters' policy was to train the slave to work and yet 'prevent him from learning to take care of himself'. Thus, writes Sowell (1981a:187), slaves over the centuries developed patterns of foot-dragging, work evasion, duplicity, theft and racial solidarity that were to remain as a cultural legacy long after slavery had disappeared, and were to handicap the Afro-Americans in the competitive world in which they later had to find their way. For blacks as a group, the greatest damage inflicted by slavery was cultural.

As Frank Tanenbaum (1947:16–17) emphasized, the claim that some men were property affected every aspect of social life. It led not to a society with slavery but to 'a slave society, not merely for the blacks, but for the whites, not merely for the law, but for the family, not merely for the labour system, but for the culture – the total culture. Nothing escaped.' Every institution had to be accommodated to the great inequality and made to reinforce it. Because of slavery whites as well as blacks had less freedom. Those Native Americans who remained in the South and would otherwise have sought wage-earning employment could find no avenue open to them in a social order which was intolerant of anomalies of status. The big plantation was built upon a finely graded hierarchy; in its internal affairs it could sometimes overlook the distinctions between freeman and slave but in its relations with the outside world that status gap could not be avoided. The other inhabitants of the state had to be divided into those whose interests were identified with the master and those who were aligned with the slaves. There had to be some unambiguous method for assigning individuals to one category or the other. The rule of ancestry did that more effectively than the assessment of appearance and socio-cultural status could do. It served the short-term needs of the planter class but it made long-term change the more difficult.

More land

The territory of the United States was greatly extended by the Louisiana Purchase of 1803 and by the terms of the treaty with Mexico in 1848. By the treaty of Guadalupe Hidalgo, Mexico gave up over one-third of its territory, and the United States obtained an area that was to become the states of California, New Mexico, Arizona, Nevada, Utah, and part of Colorado, as well as gaining all of Texas. This area was further extended by the Gadsden purchase of 1853.

The Spanish government and the Mexican government, after that country attained independence in 1821, had both made vigorous attempts to populate the Texas region through a series of land grants. Some were made to 'Anglo' (or white) Americans who were required in turn to pledge allegiance to the Mexican government and to become Catholics. While the Mexicans became anxious about the growth of Anglo influence, the settlers believed themselves to be racially superior, were angry that Mexico had abolished slavery, would not accept the conditions governing their settlement, and desired to be politically independent. In the end they revolted, and a little later the United States annexed the territory (Barrera, 1979:8–10; Estrada *et al.*, 1981:104–5). This was one of the events that led to a war which Ulysses S. Grant, subsequently President of the United States, called 'one of the most unjust ever waged by a stronger against a weaker nation'.

With the vast tracts of land which the United States acquired as a result, came a culturally and physically distinguishable Spanish-speaking population. They were spread fairly thinly over the ground, but many of them were land-owners until the Anglos dispossessed them by one means or another and turned them into a subordinate labour force who had to obtain wage-earning employment if they were to survive. One author (Barrera, 1979:39–48) proposes that they be regarded as part of a colonial labour system since they were a kind of unfree labour, paid at lower wages rates, restricted to the least desirable occupations, and were employed as a reserve labour force. Certainly this structure can properly be compared with that of black workers during the slave period and shortly afterwards; this comparison will be taken up towards the end of this chapter.

Abolition and its aftermath

The Northern victory in the Civil War of 1861–5 and the passing of the thirteenth amendment that: 'Neither slavery nor involuntary servitude . . . shall exist within the United States' (together with the fourteenth, guaranteeing the vote), marked the ending of an era and the possibility of transforming relations between whites and blacks. Legally, labour relations in the South were put on a similar basis to the North and it should have become possible to explain any differences between racial patterns in different parts of the country in terms of demography, economic structure, political relations and considerations of this kind. This prompts two questions: why was a two-category pattern maintained in the South? and why did Southern definitions of racial status become institutionalized in the North where the economic structure was so different? These questions are easily overlooked. A history of Afro-Americans is likely to take as its starting point the black sub-nation of the present day and to review the way in which it came to its present position. This is to read the present back into the past. Such a history fails to consider why the conceptions of who was black and who was white did not change as they did in other countries. It omits another dimension of historical writing, that of reading the past forward into the present.

It would be unrealistic to expect physical differences suddenly to lose their social significance, but the way was open for the blurring of the boundary between black and white. In Mexico and Guatemala the mestizos and ladinos tended to accept the Indians who adopted a 'civilized' way of life; at any rate, they erected few barriers to prevent their slowly joining the group above them in the socio-economic scale. As some blacks in the United States by their industry established themselves as more respectable than some whites, a pattern could have developed whereby people were differentiated on a basis of socio-cultural status and this could eventually have given way to differentiation by appearance, as in northeastern Brazil. Perhaps that will in the end be what happens, but for more than a century after abolition the idea seemed fantastical to people on both sides of the colour line. Though whites might think it important to reinforce the racial boundary to prevent blacks coming in, the blacks were interested in the more immediate objectives of reuniting their families, seeking satisfactory employment, adequate housing, and freedom from oppression. The boundaries that concerned them were those that excluded them from their rights as citizens. Yet, though it may not have appeared that way, there was a genuine question about whether it was possible for any group in the society to be truly equal with the remainder so long as membership of it depended upon physical characteristics and not upon a voluntary decision.

In the south after the Civil War, whites generally harboured a deep prejudice towards blacks, some of which may well have arisen from a tendency to treat them as scapegoats for the frustrations caused by the defeat of the Confederacy and the devastation of much of the countryside. White workers utilized beliefs about racial differences as weapons in what they saw as a situation of group competition. Members of the white upper class were less likely to see blacks as competitors (except for a brief period in some localities in which blacks were able to exercise their rights as voters) and more likely to want blacks to keep their distance because of the whites' concern to maintain their social status. Since there was a substantial economic and cultural gap between white and black (black income per head being about a quarter that of white, Higgs, 1977:46), whiteness will have been associated with a higher social status and this will have been one of the obstacles to a blurring of the colour line. It is impossible to write any history, however brief, of relations between whites and blacks after the Civil War without making any assumptions as to the factors which maintained the distinctiveness of the two groups. As the history is extended in this chapter, and the experience of the blacks compared with that of other minority groups, the nature of these assumptions will be seen to be more problematic than may appear at first sight, but it is best to draw attention to their importance at an early stage.

After the Confederate surrender the South was seriously disorganized.

There were no legal governments, no courts, and no money, since the bank notes issued by the Confederacy were worthless. It was in the interest of the federal government to get new governments established and to readmit the Southern states as soon as they could measure up to the requirements of Congress. To start with, the reconstruction of the South was in the hands of the President, Andrew Johnson, a former senator from Tennessee, who had been nominated as Vice-President by the Republicans to balance the ticket, and who succeeded to the Presidency after Lincoln's assassination. Unlike Lincoln, Johnson did not believe that Jefferson intended to include the blacks in the Declaration of Independence. Initially, Johnson's sympathies lay with the poor-white elements of Southern society from whom he sprang, but as President he tended to favour the white former ruling class of the South and became increasingly hostile towards blacks and towards proposals for promoting racial equality. By 1866 Congress had had enough of Andrew Johnson and the Radical Republicans took over the task of reconstruction. The Southern states were, one by one, readmitted to the Union, but in the election of 1876 doubts arose about the legality of the voting in some of them and the outcome of the election depended upon the issue. The crisis was resolved by a compromise which allowed the Republicans to keep the White House, provided that federal troops were withdrawn from the South where Democrats moved into the governors' mansions. Political control was restored to the sort of people who had exercised it before the war, and the period of reconstruction was at an end.

It was suggested earlier that in an ideal society people would behave selfishly in the market place and altruistically in the ballot box. The history of the South after 1865 illustrates what can happen when the majority behave selfishly in both the market and the political spheres. The black codes enacted by Southern Legislatures provided (at least until they were disallowed by Federal officials) a new legal basis for the old relationships of master and plantation worker; some sought to exclude blacks from the skilled urban trades. The whites had long known something of Northern customs of hiring farm labourers but they had dismissed the knowledge as inapplicable to their situation; they assumed that blacks would work only if they had the power to punish them for any shortcomings. In a radically new set of circumstances they quickly discovered that labour, particularly competent and reliable labour, was in short supply, and that they had to compete with one another to get good workers (Litwack, 1979:364–71, 420–37). To start with, landlords resented the new bargaining power of the blacks and responded by forming combinations (or 'cartels') in which, for example, they agreed not to allow tenants more than one-eighth of the net proceeds of the sale of the crops they raised. These attempts failed, perhaps because the landlords demanded too much, but certainly because of the overall labour shortage and the landlords' inability to force other landlords to follow a common policy in a market geared to individual competition. An analysis of the evidence about wage rates in Southern agriculture between 1898 and 1902 found very little difference in the wages of blacks and whites; the productivity of the two groups was similar and white farm workers had no alternative but to accept the same terms of employment as blacks (Higgs, 1977:64–6). Attempts to prevent the purchase of farmland by blacks also failed.

The job market for skilled tradesmen in the cities permitted a greater measure of discrimination where trade unions were able to establish monopoly power. Not all craft unions discriminated, and not all that tried to exclude blacks from a particular occupation were successful. The US Labor Department recorded information on 50 strikes which were called during the last two decades to resist the employment of blacks; 38 of these failed to secure their objective. But often, and perhaps particularly in the South, such conflicts never occurred because the employers, fearing trouble from the white employees, refused to hire blacks in the first place. The key to the lesser incidence of racial discrimination in Southern agriculture, what Robert Higgs (1977:59) calls the black man's 'most precious jewel of emancipation' was mobility. He could get equal terms by finding another landlord. This may sometimes have been fairly expensive, for it could entail making many enquiries, and it could sometimes have been risky. The vagrancy laws could be so used as to make it dangerous for a black man to withdraw from his employment, to dispute an employer's statements, to sue for wages due, or to challenge a storekeeper's account of a debt. One incident suffices to explain why: a black man convicted of stealing a potato valued at 5 cents was sentenced to a fine of $25 or six months' labour on the chain gang.

The greatest obstacles to black progress stemmed from their inability to achieve free and equal participation in the political processes, of voting, holding office and influencing the exercise of governmental power. Whites enforced the laws so as to keep the blacks subordinate. They saw that much less money was spent on black schools. As Higgs (1977:124) writes, 'even if competitive forces in the labor market assured black workers a wage commensurate with their productivity, the fact remained that illiterate, ignorant, and untrained workers were simply not very productive'. Unequal spending on schools was a major handicap to black progress. It is impressive, therefore, that on Higgs' calculations (1977:102, 117, 126; 1978:99) between 1867–8 and 1900, black real income per head probably more than doubled and that black incomes grew more rapidly than white. Blacks were a long way behind, with an income per head in 1900 possibly about 35 per cent of the corresponding white level for the United States as a whole; they were slowly catching up, but one obstacle was that the disappointments were so frequent that they could sap the will of men and women to continue trying. A vicious circle was created when discrimination reduced black competitiveness and thereby evoked more discrimination.

The 1880s appear to have been a decade in which blacks and whites in the North were mixing on a basis of greater equality than ever before. A series of visitors very favourably contrasted the position with that obtaining in the South, including a black journalist who returned after a visit to his native South Carolina an astonished man. He had watched a black policeman arrest a white man 'under circumstances requiring coolness, prompt decision and courage'. Testimony about mixing in restaurants, places of entertainment and cemeteries was reported even from Mississippi (Woodward, 1957:17–24).

Yet, in the struggle for power in the political realm and for the conscience of the nation, the newly won rights of blacks were being cut back. Of major importance was a sequence of three Supreme Court decisions which virtually deprived the blacks of the rights conferred upon them by the fourteenth amendment. These were the 1873 judgement in the *Slaughter House Cases*, which curtailed the privileges recognized as being under federal protection; the 1883 declaration that the Civil Rights Act of 1875 was unconstitutional; and the 1896 affirmation in the vital case of *Plessy v. Ferguson*. Plessy had objected to being required to ride in a separate 'Jim Crow' coach, maintaining that this stamped him with a 'badge of inferiority'. The Supreme Court dismissed his appeal, holding that it was not unconstitutional for blacks to be offered only 'separate but equal' facilities. These facilities can rarely have been equal in any significant sense. So the colour line was legitimated and extended. In courts of law separate Bibles were used for white and black witnesses to take the oath. In restrooms, water fountains, cinemas and theatres, the races were segregated. Public parks were opened occasionally for a 'Coloured Day'.

The 'Redemption' of 1876 was achieved under the leadership of the Southern upper-class conservatives who were able to establish the improving public atmosphere of the 1880s. Lower-class white attitudes were much less favourable. Before the decade was out, the Conservatives were losing their grip; a sequence of bad harvests led to agrarian impoverishment and to a storm of discontent which expressed itself in a new political movement: Populism. Initially the Populist white farmers espoused the cause of the blacks; their leader, Tom Watson, told the two races: 'You are made to hate each other because upon that hatred is rested the keystone of the arch of financial despotism which enslaves you both.' For a time, blacks and Southern poor whites experienced a degree of fellowship. The conservatives became desperate: willing to use any weapons to defeat this new threat, they made common cause with the blacks' enemies. They bought black votes, or, in black sections, recorded black voters as polling on their side whether or not these voters went near the polls. Since the blacks were not strong enough to defend their political rights, and since the existence of those rights seemed to invite such fraud, the whites agreed that these rights should be abrogated. By 1904 Tom Watson was supporting black disfranchisement so that whites should be able to divide on the political issues. The extent of such moves can be gauged from the speech of a Pennsylvania congressman in 1901 when he declared: 'In the seven districts of Mississippi the total vote cast for all Congressional candidates in 1890 was 62,652; in 1898, 27,045. In the seven districts of South Carolina the total vote in 1890 was 73,522 and 28,831 in 1898. In the six districts of Louisiana 74,542 in 1890 and 33,161 in 1898.' He added that one member of the House representing six counties in South Carolina, with an 1890 population of 158,851, had been elected on the votes of 1,765 persons (Deloria, 1981:14).

The agrarian impoverishment of the 1890s caused white farmers to flock into the cities, with consequences similar to the migration in South Africa a little later. In Greensboro, North Carolina, white employers fired blacks from lumber, woodworking and furniture factories to replace them with white men and boys. At the same time white women were given the jobs which black women had held in the tobacco factories. Whereas in 1870 nearly 30 per cent of Afro-American workers in Greensboro had been employed in skilled occupations, by 1910 the figure had dropped to 8 per cent. In 1884 16 per cent of the black labour force had held jobs comparable to those of whites in city factories but by 1910 not a single black was listed as a factory worker despite the greatly increased employment in textiles (Chafe, 1980:15).

In 1890 income per head in the South was about half that in the United States as a whole. Cotton prices averaged 7 cents a pound that decade. Gradually the price increased, jumping to an average of 25 cents a pound during 1916–20, and though the 1920s saw a recession, the relative position of the South improved so that by 1950 Southern real income per head had reached about seven-tenths of the national average. Spending on black schools declined sharply during the period 1890–1915, which will have put blacks at a greater disadvantage in seeking work (indeed the quality of black schools may not have regained the 1890 level until after 1945 – see Barry R. Chiswick's comments in Freeman, 1974:559). Nevertheless, blacks and whites both participated almost equally in the advance, as can be seen from several economic indices, though the gap between them remained steady. This gap explains the one index on which the figures for blacks and whites sharply diverged: that of migration out of the South, which by the 1940s had risen to 17 per cent per annum for blacks compared to 3 per cent for whites.

As Robert Higgs (1978:100) concludes, 'during the first half of the twentieth century in the South, the battle for achievement of racial economic equality had been fought and lost.'

There is good reason to believe that the whites wished to keep blacks in a subordinate position, but it is also clear that in competitive markets white employers were obliged to offer black workers the same wage rates as white workers whether they liked it or not. That they were forced to treat them equally in market relations may possibly have increased their determination to maintain a hard boundary in racial relations, but there is also evidence that, where the option was open, whites were more concerned to make money than to cultivate their prejudices. White shoppers would not pay more for goods so that they could be served by a white instead of a black in a store, and not many blacks responded to appeals to spend their money in black-owned stores if the prices there were higher. Robert Higgs shows that three important conclusions can be drawn: firstly, that it was uncommon for a Southern employer to pay blacks less than whites for doing the same work under similar conditions; secondly, that the black labour force was concentrated in segregated areas and occupations in which blacks gave neither orders nor advice to whites. Thirdly, that colour lines and black earnings moved backwards and forwards as population movements affected the composition of the labour market. Statistics concerning non-farm occupations in 1900–9 reinforce those from agricultural employment in suggesting that although there was no wage discrimination, blacks were concentrated in the lower paying regions, the lower paying industries, the lower paying services and the lower paying jobs within them. The reasons for the initial location of the blacks in the South, and in that part of the South which benefited least from industrialization, were historical. The reasons for their other disadvantages were their lower levels of skill (because of less schooling and less training) and that a white employer, faced by two job applicants of apparently equal ability, would choose the white one. Any good jobs which were in the gift of state and local governments were reserved for whites.

These considerations help explain why there were certain general variations in black wages and incomes, but they do not account for particular cases of black disadvantage stemming from lack of political power. Mobility might be the most precious jewel of emancipation but not everyone could benefit from it 60 or 70 years later. Individual black men isolated from kinsfolk and ignorant of how best to look after their own interests were at times captured and subjected to peonage with the cooperation of local judges and police officers (Daniel, 1972). Walter White, Secretary of the National Association for the Advancement of Colored People, reporting on an investigation into events in Mississippi, wrote 'the most significant injustice is the denial to Negroes of the right to free movement and of the privilege of selling their services to the highest bidder' (Daniel, 1972:163). Allison Davis and his colleagues (1941:401, 378, 261) maintained that intimidation had bred in the black man a reluctance to press for his rights. They were sure that upper-class whites could use political pressure to depress black wages in the industrial sector so that they would not have to be raised on the farms. Then when, during the depression, whites set out to take over jobs previously regarded as being for blacks, they could resort to violence whereas it was dangerous for blacks to reply in kind. The market may have worked to reduce racial inequalities, but its operation was significantly qualified by white political power.

How then are racial inequalities ever reduced? Robert Higgs (1978:112–16) shows how the concept of equilibrium as this is used in economic theory can be brought to bear illuminatingly on the limited range of historical evidence. At one point in time there will be a given number of workers seeking employment and a given demand for labour by employers. The relation between demand and supply will be the main factor determining the level of wages, and the labour market will be in equilibrium. Consider what then happens if there is a major change either in supply (because a lot of workers emigrate or because there is a war and they are recruited to the armed forces or to war industries) or, for that matter, if there is a major change in demand (on account of a sudden depression). After such an event a new equilibrium is established. The important question, though, is that of how to move from one equilibrium to another without depending upon some extraneous and undesirable convulsion, like a war, to shake up the system and force through the changes that are desired.

The list of factors which can operate so as to maintain an economic equilibrium incorporating racial inequality and slowing down the competitive forces that might reduce it is quite a long one. In the first place, whites in the South displayed an aversion from any contact with blacks except in relationships in which they played the superior part. Since there were some relationships which had to be treated differently they came to an understanding that conduct in certain situations, in particular those which might imply a claim to social equality or which involved relations between black men and white women, were to be judged by racial criteria and black subordination was to be enforced. Conduct in other situations, such as those entailing market relations, was to be regulated by non-racial criteria, such as those of economic advantage or socio-economic status. W. Lloyd Warner described the system as exemplifying 'colour-caste'. Blacks were subordinate in situations defined by caste norms, but, in others, class distinctions were recognized within the white group, within the black group, and in certain black–white contacts. Thus in a study of Natchez, Mississippi, it is reported that a lower-class white woman pointed a pistol at a respectable black professional man; he knocked it from her hand. She ran down one of the main business streets shouting, 'that nigger struck me!' (i.e. she represented it as an offence against caste norms). The woman had the black man arrested, but the judge, refusing to regard it as a matter of caste, threw the case out of court (Davis *et al.*, 1941:477; cf. Banton, 1967:143–55). The sharp differentiation between the situations in which racial norms did and did not apply made it easier for whites to maintain their preference for segregation in social relations while admitting changes in economic relations.

In the second place, whites professed many inaccurate beliefs about the capacities of blacks and often maintained these beliefs in the face of contrary evidence. That the beliefs were wrong did not make them the less important as determinants of white behaviour. If, as seems to have been the general pattern, others made life difficult for whites who did not share their attitudes, there will have been few non-discriminating employers around to create competition in new sectors. In the third place, if white employers entertained the possibility that there might be black workers able to fill job vacancies, they would often have had to take considerable trouble to search for them because many of these blacks will have been discouraged from applying; other whites will have been ready to assert that there were no blacks with the skills required and will have been quick to question the motives of an employer who searched very hard. In the fourth place, to hire blacks for what was considered a white man's job will have been likely to occasion trouble, and the behaviour of employers is often characterized by 'risk aversion'; moreover, hiring blacks could in some circumstances mean that the whole work force in a particular occupation would have to change over from white to black and there would therefore be turnover costs. Finally it should be remembered that many of a white employer's attitudes towards blacks will have been formed during his childhood and will not easily have been changed during his adult years. Nor will many employers in a region like the South have been trying to make the maximum possible profits; many will have been anxious about their standing in the communities in which they lived and reluctant to take steps they might see as putting their reputations at risk. Empirical studies of businessmen's decision-making do not bear out the academic supposition that they are constantly seeking maximum profit.

There may not have been so many factors on the black side which could help maintain a racially unequal economic equilibrium, but cumulatively they could have been very important. Most are brought together in the notion, already mentioned, of a vicious circle, in which the experience, or expectation, of discrimination, depresses black morale, encourages any tendency to live for the present, discourages saving, reduces aspirations, and diverts people's energies. It is also worth remembering that W. E. B. DuBois thought that ten years more of slavery would not have done so much harm to the development of the Negro race in America as the failure of the Freedman's Bank, so great must that discouragement have been to blacks who were trying to save money.

If considerations such as these reinforce customary expectations of employer–employee relations, then it is not surprising that when, in the form of black emigration, competitive forces began to put pressure on the Southern labour market, the employers first responded not by raising wages but by coercive measures designed to stop the emigration. Laws were passed to suppress the activities of labour agents recruiting for the North: they were required to obtain licences which were priced prohibitively high; sometimes they were attacked or prosecuted and heavily fined. The police also made mass arrests of migrants congregating at railway stations and held them on trumped-up charges in the attempt, usually unsuccessful, to make them change their plans. In the end the employers had to adjust to the new circumstances, but the strength of their resistance shows how political power can be deployed to maintain a market equilibrium and that it can take major changes coming from outside the region to reduce customary patterns of inequality.

Ethnic succession and achievement

The principal characteristic of immigration into the United States during the nineteenth century is well stated in the verse upon the Statue of Liberty:

> . . . Give me your tired, your poor,
> Your huddled masses yearning to breathe free,
> The wretched refuse of your teeming shore,
> Send these, the homeless, tempest-tost to me . . .

The immigrants were economic or political refugees coming in at the bottom of the social scale, knowing less about life in the United States than those already established and therefore less of a threat to them. Had they been not 'wretched refuse' but challengers for the better-paying jobs held by the established population, there would have been more vocal demands for restrictions upon immigration. As it was, immigrants to the Northeastern cities usually were in competition with those who had arrived just before them, and with black workers moving up from the South, and this competition often took on a group character. It retarded any blurring of the colour line there also.

Discrimination against blacks in New England and New York has a long history, and though there was some alleviation of segregation in the decades leading to the Civil War, working-class white hostility towards blacks was often fierce. The North forced the South to abandon slavery, but did not' change its own practices in any corresponding fashion. Between 1865 and 1866 Connecticut, Wisconsin, Minnesota, Kansas, Ohio and Michigan refused to grant blacks the right to vote. Ironically, prejudice against blacks was strong in the region close to the northwestern frontier of settlement, particularly in the states of Ohio, Indiana and Illinois which passed laws to restrict competition from the few black residents, and further laws to prevent any more blacks settling there. Many of the settlers there had previously been non-slave-holding whites in the upper South; they had some experience of competing with slave labour and wanted no more.

Between 1820 and 1919 about 33 million immigrants entered the United States. They came in waves: the Irish formed the bulk of the influx between 1820 and 1859, after which the Germans became the largest group for three decades. Immigration from Scandinavia rose to its highest relative strength in the 1880s; in the next three decades to 1919, Italians, and Jews from Russia, overtook the Germans, though there was also at this time substantial immigration from Austria-Hungary. Each ethnic group had its distinctive characteristics. Those who came in the first part of the century found a largely agrarian country in which, towards the end of that period, there was work in the construction of railroads and canals. These conditions offered opportunities to the Irish, who, lacking the capital and the skills needed to start up as farmers, and unable to compete successfully with more skilled English immigrants for artisan occupations, most often became manual labourers. German immigrants brought with them more capital, and, like immigrants from Britain, they were better able to move on to other parts of the United States instead of remaining in the northeastern cities. The Scandinavians, too, intended to continue as farmers and moved on to the northwestern frontier settling in greatest numbers in Minnesota.

When, fifty years after the Irish, the Italians and Jews arrived, they found an already industrial economy. Apart from openings in transportation, construction, metal and other heavy industries, there were opportunities for them – which had not been available to the Irish – to move into office work and the professions. Until the end of the century at least 90 per cent of all black Americans lived in the South, though by 1860 the half-million 'free persons of colour' were almost equally divided between South and North; after the war the numbers of blacks in Northern cities increased slightly but in 1880 they were only 1.6 per cent of the population of New York, 1.3 per cent of Chicago, 3.7 per cent of Philadelphia and 1.6 per cent of Boston.

As William J. Wilson (1978:48–50) has recently emphasized, much of the prejudice which blacks encountered in the North was associated with competition for jobs. He says that the violent attacks upon blacks in the draft riots, which in 1863 entailed the killing of a thousand people, were prompted by Irish resentment at being forced to fight in a war which was expected to lead to the abolition of slavery and a mass influx of black workers who would weaken the position of other workers. The Irish repeatedly voted against proposals to extend political rights to blacks and successfully eliminated blacks from many low-paying occupations. In 1862, for example, 'Irish longshoremen in New York informed their employers that all Afro-American longshoremen, dockhands, and other types of workers must be dismissed summarily, otherwise the Irish would tie up the port'.

As the economy grew and competition eased, so the period between 1870 and 1890 became one of relative racial friendliness. Civil rights laws in the state of New York gave blacks the right to vote, made segregation unlawful, legalized intermarriage and admitted black men to juries. Racially mixed residential areas were not uncommon. In Detroit, blacks were able to vote and their upper class had 'interaction with whites on a regular and equal basis' – having attended high school and college in an integrated setting. Black physicians and dentists 'had mostly white practices' while in politics there was a 'regular election of black men to public office in Michigan in the 1870s'. In Illinois by 1885 there was 'a public opinion strong enough to raze all of the discrimination laws from the state's statute book', while the evidence testified to easy contacts, and to marriage across the colour line (Sowell, 1981b:71). The racial boundary, it seems, could be blurred when the proportion of blacks was small and people met one another on the basis of equal status.

Black emigration from the eleven states of the southeast rose from 99 thousand in 1870–9 to 110 and 312 thousand in the next two decades. After falling back to 267 it rose to 577 in the decade of the First World War, continuing at 926 and 463 before jumping to 1,515 and 1,459 in the two decades following 1940. The effects of this influx upon the black community in the North were disastrous. The physical health of the black newcomers may not have been quite so bad as that of the Irish when they arrived, and their standards of hygiene and general social respectability may possibly have been not quite so low, but the standards of the majority society had improved in the meantime, so the whites tried to keep them at a distance. High rates of disease, alcoholism, and homicide so ravaged the black communities at the beginning of the new century that many observers predicted the eventual extinction of the race. Many contemporary Northern blacks openly blamed the newcomers for the hardships that began to afflict blacks as a group, while a distinguished black historian predicted: 'The maltreatment of the Negro will be nationalized by this exodus' (Sowell,

1981a:212, 1981b:73). The hardships were experienced in almost every sphere of life. Black residents were driven out of mixed localities 'by neighbourhood improvement associations, economic boycotts, frequent acts of violence, and later, restrictive covenants'. In New York City after 1900 there was a sharp increase in the number of legal suits brought by blacks complaining of discrimination in hotels, restaurants and theatres. White churches which had admitted blacks to their congregations, attempted to ease them out. Racial conflict intensified in the job market: if, during a strike, an employer brought in strike-breakers and a small minority of them were black, the incident could be publicized so as to reinforce the stereotype of blacks as strike-breakers (Wilson, 1978:63–4). Unexpectedly – and this is an important issue – it is not certain that the reverses which blacks suffered at this time in political and social relations were mirrored in the economic field. Thomas Sowell (1975:52) contends that there is little evidence to prove that the great mass of the black population advanced more rapidly economically during what from a political point of view was the best historical period, or that black economic advance could be halted in the worst of political periods.

Some immigrant groups have been more successful economically than others, as can be seen from the adjoining Table 3. Note, however, that it reports average family income. A group in which the average age is high and families are large, may have several people contributing to the income. A more recent immigrant group with many children, or one with many households in which there is no father-figure and the mother is the head, may have few income earners relative to the mouths to be fed and will appear poorer even though the earnings to employed members of the group are no lower than those of other groups. While about 20 per cent of Native Americans are age forty-five or older, twice that percentage of Polish-Americans are over fifty-five and this must contribute to the disparity in the income figures. The proportions of families with three or more income earners are one in thirteen among Puerto Ricans, one in ten among Native Americans, one in eight among whites, but one in five among Chinese. High fertility rates mean low incomes per head, but fertility rates tend to fall as each group adjusts to life in city neighbourhoods. In 1910 Jewish women aged 35 to 44 had the same number of children (5.3) as Mexican-Americans today, and more than blacks (4.2), the Irish (3.3), or the national average (3.4). By 1969 Jewish fertility in that age-bracket had been reduced to 2.4; Mexican-Americans, who were experiencing continued immigration and were less urbanized, had come down mightily to 4.4, while blacks (at 3.6) had come closer to the Irish (at 3.1) (Sowell, 1981a:6–8). By 1979 the fertility of women of Spanish origin was below that of black women.

Table 3: *Family income index, by ethnic group, in 1969, United States*

Jewish	172
Japanese	132
Polish	115
Chinese	112
Italian	112
German	107
Anglo-Saxon	107
Irish	103
Total UNITED STATES	100
Filipino	99
West Indian	94
Mexican	76
Puerto Rican	63
Black	62
Indian	60

Source: US Bureau of the Census and National Jewish Population Survey. This table is reproduced from Sowell, 1981a:5.

The factors which may possibly explain differences in the social and economic achievements of ethnic minorities have recently been examined by Alice Kessler-Harris and Virginia Yans-McLaughlin (1978). It would seem as if the amount of capital a group had on arrival was less important than the skills its members possessed and the appropriateness of their previous social experience to the environment in which they found themselves after entry. The Jews who immigrated in 1900 had substantially less money than members of other groups but the Jewish group had the highest population of skilled workers. A high level of skill had earlier enabled German, English and Scottish workers to take advantage of opportunities denied to the Irish, yet by the 1880s the Irish were starting to catch them up. By contrast, the Jews, whose skills as tailors were valuable in New York's expanding garment industry, managed to build upon their initial advantage. Of course, there were often important differences within national groups; northern Italians were better adjusted to urban living than southern Italians, for example. Jews and Italians had the disadvantage of having first to learn English, but this seems not to have been a serious handicap and they soon equalled or surpassed the mobility rate of the Irish. Nor were rates of literacy closely associated with achievement, though attitudes towards education were crucial. The Italian countryman, suspicious of modern ideas and fearful of the extent to which Americanization would disrupt the integrity of the family, withdrew his children from school as soon as possible. Jews, whose landless condition and religious training had taught them to respect learning, hungered for education.

Living conditions in the New York tenements improved from the 1860s to 1900 and the Irish and German tenants gave way to Jews and Italians. One observer reported that 'the visitor of 1900 could go about dry-shod, at least, in tenement yards and courts where 35 years before the accumulation of what should have gone off in sewers and drains made access almost impossible'. Whether such differences affected mobility it is difficult to say. Nor does it seem that the cohesiveness of an ethnic group, by itself, had any effect though immigrants surely benefited when there was an established community of *landsmänner*, large enough not to be overwhelmed, who could help them settle and provide guidance. Group life based on religious or secular institutions, could look after the unfortunate and stimulate and assist the ambitious, but it could also lead members' energies into directions which retarded economic advance. Success in the political field did little if anything to assist such advance. The Boston Irish, who controlled that city politically from the 1880s onwards, were twice as likely as any other group, native or foreign, to be low-level manual workers in the 1890s, whereas the Jews were not handicapped by their preference not to organize politically.

Minority and lower-class groups experiencing long-term family instability after the initial migration and settlement crises are rarely high achievers, but the converse has not been proven. Among the Jews, stable and supportive families, along with respect for individual achievement, provided a launching pad for the able youngsters, whereas family strength among the Italians seems to have discouraged mobility because the highly individualistic American values threatened the Italian pattern of equality within the family. Prejudice played a part in limiting job options for members of all groups except the English. The Irish suffered more from this than other European groups but Kessler-Harris and Yans-McLaughlin consider that the cultural assets immigrants brought with them had as much to do with explaining future success as the negative effects of job discrimination.

When the National Advisory Committee on Civil Disorders came to report on the urban riots of 1967 its members chose to address 'a fundamental question that many white Americans are asking today: why has the Negro been unable to escape from poverty and the ghetto like the European immigrants?' They answered the question with five points. Firstly, when the European immigrants were flooding in, America needed great pools of unskilled labour, but since then, and especially since the Second World War, the economy had matured. The Negro migrant arrived too late. Secondly, Negroes suffered from a prejudice so pervasive that it formed a special barrier. Thirdly, they claim (contrary to Kessler-Harris and Yans-McLaughlin) that political representation brought economic benefits to the European immigrants. By the time the blacks arrived the great wave of public building (often under municipal control) had come to an end; reform groups were reducing the power of the political machines. Because of prejudice the blacks were less well represented politically and the rewards of representation were lower. Fourthly, the European immigrants came at a time when material aspirations were low, families were large and supportive so that men could find satisfactions in family life that compensated them for the life they had to lead in the workplace. Blacks came to the city under quite different circumstances. Fifthly, they stressed the factor of time. Those immigrants who came, like the blacks, from rural backgrounds, 'are only now, after three generations, in the final stages of escaping from poverty . . . Negroes have been concentrated in the city for only two generations, and they have been there under much less favourable conditions.' So the Commission concluded: 'What the American economy of the late nineteenth and early twentieth century was able to do to help the European immigrants escape from poverty is now largely impossible. New methods of escape must be found for the majority of today's poor' (Report, 1968:282). It is a conclusion to which this chapter will return, though it is uncertain whether the new methods have been found.

Political changes

The First World War brought a halt to immigration, an increase in industrial employment, and new opportunities for black Americans. Racial competition for jobs, housing, and social facilities like beaches, parks and playgrounds, gave rise to a series of riots after the war. In the depression of the 1930s Roosevelt captured the black vote that previously had been committed to the Republicans as the party of Abraham Lincoln; nevertheless, the ratio of black income to white fell during the period of the New Deal because of the depressed job market. The exclusive boundary against blacks was hardened by the pressure of competition while the relative weakness at this time of the black internal boundary is suggested by attitudes towards those mulattos who 'passed for white', usually in order to obtain work or to compete with whites on equal terms. These attitudes are described in a study of black Chicago started at the end of the 1930s (Drake and Cayton, 1945:159–71) in which it is said: 'There is not a single Negro family known to the authors that has not been aware of instances, sometimes scores of instances, in which friends, acquaintances, or relatives have crossed the color-line and become white – "gone over to the other side" as Negroes phrase it.' It was relatively easy, they suggest, for whites to become socially accepted as blacks; the main problems of a black person who wished to pass for white were psychological, since he or she was unlikely to be 'exposed' by other blacks, particularly if it was thought that the person was passing for economic reasons. Black men were more likely than black women to pass for non-economic reasons, and they also tended more frequently to revert to a black identity later. However, passing was not based upon a social exchange such as the status change of a mulatto Brazilian who was regarded as white because he was well-to-do. Passing was a consequence of a social rule which defined Negro status in terms of ancestry and which became socially unrealistic when the amount of black ancestry was too small to be evident in a person's appearance, and when, because of urban living, others knew neither the actual ancestry of the person, nor the appearance of relatives and others living in that person's household.

By the 1940s it was far too late for any mulatto escape-hatch to develop in the United States. Whites throughout the country had become accustomed to the prevailing definition of racial status. So, too, had blacks. At the beginning of the century W. E. B. DuBois had posed the Negro dilemma: was the better strategy that of strengthening the inclusive boundary and promoting separation (the nationalist strategy), or was it better to concentrate upon trying to weaken the exclusive boundary (the integrationist strategy)? Over the years the dilemma had sharpened; the inclusive boundary had been much reinforced and the exclusive one weakened only slightly.

A substantial black ethnic revaluation movement started to gain momentum at the end of the 1950s. The economic demands of the Korean war had helped black employment and the urbanization of the black population proceeded apace. In 1910 one-fifth of the black population was urbanized by comparison with one-half of the white; by 1960 equal proportions lived in metropolitan areas, and since then the black urban proportion has increased, though there is now a contrast in that most urban blacks live inside central cities and most urban whites outside. Urbanization provided a better base for black political movements, in association with the improvement in the media of mass communication (notably television) and with the stimulus provided by the admission of many new African states to the United Nations; black self-confidence was boosted and the possibilities of political action were enhanced. At a time when white ethnic consciousness was declining (because it had been sustained primarily by internal processes) black consciousness was increasing, with the proviso noted by Martin Kilson (1975:237) that blacks were hesitant about whether they did indeed possess a full measure of ethnic attributes. As a result of their historical experience, blacks were more inclined to doubt and deprecate their ethnic identity than other minorities (see also Lincoln, 1974:122–3). Perhaps the tide turned with the Montgomery bus boycott. The Federal Supreme Court had already declared in one of its most celebrated decisions, that 'in the field of public education the doctrine of "separate but equal" has no place'. That was in 1954, but not much had happened to change the national pattern by the end of the following year when Mrs Rosa Parks was arrested for refusing to give up her seat on a bus. In response, the blacks of Montgomery, Alabama, walked to their destinations for a whole year, until the rules were changed. The campaign was led by the Rev. Martin Luther King, Jr and it brought him to a position of national leadership. Then one day in 1960 four black students sat at the lunch counter in a Greensborough, North Carolina store and waited to be served (Chafe, 1980). Within a month thousands of black and white students 'sat in' at lunch counters throughout the south and began a wave of sit ins, drive ins, wade ins, play ins, kneel ins, pray ins, and so on, wherever services were segregated. The next year the Supreme Court held discrimination against inter-state travellers in bus terminals to be illegal and set off the 'freedom rides' to dramatize the law's requirements. The vicious assaults on freedom riders were publicized, raising the political temperature and stepping up the pressure. Demonstrations in Birmingham, Alabama, were brutally dispersed; the President had to send in federal troops, as he had to enforce desegregation in some Southern universities. A famous 'March on Washington' in 1963 which brought out 200,000 marchers, was followed by the bombing of a Birmingham church in which four little girls were killed. The marches continued.

The administration of President L. B. Johnson, by committing itself to the introduction of stronger legislation, inaugurated what has been called a second Reconstruction. The Civil Rights Act of 1964, passed after the assassination of John F. Kennedy, banned discrimination in public accommodations and employment and made it possible to deny federal funds to those who engaged in discrimination. The Voting Rights Act of 1965, passed after the beating to death of the Rev. James Reeb in Selma, Alabama, restored the franchise to blacks in the South, though others were to die before it became easier for blacks to get their names onto the registers. The Fair Housing Act was passed in 1968, only one week after the assassination of Martin Luther King, although for years there had been unsuccessful attempts to persuade Congress to act against housing discrimination. In 1966 a national controversy had erupted over the slogan 'black power' launched by Stokely Carmichael on a Southern freedom march, and Afro-Americans, beginning with the activists, started to describe themselves as 'black' instead of 'Negro'; young blacks turned to African costumes, hairstyles, and 'black studies'. The call for 'black power' was effective in winning black support, partly because it made whites anxious. These developments occurred against a background of increasing, and well-publicized, violence in the cities. In 1965 an encounter between policemen and a black citizen ignited a riot in Watts, Los Angeles, that led to 34 deaths and $35 million in damage. Eight major disorders occurred during the first nine months of 1967; one in Newark led to 23 deaths and $12 million in damage; one in Detroit caused 43 deaths and possibly $54 million in damage. These riots must have reflected upon the image of the United States overseas and may have troubled the American conscience more than they troubled the economy.

The National Advisory Commission appointed to report on these disorders, declared that the blacks 'acted against local symbols of white American society, authority and property in Negro neighbourhoods – rather than against white persons':

> What the rioters appeared to be seeking was fuller participation in the social order and the material benefits enjoyed by the majority of American citizens. Rather than rejecting the American system, they were anxious to obtain a place for themselves in it.

Seeking to explain why it happened, the Commission described 'certain fundamental matters':

> the most fundamental is the racial attitude and behaviour of white Americans . . . White racism is essentially responsible for the explosive mixture which has been accumulating in our cities . . . At the basis of this mixture are . . . discrimination . . . black in-migration and white exodus . . . the black ghettos.

The convergence of many factors made the role of the police difficult. Almost invariably the incident which started the riot had been routine arrests for minor offences of blacks by white police, but the police were not merely the spark that set off the rioting. To many blacks the police symbolized white power, white racism and white repression; this did faithfully represent the attitudes of many policemen. The Commission put forward a long list of recommendations for action in the fields of employment, education, welfare and housing.

Under President Richard M. Nixon from 1968 the focus of national attention moved elsewhere, but it was during his administration that the Office of Federal Contract Compliance in the Labor Department developed and enforced a system of 'goals and timetables' which, in effect, required those who received federal funds, as did most universities, to attain quotas in the employment of minorities. This requirement was bound, sooner or later, to be brought by the Supreme Court to decide whether making special allowances when considering one applicant's claims constituted discrimination against another. They pronounced on the issue in 1978 in the case of the *University of California v. Alan Bakke*, but the Court was evenly divided and its message for the nation uncertain. Two subsequent judgements in the cases of *United Steelworkers of America v. Weber* and *Fullilove v. Klutznik* were unequivocal in upholding the legality of a training programme with a 50 per cent black quota and the constitutionality of a federal law requiring 10 per cent of the public construction funds distributed under the affirmative action law to go to minority contractors.

Cities in North America tend to be more spread-out than cities elsewhere. The residential density is low; public transport is limited; most people go around by private motor car. To get children to school it is necessary to provide a free 'school bus' service. The existence of such a service has been used to promote racial integration in schools, for, if the children have to ride in the buses anyway, they could be taken rather longer distances if in this way it became possible to adjust the population of the school and get a better mixture of black and white. Influenced on the one hand by evidence that those who held power in the South would not willingly obey the law, and on the other by the findings of social science research which seemed to indicate that the segregation of classes was harmful to the education of black children, federal courts increasingly ordered changes in the boundaries of school districts to increase the scope for engineering racial proportions. Eventually they reached the position where they seemed to be saying that every school should have a black minority and no school should have a black majority. Whether the benefits have been equal to the costs is a matter for debate. Concluding his review of the outcomes, Nathan Glazer (1975:121) maintains that one thing, at least, is clear: integrating the generally lower-income whites of the central city with lower-income blacks, particularly under conditions of resentment and conflict, achieves nothing in educational terms, while the general effect of busing is to cause many parents to move their children to private schools.

A major force behind the political struggle which sustained these changes was the boost which the events of the 1960s gave to black morale. The older generation was less easily persuaded. The Afro-American Senator Edward Brooke said of the 'Black Power' call: 'That slogan has struck fear in the heart of black America as well as in the heart of white America . . . The Negro has to gain allies – not adversaries.' The movement was led by middle-class blacks who felt that at this moment in time it was worth risking assault or imprisonment to try to secure a greater measure of justice. A large proportion of the black population became willing to engage in sit ins and demonstrations. Black leaders did not encourage rioting (it should always be remembered that there are important tensions within the black population and that blacks suffer more than proportionally from the criminal actions of other blacks), but they were ready to stress the resentments that underlay rioting and the need for drastic reforms if these were not to occur. The new political stance was accompanied by a stress upon cultural styles that would highlight black distinctiveness such as African hairstyles and costume, soul music and the like. Afro-Americans began to cultivate their ethnic attributes.

Middle-class blacks were also the main beneficiaries of many of the new policies. While the increase in black solidarity shifted the political balance between black and white to the former's advantage, it left considerable ambivalence amongst blacks about how far anti-white activism should be carried. The basic structure of white-black relations was changing (for example, in the 1960s the number of blacks in white-collar and skilled occupations increased by 76 per cent compared with an increase of 24 per cent for whites). But attitudes changed in more complex ways. It is probable that support for passing declined, for blacks expected other blacks to be proud of their racial identity. As the barriers to intermarriage between blacks and whites were reduced, so their frequency increased, despite suspicion from many blacks. The 1960s saw a 26 per cent increase in such marriages (Kilson, 1976:369). It is difficult to assess subsequent trends since many states no longer record the race of couples at marriage. Data from 34 states for 1979 indicate that white males married white females 522 times more often than black females; black males married black females 22 times more often than white females; white females married white males 183 times more often than black males; black females married black males 63 times more often than white males. Several states, including California and New York, are not included in these figures and it is probable that the rates of intermarriage there are higher; in New Jersey, for example, they were nearly twice as frequent as in the other states where records were kept.

The position of blacks in the housing and employment markets will be considered from a slightly different standpoint in subsequent chapters. Here it is important to note that recent changes, whether accelerated by government policies or simply the result of long-term trends, have led to greater inequalities within the black population, and a greater measure of overlap between successful blacks and members of the white population. Since the experience of disadvantage holds a minority together while success causes it to disintegrate, this may in the long run affect the distinction between black and white. According to William Julius Wilson (1978:152–3) black life-chances now depend much more upon class position; with changes in the structure of the economy, competition between lower-income blacks and whites has shifted from the sector of employment to the sectors of schooling, housing, and municipal politics. This interpretation suggests that the significance of racial distinctions will, in due course, decline in these other sectors and class affiliation become correspondingly more important. Wilson draws upon findings which suggest that by 1973 the importance of family background on black educational achievement was similar to that among whites. Where black home circumstances were supportive of education, this was being passed on. Fewer young blacks graduated from high school but the percentage going on to college of those who did was equal to that of whites. Kilson (1981) draws similar conclusions from some other sources. Whereas by the end of the 1970s female-headed families constituted about 15 per cent of all families, among blacks it had risen to 41 per cent. This family form, he says, displays a seemingly endemic incapacity to foster social mobility. At the other end of the scale the proportion of black families among those with incomes of $25,000 and over per annum has been increasing. The general picture is that of a black middle class increasingly resembling the white middle class, whereas no changes are occurring which hold out any prospect of alleviating the unique problems which so comprehensively restrict the opportunities open to the black poor.

Preliminary reports from the Census Bureau indicate that by 1980 the population of the United States had risen to 226.5 million. Of this number 188 million were counted as whites, 26.5 million as blacks, and over 15.5 million as being of Spanish origin (60 per cent of these being Mexican and 14 per cent of Puerto Rican origin). The population of Native Americans, or Amerindians, had risen to over 1,360,000; other totals included: Chinese, 806,000; Filipino, 775,000; Japanese, 701,000; Asian Indian, 362,000. It was notable that, of the major groups, the white population was the oldest, whereas 32 per cent of the population of Spanish origin was under 15 years of age. As these young people pass into the age range in which they have children, the proportion of the total population which is of Spanish origin will expand considerably.

The Hispanic population is concentrated in the states of California, Texas and New York, but as Hispanic-Americans spread out into other parts and increase as a proportion of the total population, and as the Native Americans do likewise, these trends will help modify the assumption that the entire population can be assigned to either the black or the white category. This assumption has been bewildering and hurtful for many Hispanic and Native Americans. Joseph P. Fitzpatrick (1971:101), speaking from a long experience with their struggles, concludes that 'nothing is so complicating to the Puerto Ricans in their effort to adjust to American life as the problem of color'. They came from a society which resembles that of northeastern Brazil in that appearance is but one factor determining a person's status and class is more important than colour.

(Though Puerto Ricans tend to be of lighter complexion than people in northeastern Brazil.) The difficulty they can experience in adjusting to a two-category system of racial assignment (as illustrated in the autobiography of a young man of dark complexion, Thomas, 1967) casts an unexpected light upon the magnitude of the conditioning to which Afro-Americans have been subjected in the socialization process and upon the psychological costs to blacks of their subordination.

Interpretations

In the discussion of racial and ethnic relations in the United States during the past thirty years, the most central issue has been that of differential economic attainment. What underlies the placing of groups in Table 3? Why have Afro-Americans not advanced faster? There have been many answers. A convenient classification of them is that employed by Mario Barrera (1979:174–212). He calls them deficiency theories, bias theories, and structural discrimination theories. These are not to be found only in the form of explicit theories. Anyone who constructs a historical account of racial inequalities in the United States must make use at the very least of some set of assumptions as to the nature and cause of such inequality. It should also be remembered that many interpretations of current racial inequality will contain elements of all three theories, though with differing emphases.

Deficiency theories

The most obvious examples of deficiency theories are those maintaining that particular groups are less advanced culturally and economically because of biological deficiencies in their make-up, such as those described earlier as Typological and Selectionist Theories. Arthur R. Jensen has suggested that there may be different kinds of intellectual ability, and that the lower average I.Q. scores of black Americans may be due to a lower capacity for abstract reasoning genetically transmitted in that group. If a capacity for abstract reasoning is important to economic achievement then a lower average ability in that respect could explain some features of recent black history. This possibility has been examined by Thomas Sowell (1978) who shows that when white immigrant groups were new to the country their I.Q. scores were low; as they have come to prosper, their scores have risen, demonstrating that in the comparison of such groups (if not in the comparison of individuals) ability to score well in I.Q. tests may be a consequence of economic achievement and not the cause of it. For example, a study of 60,000 children in twelve cities in 1910 found that

Polish Jews were more often below the normal grade in their age than any of the other ethnic groups studied; 67 per cent of these Jewish children were scholastically retarded. A leading psychologist declared in 1923 that army test results tended to 'disprove the popular belief that the Jew is highly intelligent'. Since the scores of this and other groups have improved over time, there is no reason why black averages should not follow the same course. Black orphans raised by white families have I.Q.s at or above the national average. Other evidence suggests that an interest in abstract as opposed to concrete problems may be culturally determined. Sowell regrets the hostility towards I.Q. tests generated by the Jensen controversy, since they can offer clues to the sources of education and social problems. One example he gives is that, among blacks who failed to come up to army mental standards, three-quarters were from families of four or more children and one-half from families of six or more children.

As an example of a cultural deficiency theory, Barrera cites arguments advanced by Edward C. Banfield, who draws inspiration from the 'culture of poverty' thesis to argue that inequality can in part be attributed to economically relevant cultural differences. It is more interesting here to discuss, as a kind of cultural deficiency theory, Thomas Sowell's application of the theory of human capital associated with the Chicago school of economics. According to this theory, when people invest by using their resources to make roads, build houses and purchase machinery instead of using them for consumption, they create physical capital. When they use resources to train people and improve their capacity to produce, they create human capital; this consists not only of investments in formal education but of the acquisition of 'know how'. Some groups and some families have long histories as traders or small businessmen; in such groups children learn as they grow up a great deal that will be useful to them in their adult occupations. The notion of human capital is thus highly elastic, but it is also relative to particular modes of life. For immigrants who move into big cities, prior experience of urban living is a form of human capital, but experience of farming is a useless asset. Were two groups with these different backgrounds to move to the countryside, the tables would be turned.

In his book *Ethnic America*, Thomas Sowell has presented a series of histories of the Irish, Germans, Jews, Italians, Chinese, Japanese, Blacks, Puerto Ricans and Mexicans in the United States. Their most striking common characteristic, he says, is that their economic circumstances improve. Progress is generally taken for granted in the United States, but it still has to be explained. Sowell's explanation heavily emphasizes the 'supply side', interpreting progress as a consequence of improvements in the quality of the labour supplied as immigrants acquire new skills and the sort of work habits that bring reward. The possibilities of progress being held back by bias or being substantially influenced by structural factors are presented as relatively unimportant. In order to follow his argument it is necessary to appreciate the distinction between two kinds of discrimination. Categorical discrimination is practised when someone treats less favourably everyone who is assigned to a particular category simply because they are socially defined in this way. Statistical discrimination is practised when someone treats less favourably people assigned to a particular category in the belief that there is a lesser likelihood of people in that category having the qualities important to the selection that has to be made. The difference is one of motive (see Banton, 1983 and pp. 369–70 below). Sowell's view in effect, is that, as the supply of a minority's services improves, categorical discrimination becomes too expensive and will give way to statistical discrimination, the incidence of which will be gradually reduced as the probability of their being unsatisfactory diminishes, starting in situations where demand is high relative to supply.

Sowell believes that 'not only history but also economics argues against the widespread assumption that group income differences are largely a function of discrimination, rather than human capital differences or differences in age, geographical distribution, and other factors. Translating subjective prejudice into overt economic discrimination is costly for profit-seeking competitive firms.' He adds that, despite the supposedly crucial factor of the frontier in the history of opportunity in America, some of the most successful groups either did not come near it or arrived after its closing had supposedly slammed the door on upward mobility. Though education has also been regarded as crucial, the most successful groups first rose by their labour and business sense, and only later could they afford to send their children to college (Sowell, 1981a:291–2, 274; 1981b:19–20).

Interpreting, from this standpoint, the history of Afro-Americans, Sowell argues that the effect of enslavement was to destroy much of the human capital that Africans brought to the New World. Their sense of personal responsibility was destroyed. Lack of initiative, evasion of work, half-completed tasks, unpredictable absenteeism, and abuse of tools and equipment, were pervasive under slavery and continued after it. Migration to Northern cities entailed a traumatic change to which other groups took generations to adjust. The social pathology of violence, alcoholism and crime that afflicted them reappeared among blacks, and the established population drew back from the other groups in the same circumstances. The separation of groups at work or in the neighbourhood should be seen as part of a pattern of preference related to culture, respectability and other general social characteristics rather than as a product of beliefs about natural superiority and inferiority. Nor is Sowell worried about segregation in schools, maintaining that groups with different attitudes towards education perform much the same way whatever the mix in the classroom. He finds no grounds for believing that either cultural persistence or group advancement has been promoted by making cultural distinctiveness a controversial issue and cites evidence to the effect that the use of quotas in employment policy has done little or nothing beyond what had already been achieved under the 'equal opportunity' policies of the 1960s. Thus in his view the strategies pursued by most black leaders in recent times have been quite misguided. Blacks now are about where the Irish were one hundred years earlier, and their salvation lies in individual self-improvement (Sowell, 1981a:200, 211, 289, 285, 295, 223, 193).

This analysis and prescription is strengthened by a comparison with the histories of Chinese- and Japanese-Americans. In the nineteenth century both China and Japan were politically and militarily humiliated by Europe and the United States. Chinese workers were brought to the United States in conditions of quasi-slavery such that President Grant in 1874 said: 'The great proportion of the Chinese immigrants who come to our shores do not come voluntarily, to make their homes with us and their labor productive of general prosperity, but come under contracts with headmen who own them almost absolutely.' The prejudice against them shown by white workers was often based on a realization that it was difficult for a free man to compete in the market place with such a worker. Chinese were, in 1882, the first ethnic or racial group to be specifically barred from entering the United States as immigrants. Those who were in the country already were allowed to take only the hardest, dirtiest and most menial jobs. Throughout the west, Chinese who tried to work as independent goldminers were forcibly driven off the mine fields by white miners, often with great violence. Mobs of whites sporadically sacked the urban Chinatowns. In Los Angeles, in 1871, such a mob shot, hanged, and otherwise killed about twenty Chinese in one night. Chinese men were trapped in the United States, without womenfolk, at the mercy of Chinese bosses, unable because of poverty to return to their homeland. Many thousands of them had to live out lonely lives as residents in a country where they neither were wanted nor wanted to be. At the same time the shabby-looking, lice-infected and violence-prone Chinatowns were used by anti-Chinese elements as arguments for continued immigration restrictions although the existing restrictions were largely responsible for the conditions that were the subject of complaint. It was a bad case of blaming the victim (Sowell, 1981a:133–42; Peterson, 1978; Markus, 1979).

Japanese immigration got off to a better start because the first immigrants were officially selected and their government was able to watch over their interests. Their thrift, diligence and ambition made them very effective competitors and evoked antagonism. The American Federation of Labor would not allow Japanese workers to join or to form segregated locals (i.e. union branches). American farmers and businessmen turned against them so that though they prospered it was in small and scattered, often rural, communities and when, in December 1941, Japanese airplanes attacked Pearl Harbour, Japanese Americans had few influential friends and many bitter enemies. The result was a policy of internment thought necessary for the country's security, and the construction of the first concentration camps on United States soil. Some 110,000 persons, of any degree of Japanese descent, men, women and babes in arms, were put into camps behind barbed wire and guarded by armed soldiers (the story was little different in Canada). No charges were brought against individuals. They lost property worth $400 million. One of the foremost constitutional lawyers called it 'the most drastic invasion of the rights of citizens of the United States by their own government that has thus far occurred in the history of our nation'. Yet, remarkably, their morale held, and somehow, the younger generation emerged from the camps better prepared to enter new occupations, reducing their previous isolation.

Sowell says that today one quarter of all employed Chinese-Americans work in scientific and professional fields. More of them work per family; they have more (and usually better) education; but if these advantages in working and education are held constant, they have no advantage over other Americans. The reasons for Japanese success are similar (Sowell, 1981a: 152–79; Peterson, 1978). He implies that there is nothing special about these groups; others, with similar attitudes, could do as well.

The parallels between Chinese- and Japanese-Americans on the one hand, and the Afro-Americans on the other, are not close enough to give Sowell's arguments very substantial support, but they do make them somewhat more persuasive. However, three serious and general objections or qualifications need to be stated. They concern Sowell's view of markets; the speed with which, in some markets, supply and demand adjust to one another; and the importance of structural considerations.

The picture of markets which Sowell presents is decidedly partial and very much an economist's abstraction. When he discusses 'non-competitive markets' his examples are all of instances in which the government, a state-regulated industry, a public utility or some non-profit-making institution, fails to act as a private entrepreneur in a competitive market might have done. Nothing is said of other forms of monopoly or of the segmentation of certain kinds of markets. Nothing is said about the place of government in acting against trusts and in promoting fair competition. There is no recognition of the way, in many areas of business, government is obliged to play a regulatory role. The reader is told that 'government provides a legal framework within which transactors can make their own economic decisions'

(Sowell, 1981b:46–50, 103–24). Some of those transactors could be monopolists, others could be people wanting to compete in a market but frozen out. When Sowell describes how 'government can reduce the options available to the transactors', he does not mention that the government can increase costs to those who discriminate.

Some markets adjust more quickly than others and they may change more rapidly when moving in one direction than when under pressure to go the opposite way. It is not difficult to accept what Sowell says about the reactions of white residents to the influx into a neighbourhood of blacks with lower standards of living and behaviour, but it has to be remembered that these same whites had earlier been living alongside blacks against whom these complaints could not reasonably be brought. Why did not the market work for them? They were, to start with, victims of statistical discrimination but then it changed and became categorical, since respectable blacks moving into previously all-white neighbourhoods could be harassed, have their windows smashed and be put in fear of their lives; the market did not help them. A vicious circle can be established whereby whites with an initially low preference for segregation come to identify blacks more firmly with low standards and declining property values, so that their preference for segregation increases and becomes unresponsive to any improvement in the standards of the black people who would like to move into the neighbourhood. House-owners may have insufficient information about prospective purchasers, insufficient information about the feelings of the residents, can set a high value on risk-aversion, and regard movement to another district as entailing financial and personal costs greater than any economic benefit from a sale. Under such conditions a housing market which moves quickly towards white exclusiveness will not necessarily reverse itself when the conditions which caused the initial change have disappeared. Since housing segregation is important, both directly and indirectly, to many forms of racial inequality, Sowell's account gives much too optimistic an impression of the chances that this will be rectified by the processes he describes.

Finally, while it may be true that some of the most successful ethnic groups did not benefit from the opportunities associated with the moving frontier, differences arising from geographical distribution deserve more emphasis. Some of the success of the Chinese and Japanese can be attributed to their having settled on the west coast rather than the east, and to their having been in the right position to take advantage of the economic opportunities that opened up there. It is relevant to recall the significance which Higgs attributes to the Afro-Americans having been placed from the beginning in an unfavourable geographical location. As he writes (1978: 109), for them 'to grasp the emerging opportunities seemed almost always to require relatively more investment: to migrate to the cities or to the North; to finance a decent education out of their own pockets; to establish a business as a chance to participate in existing white enterprises'.

Sowell offers an interpretation of minority progress which is of little use for explaining periods of retrogression; if it is to be brought down from its highly generalized level and applied in the analysis of job markets in particular occupations as they are conditioned by local circumstances, many other factors will have to be incorporated in the framework. Sowell's simplifications of the issues will seem less justifiable.

Bias theories

As examples of bias theories, Mario Barrera cites the Report of The National Advisory Committee on Civil Disorders for its focus on 'white racism' and Myrdal's analysis in *An American Dilemma*, but the great bulk of writing by United States sociologists and social psychologists puts forward white prejudice as the main explanation of racial inequality.

Opinion polls and other attitude studies show a steady diminution in the hostility expressed by whites towards blacks, and indeed towards most minorities. In 1968, for example, 32 per cent of whites in a national survey said that whites had a right to keep blacks from living in their neighbourhoods; by 1978, support for this proposition had dropped to 5 per cent of the white population. Conversely, the number of whites believing that blacks had a right to live anywhere they could afford went up from 63 to 93 per cent. Between 1958 and 1978 the Gallup poll found a parallel rise from 42 per cent to 81 per cent in the number who said they would be willing to vote for an Afro-American as president (Wattenberg and Gergen, 1980).

Another analysis has found that during the period 1970–2, when the white backlash was supposed to be fierce, there was instead a leap forward – especially in the South – in the kinds of attitudes expressed by whites. Since 1972 there has been a return to the slower but nevertheless steady rate at which racial tolerance has been increasing. Some 37 per cent of the increase in racial liberalism over the years 1963–78 can be attributed to the entry into the adult population of a new generation with more education and new attitudes. Much of the remaining increase can be traced to a modification of attitudes on the part of older people; it may also have been part of a broader movement towards the liberal position on social issues generally in which the rejection of official views about the Vietnam war may well have been influential (Taylor, Sheatsley and Greeley, 1978). While the Presidential election of 1981 may have signalled a reaction on some of these issues, it is unlikely to have reversed the long-term trend in white opinion about relations with Afro-Americans.

Opinion polls and attitude studies are not always good predictors of how people will behave in real situations, so it is interesting to read Thomas Pettigrew's summary (1981:249–50) of the results of some experimental studies. One, conducted at a supermarket, confronted people with a situation in which either a black or a white middle-aged woman dropped her packages, apparently accidentally, in front of people going into the store. Whites stopped and helped the black woman as often as they did the white but they picked up all the white woman's groceries on 63 per cent of the occasions compared with 30 per cent for the black woman. In a second study, registered members of the Liberal and Conservative parties of New York State were telephoned and asked for help. Liberals helped the caller who sounded like a black man as often as the caller who sounded like a white; Conservatives helped the white man more frequently (on a ratio of 92 to 65); but Liberals hung up the phone without listening properly to the caller more often than the Conservatives, and more often for the black caller. One study attempted to take account of social class differences also. Black and white men, carrying canes, fell, apparently unconscious, in New York subway cars, pretending to have heart attacks. Those who looked respectable were helped by other passengers equally often, independently of the race of the sufferer or the helper; but, when those who collapsed appeared to be of lower status, smelled of alcohol, and carried a bottle wrapped in a brown bag, they were more frequently helped by people of their own race (Gaertner, 1976; Wispe and Freshley, 1971; Gaertner and Bickman, 1971; Piliavin *et al.*, 1969).

These findings, in line with others, support the conclusion that categorical discrimination against blacks is declining; whites are now more inclined to see the black category as sub-divided, especially by socio-economic status; while the incidence of statistical discrimination against the different sub-categories varies, being higher towards low-class blacks. The findings imply a shift from the drawing of exclusive boundaries against blacks based upon the criterion of descent towards one in which racial boundaries, though enforced in some spheres, are considered irrelevant in others; and towards one in which a person's claims upon another's sympathy are based, not upon ancestry but on appearance – counting social characteristics as well as skin colour.

Structural theories

As examples of structural theories of racial inequality in the United States, Barrera describes two, the caste–class theory of W. Lloyd Warner (really a model rather than a theory, and not so very different from that of Myrdal which is called a bias theory), and the internal colonialism theory elaborated by Robert Blauner. According to the latter, the position of racial minorities like Mexican-Americans, Puerto Ricans, and Afro-Americans, is fundamentally similar to that of peoples subjected to colonial rule. Colonialism is defined as 'a structured relationship of domination and subordination, where the dominant and subordinate groups are defined along ethnic and/or racial lines, and where the relationship is established and maintained to serve the interests of all or part of the dominant group' (1979:193). The nature of this argument can be clarified by comparing it with Thomas Sowell's presentation of the Mexican-American minority and the processes in which it is involved. First, though, it may be well to point out that there is no generally agreed name for the group acceptable to all its members. The more politically radical members mostly prefer 'Chicano' (an abbreviation based upon the pronunciation of *Mexicano* in Spanish) but the Mexican-born are the more inclined to see themselves as Mexicans, while some of the long-established American communities prefer to be called Hispanic-Americans, Latins or the like.

It is thought that there are about seven million Mexican-Americans, two million of them being 'undocumented' workers who have crossed the border illegally and found work. About half live in California, and many of the remainder in other states of the southwest. Many descend from people who lived in this region before 1848 when it became part of the United States. Others descend from the first wave of immigration in the early twentieth century which brought men to work on the railroads, in agriculture, and in the mines. The jobs they took were the hardest and the least-paid, but they could earn much more than in their home country, and it was impossible to prevent border crossings by those determined to come north. Many immigrants came intending to stay for only a short while and many were recruited by labour contractors who brought in work crews under the strict control of a 'coyote' or headman. Sowell notes that in the early period such crews were marched through the streets of San Antonio under armed guard. Laws to control labour contracting and exploitation were widely evaded. Since Mexican-Americans were physically distinct, illiterate, and lived in primitive conditions, they were viewed with repugnance by Americans in the southwest, especially in Texas, and by the more acculturated, often lighter skinned, Mexican-Americans who were better established. Those immigrants who lived in family groups had many children, even by the standards of the times, and were slow to learn English. When, after the First World War, the economic depression deepened, a systematic campaign was undertaken to deport Mexicans, and those sent back to Mexico included many who were United States citizens.

A second wave of immigration started when the Second World War absorbed millions of Americans into the war effort. A contract labour scheme, the *bracero* programme, was initiated in 1942. Then, after the war, a new series of deportations started, though this time citizenship rather than indigence was used to determine just who was to be expelled. Although expulsions have continued, a third wave of immigration can be dated from 1970, encouraged by the growth of American legal and social agencies ready to protect and defend illegal immigrants, and tolerated because of fears of offending the Mexican government and public opinion. Though there are important variations from one state to another (such as between California and Texas), Mexican-Americans have become increasingly urbanized; incomes have risen, not only absolutely but relative to rising incomes in the United States as a whole; comparisons are made more difficult by the proportion of women seeking employment and the high rates of male unemployment.

Thomas Sowell concludes (1981a:262) that the long time required for immigrants from Mexico to catch up with native-born Mexican-Americans in income (about 15 years) shows the importance of human capital. He writes: 'These internal patterns raise serious questions about common assertions that Mexican-Americans' income differences from [the] general population are largely or solely caused by employer discrimination . . . Mexican-American men have incomes about as high as, or higher than, other American men with similar educational qualifications, through the high school level.' As he also observes, it is more difficult to make comparisons that take account of the illegal immigrants who, because they are undemanding, appeal to many employers. Characteristically, he adds that the extension of the minimum-wage law to agricultural workers in 1966, increased costs to the employer of hiring legal immigrants or native workers when illegal immigrants were available for work. The best policy, he implies, is for the government to allow an unregulated market to distribute its rewards.

Those who are sympathetic to interpretations in terms of internal colonialism argue that in the second half of the nineteenth century Chicano workers were concentrated in the sorts of unattractive jobs elsewhere undertaken by blacks, and that both groups suffered downward mobility at this time. Barrera (1979:3) writes:

> studies which attribute occupational stratification to
> educational deficiencies among racial minorities are seriously
> misleading in that they do not take into account the
> historical conditions under which the pattern of segregated
> and inferior schooling for minorities was established. If it
> can be shown that such patterns were deliberately instituted
> and that the interests of certain groups, such as agricultural

and industrial employers, were involved in their establishment, a very different light is shown on the pattern of racial inequality.

According to this view, the conquest of the southwest can be understood only as an expression of a dynamic and expansive American capitalism. This economic order then creates structures of labour relations designed to exploit colonial workers even more than the workers of the metropolitan economy.

Chicano workers, and particularly the undocumented workers, have suffered from two particular disadvantages. Firstly, they have been in a weak bargaining position in the labour market, unable to obtain the wage rates available elsewhere, both because of the nature of their employment (as in agriculture) and because they were in regions where trade union organization was weak. In 1982, for example, two men, blacks this time, were sentenced to life imprisonment for kidnapping, slavery, and holding migrant workers in involuntary servitude on a farm in North Carolina, but it is believed that many offences of this kind are never brought to court. Secondly (and this applies also to Puerto Ricans), they were part of a continuing immigration bringing in workers with low standards who depressed the reputation of their group; moreover, they came from relatively undeveloped countries in which United States companies had such substantial investments that it often seemed as if their economies were subordinated to United States interests. For such reasons, migration was likely to continue and the assimilation of the groups in the United States be retarded. Because of their weakness in the market, Chicanos had contributed more than proportionately to economic growth in the southwest, while in recent years it has appeared as if their gains in average income and occupational status during the 1950s and 1960s were not maintained during the 1970s. The recession forced the Chicanos into occupations for which the labour demand is likely to decline and bring down relative wage levels. Mexican-Americans were taking more than their share of the hardships. Lacking technical and economic skills they were being increasingly limited to the secondary labour market with its unfavourable wage rates, limited fringe benefits, and general instability (Estrada *et al.*, 1981:128–39; cf. Bonilla and Campos, 1981). Changes in the demand for labour may be creating a marginal labour force of unemployables caught in a vicious circle which will transmit the disadvantages to the next generation.

Seeking to account for the differential economic attainments of the various ethnic minorities, interpretations in terms of internal colonialism stress that the weakness of minority workers leads to their exploitation by employers; majority workers fear that employers will use them as a reserve army upon which they can call to break strikes and weaken the bargaining position of majority workers. The latter then are the more easily deluded by racial ideologies developed to divide the working class. It is at this point that Barrera's discussion of structural theories divides into two. In so far as such theories point to features of the labour market overlooked by deficiency and bias theories, and in so far as they illuminate ways in which present situations are influenced by historical events and connections with markets overseas, structural theories bring into focus factors which should enter into any interpretation and are not incompatible with the propositions advanced in connection with the other theories. But when structural theories are subsumed in a larger enterprise of explaining the development of American capitalism, and this is viewed as a process exemplifying laws of a kind which Marx and Lenin claimed to discern, something else is afoot. Structural theories are then being cast as part of a philosophy of history based upon dialectical materialism, one which claims to incorporate everything that is valid in the deficiency and bias theories and is not to be compared with them as if dealing with observations on the same level of social reality.

Conclusion

Readers who approach the history of the United States from different standpoints will draw from that history different conclusions, but this chapter should have demonstrated that any study of the relations between racial and ethnic groups needs to pay close attention to patterns of competition. From an early stage competition between whites was on an individual basis and this, in line with the analysis in Chapter 7, tended to reduce the initial differences between those ethnic groups which were accounted white. Similarly there was individual competition within the Native American, Afro-American, Hispanic-American and other groups set apart by the whites. Between these groups there was group competition. Whites treated Afro-Americans differently as a group because that way they could make more profit from the use of their labour power. They treated Native Americans as a group in the first place because they wanted the land which was the collective property of Indian nations, but in the second place because the Native Americans appeared to have little contribution to make to economic development.

Slavery provided a clear-cut example of group competition because it identified the free and slave status with what were defined as racial characteristics in a two-category system. The tensions between white employers and white workers were displaced onto the blacks. A pattern was established that survived the ending of the economic relations which gave rise to it in the first place. This chapter has tried to establish that the difference between the various groups can be usefully and adequately represented in terms of the maintenance of exclusive and inclusive boundaries. There are continuous pressures to change these boundaries, both to reinforce and to dissolve them, so it is necessary to explain why they take the form they do. According to one view, market forces are working rapidly to eliminate all differences other than those which people as members of groups wish to maintain and for which they are willing to pay. Yet the transition from group to individual competition is not easily accomplished. One reason for this is that differences in privilege tend to strengthen group boundaries. Because minority members earn less, social association with them is less valued and they are thought of as different. This feeling then puts a break upon their economic advance and slows down the effect of market forces. It is in periods when the demand for labour increases, relative to supply, as during wartime, that minority members gain access to new kinds of employment and the scope of individual competition increases fastest.

11

Ethnic alignment in Great Britain

The first occasion on which a black person figures in British historical records comes from Scotland where, in 1507, King James IV invited a black woman to preside over a tournament. She was probably the one mentioned in a poem by William Dunbar (the first man, incidentally, to use the word 'race' in English) which says that when clad in rich apparel, she blinks 'als brycht as ane tar barrell'. As queen of the tournament it would have been to her that the knights raised their visors, and it would have been her virtues that some of them defended at the sword's point. When a historian referred to these events in 1901, he found it 'well-nigh incredible' that James, 'the very pattern of a Paladin of chivalry', should have done this – and apparently have repeated the event in the following year (Paul (ed.),1901: xlviii). This tells us as much about racial attitudes in 1901 as four hundred years earlier. In some sense which remains to be explored, whites came to scorn blacks much more by the beginning of the twentieth century and, in a complicated way, attitudes have changed again during that century.

Changes in white attitudes

Later in the sixteenth century there are records of five blacks brought from West Africa to learn English so that they could serve as interpreters. The Spanish wars seem to have resulted in the introduction of some blacks into Britain and Queen Elizabeth I ordered their deportation in 1596, though there is no good evidence of black slaves in Britain before 1621 (Shyllon, 1977:6). There was in Britain at that time a powerful, widespread, and ancient tradition associating black-faced men with wickedness. There were also dark-skinned people called 'Moors' who had an accepted part in the world of pageantry. In at least ten of the London Lord Mayor's pageants between 1519 and 1624 Moors served as bogey-man figures to clear the way before the main procession. A fair amount can also be inferred about racial attitudes in this period from Shakespeare's plays, notably *Othello* (Hunter, 1967:142, 145; Jones, 1965; Mason, 1962).

Evidence about white attitudes towards blacks in this period has to be gleaned from varied and uncertain sources; it would seem that British people entered the sixteenth century with a very unfavourably stereotyped image of blacks as people of doubtful humanity, and as heathens lost in wickedness and ignorance. This image gave ground to the contrary evidence of experience, and was for a time succeeded by the very different image of the Noble Savage. Those Englishmen who took part in the African slave trade became very well aware that blacks were people with a human nature like their own. In Britain there was hostility towards all foreign workers who appeared to compete with the native people for occupation or profit. The historical records fill out in the eighteenth century because many Englishmen who had prospered as the owners of sugar plantations in the West Indies returned to their home country bringing with them black servants who had been domestic slaves in the colonies. It became very fashionable to have a black attendant. Though slavery was established according to colonial law there was doubt as to whether this law could be enforced by English courts in the absence of any English law authorizing enslavement. Many of the servants ran off and a black community of perhaps 14,000 persons formed in London by the 1770s, concentrated in St Giles' parish, Mile End, Paddington, and along the riverside (Walvin, 1973:48; Shyllon, 1977:102).

Britain was at this time a society in which there were substantial inequalities in the distribution of wealth and prominent differences of rank. By the standards of later centuries the opportunities for someone to climb to a higher position in the hierarchy were not great. In a world given to genealogical thinking, even illegitimate descent from a king or a great noble could confer a measure of honour, but descent from slaves or from a heathen nation was dishonourable. In inter-personal relations, rank also depended upon association with the powerful. In dealings with working-class whites, the black attendants of aristocrats and West Indian nabobs doubtless benefited from their relationship with people of higher status.

At this time the human status of black people was unquestioned. It was a new development when, in the late eighteenth century, a small minority of whites, mostly connected with the West Indian interest, began to disparage blacks in stereotyped terms as 'a dissolute, idle, profligate crew'. The most vociferous was Edward Long, who asserted that 'the lower class of women in England, are remarkably fond of the blacks, for reasons too brutal to mention; they would connect themselves with horses and asses, if the laws permitted them. By these ladies they generally have a numerous brood.' He went on to express the fear that the English blood would become contaminated by this mixture which might spread to reach 'the middle and then the higher orders of the people' (reprinted, Walvin, 1971:68). But this and similar testimony shows that there was little resistance to intermarriage and reveals a conception of society powerfully structured by class as well as racial differences.

Some writers (e.g. Shyllon, 1977) contend that English attitudes displayed, from the very beginning, a fierce racial prejudice heightened by sexual anxiety that was untouched by the differences between a preindustrial and an industrial social order. Anthony J. Barker's recent (1978:157–200) research tells heavily against such a view. Other pro-slavery writers repudiated Long's racialism. Pro-slavery and anti-slavery publicists agreed that the African was no more amenable to the regimentation of slavery than any other man. Opposing propagandists were united in considering Africans culturally rather than biologically backward and in thinking that if African society could not be reorganized along European lines it would, in the long run, be to the advantage of Africans for them to be removed from that society. What divided them was their disagreement about whether the slave trade was a proper means for enabling Africans to realize their full human potential in some other environment. As wider sections of the population were drawn into the campaign against the slave trade, against colonial slavery, and then for the emancipation of black slaves in the United States, the black man came to be seen above all as a victim. Englishmen saw black enslavement as symbolizing the forces which thwarted individual liberty in their own society. The abolitionists were sometimes patronizing towards black American visitors, but this was partly attributable to class differences and they were watchful for racial discrimination in British society. They found very little, and there are frequent references to the reception, reluctant though it sometimes was, of black people in 'polite society'. The native black poor lost the paternal protection of high-status employers and patrons; as they struggled in the less secure and more individualistic world of the self-made entrepreneur and the wage-labourer, they found themselves isolated in the anonymous and less hospitable neighbourhoods of the growing cities. They were less often in contact with literary English people and so there were fewer published references to them. Since they presented no threat to any group interest they evoked no group hostility (Lorimer, 1978:21–44).

In the latter part of the nineteenth century a black skin colour started to acquire a new and less favourable significance. The black poor seem not to have constituted any distinctive group at this time but there is an appreciable body of evidence based upon visits to the country by articulate, refined and gentlemanly blacks, often from the United States. Up to the middle of the century these visitors found that it was their social position, not their colour, which determined the quality of their reception, but towards the end of the 1860s there was a change of mood in the country. Douglas Lorimer's conclusions about this add detail and precision to Philip Mason's interpretation of social changes over a longer period. Mason suggests that in the early eighteenth century men took it for granted that they were not equal yet behaved as though they were. Close association could not overcome the certainties of distinction based upon rank. By the end of the nineteenth century it would have been unusual to hold that there were innate differences between Englishmen, and yet eccentric to behave as though there were not. There was a growing aloofness evident in the belief that the lower classes smelled, and servants were kept firmly below stairs. Economic growth enabled the rich to lead a more separate existence and to resist challenge by erecting physical barriers that prevented others from seeing how similar they really were (Mason, 1962:12–38). Lorimer finds that the change in the social structure implied for blacks a transition from ethnocentrism to racialism which can be dated more precisely.

The 1860s seem to have been a time when economic and social changes increasingly led the population to see chances for social mobility. The opportunities for schooling were being extended. Literacy was growing and there was a burgeoning popular literature. More men were being given the vote. Competitiveness was on the increase and it is to be expected that people would have taken advantage of skin-colour differences if they could turn them to account. There were stimuli from overseas: the Indian 'Mutiny', the American Civil War with its racial connotations, and the Jamaican uprising of 1865, probably strengthened sentiments of white superiority giving point to the doctrines of racial typology. The stereotype of the black man as carefree, immoral and ignorant was magnified by Negro minstrel shows and possibly underlined by the religious changes reflected in the campaigns for Sunday observance, moral reform, teetotalism, and anti-Catholicism. Wealthy merchants and professional men who had been climbing the social ladder found it difficult to enter the higher ranks. These men, or their sons, had to elaborate and cultivate the ideal of the English gentleman. Those who were climbing identified blacks with the lower orders and many of the working people felt that, though their status was low, at least they were one step higher than the blacks. A visitor from Sierra Leone at the end of the century was clear that the worst areas for racial hostility were the lower-class suburbs where a black person attracted the abusive cat-calls of boys and factory girls (Lorimer, 1978:45–68; 201–11).

The imperial relationship popularized the image of blacks, browns and yellows as people who, overseas, were ruled for their own benefit by whites. But it comprehended another message that there were maharajahs, chiefs and potentates in these countries who could claim an upper-class status and were powerful enough to require diplomatic consideration. Their sons, like Jawaharlal Nehru, might attend English public schools, and, like Ranjitsinhji be acclaimed for their skills as cricketers. There might be racial discrimination in England, but the Aga Khan, for example, was unlikely to be much affected by it. It is also to be remembered that three Indians have been elected to the House of Commons to represent English constituencies, the first of them, Dadabhai Naorji, was Liberal M.P. for Central Finsbury from 1892 to 1895, and the others were a Conservative and a Communist who were elected to East London seats in 1895 and 1924.

The First World War offered colonial seamen a chance to leave their ships in British ports and sign on again at the higher rates prevailing in these ports, but after the war there were fewer ships sailing and white seamen wanted all the jobs. There were riots in several ports (Little, 1948:57–67; Holmes, 1975). A somewhat different perspective on the events of the time can be obtained from the career of John R. Archer, a Liverpool-born black man who was elected Mayor of Battersea in 1913 and who became a significant figure in London left-wing and Pan-Africanist politics (Kosmin, 1979b).

The black population of Britain remained tiny, and the general British assumption up to and during the Second World War was that coloured people, whether black or brown, belonged overseas. The war saw some changes with the arrival of West Indian and black American servicemen. The United States Army was then a 'Jim Crow' institution with segregated units and mostly white officers for the black troops. Because of the United States influence there were places of entertainment that started to operate a colour bar to the detriment of the black British. There were vigorous protests but the British War Cabinet was unwilling to put pressure on the United States and took no effective action. The feeling that other issues should be neglected during wartime may have prompted some increase in racial tolerance but many blacks could not accept the ever-present possibility of discrimination in a society which professed to disapprove of it. They found this hypocritical and said that they preferred open discrimination since then they knew what to expect (Thorne, 1974; Smith, 1980).

Race and employment

Post-war black immigration to Britain began in June 1948 when the *S.S. Empire Windrush* brought 492 Jamaicans to Tilbury Docks. About 120 of them were ex-RAF servicemen who had been home on leave after having been demobilized in Britain. Some of them had been intending to return anyway, others had been disappointed by the lack of opportunity for them in Jamaica. There were few passenger ships bound for England, and, when Jamaicans learned that one was coming with vacant berths on the troop deck, the available places were booked up in two days. It was an unexpected development which took the British government by surprise. In Parliament it was suggested that if other West Indians had ideas about immigrating there should be checks in their homeland to make sure that they would be suitable for employment. The Secretary of State for the Colonies replied:

'We recognize the need for some vetting, but obviously we cannot interfere with the movement of British subjects'. Then he added, 'It is very unlikely that a similar event to this will occur again in the West Indies' (Eggington, 1957:61). Twenty years later *The Sunday Times* tracked down the *Windrush* men and found half still in Britain, spread out across the country and mostly married with children. The others had gone on to the United States and Canada, or back to Jamaica.

It is sometimes argued that unfavourable images of coloured people were culturally transmitted within the experience of growing up and being educated in Britain. Generations of Britons learned, says Lawrence (1974:55), not only that it was good to be British but that it was unfortunate and a sign of inferiority to be black. This may have been so, but the imperial-colonial relationship also meant that many white British people felt a sense of obligation towards coloured people from Commonwealth countries that they did not feel towards coloured people from non-Commonwealth countries; this sense was paralleled by the belief that Britain derived benefits from the relationship and that it would be foolish to damage it. Nor did British people fail to recognize that there was a class structure in the societies that were to some degree subject to white rule. Many of the dark faces in London and other university cities were known to be the faces of students who would in due course be returning to occupy influential places in their own societies. Their goodwill could be important. In 1951, PEP (a policy group with strong official links whose proper title was Political and Economic Planning and which now continues as the Policy Studies Institute) started a study which drew attention to the increase in colonial students from about two thousand in 1946 to over ten thousand by the beginning of 1955. Though their report does not acknowledge this, one concern was that the racial discrimination the students experienced, and the attempts of Communist activists to introduce them to revolutionary politics, could convert a group that might be a political asset into a liability. The British Council and other unofficial bodies were encouraged to interest themselves in the welfare of these students. After 1948 the number of West Indian workers resident in Britain was increasing and the trickle of West African stowaways also received much publicity, but there was a significant change when, later in the 1950s, the image of the black man as student gave way to the image of the black man as a relatively unskilled worker taking the jobs that white men did not want.

A government social survey in 1951 revealed that only twenty per cent of the British public knew the difference between a Dominion and a Colony. Visitors from Australia, New Zealand and Canada at this time were irritated to find that they were sometimes referred to as colonials. In the survey those who did not know the difference between a Dominion and a

Colony had this explained to them and, in answer to a further question, 74 per cent replied they believed Britain would be 'worse off' without the colonies (five years later the proportion had fallen slightly – Banton, forthcoming).

When the possibility of restricting immigration was raised, one of the major obstacles was the political commitment to the principle that British citizenship conferred the right of entry into the United Kingdom. The possibility of legislation was first considered in the cabinet in 1950–1 when Clement Atlee's Labour government was in office. A cabinet committee reported that restrictions were unnecessary for the time being. The difficulty, they said, was that 'any solution depending on an apparent or concealed colour test would be so invidious as to make it impossible of adoption'. The matter was raised again early in 1955 under the Conservative government of Harold Macmillan, which also decided against legislative controls, preferring to persuade West Indian ministers to try to regulate the migrant outflow. When eventually the Cabinet agreed to bring in what became the 1962 Act, the Prime Minister was surprised that the Secretary of State for the Colonies did not oppose the measure. The history is important for other reasons. As Nicholas Deakin observes, had the Conservatives legislated in 1955 (or Labour in 1952) they could legitimately have presented the move in terms of the control of immigration and no more, since there would at that time have been no substantial domestic racial relations problem. By waiting six years the Conservatives delayed until it had become a matter of preventing the entry of British subjects with black or brown faces rather than white (Deakin, 1975). Some commentators have seen in British policy a progressive development closely related to changing circumstances in the job market. This makes little allowance for the sorts of considerations which tipped the balance against legislation in 1951 and 1955, but in favour of it a few years later. When the detailed political history of decisions in this period is written it may show that important decisions depended upon short-term expediency and personalities as well as on economic rationale.

Among the British public at large there may well have been a shift in racial attitudes round about 1958. Table 4 sets out the responses to opinion polls. The 1951 poll asked: 'Provided there is plenty of work about, do you think that more coloured people should be encouraged to come and work here?' Similar wording was employed in 1956, but the 1958 and 1961 polls asked whether immigration should be free or controlled (Banton, forthcoming; Rose *et al.*, 1969:594).

Rather than establishing any particular shift in the late 1950s these polls reveal a progressive decline in support for free entry until by 1968 it had dwindled to almost zero, but there are reasons for suspecting that the public

Table 4: *Free entry for immigrant workers from the colonies?*

	1951	1956	1958	1961 (May)
'Yes'	38	37	21	21
'Yes, providing there *is* work', etc.	8	35		
'No'/Immigration to be controlled	38	18	65	73
Other answers	10	9		
Don't know	6	1	14	6

re-evalued the imperial-colonial relationship at the end of the 1950s. The Conservatives committed themselves to a policy of decolonization in 1959. The West African colonies were by then set on course for independence and those in East Africa were to follow. Britain did not enter the European Community in 1956 when she might have done, but it was being argued with growing force that the country's economic interests pointed to the development of economic relations with Europe at the expense of preferential trade with Commonwealth countries. In 1956, 71 per cent of people questioned considered that, as British subjects, coloured colonials should be given preference over European immigrant workers but the possible disadvantages of a relationship which gave citizens of the colonies a right of entry were starting to attract attention. In 1955 the number of immigrants from Jamaica rose three-fold and there were nearly eight thousand from India and Pakistan, countries that previously had not contributed enough for them to be worth counting separately: were they to provide as big a surprise as the West Indians? 1958 brought much publicized rioting in the Notting Hill district of London, suggesting that black settlement entailed trouble. Since then the ideological attack on 'colonialism' has gathered strength until many British people wish to forget that their country ever had colonies or feel guilty that it should have done, but this was not the mood of the early and middle 1950s.

The primary element in twentieth-century British attitudes has been an extension of their attitudes towards previous immigrants, of whatever colour; namely, resentment and fear of their ability to damage the interests of the native people by competing with them for jobs and other resources. There have been few situations anywhere in the world in which immigration has not prompted some degree of hostility based upon competition, but in the British case, as in some others, the distinctive appearance of the incomers has meant that even their British-born children have sometimes been regarded as illegitimate competitors with more restricted rights than white people. The degree of this resentment is associated with the intensity of the competition. To understand this it is necessary to begin with an appreciation of the state of the economy, particularly with respect to the trade cycle and the pattern of structural change. In an industrial society new industries are likely to be starting up continually and others declining. Workers have to be attracted to learn new skills and move to new jobs. In a depression ways have to be found of reducing employment or reducing wages. According to a simple model of the economy the main regulator for reflecting change is adjustment of wages, in both real and relative terms. In times of prosperity workers may be the less inclined to work unsocial hours or do dirty jobs, so wages in these occupations should be increased relative to others to even out the balance of supply and demand. It never works quite like this, of course. In the early phases of industrialism wage determination was affected by the greater bargaining power of the employer. With the rise of trade unions there appeared situations in which the bargaining power of the unions was the greater. National agreements might be reached which pitched wages too low in some localities and too high in others. Another complicating factor has been the possibility of using capital to invest in labour-saving equipment. The greater the demand for labour, the more wages will rise and the more quickly will it become economic to invest in such machinery.

In the early 1950s the demand for labour in the expanding sectors of the English economy ran far ahead of the supply. Interviewed on the subject, one West Midlands manager replied:

> The big influx of immigrant labour began in 1954. At this time you couldn't get an armless, legless man, never mind an able-bodied one. Any worker could leave the works and get a job literally within three or four minutes simply by going to the factory next door. We tried recruiting Irish labour but this didn't come off (Wright, 1968:42).

In a period of growth workers are likely to abandon unpleasant jobs in order to move up the scale into the kinds of employment they find preferable. The employers' options are then to change wage relativities, to buy labour-saving equipment, or to use immigrant labour. The first of these can be difficult in the British structure of labour relations; the second depends upon the availability of the equipment and confidence that the market for the product is stable enough for the investment to be recouped in due course; the third can be the easiest solution for both the employers and the unions, and it is particularly attractive if the labour shortage is thought to be temporary. If immigrants are introduced during the boom they can do the dirty jobs and work the night shifts until the economy slackens off, when the native workers will again become interested in this kind of employment. If at this stage the immigrant workers can be sent away and no others are admitted, this will suit all parties in the receiving country. It never works quite like this either.

Unless the slump follows quite quickly after the boom, a more likely sequence is for the immigrant workers to adopt the job strategy of the native workers. They take the dirty jobs when there is no alternative, but as soon as they get a chance they move up the scale of preferences into more attractive positions. They also adopt the consumption habits of the native people. In so far as they succeed in doing this, there is again a shortage of workers willing to do the dirty jobs, so this sets off a new wave of immigration, perhaps of workers from a country a little more distant than on the previous occasion. As W. R. Böhning (1972:55) shows, this process of taking in a new bottom layer could go on almost indefinitely if economic and political circumstances permit.

The British economy has not achieved sufficiently sustained growth since the mid-1950s to furnish a good example of the inter-relations between full employment, wage relativities and immigration. Actual experience has not always coincided with the model, but immigrant workers were first drawn in as a replacement labour force in the more marginal industries where wage levels were insufficient to attract British workers (Peach, 1968), and they were spread across a range of employment. This strengthened the tendency for them to seek housing in the declining inter-city zones. The employer's position seems generally to have been one in which, other things being equal, he would sooner offer employment to local workers. In the West Midlands study just quoted the author refers to two factories on the outskirts of the industrial centre which did not employ coloured workers because they could get local ones. According to the Personnel Manager of one of them, the position had been discussed with the workers, who, like the employers, 'weren't against employing coloured labour, but didn't see any reason to do so while there were local people out of work'. In this kind of situation immigrants can obtain work only either by working for less wages or by working better than the local employees.

In practice the dilemma is rarely so stark. The job preferences of immigrant workers may differ from those of native workers, particularly with respect to the non-monetary aspects of reward. When West Indian women first sought employment in Britain there was a general labour shortage in hospitals for nursing, catering and cleaning staff. Since hospital work had a higher status in the eyes of West Indian women, the combined monetary and non-monetary rewards were enough to attract black women workers although they did not attract white women. Since that time, West Indian women have been less inclined to see hospital work as conferring status and their job preferences have moved closer to those of the native women. In the West Midlands study there was a metal works and a foundry whose policies were to promote their own employees when a skilled vacancy arose, rather than engage an already skilled worker from outside. The worker who took such an opportunity would have to learn the trade, taking a less-well-paid position with prospects of obtaining significantly better pay before very long. Yet many of the local workers were unwilling to take such an opportunity. Those who were, whatever the colour of their skin, could move ahead (Wright, 1968:48). Most workers, like most managers, do not respond as quickly as they might to new opportunities. There are always the risks and the inconvenience to be considered. It is unlikely, in view of the competition at home and overseas, that wage relativities could ever have been adjusted sufficiently rapidly in the 1950s to ensure a sufficient supply of workers for the unattractive jobs. It has also become apparent since then that in all industrial countries with a welfare system – throughout Europe and in many parts of the United States – the local people will prefer to live on unemployment benefit rather than take jobs they find distasteful. The tastes of immigrant workers may, for a time, be different, so they offer a solution to a problem which the economy of the receiving country cannot handle on its own.

There is also the possibility of capital investment as an alternative either by automation or by de-skilling. If an unskilled, low-wage labour force is available it may pay employers to re-design their production process so that they break down relatively skilled jobs into unskilled ones, employ more workers and still break even. In the 1950s there were many predictions that automation would render the unskilled worker redundant. All jobs would require a significant period of training. These predictions have not been borne out and a more recent tendency towards trans-national production has meant that some kinds of work are taken to the countries where the cheapest labour is available instead of bringing the labour to the work. For example, trousers are cut out on automatic machines in West Germany, flown in air-containers to Tunisia, where they are sewn together and packed, and then flown back to Germany for marketing. An American electronics company may produce masks and wafers for integrated circuits in the United States (this being a highly automated process), fly them to Southeast Asia where they are soldered into capsules (which is labour-intensive) and then bring them back to the United States for testing and sale (Castles, 1981:411). Trade unions in the United States which then lose this opportunity of employment for their members, call this the 'run-away shop'.

The inter-relations of investment and employment may be complex. In a study of the wool textile industry in Yorkshire it was found that new capital investment and the employment of immigrants had gone hand-in-hand. Because immigrant labour (from Pakistan) was available, firms had considered that it would be economic to install expensive new equipment which, if it was to pay its way, had to be operated for 24 hours a day. The local workers would not have been willing to work shifts through the night at the wages the employers could afford to pay, but the Pakistanis were willing; without them the industry would have contracted more rapidly (Cohen and Jenner, 1968).

Differences in the pre-migration work experience and cultural background of immigrants may influence their work preferences, their occupational abilities and their attractiveness to employers. In the East London clothing trade each employer interviewed testified that Pakistani and Indian workers were very quick to learn and adaptable (most of those referred to as Pakistanis will have been from what is now Bangladesh). There was a definite preference among clothing employers for Asian over West Indian workers, but in the building and furniture trades opinions were exactly the opposite and Asians were considered to be lazy and indolent (McPherson and Gaitskell 1969:27). Asians would have been at a disadvantage in occupations requiring collaboration with the English since so many could not speak English. This would have been less of a disadvantage in the West Midlands foundries where work was related to a mechanical process and if necessary a team of Asian workers could work under the leadership of one of their number who spoke the language (for a graphic account of how little communication might be necessary, see Wright, 1968:161–4).

When immigrants from a particular country are heavily over-represented in a particular occupation it is tempting to attribute this to their particular group characteristics and conclude that the French are naturally adept at cooking, that Asians are accustomed to working in high temperatures but do not have the physical strength that gives West Indians an advantage in the building trades, and so on. It is easy to over-estimate the importance of such explanations which seem the more plausible because they are used to account for occupational specialization after the event. When people grow up in a family that has been accustomed to running a small retail business they do acquire the sort of understanding that has enabled Jews, Chinese, Lebanese and some Asian groups to be successful competitors in African and West Indian countries where business traditions and attitudes have been less developed. But, apart from this, pre-migration characteristics are less important than they appear. The Chinese, Italian and other ethnic restaurants in Britain are not usually run by people who were restaurateurs in their home countries. They need some culinary expertise at the start but this is only one among many requirements, and ethnic cooking styles are quickly adapted to the tastes of customers in the countries in which the restaurants open. When an immigrant group establishes itself in a new country its members look for opportunities that are not being exploited effectively by the native population. These are the niches in the contemporary economic structure in which the competition is least vigorous. Having secured a foothold in such a niche, the group seeks to build upon its success and perhaps to obtain a monopoly upon this kind of work. Its members may then come to define themselves in terms of their occupational speciality.

An interesting example of the interaction between immigrant community values and economic opportunity is provided by the history of the Jewish minority in Britain over the past one hundred years. Surveys conducted between 1895 and 1908 found that before migration 29 per cent had been making clothes, so the immigrants could draw upon existing skills in moving into this trade in Britain. But probably more important were the cultural aspirations of the group. They did not see themselves as permanent members of the working class but were willing to save and plan so that they or their children could enjoy a middle-class existence. The experience of discrimination was not a novelty and they distrusted the hierarchically organized industries in which this was so often found, preferring occupations that would give them independence. It often surprised observers to find that among the Jews the greatest ambition was not to earn higher wages but to become a master. Barry Kosmin (1979a:47) notes that unlike the master, the worker can earn only as long as he is employed, and that the Jewish tradition placed a very high value on independence. Jewish businesses are concentrated in clothing, footwear, timber and furniture, leather and furs. In 1945 estimates suggested that three times as many Jews were self-employed as were non-Jews, while some more recent surveys point to an even greater difference. The post-war years have seen a large-scale entry of Jews into the professions, especially as doctors, lawyers and accountants (often starting business from the box-room of a suburban house, causing some observers to call accounting 'the home-tailoring of the late twentieth century'). Particularly interesting is Kosmin's explanation of why taxi-driving has become a Jewish trade *par excellence*. As he says, it offers a wide variety of working relations, relatively easy entry and complete independence. It can be a full-time or a part-time occupation; it offers great scope for initiative and gives maximum financial return for work invested. From first entry into the trade, the driver has self-employed status, belonging to a democratically organized, socially classless occupation which encourages social mixing and permits high earnings while allowing the driver freedom to reside where he wishes. The account is interesting also because it is so unusual for a minority to preserve such a distinctive set of shared attitudes in an industrial society.

By the post-war period Jews had come to form 3 per cent of the population of London and slightly more than that percentage of the population of Manchester. By 1966, persons born in the West Indies, India and Pakistan constituted 3.2 per cent of the population of Greater London and 2.8 per cent of the West Midlands conurbation. There were attacks on Jews in Leeds and elsewhere before 1914 and then in the 1930s they were gravely threatened by supporters of the British Union of Fascists. New Commonwealth immigrants have been subject to individual attacks but a comparison of the experience of the two groups in this respect is difficult and perhaps fruitless. What is more striking is that the New Commonwealth immigrants should have been seen by many members of the majority to pose a threat to their society far more fundamental than any consequence of Jewish immigration.

The politics of immigration

It is easy to be wise after the event, but in retrospect it begins to look as if it would have been better had the British government introduced immigration controls in 1952 or 1955, provided they were non-racial and treated all Commonwealth entrants alike irrespective of the country from which they came. British political leaders have, after all, been faced with a new and difficult kind of problem, that of changing British self-images and recreating them on a basis that made a person's skin colour irrelevant in competition for jobs and houses and in everything pertaining to the rights of a citizen. Had a major political party identified this as a priority issue, and taken successful steps towards a solution, they could scarcely have expected to be rewarded by the electorate. If they were unsuccessful, their electoral chances would have been badly damaged. So it is not surprising that they should have temporized. In each of three national opinion polls held in connection with the elections of 1963, 1964 and 1966, it was found that over 80 per cent of respondents felt that too many immigrants had already been let into the country (Butler and Stokes, 1969:420–5). The evidence is open to more than one interpretation, but it seems as if the primary component was one of hostility towards immigrant workers as rivals for scarce resources. At this time the number of British-born workers leaving the country exceeded that of New Commonwealth workers entering, and there were also substantial numbers of people from European countries obtaining work in Britain, but hostility focused on the New Commonwealth entrants because their colour demonstrated that they did not belong. Important though the sense of competition may have been, it does not explain the reactions, ranging from vague unease to bitter resentment, felt by many people living far from the areas of settlement and often beyond the age at which they would be competing for jobs or houses. They disliked the very idea of a black or brown Englishman. That so many Jews had been allowed into the country might be a pity, but at least they did not draw attention to themselves. They were hard-working, cultured people who could, if necessary, be assimilated. But the black and brown people did not, in general, have the Jews' positive attributes; their colour was an indelible mark of their different origin which would still attract attention even if in every other respect they behaved like the native people; if they were to intermarry that same mark would be noticeable for many generations until the whole nation had become slightly coffee-coloured. For a generation that had been brought up to believe that a white skin was something to be proud of, there was no reason for people to want to change their national self-image and a good reason for wanting to stay as they were.

It is far from certain that if controls had been introduced in 1952 or 1955, the issue of immigration could have been kept separate from that of national identity, but there can be no question that in the following decade the two issues became confounded and mention of 'immigration' came to mean 'coloured immigration' as far as the British public was concerned. Daniel Lawrence argues that each tightening of immigration control in the 1960s will have been interpreted by many white voters as confirmation both that the situation had been allowed to get out of control and that the politicians of both parties responsible must have been out of touch with the wishes and day-to-day problems of ordinary people to have allowed this to happen (Lawrence, 1978:47). In 1978 an opinion poll recorded that 86 per cent of the population considered that too many immigrants had been admitted. Majorities exceeding 80 per cent were found against the admission of the parents, and brothers and sisters of those immigrants who had settled; 77 per cent were opposed to the suggestion that the children of immigrants should be allowed to join their parents once they were over 18 years. The general view among the specialists is that the issue of coloured immigration had little effect upon voting behaviour in the elections of 1964, 1966, 1970, 1974 and 1979. Lawrence argues that this was because many electors believed that there was little to choose between the two main parties on this matter, and that the failure of the parties to respond to popular sentiment has contributed to the general disillusionment with the party-political structure, evident in a decline in the numbers of people voting that is without parallel in any comparable western democracy.

Such a conclusion is strengthened by the support shown for Enoch Powell. In March 1968 only one per cent of those interviewed in a poll considered him the man best suited to lead the Conservative Party. The following month he delivered a much publicized speech on the evils likely to follow from New Commonwealth immigration and in four subsequent polls between 67 and 82 per cent of respondents declared themselves in favour of his views. Within five months he was running neck-and-neck with Edward Heath in popularity for the posts of party leader and Prime Minister. His appeal has been not to a minority of extremists, but to a majority of the British population and it may have helped the Conservatives to their unexpected victory in the 1970 election. It might be thought that this interpretation is refuted by the failure of the party most clearly hostile to the settlement of New Commonwealth immigrants, the National Front, to attract significant electoral support, but Lawrence argues, with justification, that this party has never managed to achieve sufficient respectability to be seen as an alternative to the major parties. Traditional Conservative and Labour voters either abstain or reluctantly vote according to old loyalties rather than cast a ballot for a National Front candidate.

There have been very few attitude surveys which provide any measure of the extent and character of racial prejudice in the British population. The main one was conducted in 1967 for the volume *Colour and Citizenship* (Rose *et al.*, 1969:551–604) but the findings were presented in the form of a comparison of the characteristics of the more prejudiced with the less prejudiced. This deflected attention from the question of whether the less prejudiced do not also have prejudices and make distinctions between blacks and whites which could be of importance. Reanalysis of the replies given by the 500 respondents interviewed in Nottingham has shown that 55 per cent believed there ought to be special immigration regulations for coloured people. They were asked if they thought that named groups took more out of the country than they put in: 65 per cent thought this of West Indians, 61 per cent of Indians and Pakistanis, but only 38 per cent of Greek immigrants. When asked if they considered the British to be superior to named groups, 66 per cent thought them superior to Africans, 58 per cent to Asians and 25 per cent to Americans (but it was not clear whether respondents interpreted the question as asking about the innate superiority of the people or about their way of life and technological accomplishments). When asked if they thought colour would ever become unimportant in the way people thought about each other, 8 per cent replied in the affirmative, whereas 62 per cent felt that the colour distinction would always be important.

Another very important matter on which there is as yet no survey information concerns the scope which might be allowed in British society to what in the United States is sometimes called the 'hyphenate'. It is sometimes suggested that, say, Indian-Britons should be recognized as having a distinctive identity; while this seems only reasonable to people from parts of North America where such groups are a familiar aspect of social life, it implies a demand that many English people would not willingly concede. They have never seen theirs as a country of immigration. With a more uniform climate, a denser population and a more comprehensive system of social ranking than many others, England has been a relatively homogeneous society and those who help manufacture the national self-image have perhaps presented it as being more homogeneous than it actually is. Ethnic identities have been legitimate only in the restricted sense that individuals are accepted as being Scottish, Welsh and Irish as well as British, but such recognition does not confer any particular rights and is relevant only to informal social relations. Jewish children, like those from other religious minorities, have not been required to take part in religious services or teaching in schools, but this has not been seen as an ethnic matter. Any minority can organize a private school to teach subjects in which it has an interest, but, if acceptance of children as Indian-Britons were to mean the conferring of a right to special teaching in public schools maintained from the taxes, this would raise questions about where the line is to be drawn between private liberty and public entitlement. Hyphenate identities have not hitherto been legitimate in Britain in the same way as in some other countries. The attempt to organize Scottish and Welsh political parties on an ethnic basis runs counter to the assumption of an electoral system oriented towards a two-party opposition, but it has been justified by the possibility of territorial separation; the idea of ethnic political organizations without that possibility seems even more in conflict with the assumptions of the political system. Claims that such identities should be recognized are also regarded with suspicion because they seem to question the assumptions that England belongs to the English, and that anyone who wants to share the opportunities presented by life in England should therefore seek to become English; if a group of people want to live as Indians then by this logic they should go and live in India.

Immigration control has been seen as a way of excluding coloured would-be settlers and there has been a widespread tendency to see all black and brown people, whether born overseas or not, as immigrants. Nevertheless hostility towards the admission of coloured immigrants does not necessarily imply hostility towards black and brown people as individuals. When members of the public are asked on their door-step to answer a pollster's question, they respond to a more abstract stimulus than that of finding in their daily routine that someone whom they meet in a standardized relationship happens to be of a different complexion. There is discrimination both in the appointment of people to positions and in the organization of work. There has been a series of strikes in which Asian workers have alleged discrimination on the part of white workers and of trade union officials, but there have also been industrial disputes in which trade union solidarity has brought black and white workers together. One student of ethnic relations in the work place reports that though the workers in a London food-producing factory denied that ethnic group membership was relevant in the factory, observation suggested a more complicated pattern. When workers were together with members of their own group they regularly abused other groups as 'stupid', but in mixed settings they took care not to draw attention to ethnic differences. By way of exception, a West Indian worker and a white man who were close friends would attract attention by exchanges such as 'You black bastard!' – 'Shut up, white man!' as a way of signalling to others that they were friends, because only in that event would they be able to speak in such terms without causing a dispute (Donnan, 1976).

The politicians who, in the middle or late 1960s, tried to assess the nature of British racial attitudes in order to formulate a policy, had to balance conflicting signals. On the one hand, it appeared as if black and Asian immigrants were finding places for themselves without arousing very much friction. There were signs of a reluctant public acceptance, but one that was slowly growing. On the other hand, opposition to coloured immigration was fierce and there was the possibility that it could spill over into the domestic situation with disastrous results. There was therefore justification for the stance summarized in Roy Hattersley's words about limiting immigration: 'Without integration, limitation is inexcusable; without limitation, integration is impossible' (Rose *et al.*, 1969:229) but no one seemed to have a good answer to the question of how a policy of integration might be implemented. From a sociological viewpoint the problem was that of the cyclical effects of disadvantage, which is another way of referring to the pattern which Gunnar Myrdal (1944:75) called the 'principle of cumulation': 'white prejudice and discrimination keep the Negro in low standards of living, health, education, manners and morals. This, in its turn, gives support to white prejudice. White prejudice and Negro standards thus mutually "cause" each other.' In the British case, men and women were arriving for whom there were jobs but no houses. According to one argument, if the British government wanted their labour power it should have been ready to provide them with housing and such other facilities as were necessary to permit them to live on equal terms with other members of that society and to become integrated into it. To admit them without such assistance was to exploit them; they would be entering a competitive system with so much of a handicap that they would be unable to catch up. The danger was that they and their children would then be thought of as people who naturally belonged at the bottom of the social scale and it would be the more difficult ever to escape from this trap.

Yet even if politicians understood this, how were they to explain it to the voters? It is doubtful if even the most massive publicity campaign would have succeeded. If the voters had been told at the same time that more workers were emigrating from the country than were entering it, other politicians would have argued that immigration must be halted in order to reduce emigration. Popular beliefs that people had become entitled by years of residence and military service during the war to the benefits of the welfare state would have dominated every other consideration. Any suggestion that immigrants should come anywhere else but at the end of the queue for local authority housing – for example – would only have intensified the hostility to the very principle of admitting immigrant workers; it would probably have affected attitudes to workers who had already entered as well as to possible future entrants.

Was the prejudice of the British public so deeply-rooted and so extensive that without special measures coloured immigrant workers were bound to be trapped at the bottom of the pile? The evidence available in the later 1960s did not suggest that the position was so desperate. Britain had never known the institutionalized segregation that obtained, at one time or another, over so much of the United States, and by the standards of that country there had been scarcely any racial violence. Britain was a hierarchical society in which the native white population was differentiated by socio-economic status but permitted a significant measure of social mobility. New groups, even if of different complexion, could surely be absorbed into such a social order so long as there were opportunities of employment? There were two particular sources of evidence. The first, in point of time, was a study of discrimination in employment, housing and the availability of services like insurance, which was carried out in 1966–7 by Political and Economic Planning (Daniel, 1968). This research established beyond question that there was discrimination against black job applicants. Tests were conducted using an Englishman, a Hungarian, and a West Indian who applied for various services. In a sample of 30 instances in which a job vacancy was unfilled, there was discrimination against the Hungarian 13 times and against the West Indian 27 times; in applications for housing, discrimination against the West Indian occurred more than twice as frequently as against the Hungarian. Moreover the findings suggested that the more anglicized and the better qualified a person was, the greater the chance of discrimination. This evidence was interpreted as showing that discrimination against black people was so serious as to justify legislation but not so extreme that measures to make discrimination unlawful and expensive could not succeed. It made possible the passing of the 1968 Race Relations Act which provided the first effective provisions against discrimination (cf. Rose *et al.*, 1969:511–50).

The second source of evidence was the 1967 survey already mentioned, which took a central place in the policies advocated in the book *Colour and Citizenship* published two years later. In this survey, people's tendency to prejudice was measured by their responses to four key questions: (i) whether they would avoid having coloured people as neighbours even if they were professional people; (ii) whether they thought most coloured people in Britain inferior; (iii) whether coloured people should get council housing;

(iv) whether landlords should refuse to let rooms or flats to coloured people even if they were otherwise acceptable. Much less weight was attached to hostile answers to supplementary questions when constructing a scale of prejudice. These other questions asked whether a coloured worker should be made redundant before a white worker, whether there should be separate immigration requirements for coloured people and so on. The methods used to analyse the survey have been subject to very severe criticism (Lawrence, 1974:46–59). They led to a lower assessment of the incidence of prejudice than otherwise would have been obtained, suggesting that three out of every four native whites were entirely or predominantly free of colour prejudice. This in turn led to the statement in the book's conclusions:

> First, the extent of tolerance in Britain cannot be stressed too
> often and is indeed one of the major facts of the actual
> situation which has to be communicated to people whose
> anxieties on this score may stem in part from the mistaken
> view that there is not only widespread anxiety about coloured
> immigration but widespread hostility towards coloured people
> as such. What is needed in short is not an effort to make
> people unprejudiced, but rather to remind them that they are
> unprejudiced (Rose *et al.*, 1969:737).

This reassuring picture of English virtue received extensive coverage in the press, while another view of the same evidence, putting more weight upon some of the other responses mentioned earlier, could justifiably have described a fund of prejudice that in certain circumstances could be transformed into 'widespread hostility towards coloured people as such'.

One difficulty lay in the unsophisticated state of social science knowledge. General opinions expressed in the abstract setting of an interview are poor predictors of what people will do in real situations. But more relevant was the question of whether, by providing leadership, the politicians could reinforce the positive elements in public attitudes. If you tell people that they and their fellows are tolerant, they are more likely to behave in a tolerant way than if you declare that everybody is intolerant. One of the charges brought against Enoch Powell was that, by the way in which he described apprehensions about immigration, he made hostility towards immigrants respectable. In his view it was a politician's duty to act as a mouthpiece for inarticulate constituents, voicing their fears. Others said that politicians are responsible for the consequences of the way in which they advance their views. They thought that if racial questions were continually in the spotlight this would increase consciousness of group differences. It would be better to encourage local activity adapted to the problems of different cities and neighbourhoods.

The alternatives confronting the New Commonwealth immigrants of the 1950s and 1960s were fairly clear. Either they could see themselves as migrant workers with a better opportunity to save money than in the homeland to which they would later return; or they could present themselves as immigrants in a white man's country where they could never hope to be influential. They were too few in number and too divided among themselves to be able to achieve much by political activity. Nor could they hope to change the negative image of coloured people so widespread in Britain. They could gain social acceptance only on the terms set by the white majority who expected newcomers to conform to their values and conventions, but this same majority would be tolerant of minority groups that kept to themselves and caused no trouble. Such a situation might well change when a second generation of British-born New Commonwealth settlers came to the fore, but until that time members of the racial minorities would have to pursue their individual interests and support one another on a family or small-group basis.

The migrant's choices

In Chapter 7 the social organization of migrant groups was analysed in terms of their relative orientation towards the sending and receiving societies. This is to examine the process of migration not from the beginning but from a position more like half-way along. Those who have analysed the ways in which migration gets started have often distinguished between the 'push' factors in the sending society and the 'pull' factors in the receiving society, but neither of these has any force until the potential migrant is aware of the possible destination as one that has attractions compared with the sending society. If there is already a tradition of migration, that makes the process much easier since it usually provides not only the psychological element in the motivation but often the material possibility as well; the first migrants may then send back money to pay the passage of those who are to join them.

To start with, the migrant interprets information about the receiving society in terms of the values of the sending society. The amount he can earn in new employment seems munificent and he plans to use it to achieve the goals of his existing life without realizing that in the new environment he will acquire new goals. The 'reference groups' by which he measures himself are located in the sending society, as indeed are many of the informal social controls upon his behaviour when in the presence of fellow migrants. For a long time he expects to return to the society from which he came, but often his commitment to this weakens and there is a period, perhaps of decades, in which he talks about going back while all the time allowing ties to build up which bind him to life in the society in which he has settled. If he has children growing up in the receiving society this may well tip the balance towards settlement. This is the course which is being followed by many, but by no means all, of the migrants from Jamaica and other West Indian islands who have settled in Britain. Many of the Pakistani groups, on the other hand, are oriented towards return, while the Sikhs are in between: they are building up a distinctive migrant community within the receiving society in the attempt to transplant their culture.

Chapter 7 drew attention to the strength of the forces within the life of the receiving society which reward the newcomers who conform to the expectations of that society. Successfully to resist those forces over several generations, as isolationist groups like the Amish have done, requires a tremendous commitment to the group and powerfully distinctive institutions. Few groups have been able to transplant their culture into an industrialized society; most have, in the end, changed their way of life to resemble that of other groups around them. But a new factor has been at work recently. Because of the great improvement in world communication and transport it is possible for migrants to stay in touch with their homelands and their relatives there; to pay short return visits is no longer prohibitively expensive. In some ways, too, the receiving societies have become more tolerant of cultural diversity so that the pressures to conform are less extensive.

The migrant usually takes his homeland culture for granted. He may be unaware that the customs of other groups are different from those he knows. When he finds himself among strangers he turns to people from his own country as people whom he can understand and trust, and people who can understand him. A man from a neighbouring village whom he would once have viewed with profound suspicion is greeted like a long-lost brother. The boundary line round his friends is expanded to incorporate new people like this, but in individual instances it is often expanded too rapidly. The migrant trusts some other migrant who professes solidarity based upon common origin or appearance, and he gets duped; so there is suspicion within minorities as well as between them and others. Where there are people from many ethnic groups, it often happens that some groups get more of the good jobs, sometimes because they are better educated. In these circumstances group membership has status connotations and migrant groups are drawn into the receiving society through its class structure. Ethnic boundaries come to be aligned with those of socio-economic stratification.

Jamaica, like so many of the societies of the Caribbean, took shape as a vast organization for the production of sugar, a crop which employed more labour per acre than almost any other crop in the world. Africans were imported to grow and harvest it and, when the ending of slavery meant that the plantations could no longer obtain all the labour they wanted, Indians and Chinese were introduced as indentured workers. Some islands were almost completely dependent on the sugar crop; like Barbados, where at one time it contributed 97 per cent of the value of their exports. With the decline in the demand for sugar, and the lower price obtained for it, such countries had to look for other sources of income. Jamaica had alternative crops and hoped to benefit from the development of the bauxite mining industry and from tourism. But it was caught in the trap of a population growing much faster than the economy. With a young population, the birth rate in 1960 was high (42.9 per thousand compared with 16.9 in the United Kingdom the previous year) and the death rate low (8.9 per thousand compared with 11.7). For every thousand people, there was in Jamaica an annual increase of 34 compared with 5 in the United Kingdom. To create a job for a new worker demanded a capital investment of about £2,000 and, as many of those jobs would have brought wages of less than £3 per week, they could not have generated much purchasing power. Unemployment increased steadily, being accelerated by mechanization on the sugar estates, and this was the major pressure behind the growing army of would-be migrants. They looked not only towards North America and Britain, but to other Caribbean islands like Trinidad so that the demand of some countries for freedom of movement within the West Indies Federation, and the resistance of others, became one of the main political obstacles to the success of that organization (Davison, 1962:39–41, 46).

For the migrants on the *Empire Windrush*, and in the following decade, Britain offered much better economic prospects than Jamaica. Not every migrant was able to take advantage of those opportunities, but most succeeded sufficiently to want wives, children and other relatives to follow them, and were able to help with the passage money. This gave rise to what has been called the 'rachet effect'; the more people who emigrated from a locality, the more this encouraged others to follow them (Davison, 1962:8). In the early stages the West Indians who came to Britain included a high proportion of skilled men, a far higher proportion than in the population of the sending societies; though the proportion of unskilled rural migrants later rose, it seems as if at all times it was the better-educated and socially ambitious people who made the journey. They may not have had a clear idea of what was awaiting them, but on arrival most adapted successfully and, even those who decided after all that Britain was not for them, seem to have felt that they gained from the experience. A Jamaican sociologist who interviewed returning migrants on a ship bound for Kingston reported that one of the real surprises to emerge from his discussions with them was the absence of any hard feelings towards Britain, except from those few who were blaming others to excuse their own failures. Not one person admitted that he had any great difficulty getting a job or that there was any discrimination on the factory floor by the managers. They seemed to take the existence of prejudice for granted, resenting it on the occasions when they suffered from it, but concluding that nothing was to be gained by worrying about it. Almost all claimed to have got on well with their workmates (Patterson, 1968:76–7).

Nearly half the migrants on the *Empire Windrush* had nowhere to go in Britain, so the government accommodated them in the mile-long underground shelter at Clapham Common in the borough of Lambeth. The next day the first of them obtained work, as a night watchman, and within three weeks all the others had done likewise. They moved out into lodgings in the neighbouring district of Brixton which quickly became the major area of black settlement (Eggington, 1957:63–9). Official statistics furnish little information about the sorts of work they obtained. Like members of the other New Commonwealth immigrant groups they could be expected to move towards those industries in which there was a high demand for labour of the kind that they were able and willing to provide. They served as a replacement workforce, taking the places of white workers who were seizing opportunities to move to more attractive jobs and better residential areas (Peach, 1968:92–100). Official statistics for later years show rather more immigrants employed in vehicle manufacture and the category 'transport and communication' which is doubtless due to consistently high demand for non-skilled manual labour in these industries.

An analysis of information collected in the 1972 General Household Survey (Chiswick, 1980) compared the earnings of white and coloured males after making allowances for differences in the number of hours worked and other variables. Holding schooling and demographic variables constant, it found that the earnings of white males were 25 per cent higher than those of coloured males, whereas foreign born white men had 6 per cent higher earnings than native-born whites; coloured immigrants had 19 per cent lower earnings than native-born whites, but native-born coloured men had earnings only 3.7 lower than native-born whites and because of the small sample, the difference was not statistically significant. This finding implied that racial differences in earnings might narrow in the next generation. Two years later a PEP survey found that the earnings of male West Indians were 92 per cent, and those of minority men in general 91 per cent, of the earnings of white males. The sample was based on census enumeration districts in which the proportion of minority residents reached 2.2 per cent or more and therefore under-records the 24 per cent of the ethnic population dispersed in areas of lower concentration. It excludes the higher-earning minority members but this is more than counterbalanced by the exclusion of higher-earning whites.

Table 5 *Income by socio-economic and ethnic group: Great Britain*

Socio-economic group	Males		Females	
	White	Coloured	White	Coloured
Professionals	107	80	68	68
Employers and managers	94	61	53	53
Non-manual white collar	64	58	35	39
Skilled manual	60	56	28	31
Semi-skilled manual	51	54	24	34
Unskilled	45	51	18	29
All groups	67	58	31	36

Mean weekly income 1975–8 in £s

Source: General Household Survey, quoted from Field, *et al.*, 1981:31

The PEP survey compared the proportion of whites and minority men in different occupational levels. Forty per cent of the whites and 8 per cent of West Indians had professional or white-collar jobs; 42 per cent of whites and 59 per cent of West Indians were skilled manual workers; 18 per cent of whites and 32 per cent of West Indians were semi- or un-skilled manual workers. If it is remembered that 19 per cent of the West Indians said they had been in Britain for more than 14 years, 42 per cent for 12 to 14 years and 25 per cent for less than 12 years, then these figures can be interpreted in either of two ways. They can suggest that West Indian men coming from a very different environment, with very little capital or sources of assistance, and having to contend with racial discrimination and other handicaps, have nevertheless adjusted rapidly and been very successful in a competitive situation; in other words, the figures record an impressive degree of black achievement. Equally it can be argued that had it not been for discrimination the differentials would have been much smaller, and that the figures are to be read as a criticism of the receiving society. There is no objective basis for contending that one of these interpretations is better than the other.

Table 5, based on a later and national sample shows minority males to have higher earnings in the bottom two occupational categories, doubtless because more of them are in the younger age categories, more work extra hours, and more work shifts. Among minority women, unlike the men, earnings are equal in the higher occupational categories and higher in the lower ones, probably because many native women work only part-time. Overall, the evidence is consistent with the view that, while minority workers are represented in a wide range of occupations and industries, they are concentrated on the lower rungs of the occupational ladder for each kind of job. It also has to be remembered, firstly, that one income may have to be used to feed more people in the minority households. The PEP figures of the number of persons per working adult were: 1.17 for whites, 1.49 for West Indians, 1.87 for Indians, and 1.72 for Pakistanis and Bangladeshis. Secondly, many minority workers, particularly Asians, send remittances to help support relatives in the countries of their birth. Thirdly, minorities tend to pay higher rents than whites although their accommodation tends to be inferior. The question of minority housing is examined in greater detail in the next chapter.

Anyone who leaves his or her homeland for another four thousand or more miles away takes a big decision. The advice and help of relatives and friends is usually crucial to the decision to settle in a particular locality, and to the cultivation of new social ties. Jamaicans have usually settled in neighbourhoods where others from their island have pioneered the way, but Jamaicans have provided the largest group of West Indian immigrants and they have spread out more. Migrants from the smaller islands have been more limited in their areas of settlement. For example, of the 4,000 or so migrants from Montserrat in England in 1965–6, about 80 per cent lived in three boroughs of north and east London (Philpott, 1973.167–8). In Britain the migrants find most of their friends from among people from the same homeland; they think of returning there and are bound by social controls still rooted in the homeland. If a man misbehaves, this is liable to be reported to his kinsfolk in the homeland who may remonstrate with him. If the offender is aware that the people whose good opinion he used to value know of the complaints, he is more likely to feel ashamed. Outside the work environment migrants may have little contact with the English or even with migrants from other parts of the West Indies, about whom they may have prejudices of their own. Thus a social anthropologist reports that when one mother in a Montserrat village received ten pounds through the mail from a Jamaican in London, seeking her permission to court her daughter who also lived in London, the woman kept the ten pounds but sent a letter to her daughter telling her to have nothing to do with Jamaicans, 'the wickedest people on earth' – though she had never seen one (Philpott, 1973:171). Relations with people from other islands may build up through membership of the same church, sports club or through the friendships of the children, while friendships with members of the majority society may start from the work place. According to a national survey in 1979 West Indian males were married to West Indian females 3.2 times more often than they were married to females of British ethnicity. African, Indian and Pakistani males were married to females of their own ethnicity 4.0, 9.5 and 10.3 times more often than to females of British ethnicity. West Indian, African and Indian females were roughly half as likely to be married to men of British ethnicity by comparison with the male members of these minority groups; Pakistani females were almost six times less likely to be married to British men than were Pakistani men to be married to British females. Younger people were more likely to be married cross-ethnically, so the frequency of these marriages is increasing (Jones, 1982; cf. Smith, 1977:51–2).

The main conclusion to be drawn from this and similar information about contacts between people of similar origin but different socio-economic status, is that life in industrial societies is divided up into little compartments that are as separate as villages in an agricultural society. The media of mass communication and the apparatus of state regulation create an appearance of every citizen belonging to a mass society. Any one individual can be brought into relation with a very great number of fellow-citizens, but it is likely that the contact will occur only in a patterned and fairly formal relationship of short duration while working, shopping or travelling. The kinds of contact which lead to friendship are few and are heavily influenced by previous social ties and sharing in a common way of life with similar interests. Differences in wealth can be a much bigger obstacle than differences in political opinions. The most striking feature of racial relations in industrial societies may be the infrequency of personal contacts between people belonging to different racial categories, but this has very little to do with beliefs about race. It is a reflection of a more general social pattern.

White people in Britain often do not distinguish between Jamaicans, Trinidadians, Guyanese, Montserratians, and people from the other islands. They call them all West Indians and are more ready to assume that there is a West Indian community in an English city than to assume that there is a Scottish or Yorkshire community, or a community of immigrants from some part of northwestern Europe. It is reasonable to expect that a Jamaican will feel more in common with a Trinidadian than with an Italian, for the islands have more in common culturally than they have with Italy. But quite quickly the Jamaican and the Trinidadian will come to share something new, the experience of being treated as black people by the English. In this sense the English help to create a West Indian community where there was none before. A black American anthropologist who studied social relations involving Jamaicans and Trinidadians in north London in 1967–9 concluded that it was neither useful nor meaningful to think in terms of a West Indian, or a Jamaican, or a Trinidadian 'community'. The position was too fluid. Jamaicans and Trinidadians based some of their social relations upon ties formed before migration and unrelated to the district of settlement, but the relations had changed so that, when new kinsmen or friends from their natal districts arrived, their social expectations were rather different from the new pattern that was being established. Because of different educational standards in their home countries migrants from Barbados claimed a higher status than those from Trinidad, who in turn ranked above those from Jamaica (Pollard, 1972). There were only potential Jamaican, Trinidadian, and West Indian communities.

Social acceptance by the English was probably not high in the list of the West Indian settlers' priorities. They had their own lives to lead: trying to establish themselves in a new country and with children to bring up, there was often little time left for socializing. In such circumstances a potential community becomes an actual community only when community organizations, formal or informal, perform a service for the members which is important enough relative to the business of making a living for people to invest less energy in the pursuit of other goals in order to invest more in the building up of community ties.

Pakistan has been the source of the migrants who contrast most with the West Indians. The social organization of the working-class Pakistani migrants in Britain is based on village and kin ties and not upon their shared nationhood. They come from several parts of the country, the greatest number being from the refugee areas of Kashmir and the Punjab, particularly from the Mirpur district of Azad Kashmir. They, and the Punjabi Muslims, were in many cases displaced in the disturbances that followed the 1947 partition of India. In 1960 the Pakistani government decided to build a dam at Mangla which would submerge 250 villages in the Mirpur district. Compensation was paid to those displaced and it was used by some recipients to finance further emigration to Britain. Others came from the Chhachh area, or Campbellpur sub-district, and from parts of Nowshera sub-district. In these localities there has been a well-established tradition for young men to emigrate for a few years to earn and save money, and eventually return to their village (Dahya, 1973:244). There are smaller numbers of Pakistani migrants from other rural and urban areas (on the latter, see Jeffery, 1976). The migrants made for cities like Bradford and Birmingham where work was available and where communities had already been established, if on a very small scale, mostly by seamen who during the war left their ships in British ports in order to seek better-paid employment ashore (Dahya, 1974:84, 95).

The most detailed study of these migrants is that conducted by Badr Dahya over a substantial period up to 1967. He makes it clear that most of them were small landholders who in their districts of origin despised labouring work and the people who did it. In Britain they did not hesitate to undertake such work themselves because they saw Britain as a different social world to which they did not belong. They had come simply in order to earn as much as they could, spend as little as possible, and remit or take back the maximum amount for the benefit of their kinsfolk and friends in the homeland. But there are limits. Dahya tells the story of a migrant in a Bradford mill who refused to sweep the floor, saying: 'I can't do it'. The shop manager took off his jacket, loosened his collar, rolled up his shirt sleeves, and gave him a demonstration of how to sweep the floor, only to be told; 'Ah! It is all right for you because you are a Christian! In our country too, all sweepers are Christians. I am a Muslim and can't do it.' He would not undertake a task which could be understood in terms of the values of his home village and there interpreted so as to detract from his prestige and that of his kinsfolk. Thus the informal controls which regulate the life of Pakistani immigrants resident in Britain are rooted in the homeland and the continuing competition between kin groups there.

The head of the family exercised authority over the family members, managing its property and distributing resources to meet the domestic needs of members. He arranged the marriages of his children and grandchildren. Religious beliefs supported the conventional respect for old age and traditional authority, so that the family head was presumed to know what was best for everyone else; even a man who was in his fifties and the father of adult children complied with his decisions like the others. A family head would arrange the betrothal of a migrant either immediately before his departure or soon after he had established himself in Britain. Usually he would be betrothed to the daughter of a kinsman, or to a girl from a family of the same caste, but when a group was successful in exploiting the opportunities of migration it was able to advance its status, and marriage to girls from high caste urban commercial and professional classes, including military families, might become possible. In the more normal course of events the migrant might work in Britain for five or six years before returning to his village for a visit of six to twelve months during which he would get married. On his return to Britain he might buy a small house in the inner city if he had not done so earlier, and would there accommodate any younger male kinsman whose immigration he might have assisted. At a later stage the family head might permit a migrant's wife to join him, though she was likely to leave any female children behind. Dahya (1973:253) reported that in 1971 a man wrote to a migrant newspaper complaining that although he had been faithfully carrying out his obligations to his father in Pakistan, the latter had refused to allow the migrant's wife and children to join him. He now sought advice as to his next move.

In Dahya's view the migrant's transactions with his family head could be regarded as a series of moves in a game in which each party was trying to secure the best possible bargain. The family head wanted the migrant to save and remit money to finance further migration, to buy land, to build a big house in brick and cement, perhaps to open a shop or business in a nearby town, and certainly to raise the prestige of the family, especially by arranging marriages with families of higher status. By investing the migrant's savings in such ventures, he gave the migrant a greater stake in the social life of his district of origin and reinforced the incentives for him to return. The Pakistan government lent a hand in this by encouraging insurance companies to tap the migrants' savings and invest them in policies which on maturity were payable only in Pakistan. If the cycle could be maintained the migrant would return home on the death of the family head, perhaps to take over this position, while leaving younger kinsfolk in Britain over whom he would exercise authority. He might be even more severe, for he had experienced the same living conditions and knew the temptations to which the migrants were exposed.

This homeland orientation affected many aspects of the migrants' lives in Britain. Dahya stated that in the emigrant villages he visited in Pakistan the people had often been exploited by outsiders so that they had learned to distrust people who were not kinsmen or known relatives. The migrants brought this viewpoint with them to Britain, showing little or no interest in the possibilities of collective action to improve conditions at work or in the neighbourhood. Any formal migrant association was likely to consist of a small group of kinsmen and friends who were of urban origin, represented by a society with a general-sounding name, lettered notepaper, and secretary with a typewriter; but the office-holders were not leaders in the sense of being decision-makers for the rural migrants and did not have anything like the influence of family heads. The office-holders in such associations, being literate and more skilled in the use of English, served as intermediaries. Their wives did not observe *purdah* (on which see Khan, 1976) and were often active in the All Pakistan Women's Association. Dahya refers to a conference at which the President of the local branch of this Association contended that the dignified status which Islam conferred upon Muslim women fourteen hundred years ago had not yet been achieved by Western women. It seemed as if these remarks were a warning to outsiders to leave immigrant Muslim women alone, especially in respect of *purdah* and their lack of English, so that representatives of the Pakistani elite could retain their position as intermediaries.

The homeland orientation affected the migrants' participation in British politics. In Bradford a Conservative Party candidate solicited Asian support in the 1959 municipal election. He won the seat in the following year, believing the Asian vote to be responsible for his apparently spectacular success, though it is far from certain that this was the case. Thereafter other parties competed for the Asian vote, while the first Asian stood as an independent candidate in 1963. The Liberals in one ward adopted an Asian candidate for the municipal election of 1969 and the

Labour Party in an adjoining ward soon followed suit. In 1971 they chose Manawar Hussain for the fifth safest Labour seat in the city. His prospects seemed excellent, but Hussain came from what was then East Pakistan and the tensions were building up which led to the fighting which was to result in its becoming the independent state of Bangladesh. West Pakistani leaders accused the Labour Party of favouring the Bangladesh side in the conflict and their countrymen turned out in strength to vote for the Conservative candidate (Le Lohé, 1975:91, 106–13). Dahya observes that whereas the migrants welcomed the election of Asian candidates as a means of raising their status and securing their civil rights, they were afraid that the exercise of those rights would bring corresponding civil duties, like jury service, which they saw as more of a burden than a privilege. They would participate only in so far as this would further their aims of saving money, staying separate, and returning to their homeland.

The major threat to the possibility of their remaining separate comes from the presence in Britain of the migrants' wives and children. The children attend British schools, watch television and learn new aspirations, norms and expectations. They see English girls with short skirts, bare arms, artificially waved hair, using conspicuous cosmetics to attract male attention, and behaving in ways that in the homeland would be considered utterly shameless. The men do not want their girl children corrupted by such influences so they keep them close to the home and often send them back to their home villages at the onset of puberty. The migrants have acted so as to emphasize and reinforce their cultural distinctiveness by having their wives and children dress in the styles of a Pakistani city. They restrict their daughters' participation in certain school activities (physical education, athletics, sport) and have established Sunday schools to provide religious education, mainly for boys, while there is now a private school in Bradford run on Islamic lines, parallel to the separate schools established by other religious bodies. By stressing their distinctiveness they attract some hostility and this, in turn, makes it easier to maintain the distinctiveness.

Such measures are the more necessary because the migrants hold a basically favourable image of life in Britain. It is not surprising that prior to migration Pakistanis should have entertained a golden vision of British life in which there was no place for racial discrimination, overcrowding or menial work. When they have been in Britain for a while they talk about it with disdain as a heathen country in which there is nothing worthwhile except the opportunity to earn and save, contrasting unfavourably with the now golden image of their country of origin. To put this critical view in context, though, it is necessary to note the terms in which migrants on return visits to Pakistan described Britain to Dahya, who, as they well knew, had visited many Pakistani homes and lodging houses in different parts of

Britain. To him they said such things as 'England is a perfect country in every way except that the people there are not Muslim'. He quotes, too, a letter to a migrant newspaper after the Labour Party's defeat in the 1970 general election entitled: 'Alas! If only Mr Wilson had been a Muslim . . .' In the letter the migrant describes in sympathetic terms the TV portrayal of the former Prime Minister, with a few items of furniture, leaving No. 10 Downing Street. The writer observes that the Wilsons had no house of their own to go to and contrasts their situation with that of certain Middle Eastern dignitaries saying: 'Had Mr Wilson been a Muslim, we could have held him up as an example to Muslim leaders who live in the lap of luxury.' The migrants judge British society from their own standpoint and the features they select for criticism or praise may not be those the European would expect (Dahya, 1973:264–9). When he returns to Pakistan the migrant finds that he is expected to pay a great deal extra for any personal services, and grumbles about the way he is exploited. Slowly his attitudes start to change. His identification with the sending society weakens but he does not necessarily identify more with the receiving society. He is more likely to start identifying himself with the immigrant community newly established within the receiving society.

For the Pakistanis this process is not far enough advanced for its character to be certain. Probably it gains most momentum among those migrants who are self-employed and therefore enjoy highest prestige within the immigrant community. Muhammad Anwar (1979:131) says that he was told in 1976 that at least two Pakistani textile manufacturers in Rochdale were making enquiries about exporting garments to countries in the European Community and were looking for Pakistani contacts there. He describes the ways in which teenage boys (some still at school) were encouraged to undertake part-time work collecting the garments, delivering materials to home-workers, ironing, sewing buttons, and the like. Some migrant women worked in the mills, going out dressed in tunic and baggy trousers to work in a team directed by an English-speaking Asian woman, probably a Sikh or a Gujerati. The men might justify this by saying that the wife's wages went towards the cost of running a car, and a car enabled them to visit relatives in different districts. But the change was of greater significance than was appreciated at the time it was introduced. If wives and children contributed to the family income this reduced the power of the male head of the household; the desire to earn money became more important relative to the maintenance of traditional values so that when there was a choice between the two, the migrants were more likely to seek their financial advantage; more of the money came to be spent upon comforts for life in Britain and for gaining status in the eyes of members of the migrant community rather than in the eyes of kinsfolk and fellow-villagers back home; women and children built up their own links with the sending society independently of the senior male, and they were more subject to British cultural influences. All this ran contrary to the process of incapsulation. For the man, it meant a change from being a migrant worker to being an immigrant; from being a transient to becoming a sojourner. (A sojourner is a migrant who leaves his country of origin to work, achieve his objectives as soon as possible, and return home, but never keeps to his plan; he stays abroad while continuing to think of himself as a temporary resident – Siu, 1952.) This recalls what for many migrant groups has been called 'the myth of return'. People talk of going back and the idea of doing so remains important psychologically to their life in the receiving society, but there is little likelihood that they ever will return.

The Punjab, a state in Northern India on the frontier with Pakistan, has been the sending society for a group of migrants who have gone further than the Pakistanis in establishing an immigrant community in Britain. These are the Sikhs, followers of what was originally a reform movement within Hinduism but is now a distinctive religion. Although Sikhism officially deprecates the caste system and preaches the equality of all men before God, it has not in practice stopped the organisation of families in caste-like occupational groupings. One such grouping which has provided many of the migrants to Britain is that of the Jats or farmer caste; another is that of the Ramgarhia, or craftsmen, many of whom emigrated to East Africa and have travelled from there to Britain; there are smaller groups of Bhattras (merchants) and Mosbees (sweepers).

An account of the background to Jat Sikh emigration by Joyce Pettigrew (1972) helps explain who emigrates, and why. When a farmer with several sons dies, the sons have equal claims to inherit his land, but if the patrimony is subdivided the plots they obtain may be very small, so some of them have to find another way of making a living. Families are engaged in continuous competition with one another for honour and power (status derives from power in this society). Much of this competition centres upon making the most favourable marriage alliances possible. There is little opposition between altruism and egotism in the way the Westerner conceives these ideas, for rarely is a man faced with the problem of whether he should put first his family's interests or his own individual interests. To help himself, he has to help his kin. If he were to accumulate wealth, but did not have his kinsfolk's support, he would have difficulty retaining or enjoying his gains. Family obligations override all others; obligations to non-kinsfolk are weaker and operate on a different level of morality.

Jats are brought up to a way of life which associates land-owning with honour and political dominance, but working on the land has been a task for inferiors. Because of the continual division of inheritances, many Jats find themselves able to command less land than that to which they consider themselves entitled. They prefer to seek their future elsewhere. Though the different sections of a joint family help one another, the members of one that is poor feel embarrassed and are more likely to emigrate. So, apparently, are men in occupations of relatively low prestige, like that of schoolteacher; while a young man may be pushed into emigration when his kinsfolk fear that if he remains at home he may become an embarrassment to them (see Helweg, 1979:17). The more prestige-conscious a village, the greater its potential for emigration. Among the Jats, the various factors which determine honour and power can all be related through the common measuring-rod of money. A girl's B.A. degree, a returned emigrant's factory, an hereditary title, can all be seen as counters in the material exchange which accompanies marriage. The struggle for status leads to alliances between people of differing degrees of respectability: the lawyer mixes with the law-breaker and the doctor can be friendly with a gold dealer. Yet this is not just a question of commodity values. The claims of friendship draw upon important elements in the Jat's ideal of manliness, and these claims survive after other joint activities have ceased. Nevertheless, the fuel which drives the emigrant's ambition is still the desire for honour, and for money as a means of acquiring honour.

This explains why men leave the land, but not why they choose to come to Britain. The Punjabi villager who thinks of emigrating has a wider range of possibilities than the Mirpuri villager, for Punjabis have a greater tradition of migration both within India and overseas to Malaya, Burma, Canada, and elsewhere. The men of certain districts within the Punjab have already monopolized the opportunities for a military career, while those from certain towns have captured many of the openings in the transport industry, so it was the men of one of the remaining districts, that of Jullundur, who looked to the opportunities presented by English industry. Behind this connection is the imperial one which conferred on Indians British nationality and a right to settle in Britain when they had no corresponding right to settle in other overseas countries. The nature of the sending society also helps explain features of migrant behaviour in Britain. Like the Mirpuris, the Punjabis adopt a pragmatic attitude towards employment. At least to start with, it is status back home that matters, not status in English eyes.

The earliest phase of Sikh settlement was that of the pioneers who, between the two world wars of the twentieth century, left their ships in British ports to move inland and set themselves up as pedlars going round from house to house selling goods on credit from suitcases. Then in the 1950s mass migration got under way. It was a migration of adult males who in Britain lived in all-male households, usually residing in a house owned by a fellow-Sikh who exercised a kind of paternal authority over his tenants.

The landlord, or another Sikh who had some command of the language and had learned how to handle relations with English officials and business-people, served as a go-between and broker in Sikh–English relations as well as a patron. He would introduce a new arrival to people in the personnel departments of local factories and help them obtain work. This placed the newcomer more firmly into a client relation with his patron to whom he had to render reciprocal services when called upon, and it was the beginning of a structure of status and power within an immigrant community. At the beginning of this second phase the migrants sent home their earnings almost as soon as they were received. They worked long hours, even on occasions as much as 90 hours in a week. After a while they discovered new ways of enjoying themselves now that there was no-one around to tell tales about their misconduct. They cut their hair (instead of having it tied up inside a turban), they frequented the public houses, consorted with English prostitutes and other girls; their leisure was their own. Having remitted money to pay off the costs of their passage or to help their family's needs, they began to retain more of their savings so that they could send or take home the money as an impressive lump sum. They began to look for profitable investments in Britain to increase their capital, and an obvious course was to buy up cheap houses in the inner-city areas. Roger and Catherine Ballard (1977:33), in their description of the development of Sikh settlements, write that, to South Asian villagers, *izzat*, or prestige, is perhaps the most important of all goals. 'The most significant transformation in overseas settlements came about when these too became arenas within which *izzat* could be gained or lost. Once this occurred, all migrants had to compete or else lose face: this was the point at which the transition to the third phase of settlement, consolidation, took place.'

The Sikh migrants were not subject to the authority of family heads in the sending society like the Mirpuris. They could take their own decisions to arrange for their wives and children to migrate and for their families to be reunited in Britain. The fear that the British government would enact legislation to make this more difficult speeded up the process so that during the 1960s family reunification went ahead rapidly. A study of the Sikh community in Gravesend (Helweg, 1979:55–65, 89–90) draws attention to the implications of this for the Sikh men. As soon as the women came over they set up a hot line to the sending society, telling their sisters there about the doings of fellow-Sikhs, especially those of whose conduct they disapproved. The case of Kewal Singh is an illustration. This young man, as a dutiful son, had remitted money to his parents in the Punjab where his father had started to arrange a marriage for him. But the bride's family heard that he was often drunk and slept with English girls, so they broke off negotiations. This diminished the *izzat* of all Kewal's kinsfolk in the village since the misconduct of one person reflects upon everyone associated with him or her. A father who had taken pride in his son was now shamed by him.

In the view of the Ballards, perhaps the most important change in the third phase was that it became possible to celebrate life-cycle rituals in Britain, and among these marriage is of particular importance because it identifies two kin groups. In the homeland betrothals had to be between people of similar caste but different clan, and the standing of the two families was assessed largely in terms of the land they owned. When a marriage is arranged between two families in Britain a new preference has developed: the bride should come from a family living in a different city from the groom's parents, for the wholly traditional reason of ensuring a distance between the groom and his mother-in-law. The educational and occupational standing of the families has become more important than the amount of land owned in the Punjab. Sikh marriages have become increasingly elaborate affairs so that the authors, writing of the 1970s, say that a father can hardly avoid spending at least £2,000 on each daughter, and possibly much more, especially on dowries. This sort of competition for *izzat* drove each family to maximize its income; it strengthened the arguments for the women to obtain paid employment; it drew everyone in the family further into the English economic structure.

The 1960s also saw the immigration of Sikhs who had previously been resident in Uganda, Kenya and Tanzania where they had already adapted to life as members of a distinctive minority. Though more Anglicized than the migrants who came directly from India, they were also more inclined to wear the turban, to maintain religious practices and to cultivate those cultural features which sustained their ethnic identity. As Sikh communities built up in Britain, so an ethnic infrastructure developed of grocers, cinemas, cloth and sweet shops, goldsmiths and travel agents to serve an Asian clientele (for many migrants travelled back to the Indian subcontinent to visit kinsfolk). These establishments were followed by garages, driving schools, taxi services, insurance brokers and television repair shops. Indian groups have advanced much further in this direction than Pakistanis or West Indians. Running his own business gives a man added status within the ethnic minority. It brings a prospect of greater economic reward because he can more easily circumvent racial discrimination, while the availability of support from his family (especially in keeping a shop) gives him an advantage over competitors from the native majority.

If the migrants had held to the objectives which led them to leave the Punjab in the first place, they would have returned and not arranged for their families to be reunited in Britain. A minority did return, intending to enjoy the benefits of the capital they had accumulated, but things did not go according to plan. They complained universally of the corruption, which probably affected them the more because their absence had removed them from the network of political and economic contacts without which it is difficult to run a farm or a business successfully. Most of them continually put off a decision, and the presence of the children complicated matters. They disliked the possibility of their growing up to resemble the English but the advantages of an English education were considerable. If the children succeeded at school this brought the family prestige. If the children were sent back to the Punjab they enjoyed the warmth of the reception from their kinsfolk but they suffered from poor health because of the difference in diet; they missed the amenities of English life and did not take well to being disciplined by village grandparents or Indian teachers. The adult settlers in Britain had by this time developed a sense of pride in their homes. They decorated them with wallpaper, carpeting and matching furniture, and remodelled the bathroom in the modern style. Village life became unbearable for women who were used to modern kitchens. Moreover, the sending community and the immigrant community were growing steadily further apart. When the migrants visited their home villages they were still treated with outward respect because of their wealth, but privately they were regarded as of inferior status because their position did not derive from land-ownership. As one villager remarked: 'They are just common labourers in the factory, working like dogs, while I am a king on my land' (Ballard, R. and Ballard, C., 1977:41; Helweg, 1979:66, 93). The migrants continued to talk of returning as a way of communicating their refusal to identify with life in England, but they had nearly all decided to remain whether or not they were prepared to acknowledge this.

In the next decade some Sikhs were managing to move up the occupational ladder a little and their children were growing into adolescence. This is the fourth phase so far and it is one which focuses on the children. They are sometimes depicted as torn between two cultures. It is un-questionable that some individuals do not have the psychological strength to reconcile the contrary pressures, but they are only a minority. There is a struggle within the immigrant community about the circumstances and extent to which Western ways can be accepted. The daughter of one of the early immigrants to Gravesend remembered that as soon as her aunts arrived, a great deal changed: 'the women would come to our house and say, "Don't you think Nimi's hair should be braided now that she is ten?" or "Nimi should not go to school with bare legs, otherwise she will grow up being immodest".' Her mother had to conform, but Nimi began to react against Punjabi culture because it restricted her freedom. In another incident two schoolgirls on a bus were making a bit of a noise talking in Punjabi. An older Kenyan Asian girl reproved them and said they should sit beside the English ladies to improve their English and learn British ways.

Soon afterwards she had half a dozen Punjabi mothers on her doorstep to tell her, in a threatening way, not to spoil their daughters by encouraging them to adopt English ways and become like herself (Helweg, 1979:55, 120). In this struggle the mothers can tell someone else's daughter to mind her own business, but they soon have problems with their own daughters, for children have their special ways of putting their parents under pressure. A girl of 16 years can run away with her boyfriend and may be entitled to draw welfare benefits from the state which will make her independent of her parents. If they report her missing to the police, and the police discover her whereabouts, they will not, without her permission, give her new address to her parents. Asian parents know that children have run away like this and that it has brought shame upon their families. They do not want to run unnecessary risks and they make many concessions to their children in order to hold their families together.

A comparison of the decisions taken, consciously or unconsciously, by the migrants from Jamaica, Pakistan and the Punjab brings out some strong contrasts. First among the conclusions may be surprise that, given the population pressure in India and Pakistan, it was only a few small areas of the subcontinent that participated in the migration whereas virtually all the former British territories of the Caribbean have been involved. There are so many other localities in India and Pakistan where people simply did not see in emigration an opportunity of pursuing what they wanted from life. A decision to leave was conceived in a social, and first of all, a kinship setting. A man or woman was far more likely to migrate if that decision was supported by near kin; usually the man went first and it was largely for his family and his future family that he left the world he knew. But cultures differ in the extent to which they subordinate a person's independence to group obligations. The Mirpuri's decision-making was encompassed by his group obligations; the adult Punjabi was more independent of the parental generation and of the ties traced through them but he was still enmeshed in a competitive culture in which the competition was between family groups. The Jamaican migrant had grown up in a culture which, for historical reasons, showed a less developed and less formal structure of kinship obligations and one in which there were less potent sanctions upon anyone who neglected these obligations. The contrast was seen most clearly within the household, for the Jamaican woman was much more independent of her man than was the Asian wife; she could assert her rights as an individual whereas the Asian woman's rights were protected chiefly through the kin group.

The Mirpuri migrant had individual aspirations but they were objectives for himself as a member of a group. In Britain, it was kinsmen and fellow-villagers who helped him obtain work and housing, and showed him how to find his way around in a very strange society. He related to members of that society as one of a cooperating group and would have had difficulty managing in any other way. So long as his wife and children remained in the homeland his choices were constrained by the decision-making of the family head in Pakistan. The strategy of the sending community was to set up a rotational system whereby each migrant was called home after a time and replaced by a younger kinsman, but this was not an easy policy to implement since the balance of power started to tip against the family head. Remittances were used to build fine houses but sometimes these were left empty and locked because those for whom they were built were all in Britain. If remittances were invested in something other than land the income from them was not so easily controlled by the kin group. Local community life suffered because of the absence of so many of its members and because it was so difficult for the villagers to match the lavish spending of emigrants who returned on visits (for a striking example from Hong Kong, see Watson, 1977). Those who stayed behind had to build a new and different community life so that when migrants returned they found the society was not as they remembered it.

The Jamaican came from a society in which the ownership of land and other sources of wealth was on an individual basis. Like others brought up in a capitalistic culture, he aspired to wealth for himself and his immediate kin and if he was successful his goals changed in the course of his career. Like the Pakistani and the Punjabi, he often came from a country district, and adjustment to life in a complex urban civilization constituted a series of major problems quite independently of the operation of racial discrimination; but the Jamaican could not call upon the support of any more than a loose informal group in responding to those problems. In most ways he was the best equipped of the three to participate in British social life but because he, necessarily, followed an individual strategy and lacked the prior experience of many Asians in running businesses, he could not exploit any special opportunities in the British occupational structure. A study in Handsworth (Rex and Tomlinson, 1979:83) found that West Indians were more interested than Asians in the affairs of their homelands, much more inclined to say that they wished to return there and more likely to claim that they had definite plans to do so.

The Punjabi example is of migration decisions being taken initially in the homeland but then quite quickly being transferred to an immigrant community that was located within the receiving society but was in only a limited sense part of it. The Punjabi's aspirations were for the approval of fellow Punjabis, but the reference group changed from Punjabis in the homeland to those in Britain. To further those aspirations they competed as family groups with other family groups and as Punjabis with non-Punjabis.

They could call on kinsmen for help in raising capital to buy a house or start a business. They helped one another in celebration or in adversity. Their culture has been characterized by a high level of competitiveness; parents have to work the harder in order to provide dowries for their children. This orientation is seen even more strongly among the Gujerati migrants who have a stronger commercial tradition. In their society it is not unusual for a wealthy man to seek out others to whom he may lend money (Tambs-Lyche, 1980:171), since a man builds up prestige by putting others under an obligation to him. The culture of Asian groups can generate competitiveness in these ways, elevating those values that have been associated with the spirit of capitalism. They are often more competitively inclined than the twentieth-century English and one of the fears is that their successes will evoke hostility from less successful sections of the receiving society.

Britain's mosaic

The similarities and differences between these groups and their experiences can be examined in terms of Figure 8, classifying immigrant groups by the relative attractive power of the sending and receiving societies, and Figure 5 classifying groups by boundary and privilege. The Jamaicans start out as most attracted towards British society and its values, coming closer to the conformist orientation (box 1 in Figure 8) than the others. The Mirpuris are most committed to the sending society and can be placed in box 3, as showing a colonial orientation. All three groups were faced by English attitudes varying between incorporating and excluding as depicted in Figure 5. Most English people were willing to extend a degree of social acceptance to coloured immigrants who met their terms; in brief, the kind of cultural conformity which required an appropriate level of earnings. Their attitude often seemed grudging and reluctant, while some were openly hostile. It is difficult to characterize the English as a group in these circumstances because contact occurred only within particular relationships; urban living divides up and structures social relations in ways such that it is difficult to generalize about attitudes and social acceptance.

Over the course of time the attractive influence of the receiving society increased for members of all three groups. Among the Pakistanis, the Mirpuris responded to this most strongly by strengthening their inclusive boundary and developing the processes of incapsulation. The Jamaicans are more difficult to characterize in this way. Some have reacted to experience of exclusion by reinforcing their intention to return, while others have temporized, responding to situations as they developed. The Punjabis show most clearly a process which is also important among many of the other minorities. In between the sending and the receiving society they have created a new one, a minority community, by developing inclusive bonds based on social relations in Britain rather than on relations in the country of origin. To represent this, it would be necessary to change Figure 8 from being two- to being three-dimensional. This draws attention to a more general problem. If it is argued that the changes in each minority are unique, the appropriate way of studying them must be historical, and there is little scope for sociology. If, on the other hand, a sociological approach is to be developed, this requires some sort of framework within which minority responses can be compared. The difficulties in fitting the various minorities into the classifications of Figures 5 and 8 demonstrate that frameworks may need to be complex. They show that there are advantages in starting from the position of the individual actor and constructing a theoretical scheme in terms which will explain behaviour by identifying the influence of macro factors on the micro level.

The sequence of generations

The circumstances of excess demand for labour which made immigration politically acceptable no longer exist. If the high unemployment levels of the early 1980s persist, whites are likely to see blacks and Asians as competitors for jobs to which they, on historical grounds, have a better claim. Future developments will depend substantially upon relations in the housing and employment markets, but also upon the experience and responses of the second-generation settlers. It may therefore be helpful at this point to outline possible future scenarios as these have been seen by other authors.

One possibility has been called the 'class unity process', to identify the tendency for members of racial and ethnic strata to become incorporated in the classes of the native social structure and to define their major problems as class issues (Miles and Phizacklea, 1977; cf. Lawrence, 1974). The second is that of 'ethnic organization' (though it could be called the ethnic unity process) by which the different ethnic groups organize politically as separate units. The third is the 'black unity process' whereby all non-whites come to form a cooperating group. Both the Asian and the West Indian immigrants have been accustomed to cultural patterns in which a pale complexion is preferred, and are surprised to find that the English count as coloured every one who is non-white (and often have doubts about whether Mediterraneans are really white). The English do not draw a colour line as sharply as white Americans and usually subordinate distinctions of complexion to those of socio-economic status, but colour is important enough for many minority activists to believe that the unity of all non-whites (or at least of blacks and browns) must be the final outcome. Nevertheless there is much which suggests that this is improbable.

The various ethnic minorities have hitherto been very much aware of what divides them from one another and show more hostility towards the other minority groups than they do towards the English; for most Indians and Pakistanis 'black' is a pejorative description which they will not readily apply to themselves; while there are many incidents which evoke an alignment of non-white against white, there are also powerful forces drawing immigrants and their children into a consumer society and giving them wants and aspirations which bring them closer to the whites. The second process, ethnic unity, is expected to gain importance, especially among Asians, as the incapsulated minority communities become arenas for status competition, and they may well be a basis for mobilization for industrial and political action, but this process has also to contend with the absorptive attractions of the majority society and may not long remain powerful. In the longer run Hindu, Sikh, Muslim and other faiths may serve functions similar to those served by Judaism for the Jewish minority. Whether a distinctive religion could play such a part for the black British is much more problematical. Estimates of the probability of the first-mentioned scenario, that of minority members being drawn into class politics, tend to vary according to the writer's own beliefs about the importance of class struggles in history. Possibly the strongest case for it is that stated by Robert Miles and Annie Phizacklea (1977:506) who write

> we believe that West Indian, Indian and Pakistani workers in
> Britain have widely realized and accepted their class position as
> indicated by their voting behaviour and trade union membership
> but that this has not been matched by the response of fellow,
> British workers, nor until very recently, by the trade unions. The
> result is that on several occasions over the past few years, ethnic
> organization has been forced upon them as the only means of
> attaining their ends.

There is also scope for debate about the class position of black and Asian workers. It is possible that instead of their being absorbed into the British working class they will remain as an under-class, a reserve army of labour of the kind envisaged by those who write of internal colonialism (cf. Sivanandan, 1977).

The future pattern could incorporate elements of all these four possibilities, depending upon the extent to which the major political parties compete for minority votes, as well as the considerations already mentioned. Whatever happens, one important component will be the choices made by members of the minority second generation as they appraise the alternatives open to them. Many of these choices will be made in the context of their relations with their parents who will also be assessing the alternatives they see as open to their children. The children will often be influenced by their parents' judgements, either deferring to them or reacting against them.

In the Asian minorities the parental generation can offer greater rewards to children who follow their advice than can the corresponding generation of West Indian parents. The extended kinship network of the Asian groups can give their children significant emotional support and material assistance of the greatest importance in matters, such as those of house purchase, which are dependent upon capital accumulation. Many parents go to great lengths to assist their children and are willing to compromise in order to maintain family unity. One anthropologist who has studied a Sikh group, writes:

> Parents are acutely conscious of their powerlessness in the face of their children. They say that if they give in to their children's demands for the same degree of freedom as their English friends receive, then the children will be lost; if they are oppressive and authoritarian their children . . . will take the first opportunity to rebel . . . I have met fathers who will wait for their sons to return home before making quite a minor decision, so that they can have their say.

The same account continues: 'Children have enormous respect for their parents and are usually unwilling to precipitate inevitable shame on their parents by acting in a way which will be condemned by others.' To marry without parental consent would result in expulsion from the family group. Many of the young men who have behaved in a rather English manner in striking up liaisons with girls change radically when faced with the responsibilities to their kinsfolk that are embodied in marriage; some of them insist that their marriages must be arranged in completely traditional style and say that they do not want to meet their bride before the ceremony (Ballard, 1973:18, 22–3). Another author who confirms this interpretation, remarks on the young men who are sent back to the Punjab to visit their kinsfolk where they are received lovingly and generously as long-lost sons of the family. It reinforces their tendency to define themselves as Asian (Thompson, 1974:246). Many of the young people in England emphasize that they obtain much enjoyment from being Asian in culture and associate themselves with the Asian criticisms of the contemporary English way of life.

West Indian parents in England cannot offer their children the same emotional or material rewards for identifying themselves with the elder generation's view of how people should lead their lives. Because of the circumstances in the inner-city areas in which so many have made their homes, and the lack of the group supports which are so important to any understanding of Asians' position, a great deal of the deprivation suffered by the first generation of West Indian settlers is transmitted to the next. Cultural change among the Asians is likely to occur within an Asian framework with a desire for modernity used to select from and reinterpret the traditional heritage. Among the West Indians that heritage is much less distinctive and is a less extensive resource for those who are under pressure in a very competitive environment.

Access to the better rewarded positions in British society is characterized by what Ralph Turner (1960) has called sponsored as opposed to contest mobility. If promotion through the educational system is like a race, contest mobility is a pattern allowing all those contestants who have the motivation to keep on racing until the last opportunity before the winners are selected. Sponsored mobility is a pattern in which the most promising runners are selected at an early age for special training and thereafter have a very much higher chance of eventual success. Sponsored mobility has in England worked through the 'eleven plus' examination and what used to be the 'direct grant' schools. Promising children have been selected early, given a more academic education, helped with scholarships and subtly inducted into elite status. The route they follow stimulates competitiveness and promises high rewards in return for hard work and moderate incomes at the outset. Those youngsters who are not selected react against this by developing cultural styles which disparage intellectualism, stressing instead solidarity and immediate gratification. John Rex (1982) has recently illuminated the differences in the ways in which these influences bear upon young Asians and West Indians in Britain. Indian boys are encouraged by their parents to concentrate upon their studies. The values of their social groups resemble those of the British middle class more than of the working class so that both their culture and their family structure will support a strategy of deferred gratification. By contrast, West Indian parents are, in the main, less effective in helping their children's education; the careers which offer them the best prospects of reward are those which depend upon expressive styles, such as those of the musician, the sportsman, or, within the minority peer group, the hustler (cf. Pryce, 1977; on measurements of the comparative educational performance of minority school children see in particular Tomlinson, 1979).

It is customary to distinguish between the first generation in an immigrant minority, consisting of people born overseas, and a second generation made up of their children born in the country of settlement. There is also an in-between category technically belonging in the first generation, which can pose particular problems in a migratory movement like that of the West Indians. With them, the men migrated first, saved money, and then sent for their wives and children. Many of these young people had lived with their grandmothers from an early age, so if they were later sent to join their mothers in Britain they twice experienced separation from their mother figure (Kitzinger, 1978:44–5). Those who had completed some years of schooling in the West Indies had rarely reached the standards of their age-mates in Britain. If this section of the minority population is to be distinguished, it can, borrowing the Latin word for one-and-a half, be called the sesque generation. Many of them never caught up, and they had particular difficulty finding work. A high proportion of the Rastafarians in Britain have been drawn from this generation (Cashmore, 1979:191). Their parents complained that the permissive attitude of British people towards the disciplining of children (certainly compared with that prevailing in the West Indies) made it much more difficult for them to make their children face up to the very considerable challenges confronting them. Though the parental generation was, to start with, often critical of the sesque and second generations, in some connections they came to sympathize with their children's difficulties and to support them. In his report on the disorders in Brixton, London, in April 1981, Lord Scarman stated: 'One of the most serious developments in recent years has been the way in which the older generation of black people in Brixton has come to share the belief of the younger generation that the police routinely harass and ill-treat black youngsters' (1981:65).

Additional evidence on this is provided by a study in Manchester comparing black and white experiences of crime and the police. It found no significant differences between blacks and whites in the experience of being the victim of a crime, in the reasons for being in contact with the police or being stopped, searched or arrested by them. Blacks were somewhat more inclined to describe contacts with the police as 'unfriendly' and to complain of the way in which they had been treated 'as a person', the difference being one of 18 per cent as opposed to 9 per cent. Negative views of the police were as frequent among whites aged 16–24 years (37 per cent) as blacks (36 per cent) but older West Indians were more critical than older whites, supporting Lord Scarman's observations about Brixton. The Manchester study (Tuck and Southgate, 1981) also points to the importance of the design and quality of housing as a factor which, together with the quality of housing management, affects the incidence of crime and hence of incidents invoking police activity.

Describing the social background to the disorders in Brixton, Lord Scarman drew attention to the high percentage of children in care and of single-parent families in the black population; he wrote of the sense of disappointment in and frustration with the educational system felt by some black parents and children; he took note of the high local level of black unemployment, possibly 55 per cent for males under 19 years, and of the evidence of discrimination. And so, 'the young black person makes his life on the streets and in the seedy commercially run clubs of Brixton. There he meets criminals who appear to have no difficulty in obtaining the benefits of a materialist society.' As he also noted, this does not support the conclusion that young black people are wholly alienated from British society. At much the same time two research workers were attempting to check that possibility by interviewing samples so drawn as to tap the sources most likely to produce alienation (Gaskell and Smith, 1981). They found that, though young blacks scored higher on a scale measuring feelings of hopelessness, they recorded positive attitudes towards aspects of British society and its main institutions suggesting that they were the more inclined to feelings of hopelessness because they did *not* reject the society that treated them badly. The young blacks did not score lower on measures of self-esteem and they had not given up hope of obtaining employment. They might be more critical of the structure of white society, but their feelings towards it could not accurately be summarized as those of alienation.

The disorders which occurred in London (Brixton and Southall), Liverpool, Manchester, Leeds, Leicester and the West Midlands at this time inevitably evoke comparison with those in the United States in 1967, but while the British riots may have been a greater shock to public opinion, the physical toll was much less. In Brixton, during the two days of rioting 247 persons were arrested; 401 police officers and 48 members of the public were reported injured; 117 police vehicles and 87 other vehicles were reported damaged or destroyed. In Liverpool one white member of the public died as a result of injuries sustained when he was hit by a police car. Both in the United States and in Britain tension between young blacks and the police was central to the disorders. Lord Scarman concluded: '(1) The disorders were communal disturbances arising from a complex political, social and economic situation, which is not special to Brixton. (2) There was a strong racial element in the disorders, but they were not a race riot'; and finally: '(7) The riots were essentially an outburst of anger and resentment by young black people against the police.' It should also be noted that the level of street crime in the Brixton area was many times higher than that in other parts of London of similar socio-economic character, so that the action of the police in periodically swamping the locality with police officers who stopped anyone in the streets who aroused their suspicions was a routine response. The police considered that it was not worth while changing their policies to try to obtain a greater measure of public support for their crime patrols, and the lawful but heavy-handed approach of some individual policemen pushed youthful tolerance to breaking point. It should also be noted that many young whites were involved in the rioting and that according to some reports most of the rioters in Liverpool were white. The recent increase in youth unemployment was considered by many commentators to be one of the most important underlying causes.

A riot is not a single event permitting a simple explanation. It may be that the main cause of the attacks on the police was that of revenge for what

Scarman called 'instances of harassment and racial prejudice among junior officers on the street', but it is necessary to account also for attacks on firemen and ambulancemen. This would suggest that, once the disorders had started, they were seen as an opportunity to draw attention to grievances about established society and as a source of excitement. British cities are frequently troubled by vandalism and fighting between groups supporting rival football teams; rioting can be seen as an extension of the entertainment in which some young men will engage whenever they see an opportunity.* Once disorders are started they provide a cover for looters also, both black and white. Some witnesses at the Brixton enquiry thought the white looters were generally older, more systematic in their methods, and were from outside the neighbourhood.

The response of the British government was, like that of the United States government, to hold an enquiry. It resulted in very similar recommendations: the central government was to make available funds for programmes to alleviate racial disadvantage, particularly in education and employment.

> A policy of direct coordinated attack on racial disadvantage
> inevitably means that the ethnic minorities will enjoy for a time a
> positive discrimination in their favour. But it is a price worth
> paying if it accelerates the elimination of the unsettling factor of
> racial disadvantage from the social fabric. I believe this task to be
> even more urgent than the task of establishing on a permanent
> basis good relations between the ethnic minorities and the police
> (Scarman, 1981:135–6).

The English judge then ended by quoting the American president's address printed at the beginning of the United States National Advisory Committee Report.

Conclusion

Chapter 10 included a section comparing the various kinds of explanation advanced to account for the persisting economic inequality of Afro-Americans despite their long residence in the United States. It would be inappropriate to pose quite the same questions about racial inequality in Britain during a period when more members of the Asian and West Indian

---

* Readers in the United States should appreciate that in Britain the ownership of shotguns for hunting is very strictly controlled and hand guns are virtually unavailable to anyone. Individual and group fighting involving the use of fists and blunt instruments like sticks, kicking – at times with steel-tipped boots – and the throwing of stones and bottles, can occur the more easily because there is no fear that one of the parties will draw a gun. Fatalities are correspondingly unusual. Attacks on the police can also be risked the more readily because the police are unarmed.

minorities have been born outside Great Britain than within it; only towards the end of the 1980s will the number of people in the second generation of settlement come to equal the number in the first. In some respects it is more illuminating to compare the position of the minorities in Britain with the 'guest workers' on the European continent and migrant labourers in the United States.

On that continent (and to some extent in the United States) the incoming workers have mostly been either contract workers or illegal immigrants; in neither case have they been citizens of the country in which they work. The contract workers have had no right of residence after the expiry of their contract; the illegal immigrants have been specially liable to exploitation, and both have been used as a source of cheap labour. In Britain the immigrants have, until recently, had a right of entry as British citizens and have been eligible to vote (like Puerto Ricans in the United States). Illegal immigrants have been relatively few. Whereas migrant workers are often engaged for work such as fruit-picking which entails only limited contact with the native population (and guest workers in Germany have been housed in special barracks), in Britain the migrants have been concentrated in the cities and have been scattered over a wide range of industrial occupations. The physical differences which have caused Asians and West Indians to be seen as distinctive, in other ways than Turks are perceived in Germany, Moroccans in France, and Mexicans in the United States, constitute an extra factor to be added to those which decide their economic and political status, and are not necessarily the most important.

The first immigrant generation entered Britain with a competitive disadvantage because they lacked relevant employment skills and experience. Nevertheless, the gap between majority and minority may on balance have been smaller than that confronting the blacks who moved to the industrial cities in South Africa and the United States at earlier periods; since the immigrants to Britain were numerically a relatively small influx and there were job vacancies, they did not pose an economic threat and did not evoke the resistance which characterized South African apartheid or the United States colour bar. The question of numbers can be very important. To take an every-day example, at most colleges in the United States attended by Afro-Americans there are sufficient black students for them to organize their own dances on Saturday nights. For a black student to attend the white students' dance (or a white to attend the blacks') will be seen as something unusual and will raise questions about that student's motives. At most colleges in Britain, however, there will be relatively few non-white students; many of them may be from overseas and perhaps from countries with different ideas about dancing; if the black students wish to organize a dance of their own they may be too few to make a success of it, so if they attend the general student dance their presence is not unexpected. Interaction between people assigned to different racial categories is less compartmentalized in Britain than in the United States and very much less than anywhere in South Africa. In Britain the incidence of discrimination is less predictable than in the United States and very much less than in South Africa. As the next chapters will show, it is more likely to take the form of price discrimination than exclusion. Statistical discrimination is common, but not categorical discrimination. Since there has been no tradition of racial segregation, and since in recent decades there has been an international political climate sharply critical of racial discrimination, the prospects for racial equality in Britain should be better than in South Africa or the United States.

Chapter 4 challenged the suggestion that black–white relations in Brazil must come to resemble those in the United States, showing how the arguments of Parsons and Degler assumed that blacks constitute a natural group. If in the United States class differences within the black population come to resemble those within the white population, the goals of blacks will increasingly resemble the goals of whites of similar status. Black preferences for associating with fellow-blacks in social settings and church attendance will weaken. It is possible that, though white prejudice continues to decline, black experience of discrimination will increase as blacks demand equality of treatment in integrated situations instead of remaining within the more familiar world of black associations. If so, this will reflect the demands of blacks to be treated as whites are treated, and will take the edge off any claims to be considered a distinctive group. Most nations sustain their sense of identity because they share interests deriving from a common territory and economy; some groups, like the Jews, have a distinctive religion. Afro-Americans lack these bases for solidarity and are exposed to the assimilative influences of a consumer society. Such features can be seen more clearly in Britain; so, while events there in some respects followed those in the United States during the late 1960s, in the future some of the choices made by the descendants of West Indian and African settlers in Britain may well foreshadow changes in the social identity of Afro-Americans. Certainly the figures about intermarriage suggest this.

Even if such speculations about possible future developments are left aside, the very task of describing the British situation in terms comprehensible to someone who has personal experience only of that in the United States, reinforces the claim that race relations can be studied only comparatively. So great has been the influence of the mass media in communicating images of racial tension around the world that it is now impossible for people to contemplate developments even in their own country without being influenced by what they have learned of the United States. The facts of competition and cooperation between members of racial and ethnic groups in Britain and the United States are in vital respects quite different (though there are similarities which can be appreciated if the comparisons are carefully and explicitly formulated). At the same time the ways in which people in the two countries now think about racial relations probably resemble one another more closely than do the facts, and since ways of thinking influence ways of acting, over the course of time they make the facts more similar.

The factual contrasts are inescapable. The United States is a country of over 226 million people of whom nearly 11.6 per cent are Afro-Americans and over 6.4 per cent Hispanic-Americans. Great Britain is a country of 54 million people of whom, in 1976, 3.3 per cent were of New Commonwealth origin (West Indies 1.1 per cent; India, Pakistan and Bangladesh 1.2 per cent; Africa, Sri Lanka, Hong Kong, Malaysia, etc. 1.0 per cent). Afro-Americans have been a major component of the United States population almost from the time Europeans first settled there, but Hispanic-Americans are mostly recent immigrants. In Britain the whites are the natives. The coloured people are from Third World countries with distinctive cultures that stand in a relationship to the receiving society not unlike the relationship of Puerto Rico and parts of Latin America to the United States.

In Britain the position of the Asian groups illustrates the utility of definitions which allow for a group to be both an ethnic minority and a racial minority, since the Mirpuris, Gujeratis, Sikhs and others have in full measure all the attributes which have caused minorities elsewhere to be accounted ethnic, and yet at the same time their relations with the majority society are dominated by the racial definitions employed by members of that society. The position of people of West Indian origin is complicated in a different way. Members of the immigrant generation see themselves as Jamaicans, Trinidadians, Guyanese, Barbadians, Dominicans, Kitticians, Montserratians, St Lucians, Vicentians, and so on. They see themselves as West Indians only in so far as this definition has been forced upon them by others. Their British-born children, however, see themselves as black British and are so seen by their parents. The parallels between their position and that of black people of similar age in the United States are close and may become closer. To most of these young people in Britain (and to a small minority of young Asians) it is at present very important that they define themselves as black, for much the same reasons as this self-designation has been taken up in the United States; indeed it says something significant about white colour values in both countries that it should be so important to so many people that they define themselves in this way.

The present significance of the designation 'black' illustrates a common element in the way in which people in Britain, the United States and South

Africa now think about certain kinds of group relations. For people in Britain and the United States it recalls one of the most momentous events of modern history: the Atlantic slave trade and the enslavement of several millions of Africans in a social order which identified a pinkish skin colour with liberty and a brownish one with servitude. The contrast was then strengthened by calling it one between white and black, bringing in the historical associations of the former with purity and the latter with evil, dirt and misfortune. This emotional inheritance was challenged by the slogan 'black is beautiful'. The growing awareness among white Americans that slavery was a great historical wrong has occasioned feelings of guilt that have many consequences. Nathan Glazer (1975:177–8), discussing the growth of feeling of white ethnic identity in the United States in the late 1960s, suggests that, stimulated by Afro-American assertiveness, the descendants of the later immigrants from Europe began to reflect: 'If we are like all other Americans, then we bear the responsibility for slavery, exploitation and imperialism. If we are, however, Poles, Italians, Jews, and the like, we have our own history of being exploited to refer to in protecting our position or extending it.' The British conscience is not troubled by the country's part in the slave trade as the white American conscience is troubled by slavery (indeed the British tend to congratulate themselves upon their leadership of the struggle to end the slave trade). Those British people who feel a sense of guilt about their country's recent history are more likely to have concluded that imperial expansion was a cover for the exploitation of countries overseas. One way of alleviating any feelings of guilt that this may arouse is to attribute the wrongs to the evils of the capitalist system.

In the United States black activists challenged white values by polarizing the opposition between black and white. Many British sociologists are influenced by their example and prefer to designate everyone in Britain of Asian, African or West Indian origin as black, regardless of the fact that the Asians were not touched by the experience of slavery and, at the very least, consider this an inadequate way of designating their minorities. This readiness to designate all ethnic minority members as black seems to derive from a belief that it is in the minorities' interest to polarize group relations, but the underlying argument has never been explicitly justified. The inclusive use of the word 'black' is an out-growth of recent American history which is now being taken up in countries to which it is less well suited. It shows that even the most elementary concepts used for this study of racial relations are shaped by comparisons between countries and reflect the relations between periods of history.

12

Minorities in the housing market

Sociologists interested in quantitative analyses have carried out many studies of housing segregation, especially in the United States, but their explanations of how segregation comes about have not been equally sophisticated. In seeking an understanding of racial discrimination in market relations it can be helpful to learn from the approach of economists to consumer behaviour. The price of a house does not depend solely on the cost of construction. Some houses have greater appeal to potential purchasers because of their design, their individual character, their location and so on. Different sets of consumers likewise prefer particular brands of cigarettes. These are differences of taste. Not all consumers have the same tastes and their tastes change, both as they get older and as social patterns change. A product that appeals to popular tastes will command a higher price, while a prospective purchaser who is making a selection between several houses at the same price will choose the one which best corresponds to his or her tastes. A purchaser may prefer a house or apartment in a racially segregated area. Observers may think it deplorable that a house purchaser should be influenced by racial prejudice just as they may deplore the purchase of pornography or the expenditure of large sums on gambling, but the market consequence of tastes for particular goods or attributes are the same whether or not other people consider that such tastes ought to be eliminated.

This mode of argument has been developed furthest with respect to discrimination in employment. It is easy to understand that one male employer selecting between potential secretaries of apparently equal competence may prefer the one who looks most attractive while another may choose the least attractive one in the belief that she may be more conscientious and stay longer in the post. It is equally easy to understand that an employer may prefer, other things being equal, to engage employees of the same ethnic or racial background as himself. In so doing he exercises a taste for discrimination. The strength of such a taste can be measured in monetary terms. One employer may prefer workers of his own kind even though he could get others for 10 per cent lower wages, whereas a different employer, perhaps in a different business, may think only of incurring the lowest costs in hiring, paying, and retaining his workforce. Yet in one important respect the purchase of a house is simpler than engaging an employee and for this reason it can be better to analyse discrimination in housing first.

Every relationship between an employer and an employee is unique, so a wage forms part of a bargain between a particular employer and a particular employee. Industrial societies, for reasons of public policy and convenience, do not proceed on such a basis. The employer is usually in so much more powerful a position than the individual worker that equal bargaining about wages is difficult, while in many occupations there is too little difference in the output of different workers for individualized wage rates to be a practical proposition. So it is assumed that there is a standardized relationship between, say, a building employer and a bricklayer, according to which all qualified bricklayers are to be hired according to the same conditions of service and paid the same whether by the hour or by the number of bricks laid. This is a standardization according to the job which denies the relevance of ethnic-group membership, but, as the next chapter will consider, does not necessarily work to the advantage of minority-group members.

The position is otherwise in the provision of services based upon the characteristics of the individual for whom the service is designed. In a study conducted in England in 1966–7, an Englishman, a Hungarian, and a West Indian applied for motor insurance, each claiming a middle-class occupation, eight years' accident-free driving in Britain, and a 'clean' driver's licence (i.e. showing no record of conviction for motoring offences); each tester stated that he had not previously owned a car. In 6 out of 20 applications the West Indian was refused insurance cover altogether; on 11 occasions he was quoted a higher premium so that on only 3 out of 20 applications was his minority status ignored. The average premium quoted by the 14 firms who offered cover to all three testers were: West Indian £58, Hungarian £49, Englishman £45. Differences of this kind are possible because the quotations are individual and supposedly related to the risks of insuring the particular applicant. Why did the insurance companies want 9 per cent more from the Hungarian and 29 per cent more from the West Indian? There is no reason to believe that they possessed any good evidence to show that minority members, like young men with sports cars, were a greater insurance risk; so the differentials must have measured a subjective assessment of risk affected by stereotyped notions about the likely behaviour of foreigners and blacks. In so far as this was the case, it indicated that the market was not operating according to strictly economic criteria and that a company which did so should have been able to attract business from minority motorists and make greater profits until its competitors changed their policies.

This illustration can serve to identify differences between housing markets and employment markets. In private housing each house or apartment is unique. Even if it is of the same dimensions as another in the block, it is likely to be in different condition or in a less favoured location. The bargaining over purchase price is usually private; even if the sale is by auction, one would-be purchaser is unlikely to know very much about his competitors and their resources. In the private market the agreement to sell or rent a particular house or apartment stems from a private negotiation and the price is unique to the transaction. It resembles a company's offer to insure a particular motor car on specific terms for a particular price rather than a bargain about the wages to be paid to bricklayers. In industry, bargaining about wages is rarely private and the bargains often have to meet official criteria. The renting of housing built by municipalities and other public bodies differs from transactions in the private housing market in that the houses or apartments are more likely to be built to a standard design and rented at standard rates.

Differences in the structure of markets affect the character taken by racial discrimination. Where bargaining is individual – as over insurance and private housing – price discrimination cannot easily be detected and occurs frequently. The minority purchaser has to pay more but by doing so he can cancel out the vendor's taste for discrimination. Where bargaining is standardized, the discriminator who would be willing to hire minority members if he could pay them wages 10 per cent lower is not able to choose this alternative, so he will fill his vacancies with workers of his own ethnic background so far as he can and minority members will be excluded from employment. It will be noticed that in the motor insurance example the West Indian tester suffered price discrimination in connection with 55 per cent of his applications and was excluded from the market 30 per cent of the time. It is reasonable to suppose that where bargaining is individual, price discrimination will be the main form of discrimination; where it is standardized, the main form will be exclusion. Discrimination in either form by the majority stimulates responses from minority members which influence the structure of the market and introduce complications into the analysis.

Housing markets in the United States

The extent to which blacks are subject to housing segregation in American cities is the more notable because of its implications for racial inequality in other spheres. If housing segregation could be eliminated, there would be

Table 6: *Indices of residential segregation between whites and non-whites, 1950–1970, for central cities and selected suburbs*

	1970	1960	1950
Boston	79.9	83.9	86.5
Cambridge	52.6	65.5	75.6
Chicago	88.8	92.6	92.1
East Chicago	79.0	82.8	79.6
Evanston	78.3	87.2	92.1
Los Angeles	78.4	81.8	84.6
Pasadena	75.0	83.4	85.9
New York	73.0	79.3	87.3
Mt. Vernon	78.4	73.2	78.0
New Rochelle	70.7	79.5	78.9
Yonkers	68.0	78.1	81.7
Newark	74.9	71.6	76.9
East Orange	60.8	71.2	83.7
San Francisco	55.5	69.3	79.8
Oakland	63.4	73.1	81.2
Berkeley	62.9	69.4	80.3

Source: reproduced from Glazer, 1975:143

less need for busing and the problems of school integration would be dramatically reduced. Black incomes would rise relative to white incomes; black access to employment and to social services would improve. The magnitude of segregation can be judged from Table 6 which sets out calculations developed by Karl and Alma Taeuber. It gives indices for cities obtained by adding up figures calculated block by block. If an area is either all black or all white this produces an index of 100; were blacks and whites evenly distributed there would be an index of 0. As can be seen, the indices are closer to the upper end. They are falling slowly, though much less slowly than the rate at which the segregation of other minorities fell. The main determinant has been the massive movement of the white population from the cities out to the suburbs. Blacks have moved too, their number of suburban residents having increased from 2.2 to 3.7 millions over 1950 to 1970, but as a proportion of the suburban population they fell from 6.1 to 5.3 per cent. At the same time the quality of life available in the inner cities has declined.

It is sometimes thought that blacks are concentrated in their inner cities because they are poor, because they do not wish to spend so much on housing, or because they prefer to live together. There is good evidence against all these explanations. For example, 52 per cent of Detroit's poor white families in 1970 lived in the suburbs whereas less than 12 per cent of relatively rich Detroit black families (i.e. with an annual income of over $10,000) did so. While in 1977 black family income in Detroit was only 57 per cent that of white families, it was also the case that blacks in general could have afforded more integrated neighbourhoods and would have preferred to live in them. In this respect Afro-Americans in Detroit are no different from those in the country as a whole, for in 1966, 68 per cent of blacks in a national sample said they would prefer to live in an integrated neighbourhood. Research in Detroit has shown that if blacks fail to live in presently white neighbourhoods it is not because they overestimate the price of houses there; nor is it because they would consider that any black family moving to a mostly white neighbourhood was deserting the black community (Farley *et al.*, 1979:111). Overlapping the distinction between urban and suburban residence is the distinction between living in rented housing and being an owner occupier. Analyses of the 1960 Census data show that whereas 41 per cent of blacks in Detroit owned their houses, 67 per cent would have been homeowners if their housing-market behaviour had been the same as that of white families after allowing for differences of income and family size. In Chicago the difference was between 18 per cent and 47 per cent. An independent study in St Louis later produced figures of 32 and 41 per cent respectively for 1967 (Kain and Quigley, 1975:145, 295).

When due allowance has been made for economic differences between black and white populations, significant differences in housing remain which can be attributed only to discrimination. There is abundant evidence that real-estate agents, apartment managers, landlords and suburban developers have denied blacks access to housing in what were considered white areas. Banks and mortgage companies have been willing to lend blacks money for house purchase only in particular areas. The Federal Housing Administration and the Veterans Administration – which had the power to break with this pattern – conformed to it instead. Local governments, through their control of zoning, building regulations and land development have contributed to the maintenance of segregation. A substantial proportion of tax revenues – which could have been used for other purposes – have been spent on the construction of highways to facilitate commuting by suburban and exurban residents.

Comparisons have been made of the rents paid by black and white families which show that, within the ghetto, blacks and whites pay much the same, but relative to the quality of their housing they pay more than families elsewhere. Since blacks have difficulty escaping the ghetto, as a group they have paid more than whites for comparable housing (comparability assessed in a way which included measures of neighbourhood quality). Black residents in Chicago paid 20.4 per cent more than whites, whereas in Washington the difference was less, at 3 per cent, and by the same measure in San Francisco whites paid 0.1 per cent more than blacks. These are 1960 data, but now the techniques have been established it will be relatively easy to update them. Research workers in St Louis in 1969 found that black renters had to pay 12.18 per cent more than whites for comparable housing; black purchasers had to pay 5–6 per cent more. While only 8 per cent of the St Louis black households that moved house over a three-year period were home-buyers, 20 per cent would have been had they been white (Kain and Quigley, 1975:66–8, 294–5). These are measures of what can be called the 'colour tax': the extra amount paid by blacks because they have been assigned to a category identified by their skin colour. Even so, these assessments of the colour tax underestimate the size of the burden borne by blacks because of housing discrimination. Home ownership has been the most important mode of capital appreciation since the Second World War. The limitations placed upon blacks' opportunities to participate in the economic benefits of home ownership go far to explain differences in the current wealth positions of otherwise comparable black and white households, since these limitations can easily increase black housing costs by 30 per cent or more, assuming no price appreciation. A black household prevented from buying a home in 1950 would in 1970 have had annual costs more than twice what they would have been had they been able to purchase. In the rental sector, the burden of a rent 15 per cent higher is, after six years, a sum about equivalent to a whole year's rent, and one that could have been spent on something else. Residence in the ghetto entails, for a home owner, relatively greater expenditure on maintenance, fire, theft and auto insurance, and possibly on the journey to work. Often blacks will not even learn of available jobs far from the ghetto or will not apply because of the travel difficulties. Had the suburbs been open to middle- and low-income blacks this would have restrained the tendency for central city residential areas to become unattractive to middle-class whites. Had the latter stayed, the quality of schools and other public services would not have declined as they have. Entry of blacks to the suburbs, would, by increasing the competition for houses there, have lifted their prices, and reduced the prices of central city properties to some extent, helping to discourage whites from moving out. Increased black residence in the suburbs would have reduced the under-representation of blacks in suburban workplaces (Kain and Quigley, 1975:144, 148–50, 298–9, 320–3).

According to this reasoning, it was a major policy mistake to encourage suburbanization without insisting that it be carried through on a non-discriminatory basis. Who has benefited? Because blacks have difficulty buying into the suburbs, they have to compete for housing in the ghettos, forcing up rents there to the benefit of white landlords. The whites who might have sold suburban houses to blacks have got less and the slumlords more. The pattern of segregation enables whites to buy into white-only neighbourhoods in the areas to which they move, which is of value to them if they have a taste for being at a physical distance from blacks, but it is questionable whether they would wish to exercise this taste to the same extent if they appreciated what it was costing them, and not only in house prices; for the deterioration in the quality of life in the cities entails substantial costs in respect of welfare payments, police, judicial and corrections services, and so on. A minority of whites may benefit from the pattern but not the ordinary white suburban voter. This is what makes the American pattern of housing segregation so notable: it is not in the economic interest of the nation.

In the United States (as in many countries), most new housing is constructed for middle- and upper-income people, while increased demand from lower-income people is met by their taking over housing previously occupied by middle-income families. The Federal government took powers to enable it to subsidize new housing for poorer families by offering funds to those cities which would have such housing constructed. Large cities accepted such offers; smaller cities often did not, or accepted them only for the aged. In 1968 a new approach was adopted whereby any builder of such housing could be subsidized, and this programme, which ran for five years, produced far more housing annually than its predecessors; but some communities continued to resist any scheme that would mean the introduction of poor families from the inner cities, whatever their colour. The mayors of all suburban all-black towns were in a particular difficulty. If they opposed subsidized housing as lowering the reputation of their localities they were considered racist by some blacks, while officials keen to find somewhere to locate such units put particular pressure on existing black communities (Glazer, 1975:159–67; Rose, 1976:254). This kind of federal programme has encountered widespread resistance. It took up to ten years for important cases to work their way through the courts. Having done so, they resulted in 1979 in decisions requiring localities to abandon zoning policies that had discriminatory effects (see Civil Rights, 1980:80–1).

The Fair Housing Act of 1968 declared illegal any action concerned with the provision of housing that showed discrimination on grounds of race, colour, religion or national origin, except for a sale by an individual without the assistance of a broker or advertising, or rental of a room or apartment in a private house in which the renter lived. The ban extended to the actions of the real-estate industry, to lenders of funds and to advertising. Since many sectors of the housing market are not fully competitive, it might be more rewarding to move resources into the enforcement of this legislation. In 1982, the Supreme Court made the task of enforcement easier by its decision in *Havens Realty Corporation v. Coleman*. It declared that a person given false information about the availability of an apartment could sue under the Fair Housing Act even though this person was a 'tester' who did not intend to complete the transaction.

The dual market

Increased black demand for housing can be met without disturbing the pattern of segregation, either by blacks taking over the housing previously occupied by whites or by the construction of new homes for black purchasers. In the 1950s the former provided ten times more new housing units for blacks in the north central region than did new construction, but since then developers have built numerous all-black towns in the suburbs (Kain and Quigley, 1975:63; Rose, 1976:76). Nevertheless new construction is unlikely to contribute much to a solution if it only perpetuates the existence of distinct black and white submarkets. Attention must be paid to the operations of those who can influence the ways in which the racial composition of neighbourhoods change.

The Chicago Real Estate Board's Code of Ethics used to state: 'A realtor should never be instrumental in introducing into a neighbourhood . . . members of any race or nationality whose presence would clearly be detrimental to property values in that neighbourhood.' In 1950 the Board dropped the words 'race' and 'nationality' without changing its policy. In the mid 1950s, when in the course of urban renewal the black slums began to be demolished and black demand for housing was intense, a number of 'panic peddlers' seized on the Supreme Court's 1948 decision against racially restrictive covenants to frighten white residents in neighbourhoods close to the ghettos and to persuade them to sell their houses. They used cruder methods as well. One of the 'Block busters' described the process:

> Now we speculators and brokers, both white and Negro, went to work. One paid several Negroes with noisy cars to begin driving up and down the street a few times a day. He also paid a Negro mother who drew Aid-to-Dependent Children to walk the block regularly with her youngsters. Another arranged to have phone calls made in the block for such people as 'Johnie Mae'. Sometimes calls would consist only of a whisper, a drunken laugh or a warning – such as 'They're coming' . . . I began by sending a postcard to everyone in the block. The cards said, 'I will pay cash for your building.' That was all except for my phone number. (Fitzgerald, 1975:166).

The whites sold, many at prices far below the appraised value of their homes.

They did not sell to black people, who would have been happy to pay what the houses were worth. They sold to speculators who bought the houses with the benefit of mortgage loans and then resold them to blacks who purchased on a contract basis while the speculator retained the mortgage. A specific case which illustrates the practice is provided by Mr and Mrs Collins. In August 1960 the original owner sold his house to a speculator for $14,500 (which was probably round about its appraised value). The speculator bought it with $2,500 of his own money and $12,000 provided by a savings and loan association on the security of a mortgage. One month later the house was sold to Mr and Mrs Collins for $24,000 over a 25 year term. The Collinses could not get a mortgage from the Federal Housing Administration because this body agreed with the Real Estate Board that property values declined when neighbourhoods changed from white to black occupancy and that houses in such an area were therefore no longer good security for a loan. The FHA would 'red-line' changing areas as being 'high risk'. Banks, savings and loan associations, the major home-owners, insurance companies – even the Veterans Administration – usually followed FHA guidelines. Buying under a contract of sale the Collinses had to pay a total of about $45,000 (over $19,000 of which was interest) whereas had they been able to get a mortgage and terms similar to those obtained by the realtor they would have paid about $20,000 over a shorter period of time. The terms of the contract gave the purchaser no equity or title until the full contract was paid; the seller had the right to reclaim the property and keep all past payments if a single payment was missed; in many respects the contract-buyer's rights were no greater than those of someone paying rent (and in some respects they were less since a tenant who pays rent is not responsible for repairs to the building) (McPherson, 1972:53).

Why should the Collinses have bought the house without having it appraised? Why should they have agreed to so high a purchase price? Why should they have entered into a contractual arrangement so unfavourable to them? One answer is that, unfavourable as this was, it appeared better than the alternatives. To stay in the existing ghetto area was unattractive, as was the prospect of segregated public housing had it been available. Some brave people were willing to challenge segregation by buying into white neighbourhoods when opportunity offered, and then depending on police protection, but this was risky. The chance of getting into a new neighbourhood seemed better, even if it meant for most purchasers that the wife would have to stay at work and the husband get an evening job to keep up the payments. Another part of the explanation must be black attitudes: resignation to their lot and an insufficient appreciation of how onerous were the terms to which they had bound themselves. But the fact that black purchasers should have been buying houses at prices 75 per cent above the price they would have fetched in the white market is an indication of the extent to which discrimination was depressing the relative supply of housing.

The situation of the contract buyers changed in 1967 when a Jesuit seminarian and a small group of white college students came to live in the area, learned of the grievance, and helped them organize. Mr Collins and some others testified before the Illinois House of Representatives' Public Welfare Committee and received extensive publicity. They confronted some of the speculators and demanded that their contracts be renegotiated. Some agreed to this, but all insisted that it was not a question of race: they sold, or would have sold, homes on similar contract terms to both black and white people. One of the first sellers to renegotiate explained:

> I like the people on the West Side . . . When this thing started I never figured they would come to me because I didn't think I had done anything wrong. But they did. I couldn't believe it when they said I have cheated people. I went home to my wife and said: 'Isn't this the American system, where we make as much profit as we can?' She said, 'Yes, you're right'. Two days later she said, 'No, *you're* wrong and *they're* right'. And pretty soon I said to myself, 'No, you're wrong'.

After the West-siders' case had been publicized they were joined by hundreds of young, middle-class black people, many of them well educated, who had purchased on contract newly constructed single family homes on the South-side. Salesmen for Universal Builders were said to have insisted, even to a family with a $10,000 down payment, that contract terms were better than those allowed by a conventional mortgage. They had come to believe that they had paid more than they should have done for their homes, and had bought them on unfavourable terms. The South-siders joined what had become the Contract Buyers League, and early in 1969, this organization filed two suits: *Baker v. F. and F. Investment* for the West-side and *Clark v. Universal Builders* for the South-side. They alleged, among other things, that the defendants had violated the plaintiffs' civil rights as interpreted in *Jones v. Mayer* in 1968. (In that case Justice Potter Stewart held that 'the freedom that Congress is empowered to secure under the Thirteenth Amendment includes the freedom to buy whatever a white man can buy, the right to live wherever a white man can live'.) The defendants filed motions that the cases be dismissed, alleging that the discrimination was hypothetical; there was insufficient evidence that the plaintiffs had been charged more than white people would have been charged in the same circumstances. The judge, ruling against the defendants, said of this argument: 'It should be clear that in law the result would be obnoxious. In logic, it is ridiculous. It would mean that the 1866 Civil Rights Act, which was created to be an instrument for the abolition of discrimination, allows an injustice so long as it is visited entirely on negroes.' He held that the law had grown to define certain economic bounds and ethical limits of business enterprise and that the precedent of *Jones v. Mayer* was applicable to the facts alleged (Fitzgerald, 1975).

In 1976 judgement was delivered in favour of the West-side defendants, by an all-white jury. One of the jurors said afterwards to Jeffrey Fitzgerald (who had been following the case) 'we stated that the defendants would have charged their own mother the going rate'. Since it is the judge's task to explain the law, and the jury's task to apply the law to what they find to be the facts of the case, this suggests that the jurors had not been guided by the view of the judge who ruled against the motion to dismiss. As the same juror said, they saw it as a matter of 'economics, not civil rights'.

Before returning, later in this chapter, to the question of open housing markets and the matching of black and white preferences for degrees of integration or segregation, it can be helpful to compare the housing markets in the United States with those in Britain to see how far the same principles underlie patterns of racial discrimination.

Housing markets in Britain

The main difference between the two countries can be seen from Table 7. In Britain over a quarter of all dwellings are owned by the local municipalities or district councils; most of them, indeed, have been built by these councils and subsidized from taxation. They are usually referred to as 'council houses', though most are apartments (usually called 'flats' in England). Having been built in large numbers as 'estates', they have benefited from the economies of large-scale construction and are more economical of scarce urban building land. Tenancies are allocated by the councils according to their own rules of eligibility rather than by the price mechanism, and there is usually a queue for properties. Since a substantial proportion of the population live in council housing this sector is not stigmatized as much as residence in subsidized housing in the United States and elsewhere, though the more recent policy of permitting residents in council houses to purchase their dwellings may change this.

It should also be noted that, encouraged by government policies, the proportion of dwellings in owner-occupation doubled in the period 1947–76 and the proportion rented from a private landlord declined to almost a quarter.

Table 7 *Housing tenure in the United States and in England, percentages*

	Owner occupied	Rented from private landlord	Rented from public landlord
United States, 1972	62	36	1.5
England and Wales, 1947	27	58	12
England, 1976	55	16	29

Note: The US figure (quoted from McKay, 1977:40) reports the tenure status of households whereas the English figures give the tenure status of dwellings. Since multi-occupation is concentrated in private lettings the English figures underrecord private renting by households

Studies of racial discrimination in British housing markets make possible a comparison of the explanations of unequal access to housing to be derived from the Ecological and Rational Choice theories. With modifications, these theories could be applied to circumstances in the United States.

It is less easy to obtain from the Class theory, or any of its derivatives, any set of propositions to explain the differential position of minority members in housing markets since the Class theory seeks primarily to explain the development of capitalism and the struggle of classes within it. One study presented from this viewpoint contends, for example, that house-building in London followed the demand for labour by commercial enterprise and industrial expansion in the nineteenth and early twentieth centuries. Its decline as a manufacturing centre has accentuated the growing shortage of housing (both because of demolition and because of the increase in the proportion of one- and two-person households) and the decline in its quality (because of the cost of maintenance). The capitalist mode of production is said to ensure a cyclical productive process such that centres of production eventually go into decline and the labour force has to move in order to obtain work. Migrant labour from the Caribbean was drawn into declining areas because the skilled workers were moving out; it was part of the pattern, therefore, that it should be drawn into areas of urban decay and housing stress (Phizacklea and Miles, 1980:52–7). Such an approach could be extended by arguments about the way class-based politics influence the structure of the housing market: e.g. how easy or difficult it is for private developers to obtain land for house-building, the financing of private house construction and purchase, tax relief on mortgage payments, etc. Class-based politics may likewise influence the size of the private and public rental markets and the criteria for the allocation of publicly owned housing.

Some of the arguments to this effect may be acceptable in detail to those who favour competing theories.

Housing markets will differ from one city to another for these and other reasons. In Britain, for example, the city of Birmingham drew in large numbers of black and Asian workers during the 1950s at a time when there was a severe local housing shortage. Work was available in the engineering industry and its demand for labour fluctuated with changes in its export markets. Then there was a further inflow of Asian immigrants in the early 1970s. The Asian electorate in the inner-city ward of Soho rose from 5 in 1956 to 3,124 in 1971 and 4,593 in 1976. The Asian adult population in the middle-ring ward of Sparkhill was estimated at 50 in 1956, rising to 2,028 in 1971 and 4,559 in 1976. The city of Manchester, by contrast, drew in more gradually smaller numbers of minority workers from a wider range of countries to undertake a greater variety of work, and labour demand there fluctuated less. Many of the Asians were engaged in middle-class occupations. The immigrants settled at a time when white demand for housing was in decline and therefore caused less tension. For these and other reasons it is hardly surprising that whites in Manchester expressed less hostility towards coloured people than whites in Birmingham (Ward, 1978; Ward and Sims, 1981).

Important as these differences are, housing markets may vary less between one city and another in Britain than in the United States. Variations there are probably greater because of local government boundaries within conurbations and because expenditure by local government bodies is less subject to control by the central government than in Britain.

The Ecological Theory

The first significant study of racial discrimination in British housing appeared in a book by John Rex and Robert Moore (1967) which applied ecological reasoning in a way that did not presuppose any commitment to class as a master concept in sociological analysis. This section of the book was the work of John Rex who drew upon Park and Burgess' studies of urban ecology, expanding the focus upon competition for land use and showing how the competition is regulated by political institutions which have created a welfare sector in the national economy. Like them, he was concerned to identify general processes within the history of a single city's development. They generalized from Chicago; Rex, from Birmingham. In the reformulation of his theory which follows, the first proposition states his general axiom; the second lists four sequences which have influenced the present urban value system and the structure of the city's housing market. The subsequent propositions are empirical ones that can be utilized to explain racial discrimination in housing.

(1) Competition for the scarce resource of housing leads to the formation of groups each of which will attempt to restrict its competitors' access to housing.

(2) a The ecology of many British cities was determined by the sequence in which different classes benefited from economic growth transferring gains from the employment sector into that of housing.

 b The lower middle classes forsook the urban inner ring for suburban housing purchased with the aid of private mortgages.

 c The suburban ideal of relatively detached family life attained a very important position in the urban value system. The working class used their political power to promote the construction of municipal estates, creating a public suburbia to parallel the already existing private suburbia.

 d The houses in the inner ring deserted by the lower middle class and by those members of the working class who had obtained suburban housing, passed to a motley population consisting of the city's social rejects, including immigrants.

(3) The present position is that residents in British cities are distinguished from one another by their membership in housing classes of different strength in the private and public housing markets. In the private market, strength depends upon wealth and credit-worthiness; in the public market, strength depends upon the possession of attributes (like number of children, length of time on waiting list) which confer access to particular kinds of council housing.

(4) Blacks and Asians can obtain housing only in localities where competition is weakest and the existing population least organized to repel strangers, as in the inner ring zones (Rex and Moore, 1967:8–9, 16, 273–4; Rex, 1968).

In so far as this is a theory of discrimination it focuses on the public sector and on the prediction that minorities will be excluded from housing in that sector. There would be no difficulty in adding further propositions predicting price discrimination in the private sector and the use of informal pressure to restrict the granting of credit to members of minorities, indeed such extensions are implied in parts of the book.

This theory was a great stimulus to research because it enabled investigators in this field to pose questions that were more interesting sociologically, but it was not as well supported by the evidence as the authors claimed. The weaknesses of the empirical side of the study were exposed in an essay by Badr Dahya (1974:102–6) whose socio-anthropological research in Birmingham overlapped in time with the research of Rex and Moore. Dahya showed that the housing desires of the Pakistani immigrants reflected the values and standards they brought with them from their home countries. In their culture a landlord was of much higher status than a tenant. They did not wish to rent council housing. When they bought the larger and older houses in the inner neighbourhoods this was not because they had no alternatives but because these were the houses they wanted; nor when they sought mortgages did they experience discrimination as frequently as Rex and Moore asserted. At this stage the housing demand of the Pakistani was for owner occupation in a particular section of the housing market. It so happened that in this sector demand from whites was small so that prices were low. Rex and Moore had looked to the British socio-economic structure for explanations and had misinterpreted the frame of reference within which Asians made their choices.

The Ecological Theory drew attention to the importance of the procedures for allocating municipal housing. In most British cities, the two main routes to council housing are by the waiting list and the clearance programme. The waiting list is regulated by a points system designed to reflect housing need, but it gives little consideration to applicants who own the houses in which they live, whatever their condition, and this rule operates to the relative disadvantage of blacks and Asians. When, in the course of urban renewal, a whole area is cleared for rebuilding, the rehousing of people whose houses are demolished takes priority over the waiting list. But in many cities the council has accepted no responsibility for rehousing people occupying furnished tenancies, and blacks and Asians have been over-represented in these categories. In Manchester the rules were changed in 1970 to make them eligible, but it would be incorrect to interpret the change as the outcome of a struggle between black and Asian groups favouring eligibility and white groups opposing it – as might be inferred from the theory's first proposition. A major role was played by a multi-racial pressure group, while the housing administrators doubtless had their own ideas about what, seen in long term perspective, would constitute good practice (Flett, 1977:11–13; Ward, 1979). Rex's theory shows its greatest strength when interpreting circumstances in the inner ring zone on which his research was concentrated. But it should be noted that his ecological theory is comp-lemented by a subsidiary theory of immigrant settlement specifying three stages. In the first of these the immigrant is bewildered and experiences anomie; in the second he obtains personal support and satisfaction from living as a member of an ethnic colony; in the third, he is more independent, has a family life of his own, and can dispense with the ethnic colony. It is in the third stage that immigrant housing demand changes and gathers strength. Rex's interest has been in the earlier stages when the position of minority members is weakest, and he has sought to trace through some of the consequences of discrimination in housing. He argued that, since there was insufficient rented accommodation, immigrant landlords found it economically viable to buy the larger houses for sub-division and multi-occupation, interpreting their action as a response to a constraining situation. White residents of other areas disapprove of multi-occupation and put pressure on the municipality to confine it to the inner ring zone.

It will be noticed that though Rex's started off as an ecological theory, other theories of a different kind have been added on to it though they are not stated in so explicit a manner. One indication of the change can be seen in the terminology. Burgess wrote of a zone *in* transition, fore-shadowing the change in land use associated with the development of the central business district. Rex wrote of a zone *of* transition, implying that it was the residents of the zone who were involved in a sequence of change.

The Rational Choice Theory

The Rational Choice Theory states that individuals choose between the alternatives facing them, and that their choices influence the alternatives open to people who come after them. In competing to obtain maximum advantage men utilize physical differences to create groups and categories. In its application to housing discrimination by whites, the theory has to start from white attitudes:

(1) White people in Britain compete with one another for the most desirable housing.

(2) a Demand for housing is a function of (i) price; (ii) the quality of the accommodation; (iii) the amenity of the neighbourhood.

    b Amenity is a function of (i) distance for workplace, (ii) access to schools, shops and other services; (iii) population composition.

    c Most white people in Britain, and particularly those who have children in the household, prefer a population composition of socio-economic status and pigmentation similar to their own.

(3) Where blacks and Asians are not excluded from the market, price discrimination will counter-balance any disamenity resulting from what white people see as a sub-optimal population composition.

(4) The economically weaker members of the politically powerful section of the population may combine to exclude any category of competitors whose right to compete can be challenged, e.g. the right of immigrants to council housing. Exclusion will be more effective when demand is related to supply by some means other than the price mechanism.

(5) Housing patterns will be influenced by minority as well as majority demand and minority demand may reflect different judgements about amenity.

According to this theory, newcomers will usually be at a disadvantage in entering a housing market, but, if competition is between individuals, and if the newcomers' incomes and housing preferences are not greatly different from the majority's, over the course of time they may be expected to spread themselves out over the different kinds of housing until they can no longer be distinguished from the majority in respect of their housing. The crucial factor from the side of the majority in determining the pace of this kind of dispersal, is whether the whites compete with blacks and Asians on the same basis as they compete with other whites, that is, as between one individual and another, or whether they combine against coloured people as a category in the terms of the fourth proposition.

If the competition is between individuals, a white house-seller may prefer to sell his house to a white purchaser and may hope to be paid, say, £20,000 in return. He might refuse an offer from a black man at £20,000, but if the black would-be purchaser raises his price there will come a point at which the owner will sell to him. For if the seller is reluctant to conclude a bargain which would reduce his neighbour's sense of amenity there is nevertheless some point at which the sale price would be sufficient for him to compensate his neighbours for what they consider their loss – however unrealistic such a possibility may be. Thus the level of discrimination by whites can be seen as the outcome of two factors: (i) their 'taste' for discrimination; (ii) the 'price' or cost of discrimination, in the sense of benefit forgone by satisfying the taste. If this is granted, the ordinary analysis of consumer demand can be employed (Collard, 1970:84).

Sociologists and lawyers have tended to classify behaviour as being either discriminatory or non-discriminatory. The economist argues that discrimination can occur only at particular price levels and that it is necessary to ascertain the price which people put upon their prejudice, or, more accurately, upon their taste for associating or dealing with particular kinds of people. Many elements go into the taste factor in discrimination. A man may dislike the idea of a very black neighbour more than of a light brown neighbour; he may dislike the prospect of a black neighbour less if he is to be someone of high status. The price which he puts upon his taste will help decide whether or not discrimination results. Up to this point, the analysis assumes that the whites' taste for discrimination derives from their calculation of amenity. But the white house-seeker may also conclude that the best way for him to improve his position in the housing market is to combine with other whites to exclude blacks from the sectors of the market in which whites wish to acquire housing. They might declare that only the descendants of the original inhabitants (as distinguished by pigmentation) are entitled to purchase or be allocated housing of a particular kind. In so far as they were successful, competition between blacks and whites for housing would be on a group basis, and competition between white and white or black and blacks on an individual basis. The whites would have established a monopoly over the kinds of housing they preferred and for the analysis of competition between these groups it would be necessary to refer to the theory of monopolistic competition.

The richer members of the white population will normally be able to satisfy their desire for amenity without excluding any category of competitors. The poorer members of the white population are more exposed to the new sources of competition, so they may be tempted to use their electoral power to have their competitors' access to favoured sectors of the housing market restricted. This can be effected more easily in the public than in the private sector.

Market sectors

Just as governments establish the framework within which trade takes place, so developments in the market place which powerful groups consider undesirable lead to further government regulation. Table 7 can be seen as showing how the English working class have used their political power to promote the construction of publicly rented housing on a much greater scale than in the United States. The same principle also explains the changed proportions of owner-occupation and private renting in Britain after the Second World War, though in any gross comparison between the two countries the greater scarcity of building land in Britain must not be forgotten.

After the war the British government enforced rent control legislation which pegged rents to the levels obtaining in 1939, so landlords had an incentive to sell the properties which they had previously rented. There was a post-war trend towards owner-occupation (assisted by tax relief on mortgage payments and the exclusion of most residential property from capital gains tax), but government action contributed to a situation in which the demand for rented properties exceeded supply. Since the price mechanism was not allowed to adjust the two, landlords often required 'key money' or the purchase of furniture. In 1957, the controls upon rents were removed, but tenants in unfurnished properties were given greater protection than those renting furnished rooms, flats or houses. Landlords were apprehensive about the effect of this legislation and it acted as an incentive to rent their properties as furnished rather than unfurnished. The market in the furnished sector was closer to one of perfect competition than in the unfurnished sector where demand exceeded supply. The Rent Act of 1974 (which landlords saw as restricting their powers to terminate tenancies) seems to have had a similar effect in causing landlords to sell properties they had previously been renting, and so it has reduced the number of properties available to rent.

When competition is between individuals, a member of a disadvantaged minority has to pay extra to obtain the same services. A study conducted in 1951–2 reported that overseas students seeking accommodation in London very appropriately called this extra element in the price a 'colour tax' (Carey, 1956:69–71). In describing their experience one student said that when one landlady saw that he was coloured she increased the sum she wanted as rent from thirty-seven to forty-five shillings a week. Another student, who was from East Africa, put two advertisements in a local paper which were similar except that in only the second did he mention his nationality. The first advertisement brought more replies, but he also had two answers offering the same room. The answer replying to the second advertisement specified a rent ten shillings higher. The same study showed that the taste for discrimination was highest against black students, lower for lightly coloured non-Europeans and lower still for Continental Europeans.

The accommodation sought by students at this time was in a market with special characteristics. Much of it was provided by middle-aged women who owned and occupied large houses, renting out rooms to students and lodgers. The landlady provided breakfast and an evening meal; she frequently arranged for the washing of her lodgers' clothing. Many landladies were middle-class women having inherited their houses on the death of their husbands or parents. Taking in lodgers enabled them to continue living in the houses to which they were accustomed, and to take in university students did not demean their status as much as other kinds of lodgers might have done. Their reluctance to accommodate coloured students was a compound of their apprehensions about the students' different customs and a fear for their own status. If they took in coloured students the neighbours might think they did so only because they could not get white students, and they could not get them because the standard of their rooms was not high enough. In such circumstances the colour tax can be seen as a compensation to the landlady for her loss of amenity. A landlord who did not live on the premises and rented out rooms as a business might not have the same personal feelings and could have been expected to charge whatever the market could bear.

Findings compatible with these have been reported in the PEP studies. The first of these was conducted in 1967 when it was not unlawful to refuse people accommodation on racial grounds. When enquiring by telephone about 120 properties to rent furnished, in 63 cases the West Indian tester was told that the accommodation had been let already; in 5 cases he was asked for a higher rent. When enquiring in person about 60 properties, on 40 occasions the West Indian was told that the accommodation had been let already; on 6 occasions he was asked for higher rent. Unfurnished accommodation was hardly ever made available to West Indians (Daniel, 1968:155–9). A repeat of these tests in 1973 concluded that discrimination against blacks enquiring by telephone about rented accommodation and in person about house purchase had been reduced by more than half over the six-year period (Smith, 1977:287).

Further evidence of a particularly interesting kind has been derived from a reanalysis of some of the material collected in 1970 for the Committee on the Rent Acts (Committee . . . 1971:241–440). The rents paid by 1,054 white and coloured tenants in the London 'stress areas' of Hackney, Stepney and Clapham have been examined, making allowance for variations in the conditions of the dwellings, the amenities provided, and the period in which the tenancy commenced. The areas in question are not representative of the whole country, but are boroughs where there have been substantial racial minority populations for ten to twenty years. The study supports three conclusions; (i) that coloured tenants were to some degree excluded from the market for the unfurnished tenancies which are preferred by most would-be tenants; in fact, being coloured increased a family's chances of being in furnished accommodation by 22 per cent; (ii) coloured tenants in the unfurnished sector were paying a rent 11.3 per cent higher than the white average; (iii) there was no evidence of rent discrimination against coloured tenants in the furnished sector (Fenton and Collard, 1977:3–5).

Another study of house purchasing by middle-class Asians moving into the suburban areas of south Manchester and north Cheshire matched against a sample of white households, concluded, after taking into account the quality of the dwelling, that, regardless of the length of time spent searching, the Asians spent on average 5 per cent more in purchasing their houses. This study inferred that search costs were a significant element in the situation since house agents supplied Asian would-be purchasers with details of fewer properties than were supplied to white purchasers and vendors were reluctant to sell to Asians (Fenton, 1976). Otherwise it is difficult to account for the differential since people were not thought to place a high value on a hypothetical reduction in the amenity value of the neighbourhood they were leaving (but see the reference to new unpublished research findings in Ward and Sims, 1981:229).

The general picture for minorities in England is therefore one of discontinuity between four housing sectors or markets in ascending order of preference: rented furnished from private landlord; rented unfurnished from private landlord; rented unfurnished from public landlord (though for many, especially middle-class people, this will rank below the better properties in the previous category); owner occupation. Immigrants have, to start with, been concentrated in the least-preferred sector, that of furnished renting. As they have re-united their families and increased their income, so they have moved upwards. Some have obtained unfurnished tenancies. Many West Indians have waited for council houses, but some, and many more Asians, have bought poorer quality houses in the first sector. This is where the 1970 figures from the three London stress areas are interesting. They support the impression obtained from other information that the rent controls were tighter in the unfurnished sector than in the furnished sector (it is, after all, difficult to price variations in the quality of furniture). These controls therefore prevented landlords from increasing rents to the point at which supply and demand were in balance. Some landlords preferred white to coloured tenants and since they could not get higher rents from the latter, they discriminated and rented their properties to whites, of whom there was a ready stream. Because it was more difficult for minority families to enter the upper sectors they were overrepresented relative to income in the bottom sector. Other landlords of unfurnished property may have been under less pressure from the rent controls and used the price mechanism to obtain higher rents from minority tenants, hence the 11 per cent colour tax. They could do this in the unfurnished sector because the controls, although not uniformly stringent, had greater effect than in the furnished sector where, with some minority landlords and the prospect of greater profit, a more competitive market could have been created. This reasoning is speculative, but how else are the findings to be accounted for?

The Rational Choice Theory offers in principle a method for explaining the existence of price discrimination and its level, it can predict the circumstances in which discrimination will take the form of exclusion. The imposition of a colour tax may be morally reprehensible, but it brings together willing sellers and purchasers. If minority members can gain entry to a market in this way, the tax can be expected to decline if white landlords and neighbours discover that coloured people are not so very different from whites and that it is more important to differentiate between good and bad tenants and neighbours than black and white ones. Where a colour tax is not allowed to operate landlords may prevent minority members entering a preferred housing market. In Britain upward social mobility on the part of black and Asian immigrants, and closer acquaintance between blacks and whites, may have reduced the taste for discrimination amongst the white population. The law has probably reduced the incidence of discrimination by reinforcing the view that such a taste is illegitimate. By increasing the cost to any person who is reported as having broken the law, it has forced down the incidence of discrimination, but should it be brought substantially below the level of the taste for discrimination, landlords will be motivated to find ways round the law, to withdraw from the market, or to move to that sector of the market in which a colour tax can operate.

Comparison of theories

Over the period 1961–77 the ethnic minorities in Britain improved their position in respect of housing very considerably. At the beginning of this period roughly 28 per cent of West Indian household heads were owner occupiers, 3 per cent were in council houses, 13 per cent were renting unfurnished and 56 per cent renting furnished. West Indians moved into owner occupation so that by 1971 44 per cent were living in their own properties, but this number has since fallen back, possibly because more attractive council housing has become available. In 1977 36 per cent were owner occupiers, 46 per cent in council housing (compared with 30 per cent of the general population) and the remainder renting privately: 11 per cent unfurnished and 7 per cent furnished. The extent to which they have escaped from this last kind of tenure is notable. In 1961 47 per cent of Asian households were in owner occupation, 9 per cent in council housing, 22 per cent renting unfurnished and 22 per cent renting furnished. Sixteen years later 70 per cent of Asian households were in owner occupation, 10 per cent in council housing, and the remainder renting: 7 per cent unfurnished, 13 per cent furnished.

The kind of housing tenure is only a rough measure of the quality of housing. Many of the houses owned by Asians will have been old and small cottage dwellings near the centres of cities and in poor structural condition. However, such objective measures of housing quality as are available indicate that there has been significant improvement. The percentage of West Indian and Asian households in shared dwellings fell steadily from 47 per cent to 23 per cent over the period 1961–77 (but has still to be compared with a figure of 3 per cent for the general population at the later date). Another measure of quality is the number of families living at a density of more than 1.5 persons per room; that, too, shows a big reduction in differentials so that the 1981 census may report that no more West Indian than white families are now living at this density. Asian densities are higher, but have been dropping as the last wave of immigrants has been absorbed. On the other hand, a national survey in 1977 found that 11 per cent of West Indian and 18 per cent of Asian households lacked or had to share the use of a bath or shower compared with 5 per cent of whites (Field *et al.*, 1981:13–20). Moreover, a pattern of segregation was becoming established. At the end of the 1970s in Birmingham on average 15–20 per cent of the occupants of council housing in the inner areas were West Indians (and this was where the Asians were also concentrated), whereas in suburban districts the West Indian figures were mostly between 1 and 2 per cent (Ward and Sims, 1981:232).

Can it be said that either the Ecological or the Rational Choice Theory

358   *Racial and ethnic competition*

offers a better explanation of these data? The Ecological Theory predicted that the native whites would exclude minority people from access to preferred housing. West Indians have not been excluded from council housing, but most of them have been housed in the least attractive estates. The Rational Choice Theory also predicted exclusion, and expected it to be more effective where there was no price mechanism. As it was originally formulated, the Ecological Theory neglected the possibility that minority demand might differ from that of the whites. Rex's statement assumed that everyone aspired to the suburban ideal, but he has since acknowledged that there are other value systems so that his original model requires extension (Rex, 1971:297).

A strictly ecological theory of urban land use by racial groups would differ from an economic theory in that the independent variable in the former would consist of descriptions of land, whereas in the latter it would be descriptions of parties to market relations. Rex's theory used ecological relations as a spring board for discussing more general sociological issues, but it has not been built out to allow for individual variations. The Rational Choice Theory starts from a conception of consumer behaviour which assumes that there will be differences in taste, and it has no difficulty allowing for the effect of minority demand as tending to maintain or lift house prices in areas where the demand from the majority is reduced (Collard, 1973). By analysis in terms of a variable taste for discrimination and a variable cost, the theory can take account of differences in the incidence of discrimination directed against different minorities. It also provides support for the view that the less competitive a market the easier will be the practice of racial discrimination. Thus by referring to variations in the competitiveness of different sectors of the housing market it can offer an explanation of the 11.3 per cent colour tax in the unfurnished sector of the London housing market found in the 1970 survey when there was none in the furnished sector. The explanation has not been proven, but it is at least plausible. None of the other theories discussed in this book can offer any alternative explanation. If they were to be developed so as to confront these kinds of data, they would doubtless have to add on propositions such as those which constitute the Rational Choice Theory.

Yet the task of explaining the concentration of Asian and West Indian housing in the inner city remains. To account for the Asian pattern is easier. Because of their kinship networks, Asians were fairly easily able to raise the capital necessary for the purchase of cheap housing conveniently located for their work. In their culture a man who owned his own house received more respect and they were not worried if their housing preferences were different from the whites'. If need be, they could finance their purchases by renting to kinsmen who were more recent immigrants. For them, at that time, such a purchase looked the most attractive, but over a longer period circumstances change; migrants who expected to return to their homelands after a few years postpone the journey, and as their children grow up their goals in life change. In a period of rising house prices, mortgage-assisted owner-occupation has been an avenue of capital accumulation for many British families, but in the urban inner ring house prices are unlikely to have increased, or to increase in the near future, to the same extent. Owner-occupation in neighbourhoods with poor services may prove to have been a less rewarding strategy than waiting for access to the public housing sector. If it should turn out this way, one section of the Asian population may be at a disadvantage compared with people of West Indian origin, but it will not be because they did not have similar opportunities. Inequalities can develop from sources other than prejudice.

To account for the inner city concentration of people of West Indian origin is more complicated. At one time the Birmingham housing authorities sought to avoid this by an explicit policy of dispersing minority families when they were allocated council housing. This policy was declared to be illegal under the terms of the 1976 Race Relations Act and has been brought to an end. The present pattern of allocation in British cities is the product of a series of factors best described in their own terms. They do not conflict with either the Ecological or the Rational Choice Theory but little is gained by trying to link them with these theories. In the first place, officials responsible for allocations treat some classes of applicant differently: someone whose house is being demolished for a redevelopment scheme takes priority over someone on the waiting list. Secondly, applicants are allocated accommodation that, so far as possible, meets their wishes and their needs; but there may be a relative shortage of houses of a particular kind, or many more people wanting to live in a particular estate than dwellings available. Thirdly, people are not allocated in such a way as to cause estate management problems (a family with a history of failure to pay the rent and six unruly children will generate bitter complaints if placed alongside a group of small families conscious of their respectability).

Minority families tend to be at a disadvantage because they are more likely to qualify through the low-priority waiting list. They have on average larger families, while the local authorities are often short of larger houses and flats. Some minority applicants ask to be sent to central estates because other minority families are there; if they would sooner go elsewhere and are offered a location they think unattractive, they are less likely to argue about it or wait for something better, and, once they have moved to such an area they are less likely to seek a transfer. In many cities housing visitors call at the homes of applicants to form an estimate of their needs and assess the standards maintained in the home so that they can be offered accommodation in estates of similar character, and it is possible that elements of bias creep into their assessments or into the decisions reached by officials who deal with applicants who come to the housing office. An account of the values which pervade one such office (Flett, 1979) strengthens this supposition. At the same time it should be mentioned that housing departments where research has been carried out have been unaware of the extent to which minority applicants were being allocated to the least desirable housing and that, when this has been demonstrated, some have taken remedial action (see Smith, 1977:243–84). Though this is a more distantly related matter, it should also be noted that some council estates suffer from vandalism and bad management; they acquire so bad a reputation that perhaps four out of every five people offered accommodation there reply that they would sooner continue in their present housing. These estates become housing of last resort, but usually most of the residents are white and the estates are not as badly stigmatized as some of the all-black subsidized housing neighbourhoods in United States cities.

To account for the disadvantages which are experienced by ethnic minority applicants for council housing in Britain, it is necessary to allow for relationships more complicated than those usually specified in theories of racial relations. Allocations depend upon policies formulated by committees of an elected council, advised by central government and by the professional standards of officials who are accepted as experts. The policies are implemented in a situation of variations in demand for and supply of particular kinds of housing by applicants with particular characteristics, some of which are objectively and others subjectively assessed. The subjective assessments may be influenced more by shared assumptions among low-level administrators than by overt pressure, but this is a matter of inference. The explanation of decisions of this kind has to draw upon a wide range of social science knowledge that is in no way limited to racial and ethnic contacts. This reinforces the belief that the theories are realistic.

A challenge

The Rational Choice Theory can serve as a philosophy underlying attempts to interpret the history of racial and ethnic relations in particular societies. It probably has greater potential than any of its competitors for being developed to a point at which it can predict behaviour in various kinds of market and be subjected to empirical testing, but the nature of the obstacles still to be overcome is well illustrated by the research of a political scientist interested in the conflict over the busing of children to schools with more equal proportions of black and white pupils. The example does not relate to the housing market but it poses a challenge to rational choice explanations in general.

Rational choice models have in recent years been used with considerable success to predict the ways in which people will vote (Page, 1977) but the inference that they have acted in particular ways so as to maximize their net advantages can be a tautology. To subject it to an independent test is difficult. John B. McConahay (1982) studied a dispute over a court order about busing in Louisville, Kentucky, in 1975–6. A sample was drawn and 1,049 persons interviewed. Their attitudes towards the busing order were measured. If hostility towards the order was motivated by a rational assessment of the inconvenience it would cause individuals, and of their concern for any burden which additional travelling time would impose upon their children, then scores on a scale measuring opposition to busing should have correlated with scores on a scale measuring respondents' self-interest in the intended changes. The interviews also included questions permitting three different measures of racial attitudes. Several analyses of the results were carried out. They showed that at best the self-interest variables were only weakly correlated with attitudes towards busing; one of the racial attitudes measures proved to be somewhat more strongly associated with opposition but the other two showed themselves to be very powerful predictors of it indeed. The author concluded that policy preferences are not the result of any calculation of the individuals' likely net advantages but reflected early political and value socialization, especially when this touched on matters, such as those related to race, which had great symbolic significance. He argued that when it is time to vote or give responses to public opinion pollsters, Americans react as if they laid aside their private citizen roles and assumed public citizen roles, and since they know little about the facts of the matter, they draw upon their values.

Such a conclusion must be qualified. The strength of black support for busing suggests that black and white Americans draw upon different value systems. Moreover, as McConahay reports, attitudes towards busing proved poor predictors of actual behaviour. Though 20 per cent of whites said they would engage in protests and demonstrations if the plan was changed, nothing approaching that percentage did anything of the kind. Little is known about the motivations of those who continued to protest, but it would not be surprising if they included many people with little self-interest in the matter or if they were helped by like-minded people from other districts altogether.

It is not suggested that the Rational Choice Theory can predict the way people will behave in the housing market, or in expressing opinions about busing, without information about those people's values or preferences. Such information must include some measure, however crude, of the price people put on those preferences. In the Louisville case it cost whites nothing to say they would join in protest activity whereas actually to go out and join such activity not only entailed a real cost but it included an element of risk.

People did not know how such action might reflect upon their reputations or whether participation might lead to their being drawn into situations they would not otherwise have entered. When it comes to collective activity, beliefs about other people's likely behaviour are crucial. To join a demonstration is easy if thousands of others are expected to do the same and the demonstration will be orderly so that there is little chance of its being dispersed with violence. While it is salutary to compare the power of rational choice measures with others as predictors of expressed attitudes, the more important task is to discover the relative strength of different factors for predicting particular kinds of response. Assessments of how others will react can be important in housing markets, as the next section will explain.

Open markets

In the 1960s it was believed that desegregation was possible in low-cost housing projects so long as the proportion of non-white residents did not exceed 20 per cent of the total. This was said to be the 'tipping point'. Once the point was passed all the whites left and it became a segregated neighbourhood. Subsequent research has shown how complicated can be the problems of matching the preferences of groups with different ideas about the best mixture of strangers and of people like themselves.

A study in Detroit assessed the neighbourhood preferences of blacks and whites by presenting them with a series of cards. Each had 15 houses drawn upon it. Some were marked in white, others black, while the one in the middle, which was neither black nor white, was described as 'your house'. Whites were asked to imagine that they were living in a neighbourhood with no black families and then to imagine that one black family moved in. They were shown the first card depicting one black house among 15 and asked how comfortable they would feel in that situation. Further cards were presented showing other mixtures up to the point at which there were eight black households. Black respondents were presented with slightly different cards. Sixty-three per cent of blacks preferred the card showing their house surrounded by seven black and seven white households, while 20 per cent ranked this as their second choice. The card depicting only white neighbours was least attractive to them and the all-black pattern next least. Blacks therefore favoured a relatively even mix. However, although three quarters of the whites said they would feel more comfortable with one black family in the neighbourhood, the percentage support for integration dropped as the balance changed: 44 per cent would feel comfortable if whites were slightly in the majority but only 26 per cent if they had more black than white neighbours. The percentage of whites who said that in such circumstances they would move elsewhere increased steadily: 7 per cent on the arrival of the first black family, a further 16 per cent with three, and a total of two-thirds by the time the ratio was eight to seven (Farley *et al.*, 1979).

The neighbourhood preferences of blacks and whites seem incompatible. As blacks move in, seeking the ratio at which they feel comfortable, whites move out. On these figures no equilibrium is possible and the neighbourhood will become all-black. As Thomas Schelling (1972:168–74; 1978:155–66) has demonstrated, it takes a little while to explain why this is so. Houses are being bought and sold all the time and whites will move in who are comfortable at the prevailing mix, but will leave as more blacks enter. On the Detroit figures 58 per cent of whites and 25 per cent of blacks would feel comfortable in a neighbourhood which was 80 per cent white and 20 per cent black. If the whites are 58 per cent of a representative sample and only 20 per cent of the houses are made available to blacks, 22 per cent of the houses will remain vacant. On an open market these would be bought by blacks and the remaining whites would leave. The market cannot help people attain the situation they most want: both blacks and whites will end up living apart when both groups would prefer a measure of integration. The only possible solution is a cooperative one, and would depend upon the formation of a corporation able to purchase houses and eliminate the effect of uncertainty about the effect of the transition upon prices. The corporation could buy the otherwise vacant 22 per cent of vacant houses and, if it were permitted by law to sell them only to whites, it could, at some cost, populate the neighbourhood with whites more liberal on the housing issue than the white population in general.

In practice, of course, attitudes respond to experience. It is possible that whites who say that they would not wish to have more than three black families living near them might, after experiencing such a situation, decide that they would still feel comfortable if there were four or five. The authors of the Detroit study apparently pin their hopes upon this sort of development. They stress that their findings are consistent with earlier investigations showing that whites underestimate the willingness of their white neighbours to accept close interracial contact. Eighty per cent of the whites thought that a white child and a black child should be allowed to play together in the white child's home, but only 37 per cent thought their neighbours would approve of this. Since whites over-estimate the prejudice of their neighbours they are more inclined to panic when the first black families move into their neighbourhood. In all probability this tendency to over-estimate such prejudice is influenced by risk-aversion; there is less risk in an action based on an over-estimate of the likelihood that neighbours will disapprove than in one based on an under-estimation. The same applies for blacks, who, when asked about moving into a white neighbourhood, over-estimate the probability of white hostility. Real-estate agents also prefer to avoid risks; they seem to under-estimate the frequency with which whites will accept a black neighbour or move into an area where blacks are already living. The publicizing of information about people's real attitudes towards racial integration could play an important part in the promotion of integration. Publicity given to white hostility can have the opposite effect.

Publicity about the economic implications of discrimination could also help policies of desegregation. If whites were aware that they could get better prices for selling their houses without regard to the colour of the purchaser they might find that their taste for discrimination was less important. Black demand for home-ownership and for housing in mixed neighbourhoods has probably been under-estimated in the past. If it were easier and less risky for blacks to move out of the ghettos their readiness to spend money on housing might turn out to be greater than previously thought.

Conclusion

This chapter has served both to analyse the determinants of racial relations in a crucial field and to illustrate what can be involved in the attempt to develop theories of racial and ethnic relations to the point at which they can be tested. It shows how inadequate are crude conceptions of racism. To explain why discrimination exists at different levels in different sectors of the housing market requires a balancing of individual prejudice against the costs of different alternatives in situations in which people are imperfectly informed about the likely behaviour of others, and in markets powerfully influenced by the policies of local governments and financial institutions. The same principles can be used to explain discrimination in the otherwise very different circumstances of housing in British and United States cities. The analysis provides additional grounds for believing that, where blacks and whites are able to compete equally for housing, the boundaries between their groups will be weakened; but where they compete as groups the opposite happens: prejudice is reinforced, people fear the risks of breaking with group expectations, information about the attitudes of others may become less reliable, and the market be structured in ways that permit change only at the geographical margin of the ghetto.

Chapter 5 maintained that sociologists should seek out situations in which one theory can be confronted with another. This discussion has shown how difficult it can be, in the present state of knowledge, to find situations in which different theories of racial and ethnic relations offer different explanations of the same observation. It suggests that the areas of overlap between the eight theories that have been set out in propositional form are smaller than might appear. When the attempt is made to compare two of them, the explanation of the initial problem only reveals other problems which are further removed from the initial focus on race and ethnicity. The pursuit of these problems takes the research worker into other areas of social science and weakens any assumption that racial and ethnic relations are a special kind of relations. In so doing, it reinforces one of this book's main contentions.

13

Minorities in the employment market

In countries like the United States and Great Britain there is abundant evidence that the average earnings of whites tend to be higher than those of blacks and the earnings of males higher than those of females. Since incomes differ in accordance with qualifications, education, age, union power, occupation and region, as well as with race and gender, to weigh one factor against another while allowing for historical variations in economic circumstances is a complex task. Nor is it easy to discover what are the real determinants lying behind what appears to be a racial factor when this is compared with something else. It may be that the proportion of blacks with sought-after qualifications is relatively low and that the average quality of the black labour supply is therefore lower than that of the whites. It may be that white employers discriminate between blacks and whites and that there is a difference in the demand for the two categories of labour.

The main factors on the supply and demand sides which have been identified in the debate about the causes of racial inequalities in earnings are set out in Figure 10. Much of this debate has so far consisted of attempts to demonstrate the possible importance of particular components and much more remains to be done assessing the extent to which different components interact and complement each other in the explanation of particular inequalities. Some participants in the debate have emphasized the supply side and would discuss this first. However, it is easier to discuss factors on the demand side by drawing upon analyses developed in the United States, whereas a discussion of inequalities in Britain, where many of the blacks are recent immigrants, introduces new factors on the supply side; it is therefore convenient to open this chapter with an examination of factors on the demand side and with theories of discrimination.

Economists often define discrimination in a way which suits their purposes and diverges from its legal usage. English law – which has followed the law of the United States in this field – defines racial discrimination as present when, on racial grounds, someone treats another 'less favourably than he treats or would treat other persons'. It has been extended by the concept of indirect discrimination to cover the unjustified

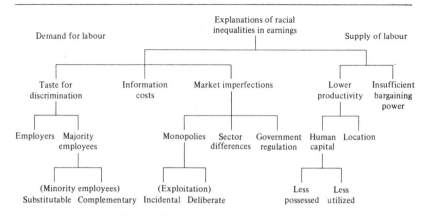

Figure 10 Explanations of racial inequalities in earnings

imposition of a requirement or condition with which members of another racial group can less easily comply. It is only actions and practices which can be declared unlawful because discriminatory. If members of a minority are on average less well qualified, their earnings will be lower than those of the majority; this will be inequality, but it will not be evidence of discrimination. When economists identify an inequality which cannot be accounted for by differences in qualifications or other characteristics of the minority labour force, they regularly infer that the difference is due to discrimination without necessarily identifying who discriminated or when the discrimination occurred.

Sometimes they infer that the characteristics of the minority labour force are an outcome of previous discrimination. If no qualified blacks apply for a post because none have been trained, the employer has not discriminated; if none have been trained because none thought it worthwhile acquiring the training, those responsible for training have not discriminated; but why did no blacks think it worthwhile undergoing training? Was it not because the pattern of white discrimination was so strong that it persuaded them or their parents that blacks would never be allowed to obtain that kind of job? Since blacks have lived in the United States for so many more generations than most of the white ethnic groups, what other explanation can there be for continuing economic inequality apart from some unsubstantiated deficiency theory? To argue like this is to make the concept of discrimination serve a political and moral end. It leaves unanswered a series of questions about the points in the economic and social structure at which discrimination occurs, and why. To say that 'society' has discriminated is only to evade the problems. Discrimination is only one of the sources of inequality between racial groups (and between men and women); any policy to reduce inequality is unlikely to succeed unless the nature and influence of every relevant factor has been analysed.

The taste for discrimination

Theories of discrimination have been seen as falling into three categories, according to whether they start from tastes and preferences, from information costs, or from market imperfections (Oaxaca, 1977).

The first comprehensive theory was that advanced by Gary S. Becker (1957) who based his analysis on the proposition that individuals have a 'taste for discrimination' in the sense explained in Chapter 12. White employers, it is said, would sooner have whites working for them than blacks, and white workers would sooner have white workmates. An all-white workforce would have for them an amenity value, just as a house in a conveniently situated and high-status residential neighbourhood has an amenity value in the eyes of a potential house-purchaser. White workers who are required to work alongside blacks may leave their employment unless they are compensated for the disamenity, just as they will object to working in unpleasant conditions unless they receive additional reward. An individual is said to have a taste for discrimination if he acts as if he were willing to pay extra or to forfeit income in order to avoid transactions with people assigned to the category against which the discrimination is practised. In this way a disposition to discriminate is measured by its effect on actual behaviour in a situation of choice.

Becker began by imagining a society consisting of two racial groups, blacks and whites, with similar work preferences. The whites preferred to avoid associating with blacks, so a white employer would, other things being equal, engage blacks only at a lower wage. Assuming that he employed both whites and blacks, he would pay whites rather more and blacks rather less than they would receive in a colour-blind labour market. Though it started as a model of a single society, Becker's model came to represent a situation in which a white society rich in capital traded with a black society rich in labour. Though the whites lost income because black productivity was not fully utilized, both parties benefited from the trade.

The economist who employs Becker's model can assume that white employers have a taste for discrimination while white workers and consumers of the product do not; equally, he can assume that either white workers or the consumers have such a taste and that the other two parties do not. It is not necessary to follow through such possibilities, but it should be noted that some outcomes depend upon whether black workers are substitutable for white. If black workers are as productive as whites in a particular occupation and will work for lower pay (because they face discrimination in alternative employments also) it will be in the employer's interest to replace that section of his workforce with black workers, and this will be easier to do if the section is a segregated one. If, however, the black workers are complementary to the white workers instead of being potential substitutes (e.g. because they act as assistants to more highly skilled workers), the white workers will want extra pay as compensation for having to work with blacks. The outcome of a white taste for discrimination when black workers are substitutable will therefore be workplace segregation, and when black and white workers are complementary it will be an increased racial wage differential.

Information costs

Hiring workers must always entail some uncertainty about how they will perform. A reference from a previous employer and a record of steady employment may indicate that one applicant is likely to stay longer in a job than another. The assigning of applicants to social categories may be thought to have similar implications. A middle-aged man may be expected to stay longer in a job than a young woman. An employer may believe black workers to be, on average, less reliable than white workers; the belief may have a foundation in fact, in that he may have had previous experience of unreliable black workers, or it may be that, for any of several incidental reasons, black workers actually are less reliable. This is a comparison of averages and it must be unfair to some individuals in the category thought to be unreliable.

Consider the situation in which two equally qualified people apply for a post. One belongs in a category in which the expected probability of being dismissed for unsatisfactory work, time-keeping, or cooperation with others, is 5 per cent, whereas the second belongs in a category with a 15 per cent probability of proving unsatisfactory. The rational employer will engage the first person, and, on successive occasions, people like him, because in that way he can avoid the costs of hiring and firing an additional 10 per cent of his labour force. Eighty-five per cent of the applicants from the second category would have proven just as satisfactory as the 95 per cent of the former who stay the course, but they are not hired because of the objective characteristics of the categories to which they are assigned. They are the victims of statistical discrimination.

In such circumstances discrimination arises from the costs of obtaining information, not from any presumed taste for discrimination. In many situations it is not worth the employer's while to spend time and money investigating the claims of job-applicants and subjecting them to aptitude tests. The profit-maximizing employer will want basic information from applicants and he may also regard category membership as an effective criterion for screening out the kinds of employees he is seeking. There is no incentive for him to incur extra costs in searching for potential employees among a section of the labour force with which he is unacquainted. If the employment of black workers causes white workers to leave, the employer may incur additional turnover costs in changing over from a white to a black workforce. If, like many employers, he is 'risk averse', being anxious to avoid a risk of unknown magnitude, he may choose an alternative which, objectively seen, will not bring him maximum profit (Arrow, 1972:99–100).

Statistical discrimination may enable the employer to reduce his costs of recruitment but, if other employers behave in a similar fashion, they transfer a burden to society as a whole by creating a disadvantaged minority. Economists distinguish between costs that are internal to a transaction and those that arise externally. Statistical discrimination results in the under-utilization of human resources and reduces the total income of the society. It gives rise, as an externality, to a public cost that can be compared with that of pollution.

Market imperfections

Calling something a 'market imperfection' will, for many people, imply that the thing in question is undesirable. It is easily assumed that all monopolies are bad. Yet some restrictions upon competition are now taken for granted in industrial societies, and none more than those on which the professions are based. Some doctors and lawyers have taken to drink, or for some other reason become incompetent or unable to provide a service as good as that which might be obtained from other people with lesser qualifications. In a free market citizens would be at liberty to engage anyone they wished to remove their appendixes or to present their cases in court. They are denied this power by rules which, with the backing of the state, enforce a monopoly allowing only qualified people to practise. The professions in turn charge their clients according to standard scales of fees and, while there is a pricing mechanism which controls the demand for the services of the most skilled practitioners, the relationship between the professional and his client is conducted on a basis different from that between seller and buyer. Few citizens complain. The person who wants his appendix removed is disinclined to take a risk with someone who has never previously carried out such an operation. He is content that doctors should have a monopoly over the practice of medicine provided it is supervised by the legislature. Members of many other occupations which do not possess all the attributes of a profession, like policemen, nurses and university teachers, probably provide a better service from being paid according to set scales with considerable security of tenure than would be the case were their performance subject to continuous (and costly) monitoring so as to base their pay upon their weekly product.

Craft guilds are an equally historical example of monopoly. The bakers, cordwainers, drapers, glovers, haberdashers, mercers, plaisterers, salters, skinners and vintners were corporations based upon the possession of valued skills. A craftsman who had spent years learning the 'mysteries' of his trade did not want to find himself in sudden competition with an apprentice whom he had three-quarters trained. He was willing to teach others his skill only if he could be sure that he would not, in so doing, weaken his own market position. In modern times workers are just as anxious to defend their job interests. Technological innovations may enable the same quantity to be produced by fewer people but it may be impossible to make use of them unless the existing workers are compensated for the potential earnings, security or privileges which they surrender.

Some monopolies, such as the sale of postal services, are maintained by governments. Almost invariably, the only armed services permitted are those owing loyalty to the head of state, and the government controls policies for recruitment to the army and navy as it does to other forms of state employment. Some monopolies, of which the telephone service is often an example, are based upon the advantages of having uniform technological provisions throughout the country. Such an institution (as was the case with the American Telephone and Telegraph Company, A. T. and T.) may follow recruitment and promotions policies which favour white males and display indirect discrimination. Another possibility is that a monopoly, or a cartel formed by a group of employers, discriminates deliberately in order to make a financial gain. Monopolists use their power in the market place (backed, often, by political power) to make unequal bargains by which their employees receive lower wages than they would under conditions of perfect competition. Reference was made in Chapter 10 to the attempts of white landowners in the South in the late nineteenth century to form such cartels. They failed, but under different conditions there can be different outcomes. One theory of racial inequalities in earnings is that income which might otherwise have been received by black workers is appropriated by their white employers, but it is equally possible that white workers benefit most from the exploitation of black workers, as was discussed in Chapter 9 with reference to South Africa.

Market imperfections also result from the way technological change affects the structure of the labour market by increasing the relative profitability of particular industries. One industry may be declining because of changed methods of production, competition from overseas or reduced demand for its product, while another industry that is favoured by the pattern of change may be making greater profits and paying its employees higher wages. Two such industries may recruit their workforces in different ways. An industry in what is called the secondary sector, employing many unskilled workers, with a relatively stable technology and a high expenditure on labour relative to capital equipment, will have a management anxious to minimize the wage-bill. If there is a plentiful supply of labour, workers will compete with one another for employment and this will be offered to those willing to work for the lowest wages. An industry with the opposite characteristics is said to belong to the primary sector. Its management will spend much more on employee selection and training and an internal labour market will be created with offers of promotion within the corporation for those who keep abreast of technological change. The management will seek to minimize (relative to its level of output) both the cost of training and that of wages; workers will compete with one another for jobs on the basis of their relative position; if applicants are lined up in order of their qualifi- cations, with those in front being the persons who can be trained most cheaply, then the posts will go to those at the head of the queue. Lester C. Thurow (1975:75–154) presents this as a distinction between job-competition in the primary and wage-competition in the secondary sectors and shows that it is crucial to an understanding of inequality in the employment market.

A third set of components in the demand for labour is constituted by government regulation, for governments draft the laws regulating employ- ment. They finance occupational training and services which put potential employers and potential employees in touch with one another. They provide financial assistance to certain industries. The laws determine how disputes are conducted and how much power a trade union can wield if it wishes to defend discriminatory practices. Many economists in the United States are sure that the law prescribing a minimum wage operates so as to restrict job opportunities for minorities, especially for young blacks. Governments, by their control of law enforcement, can either permit employers to discriminate racially or make it expensive for them to do so.

Human capital

The nature of the human capital theory has already been outlined in Chapter 10 in the discussion of the interpretations put forward by Thomas Sowell. In seeking the causes of racial inequalities in earnings it looks to the possibility that a group receives lower earnings because its labour is less productive. In a perfectly competitive employment market there is no place for racial discrimination. Even if a substantial majority of employers preferred not to engage workers from a particular minority this would not, of itself, be enough to establish a pattern of racial discrimination. One employer who did not share their feelings, or who regarded such feelings as irrelevant to business transactions, could open an establishment employing minority labour, make high profits, and either drive his competitors out of the market or force them to change their policies. Since there are minority businessmen willing to lend money to minority entrepreneurs, as well as profit-seeking majority businessmen, the persistence of discrimination in what is ostensibly a competitive market calls for some stronger explanation than a supposed taste. The human capital theorists find the explanation in differences in the productivity of labour which can be traced to different investments in training.

Economically successful parents can give their children a better start in life. The easiest way of measuring the investment in the education of a given category of people (by the state, by the parents, and by the individuals themselves) is to ascertain the proportions completing different numbers of years in school and by the qualifications obtained. However, human capital includes other factors, notably the motivation to work (which has earlier been discussed as competitiveness and which is included in the more general notion of a work ethic) and the ability to persist in the face of discouragement, which may in turn be related to the emotional support people obtain from their families and friends. Those who emphasize variations in human capital investment as an explanation of racial inequalities maintain that, as minority productivity increases, so do minority living standards, and then the majority's taste for discrimination against minority members declines.

Lower productivity may stem not from differences in human capital so much as from differences in the utilization of their work capacities by different groups. While professional women tend to be as keen to maximize their incomes as their male counterparts, there are other women who regard paid employment (especially those who undertake only part-time employment) as a social activity and a supplement to other household income. The women of different racial and ethnic groups vary more than the men in what are called their labour-force participation rates.

An illustration of some of the difficulties that can arise where both discrimination and different attitudes towards work can contribute to inequalities of earnings is provided by a United States study of differences between male and female earnings. The author follows Becker in defining the discrimination co-efficient as the gross wage differential between two types of perfectly substitutable labour. He calculates the likely effect upon wages of the differences between male and female workers in respect of work experience, absence because of child-rearing and housework, part-time working, industry in which employed, region, migration history, health, and other personal characteristics. This leaves a residual 74 per cent of the wage differential between white males and females, and 92 per cent of that between black males and females, which is unaccounted for; so it is attributed to discrimination. The author concludes that 'in the absence of sex discrimination as we have defined it, the average female wage as a percentage of the average male wage would be 88 per cent for white females and 96 per cent for black females (the current percentages are 65 and 67 per cent for whites and blacks respectively)' (Oaxaca, 1973:147–8). The crudity of the comparison lies in its treatment of women workers as sharing male job preferences. In the United States both males and females have the option of seeking full-time employment or filling the role of 'home-maker'. For cultural reasons the latter appeals to relatively more women than men. For educated women the possibility of pursuing a career may be more attractive than that of being a home-maker. For women who can obtain only relatively unattractive unskilled work the alternative may be more appealing. So the resulting pattern of inequality will in some measure reflect choices that women have made.

The productivity of immigrants may differ from that of native workers for several reasons. The work skills immigrants have acquired in their countries of origin may not be transferable to their new country or may not be in demand there. Immigrants may also be self-selected in terms of their abilities and motivation for economic advancement. Those who migrate to better themselves are more likely than are refugees to have transferable skills. Barry R. Chiswick (1980) has demonstrated that when immigrants first arrive they have lower earnings than the native-born with similar demographic characteristics. The difference is greatest for refugees from countries with different languages and economic structures. With the passage of time self-selected economic migrants overcome the obstacles and after eleven to sixteen years their earnings exceed those of comparable native workers. Some of the greater innate ability and motivation of the economic migrants is transmitted to their children; their sons earn 5 to 10 per cent more than the sons of native-born parents.

Immigrants need to be distinguished from migrant workers and particularly from 'target workers', who migrate to earn a particular sum in as short a time as possible and then return. They are attracted to employment in which they can maximize short-run earnings by working additional hours and are less concerned about job-security, promotion prospects and the like. Their labour supply is distinctly different.

Location

It has already been noted that technological change affects the labour market by affecting the profitability of particular industries. There is plenty of evidence to show that some inequalities in earnings should be attributed to variations in the return on capital investment in different regions and industries. As a source of inequality, such variations arise from the interaction between the demand for and the supply of labour, but they can be regarded as belonging on the supply side since in a perfectly competitive market workers would migrate from the low-paying to the high-paying regions and industries, and the differential would be reduced. If there is a regional differential it is because workers have other reasons for not migrating.

Bargaining power

Earnings are affected by differences in the relative bargaining power of employers and employees. In some occupations it is relatively easy to organize a trade union and ensure that everyone who follows that occupation is a member. In other occupations, like that of farm worker, unionization is difficult. There are also regional variations in unionization. A powerful union may be able to increase the earnings of its members relative to those of workers in occupations which cannot mobilize so much bargaining power.

Discussion

Becker's model of racial discrimination as resulting from trade between a white society and a black society has been criticized by Thurow who objects that: 'Racial discrimination occurs in one society not two. The dominant group controls much more than its willingness to trade or not to trade . . . The minority group may have few options and certainly not the option of refusing to trade.' Moreover, the desire to avoid association with blacks applies more to some relationships than others. 'The discriminator may want to work with, buy from or hire Negroes, but he insists on specifying the relationships under which the two parties will meet and how the Negro will respond . . . The discriminator may prefer to hire Negro maids, Negro garbage collectors, or to work with Negroes if he can be in a position of authority' (Thurow, 1969:117). Social psychologists have demonstrated that people can derive emotional gains from being socially elevated over others. They have also shown that many individuals will express a desire to avoid association with members of groups of whom they have no experience, and even of non-existent groups with made-up names. This does not demonstrate that there is no taste for discrimination, but it is a warning against an over-simple conceptionalization of it.

The limitations of such an explanation are further highlighted by a consideration of discrimination on grounds of sex. Women do not enjoy a position of equality in the employment market and some of this difference is due to discrimination. People may seek to maximize their income so that they can consume more, but in most households there is little difference in the consumption privileges of husband and wife: they share their goods and services. Why then, asks Thurow, should men discriminate against their wives and other men's wives? As he says, if consumption was the sole economic goal, most men, and certainly all men who were married or who planned to marry, would have an enormous vested interest in eliminating such discrimination since by so doing they could raise their consumption standards without having to work any harder themselves. Perhaps sex discrimination is different from racial discrimination, but it should be possible to explain both in terms of one theory of earnings inequalities.

The Becker model assumes a competitive market, and, while it is possible to allow for many imperfections in actual markets, there is still a substantial difficulty in explaining why there are not enough non-discriminatory employers. This model also treats tastes as revealed preferences, as influences upon behaviour which can be inferred from that behaviour and are not independently known and measured. Everyday experience suggests that tastes of this kind are not very stable; they exist, but are they so influential that they can support an explanation of the massive inequalities found in real situations?

In place of Becker's, Thurow proposes what he calls a monopoly model. There is room for debate about whether the two are really distinct, since perfect competition and monopoly are for many purposes the opposite ends of a single scale. To a sociologist, the work of both authors is firmly within the neo-classical tradition of economic reasoning; though Becker himself has little to say explicitly about monopoly, Thurow's proposals are compatible with his model and some may be drawn by inference from it. The competitive model as Thurow presents it, treats whites as wishing to be physically distant from blacks; in the course of seeking this goal they establish a pattern of relations that has the incidental effect of increasing white incomes. In the monopoly model, according to the argument in Thurow's first book (1969:118), a white discriminator seeks 'to maximize his gains from discrimination, including economic gains and increases in social distance', i.e. to maximize his own utility (which is a combination of material gains and psychic gains stemming from his personal taste for discrimination) and in order to do the former he takes advantage of the prejudices of others to create market situations, like monopolies, which are to his advantage. In his second book, Thurow (1975:164) gives more prominence to the whites' desire to be socially distant from blacks. One reason for their wishing to raise their incomes is that this will contribute to greater distance. They discriminate knowing that in this way they can raise both their money incomes and their psychic incomes (from maintaining a position superior to blacks in the scale of social status). The difference between these two ways of describing the monopoly model is not of great moment since the relative importance of the discriminators' desire to maximize material benefits relative to psychological benefits will vary from situation to situation and person to person, but it is worth noting, since many criticisms of the neo-classical approaches represent the desire for financial gain as both the driving force and the origin of the psychological valuations. They contend that the discriminators want the money, and since the maintenance of distance between the races helps them make greater profits they are brought, by conscious or unconscious processes, to seek distance as well. Thurow's second formulation is reversed.

According to Thurow's model whites collude in order to raise their incomes at the expense of blacks. It faces two difficulties. Firstly, where is the evidence of collusion? If it is an inference from what actually happens, is this any more reliable than the inference of a taste for discrimination? Secondly, it is never easy to maintain a cartel (for that is what Thurow really has in mind) when it is in the interest of individual members to break away because by so doing they can make greater profit. Thurow's answer is that the main mechanism for enforcing such practices lies in the way its various forms interlock. Social pressures may sometimes explain why blacks are not hired but it is more likely that the employer never faces a situation in which he has to ask himself whether it would be better to hire a black or white worker. The economists' phrase 'other things being equal', which is so necessary for analytical purposes, makes too large an assumption. Rarely do two applicants appear equal in everything but race. Much may depend upon whom they have to work with. The monopoly powers of white labour may prevent the employer recruiting at lower wages or may threaten trouble if he does hire someone unacceptable to the existing workforce. Since blacks have benefited less from investment in their schooling and job training, fewer will be qualified; past practice in an industry or firm may dissuade some of the few who might be acceptable from applying. If an employer seldom sees a qualified black job applicant his losses from not hiring them are minimal and less monopoly power is required to prevent the employment of the few qualified blacks who do get to the starting line.

Just as there are cyclical effects by which disadvantage is transmitted from one generation to the next, so there is a cycle within the same generation whereby discrimination in one area of society increases its incidence in other areas. 'Less schooling leads to fewer job skills, easing the problems of occupational, employment and monopoly discrimination. Together, all these forms of discrimination lead to low incomes, which makes price and human capital discrimination easier. Together, they reduce black political power and make schooling discrimination possible' (Thurow, 1975:169–70).

Competition and exclusion in the United States

Many of the economic statistics routinely collected in the United States differentiate between blacks and whites, providing a mass of data which, when analysed, may permit inferences of discrimination or of changes in the quality of the labour supply. There are few direct studies of discrimination in hiring (for one example see Newman, 1978). The area in which there is the most direct evidence of discrimination is that of the craft unions. Many trade unions representing skilled workers have negotiated 'hiring hall' arrangements with the employers (e.g. in the construction trade) whereby, when an employer wants a bricklayer or a plumber he notifies the union which then sends one of these craftsmen to him. These are also known as referral unions. These unions act like the guilds of mediaeval Europe in controlling entry to their trade in order to maintain the price which they can command for their services, but there is, in addition, an element of discrimination. The unions have the power to fix the number of apprenticeships; there is, in effect, a queue of applicants and the places are awarded to the sons and nephews of existing members, so if blacks are underrepresented to start with, they remain underrepresented.

Variations in the representation of blacks can to some extent be explained historically. The earliest known union is one formed by printers in New Orleans in 1810. Strong typographical unions were formed in all the South's major cities before 1860, in times when it would have been almost impossible for a black man to practise this craft. Some other Southern building trade unions, like the Carpenters and the Bricklayers, found it impossible to maintain their organizations after the Civil War because many slaves had been trained in these occupations. If the white workers were to strike for higher pay, they ran the risk that their places would all be taken by blacks. Therefore in those trades and places in which there were many competent black workers, the white workers had to choose between forming a union with black members (possibly in a segregated 'local') or doing without one altogether (Marshall, 1968:134–5). This, together with the greater opportunity for employers to engage non-union blacks, may be one of the reasons why fewer Southern workers have been members of trade unions. Crafts which came into existence in later historical periods when blacks were politically weak, such as the electrical, plumbing, and sheet-metal working trades, have been discriminatory from the outset and have fought hardest to avoid having to comply with federal equal-opportunity policies. For example, after the riot in Watts it was argued that as federal and state funds were to be used for the reconstruction of the locality, blacks should be admitted to the construction unions. Their officials rejected this, saying 'since Watts was not officially designated a disaster area, the unions should not take the initiative in trying to change hiring procedures'. Blacks were prevented from participating in the rebuilding of their own community (Hill, 1968:293).

The power of the craft unions is based upon the need for training, and the authority given by law to licensing boards to specify how that training shall be acquired; the unions have ensured that they have great influence over licensing procedures. It was because the craft unions resisted the entry of blacks that the first affirmative action programmes requiring fixed statistical quotas for employment were instituted by the Federal government through its power as a contractor, in the Philadelphia Plan in 1969, and many similar plans which followed (Glazer, 1975:50). Occupations which require only on-the-job training cannot be subject to entry control other than by the employers, so the so-called industrial unions have had less opportunity to discriminate and more reason to fear that if they do not admit blacks, black labour will be used against them.

In general there is less discrimination against blacks in non-referral unions than either in referral unions or in those sectors of the employment market that are not unionized (Bloch, 1977) and this can be supported by comparisons of earnings. Firstly, the effect of unionization in the building and construction trades, where referral unions are powerful, has been to reduce the ratio of black to white male wages by 5 per cent after allowances have been made for differences between the work groups. Secondly, the effect of unionization in the non-construction blue-collar occupations has been to raise the ratio of black to white male wages by about 3.9 per cent. Thirdly, the overall effect of unionization has been to reduce the ratio of white female to white male wages by 1.9 per cent and of black workers to white by 1.7 per cent. While an approach based on the measurement of inferred residual effects is inevitably crude, the differences are not very great; this has been taken to imply that unionization is not a major factor affecting black–white and male–female differentials and that it is necessary to look elsewhere for more powerful influences (Ashenfelter, 1973).

Unions are not the only bodies to utilize political power to influence market decisions. Greater discrimination can be expected in governmental monopolies, both because they are more subject to political direction or influences and because they do not have to compete with other bodies able to offer the same services. Thomas Sowell (1981b:105) notes that though in the war of 1812 Commodore Perry's crew was one-quarter black, by the 1920s there was literally not one black sailor in the US Navy. The government, he says, has changed the rules of the game for blacks in virtually every generation. The changing interpretations and violations of Indian treaties have been a historical scandal, while immigration policies have changed with the political winds.

Monopolies can also be maintained as a matter of custom. A favourite example of this in the United States is that of baseball. Until the late 1940s the major baseball teams employed only white players but once some teams started to field blacks and it became apparent that there were some very good black players available, the other teams had to hire them in order to retain their places in the leagues. An analysis has shown that most of the variation in individual salaries paid to players during the 1968 season could be attributed to objective measures of player value and that race had no significant impact upon salaries. This would indicate that where competition is on an individual basis racial discrimination is minimized. However, position by position, black players in the big leagues tended to outperform their white counterparts on the basis of batting averages and other objective measures. This suggested that for a black player to win promotion to a higher league his performance had to be slightly better than that of his white competitor; it was comparable to the 'colour tax' discussed in Chapter 12. Blacks were also underrepresented in the star playing positions and among big league managers, coaches and umpires; criteria of performance in these latter positions were probably less objective, making discrimination easier (Pascall and Rapping, 1972, but see Blalock, 1967, for an earlier analysis). Some other sports, like basketball, show a similar pattern, while blacks have also been more successful in the entertainment industry where performances are equally individualized. Theatrical agents have doubtless found it in their interest to provide shows featuring the best artists available within a given range of fees.

The claim that whites are reluctant to associate with blacks draws some support from the pattern prevailing with respect to the personal services provided for blacks by doctors, dentists, lawyers, funeral directors, insurance companies, and the like. Whites have tended to leave these sectors to black professionals and companies. Very many of the wealthy blacks have made their money by catering to a black clientele.

Studies of black representation in different sectors of the economy have found them to be more than proportionately concentrated in the secondary sector (trade, agriculture, services). Comparisons of minority and majority workers' wages, both within and between sectors, have shown that while everyone's wages are higher the more schooling they have received, minority workers benefit less from additional schooling (unless they complete high school and get to college). Wage differentials were lower in the more competitive secondary sector than in the more oligopolistic corporate sector; the colour tax was twice as great there as in the secondary sector (Beck, Horan and Tolbert, 1980).

An analysis of eight national population surveys from 1968 through 1975 confirms and expands these conclusions, showing that a great deal of the improvement in the relative earnings of blacks can be attributed to the steady improvement in their schooling. In 1920 black youths attended school for about 66 per cent of the time whites attended; and there were 56 pupils per teacher in the black schools, whereas the national average was less than 32 pupils per teacher. By 1954 the first of these differences had been eliminated and the second substantially reduced. Yet by 1970 blacks entering the labour force still had, on average, 1.2 years less schooling than whites. In 1947 black earnings were 54 per cent of white; in 1959, 58 per cent; in 1969 67 per cent; in 1975 73 per cent. They have increased because the black workforce has come increasingly to resemble the white workforce in schooling, regional residence, work experience and similar characteristics. Of that part of the growth in black earnings attributable to increased resemblance, 47 per cent is due to the improvement in the schooling of black workers. Successive cohorts have been benefiting from better educational facilities and less-qualified, older black workers have been dropping out of the labour force. Geographical location was a very important component of the explanation of earnings differentials in the recent past (because so many blacks lived in the South where wages were lower anyway). But this has been declining in its importance as the racial differential in the South has been reduced and the gap between the South and other regions has become smaller (Smith and Welch, 1978).

Up to 1975 government action seems not to have had any direct effect in reducing the racial differential. James P. Smith and Finis Welch looked to see if the rise in the black–white ratio was higher in those sectors of the economy most susceptible to governmental pressure, but found to the contrary that the rise came more from sectors unlikely to be so affected. There may, however, have been an indirect effect as improvements in welfare payments raise the threshhold below which people prefer not to seek employment. Since this reduces the labour supply it benefits those who are in the labour force and, to the extent to which white workers are not substitutes for black workers, it benefits black earnings. Since there has been a decrease in the black male labour force participation rate, the improvement in black–white earnings ratio (which takes no account of people with zero earnings) presents a more favourable picture of the overall black–white income comparison (Butler and Heckman, 1977). In particular it takes no account of long-term unemployment and the possible growth of an unemployable black underclass.

Since 1954 the level of unemployment among blacks has been rising relative to that among whites. It is sometimes argued that this is evidence of the way capitalists structure the economy so as to exploit minority workers more severely, and to utilize them in their struggle with the working class as a whole. A recent analysis of wage differentials and employment over the period 1947–75 came to contrary conclusions. It showed that the higher the level of non-white unemployment, (i) the greater the percentage share of aggregate income went to the third and fourth quintiles of households in the white population; (ii) the greater was the average white male income; and (iii) the greater were the average white earnings. This is evidence that whites benefited from the presence of a 'reserve army of labour', but suggests that it was not the rich whites who benefited. Increases in black–white differentials have been followed by reductions in the share of white family income going to the wealthiest 5 per cent of white families. Nor have these increases been followed by periods of higher corporate profit. If the percentage of non-agricultural labour belonging to unions is taken as an index of worker solidarity, then periods of increased discrimination result in a greater rather than a lesser degree of working-class unity (Beck, 1980). The increase in black unemployment seems to owe more to demographic change and the reduction in the demand for unskilled labour.

While calculations such as these are important pointers to the sources of racial inequalities in earnings, they are as yet far from complete. Slightly less than half of the increase in the ratio of black earnings to white is explained by the increasing resemblance of the two sections of the work force, and no more than 47 per cent of the resemblance factor by improved black schooling. Schooling is measured by years of attendance, which is a poor measure of the benefits attained from sitting in a classroom. The procedure can be reversed by ascertaining the level of education attained by a sample of young people leaving the school system and then looking into the factors in their previous record which are predictive of the level attained. Much research has been conducted along these lines and some of it suggests that the factors, like the socio-economic status of parents, which are powerful predictors of the relative attainment of young white people are much less powerful as predictors of black attainment. One study of Indiana schoolboys in 1969, for example, concluded that ambition developed in a different way in the families of the blacks than in those of their white counterparts (Kerckhoff and Campbell, 1977). It seems clear that while economic theories are a necessary starting point for the explanation of differences in the earnings of people assigned to racial categories they need to be complemented by sociological and psychological analyses if they are to explain how opportunities are translated into actual attainment or to account for the variations that are concealed within aggregated data.

Competition and exclusion in Great Britain

The kinds of analysis of racial differentials which have been developed in the United States are more difficult to carry out in Britain where governmental statistics usually do not differentiate by race and where the minority population is smaller, more heterogeneous, and of more recent origin. The sectors of industry are divided by the census into 27 industrial categories. The distribution of minority workers across these categories in the 1960s was not very different from that of the general population. This suggested that immigrant workers had a stronger position in the labour market than did the 'guest workers' in most west European countries. The five leading occupational categories for minority men (identified by country of birth) were labouring, engineering work, the professions, service work, and transport and communications. A disproportionate number of minority workers have been employed in manufacturing industry (such as Pakistanis in textiles), a sector more prone than others to fluctuation but which in good periods offers opportunities for extra earnings from overtime and shift work. In the PEP study 31 per cent of minority men were found to be working shifts by comparison with 15 per cent of white men. During the period 1961–71 there was a substantial rise in the proportion of minority men who were employed as engineering workers. There were some other indications of an immigrant workforce coming more closely to resemble the native workforce, but the over-all minority picture remained one of great heterogeneity. Irish, Pakistani and West Indian-born workers were concentrated in undesirable low-paying occupations (West Indians less than the others) but African and Indian-born people were often in reasonably good jobs with high levels of pay showing that racial discrimination was by no means the only explanation of racial and ethnic inequality. Other differences arose from factors affecting female employment (for example, a rise from 31 per cent to 40 per cent of the proportion of employed West Indian-born women doing white-collar, non-manual work). During that period the Pakistani female labour force almost doubled and, as these new workers took low-status jobs, their entry brought down the socio-economic status of the group as a whole and masked a slight increase in the number of Pakistani women in professional and managerial employment. The actual numbers are small, but they illustrate some of the complexities in the data (Field *et al.*, 1981:21–34; Smith, 1977:64–82; Mayhew and Rosewell, 1978).

When the representation of minorities in the workforces of particular employers is examined, other variations appear. Those establishments which already employ minority members receive far more applicants from minority members seeking work. It seems that many Asians and West

Indians never apply for work at places which do not already have minority employees. This enables those which are already mostly white to remain so, and restricts the range of opportunities open to minority workers. The PEP study enquired whether resistance on the part of white workers was a major limitation if the management wanted to employ minority workers and concluded that this was not the case. Complaints arose more frequently from the employment of Pakistanis, reflecting the cultural and linguistic differences between them and the native population. A substantial minority of employers had appointed minority supervisors, mostly but not solely to supervise minority employees; this too had occasioned few difficulties (Smith, 1977:99–101, 173–74, 187).

Over the period 1961–80 minority rates of unemployment have risen and fallen along with those of the general population, but the minority rate has been higher and has risen more rapidly when times were bad. West Indian men and Asian women are more vulnerable to unemployment than West Indian women and Asian men, who are in turn more vulnerable than whites. Some possible reasons for this come quickly to mind: the over-representation of minorities in the younger age groups (for all young people find it relatively harder to get work when there are few job vacancies); lack of skill; racial discrimination; over-representation in vulnerable kinds of job, etc. But the pattern is not uniform throughout the country and it may be that minority workers have been less inclined to register as unemployed. It is also possible that, when they lose a job, minority workers are more likely than white workers to accept the sort of employment generally considered unattractive (Field *et al.* 1981:21–25).

The craft unions in Britain do not have the powers of their United States counterparts to control entry and employment, and they have not attracted the same sort of criticism. Trade-union membership among Asian and West Indian workers in Britain is at a similar level to that of whites, and at a distinctly higher level in semi-skilled and unskilled occupations. As in the United States, official union policy is strongly opposed to racial discrimination but the headquarters of the union may do little to control local branches in which the officials encourage discriminatory practices (see Miles and Phizacklea, 1978).

A series of studies have provided direct measures of racial discrimination in Britain. One conducted by PEP in 1966–7 played a vital part in the moves that led to the passing of the 1967 Race Relations Act. A further study in 1974 found that the incidence of discrimination had declined, partly because of that Act, but still remained important in restricting minority opportunity. Actors were employed to apply for various kinds of work. In each individual test, one was a white male and the other a West Indian, an Indian, a Pakistani, or a Greek. Adopting a conservative estimate of what constituted discrimination in the offer of employment to the one but not the other, it was found that in applications for unskilled work, discrimination against Asians and West Indians occurred 37 per cent of the time, and against the Greek 10 per cent. The incidence was lower in applications for skilled work, at 20 per cent for Asians and West Indians against 10 per cent for the Greek. There was little difference in the level of discrimination against the West Indian, Indian, and Pakistani testers.

In another series of tests, a research worker replied to advertisements of vacancies for clerical work, management trainee and accountancy posts. Two similar applications have been submitted for each job, one in the name of a white British applicant and the other in the name of an immigrant. When both applicants are invited to an interview this has been treated as a case of 'no discrimination', but when one is invited and not the other this has been treated as an instance of discrimination. Such a measure probably underestimates the actual level of discrimination since some applicants invited for interview may be rejected at that stage on racial grounds. The tests conducted by PEP found that West Indians, Indians and Pakistanis all experienced discrimination at the first stage of the application in about 30 per cent of cases, by comparison with 10 per cent for an Italian applicant. This suggests that in these circumstances discrimination is based on a generalized colour prejudice making little distinction between the ethnic minorities. The lowest levels of discrimination were found in respect of minority women applying for junior clerical and secretarial posts. A subsequent study confirmed that over a period of ten years there had been little change in the response to applications for posts in accountancy and financial management. Whereas the success rate for enquiries from British and Australian applicants ran at 85 and 75 per cent respectively, the rates for African and West Indian applicants were 53 and 48 per cent, while both Indian and Pakistani applicants were invited to interview in 44 per cent of cases. When asked several months later about their procedures the companies in question replied that they treated majority and minority applicants equally (Smith, 1977:117–26; Firth, 1981).

When considering the determinants of minority economic progress in Britain much can be learned by comparing the experiences of West Indian immigrants in London and New York City. According to the 1970 census 15.4 per cent of West Indians in the New York metropolitan area were classified as professional, technical and kindred workers, nearly double the percentage (8.6%) of Afro-Americans so classified; moreover, within this category the West Indian median family income was 28 per cent higher than the Afro-American. West Indian immigrants and their children were dramatically over-represented among the black elite. Why, then, should they have been so much less successful in Great Britain? Dr Nancy Foner

(1979) maintains that three factors go far towards explaining the differences.

Firstly, a substantial part of the West Indian immigration to New York occurred early in the twentieth century so that by the 1920s approximately one-quarter of the black population of Harlem was West Indian. In Britain West Indians are only now establishing themselves, and possibly in relatively less favourable circumstances. Secondly, it would appear that West Indians migrating to the United States included a higher proportion of well-qualified persons. While many of those who went to Britain were craftsmen only about 10 per cent were white collar workers, whereas those entering the United States included 15 per cent professional and technical and 12 per cent clerical workers. Thirdly, West Indians in the United States settled in areas of black residence, opening grocery stores, tailor shops, jewellery stores, and fruit vending and real-estate operations which put them in direct competition with white businesses in the ghetto. Driven by the high motivation of the economic migrant, they were often successful. The minority population in Britain has not been large enough to offer comparable opportunity to West Indian entrepreneurs or to provide a political base comparable to that in New York, and there has been strong competition from Asian and majority businessmen.

By comparison with the United States, three aspects of the over-all situation of minority workers in the British employment market stand out: the way the supply-side factors are incorporated in the immigrant dimension; the special labour demand of economically vulnerable industries; and the similarity of the white taste for discrimination.

The first of these three aspects can be seen in the evidence that the immigrants on average are of lower skill than the native workers with whom they must compete, and, because they have not prospered in British schools, many of their children are at a similar disadvantage. This, however, is offset by the factor of location: the immigrants have settled in the localities where demand has been highest for the labour they can supply. Because they are immigrants subject to particular economic pressures and not well organized for bargaining over pay and conditions of employment, they have also been at some disadvantage in this respect.

Demand for minority labour has arisen within the context described in Chapter 11 in which employers in certain industries could not fill vacancies at the wage levels they could afford and therefore they, and their white employees, were ready to see these positions taken by immigrants. These sector differences have enabled employers, for example, in textiles, to draw a special benefit from employing minority workers.

The incidence of job discrimination varies with the balance of demand to supply, and is greatest in white-collar occupations in which there has been no shortfall in the supply of native applicants. White Britons show a distinct preference for people like themselves as colleagues in occupations in which co-workers are closely associated. This is what has been described as a taste for discrimination. It follows the distinction of skin colour quite closely. Though no directly comparable evidence has been collected, it seems to resemble the kinds of discrimination found in similar settings in the United States.

Conclusion: an assessment of the Rational Choice Theory

This chapter has shown that the characteristics which distinguish the position of racial minorities in the United States and British employment markets can be understood in terms of a single explanatory framework despite the differences in the structure of employment in those countries and in the character of their minority populations. The framework can also be used to explain the lower earnings of women workers. Earlier chapters have described how a pattern of group competition came to be established in the United States. That pattern was weakened by competition between white employers wherever white workers were unable to maintain a position of privilege for themselves, but where – as, for example, in baseball, minority members have been able to compete as individuals, the significance of group boundaries has diminished. The theoretical structure necessary to account for the advantages which can be drawn from group competition, and for the circumstances in which individual competition prevails, is complex. It can be seen as an application to this field of the general principles of rational choice theory. Neo-classical economics provides a framework but it takes as given the existence of tastes and furnishes no explanation of their origin or strength. Nor can it account for a crucial element in what has been called statistical discrimination, possibly the most important of the influences on the demand side. When someone discriminates against another because he or she is assigned to a category of individuals who, on average, are less likely to be satisfactory, the category has not been created by market processes. Individuals have defined blacks, or women, or Jews, as constituting a category of whom certain behaviour is to be expected and this has become a self-fulfilling prediction, but to explain the original definition it is necessary to examine the conjunction of sociological, psychological and economic factors in particular historical circumstances. Phenotypical variations and sexual characteristics become signs of social categories which are then taken as given in economic analyses.

To discover how the social significance attached to physical differences can be changed, it is necessary to go on and learn more about how values develop in human groups. When one group is at a disadvantage in economic competition, teaching its young people to study harder and to sacrifice present rewards for greater future gains, can increase the group's economic attainment and then lift its position in the hierarchy of group prestige. But if every group concentrates upon this sort of competition the results will be self-defeating. There is no solution so long as one group is pitted against another, and in the long run harmony must depend upon the valuation of individual rather than group characteristics.

In Chapter 6 it was observed that economic theories developed in the present using contemporary data can be employed to illuminate events in earlier periods, and that a similar relationship could be built between theories of racial and ethnic relations and the analysis of historical evidence in this field. By concentrating on two particular kinds of market, these last two chapters have shown how the Rational Choice Theory can be developed in response to present-day problems. The need to concentrate on a particular issue, like the explanation of racial inequalities in earnings, forces the research worker to clarify the relations between the different contributing factors summarized in Figure 10. The task of explaining the ways in which these factors operate leads to useful distinctions, like that between statistical and categorical discrimination. The study of how demand is related to supply in a racially divided housing market leads to the discovery that black and white preferences for residential mixing may be incompatible unless market processes are regulated in a different way. By grappling with such issues the theory is improved: it should then be possible to go back to the historical chapters 9 to 11 and re-examine the matters which they take up in the light of the more sophisticated version of the theory which contemporary analyses have made possible.

The merits of this theory in comparison with others should now be apparent. Five of them deserve particular notice. The first is that the Rational Choice Theory provides a foundation for questioning popular preconceptions. Many writers have taken for granted that they and their readers know what race and ethnicity are, and what individuals belong in which groups. They have done so because they assumed that race or ethnicity gave a common nature to all members of the group in question, and have not learned as much as they might have done from the situation of anomalous individuals who do not fit easily into the main categories, or from the commonplace observation that racial and ethnic groups are not defined in the same ways in different societies and periods of history. Sociology is ethnocentric if its practitioners operate with the folk categories of their own societies. They need to examine the categories in which they organize their observations and discard any definitions which are culture bound.

A second merit follows from the first. The Rational Choice Theory directs attention towards differences in the ways in which phenotypical characters have been used as criteria for assigning people to social categories. There have been, and are, different ways of appraising people's claims to social status. The theory can illuminate the historical processes by which these different patterns have developed (as in the different regions of the New World) by showing that each has its own logic which inter-relates with other institutions in the society. The social use of physical features can be seen to relate to market processes by an examination of the ways in which the form and intensity of competition affect group boundaries.

A third recommendation of the Rational Choice Theory is its recognition of the problematical nature of social groups. Convenient though it sometimes is to speak of groups as if they had lives of their own, there is great danger in attributing to them the desires and fears, wants and dislikes, which are felt only by individuals. All groups are, in a sense, coalitions. They are subject to continuous change and even when they appear to be static, this is because the energy of many individuals is directed towards preserving the existing pattern in the face of pressures to change. This is one of the reasons why it can be instructive to see racial and ethnic relations in terms of groups which maintain differing kinds of boundaries. It responds to one of sociology's most fundamental problems, that of comprehending the interaction of individual and society, by showing how individuals contribute to the weakening or strengthening of group boundaries and how they may cross them.

In the fourth place, it may be urged that this is a theory which, with modifications, sociology can share with the other social sciences. That they, too, have found it useful is a point in its favour. It is a theory of great generality facilitating the transfer of knowledge between subjects and with applications to empirical research in all areas of social life.

A fifth attribute of the theory is also notable: it speaks directly to the level of social policy (further discussed in the next chapter). Before deciding on a plan to reduce discrimination in a particular area it is necessary to discover the causes of the behaviour to be modified, the points at which it can most easily be influenced, and the measures which will be most effective. This means reducing the benefits which can flow to some people from discrimination, and increasing the costs. Most will respond to a change in the balance of net advantages. Equally, if funds are set aside for training programmes likely to be of particular benefit to minority members, it is necessary to understand what sorts of incentives will bring forward possible trainees. If any of the other sociological theories discussed earlier are developed to the point at which they can be applied for policy-making, they too will need to incorporate the sorts of analysis that are possible only by employing some kind of rational choice theory.

14

Policy implications

It is not unusual to hear someone say that racial relations in a particular locality have deteriorated, or that they are bad. This usually implies that there is tension, or that members of at least one racial group are dissatisfied with the share of rewards that comes their way. There is scarcely any discussion of what constitutes good racial relations, yet if policies are to be designed to improve such relations there must be some conception of the goal towards which efforts are to be directed.

One answer is that good racial relations will exist when each racial group has the same share of the desirable positions in society. Another answer is that good racial relations will exist when racial criteria have become socially insignificant and the desirable positions are distributed according to individual merit. These two may be identified as the 'fair shares for groups' and the 'fair shares for individuals' arguments. Members of unprivileged minorities are often attracted to the former position, while members of majorities find it easier to discuss the general issues and to demonstrate the virtues of the latter argument.

Fair shares for groups or individuals?

Considered in the abstract, the first argument soon runs into serious difficulties. This can be appreciated by imagining a society divided into several racial groups in such a way as to achieve equality of privilege between groups: each group gets the same share of rewards and the average income in each group is the same. The idea of racial equality does not imply that people should be paid the same for doing different work, so aircraft pilots could continue to be paid more than baggage handlers. To maintain inter-group equality in this society it would be necessary, firstly, to prevent anyone changing groups or forming new ones; secondly, to keep each group the same relative size; thirdly, to operate quotas to ensure that the same proportions of each group become pilots and baggage handlers. The principle of group equality would come into conflict with the principles of individual freedom and of fair treatment for individuals. On the other hand, a society constructed on the basis of these two last principles could perpetuate inequality between groups because of the transmission of privilege from one generation to the next.

This is succinctly expressed in Thomas Sowell's (1975:212) remark that 'economic progress is an inter-generational relay race'. Rich parents can give their children many advantages that will help them in competition with their peers. The analogy can be used to raise some further questions, for, if the rules allow one team to build up an unassailable lead, members of the other teams may lose interest and refuse to continue the competition unless the rules are revised to give them a better chance. One of the main motivations behind revolutionary movements is the desire to eliminate inherited inequality and allow all the teams to go back to the same starting line. Since revolutions occur in racially homogeneous societies, there is more reason to expect them when the competing groups are physically distinguishable and there is an extra barrier to inter-group mobility.

The most familiar form of the 'fair shares for individuals' argument is that everyone in society benefits when positions are filled by the most competent individuals, and it is therefore desirable to ignore the advantages that some competitors bring with them to the starting line. The alternative argument accepts this as one criterion, while adding that it is also in the social interest to motivate the less gifted individuals to compete to their full potential.

Failure to revise the rules to take account of changed circumstances can be dangerous, yet revision can often be very difficult. The freedom for manoeuvre of a rule-making body like a government can be very limited, and never more so than in the plural society in which the government has to perform a balancing act if it is to hold together groups which want to pursue sectional interests. Nigeria has introduced complex provisions for the election of a president, designed to secure that no one can attain this post who does not have significant support in all parts of the territory. Malaysia, as already mentioned, has rules which require fewer votes for the election of members of parliament from the rural constituencies inhabited by Malays. That country and Sri Lanka allocate university scholarships on the basis of ethnic quotas (for a review of the politics of preferential policies in such countries see Horowitz, 1983). Rules regulating competitive relations have to reflect over-riding political pressures.

The argument that each group should receive a fair share of the rewards states the case for the equality of outcomes, whereas the argument that individuals are entitled to fair shares advocates equality of opportunities. Once they are placed in a contemporary political context these two principles no longer appear quite so incompatible. The group argument is advanced in support of short-term policies while the individual argument has most force in relation to the long term. Recalling the analogy of the relay race, it is short sighted to press the claim for the reward of individual merit if its implementation is likely to cause the other competitors to withdraw or, by disruptive activity, to prevent the race taking place. When privilege is transmitted from one generation to the next the disadvantaged may have no hope of catching up. It may then be politically expedient to change the rules to reduce the quantity of privilege that may be transmitted, or to arrange a share-out to compensate those who have previously been held back. One of the difficulties with any policy of group compensation is that of determining just who is a member of the category which is to receive the benefit. An understanding of the problems entailed by group classifications can be drawn from Geoffrey Benjamin's (1976) account of policies in Singapore where, given the cultural differences between sections of the population, it ought to be easier to assign people to groups than in many other countries.

Singapore was earlier part of the state of Malaysia but was forced in 1965 to withdraw and become an independent republic because of the difficulties of maintaining a political balance in that polyethnic state. Since then the Singapore government has pursued a policy of 'multiracialism'; this accords equal status to the cultures and ethnic identities of the four main 'races' which compose the population. It is symbolized by the picture of four interlinked but differently coloured hands that appears on the back of Singapore's ten-dollar currency note. It is implemented with the aid of a system of personal records such that every permanent resident must possess an identity card which shows the race to which the holder is assigned. When the birth of a baby is registered, entries are made specifying the race and mother tongue of the child. The policy assumes that Singapore has at present no distinctive national culture of its own. The Minister of Social Affairs in 1973 stated: 'The objective of building one nation out of many races calls for an integrated national culture embodying the sentiments and values of the four great cultures that exist in our midst.' This implies that one day Singapore's sample of elements from these four cultures will merge into a single new culture, but the policy is implemented in a way which stresses the distinctiveness of the four cultures and therefore erects obstacles to any merging.

Government record-keeping and officially sponsored public entertainment (including the television service) combine to emphasize the division of the population into the four categories, Chinese, Malay, Indian and Eurasian, and they put considerable pressure on citizens to see themselves and their fellows as members of ethnic categories. There are regular cultural shows, consisting of dances or musical performances in which there must be at least one Chinese, one Indian and one Malay item. At one such show the Minister of Social Affairs declared that 'the different races must learn to be tolerant and appreciative of one another's philosophies and traditions before we can integrate culturally. Such a situation can only exist if each racial group is thoroughly familiar with and understands the other's culture.' So members of each group are supposed to cultivate the features which differentiate them from other groups, even if they do not wish to do so. That they may not, is a real possibility, for many of the cultural features that could be cultivated are hardly suitable, while others are potentially sources of political embarrassment. The Chinese speak so many dialects that the development of a group identity might best be done through Mandarin-language education; yet this would conflict with the use and official encouragement of English as the civic language. The main feature the Indians have in common is the caste system, but that is something they do not wish to discuss and which clashes with the Republic's meritocratic egalitarianism. That which most distinguishes the Malays is their profession of Islam, but for them to stress this could cause difficulty since Singapore is a secular state. The Eurasians have the only culture that has evolved in Singapore and is distinctively Singaporean, yet the more government policy demands that each race should have a link with a major culture elsewhere, and a distinctive mother tongue, the more do Eurasians come to feel that there is no place for them. Many emigrate for this very reason.

In the creation of a new national culture children of cross-ethnic marriages could play an important part, yet these children are assigned to the ethnic group of one of the parents only, usually the father. They are similarly assigned to a mother tongue irrespective of whether that is the language spoken in the home. As one person who had married cross-ethnically complained: 'I tried to put down my son as Singaporean when registering his birth, but the clerk . . . insisted that he must be put down as an Indian following what is on my identity card . . . she even put down his dialect as Malayalee . . . which is supposed to be my mother-tongue but of which I know not a word.' Children are supposed to learn a second language at school but this is based on the assumption that their first language is the mother tongue on their identity card; if this is not the case such a child will have to struggle with a third language. The policy stretches beyond the years of schooling. A civil servant whose actual mother tongue was Malay, but whose second language was English and whose ethnicity was Chinese, was refused permission to take his qualifying language examination in Malay and ordered to take it in Mandarin because he was Chinese. That he could not speak or write Mandarin seems to have been deemed irrelevant.

These may seem to be examples only of bureaucratic inflexibility recalling certain applications of apartheid, but they draw attention to difficulties that can spring from the attempt to preserve what are thought to be the distinctive cultures of ethnic groups. Other consequences that follow from the Singapore government's policy illuminate necessary implications of any policy based upon group identities and cannot be attributed simply to rigid implementation. Firstly, the policy presses the Chinese to become more Chinese, the Indians more Indian and the Malays more Malay. Each culture turns in upon itself since it has to be Singaporean and cannot develop ties with the original homeland. Secondly, the arts (or 'high' culture) have difficulty obtaining official support and financial backing. Individualistic (and therefore 'non-racial') creations are seen as irrelevant or possibly as examples of decadent foreign influence. Thirdly, the Singaporeans' image of themselves and of their history is distorted to fit the four-category model. Cultural characteristics are assumed to derive from distinctive genetic backgrounds and therefore to change only very slowly indeed. In reality people of all groups are changing as they adapt to the opportunities provided by a bustling commercial city, and this is the real basis for a commonality of culture which is growing rapidly. The official policy closed its eyes to this for at least the first decade (Clammer, 1982).

Geoffrey Benjamin's analysis of Singapore's multi-racialism shows that the disadvantages of such policies are real. Is an individual to be judged differently because he belongs to a particular group? If the customs of a particular minority are different in ways that put them at a competitive disadvantage or result in their breaking the laws of the majority society, are allowances to be made for them? If so, the rules may either be drawn in such a way that individuals are left with discretion as to their implementation, or they may specify the extent of the allowance that is to be made. An example of a discretionary allowance would be that permitting the admission to university of a minority student with slightly lower grades if that student had obtained those grades under adverse circumstances and might therefore be expected to perform better once he or she was able to study in the same environment as majority students. An example of a regulated allowance would be one which established the qualifying grade for minority students at a lower level and left little to the judgement of the person responsible for admissions. If this latter course is followed then an immediate problem is the definition of the category of persons to benefit from the regulation. Unless the policies of Singapore and South Africa are followed, whereby category membership is a matter of official record on a person's identity card, there must be some other clear-cut, administratively viable, procedure for determining whether a person who, for example, has a majority father and a minority mother counts as a member of the minority. This cannot be left to the discretion of officials. Nor can it take into account the question whether such a person has actually suffered from the disadvantages for which the regulation was intended to compensate. Once this kind of policy is adopted it creates a vested interest among those who benefit by it and wish to see it maintained even when the original justification is weakened. In mitigating one source of friction it creates another.

Group-based policies could be constructed on a voluntary foundation. Members of culturally distinctive ethnic groups, like Native Americans, may prefer to live in what has traditionally been their territory and to lead a life closer to their traditions than is the life of the majority. In that event their standard of living would probably be lower and they would voluntarily bear a cost arising from their choice. There would be a justification for denying majority members the right to come and live in the minority's area if this was contrary to the minority's wishes. Provided the minority members had the right to forsake their distinctive identity and could go and compete in the majority society without suffering discrimination on grounds of their origin, there would be none of the friction associated with disputes about how a person's race was to be recorded on his or her identity card.

Singapore's 'multi-racialism' is relatively benign in that, unlike South Africa's, it does not greatly affect the access of individuals to jobs and economic opportunities. The policies of both Singapore and South Africa, however, show how ideas about the nature of social groups founded upon those features which have characterized them in the past can be projected into the future, limiting the freedom of individuals to change their ethnic identity as they respond to new circumstances.

Some states, struggling to hold together a heterogeneous population, have adopted special rules or conventions for the distribution of political offices, or to regulate the balance of political power. Lebanon provides a striking example. There it was agreed that the president should be a Maronite, the prime minister a Sunni, the speaker of the house a Shi'ite, the vice-speaker a Greek Orthodox, and so on; the ethnic composition of the legislature was prescribed by law. For over thirty years these arrangements were a foundation for internal peace and a substantial measure of prosperity. Many forces, both internal and external, combined to upset them in 1975, but one obvious problem for which any such system must provide, is that of change. Even if people cannot alter their group affiliations it is likely that some constituent parts will, over time, become relatively larger or more powerful and will want the original bargain renegotiated. In Northern Ireland in 1922, Republicans acquiesced in a boundary which they could not accept as legitimate; over the course of time an increasing number felt unable to tolerate it further but there was no way in which all the parties could be brought to reconsider an agreement which had been imposed – as most such agreements finally have to be – by force. On an even larger scale, Canada has recently furnished a further illustration of this general problem. The British-Canadian section of the population grew much more rapidly than the French-Canadian section, but it was almost impossible to renegotiate a settlement reached over a century earlier when the two sections were of similar size.

There is an important difference between the group fair-shares argument as applied to the Lebanon and Northern Ireland on the one hand, and to Singapore and black–white relations in the United States on the other. No one is obliged to subscribe to a particular religious faith: a Maronite can if he wishes become a Sunni or a Shi'ite. Even in Northern Ireland there are interfaith marriages which usually result in the conversion of one of the parties. The main characteristic of racial relations, however, is that it is exceedingly difficult for an individual to change groups. The argument in favour of fair shares for individuals starts from this. It holds that the objective of public policy should be to eliminate any unfavourable treatment of individuals based on their assignment to particular categories when membership is not a justifiable ground for differential treatment. If a man wishes to identify himself as a Jew, a gypsy, or an Arab, he will know that this may make him unwelcome in some circles and will accept these consequences of his decision. It is quite another matter for him to be assigned to such a category when he does not identify with it, or for his presumed membership in a private group to be used as a reason for denying him equal treatment in the public domain. In that domain what matters is whether someone is a good citizen; in employment a good worker or employer; in housing, a good tenant or landlord; it is these distinctions that should be to the fore. If the assignment of people to social categories on the basis of their appearance or ancestry is to be diminished, remedial policies should not reinforce the very categories that have to be transcended.

One way of transcending racial categories is to support any tendencies that lead to their multiplication. If people who occupy an intermediate position between two categories want to be recognized as a distinct group, then a policy which permits them to be so classified weakens the element of constraint that would otherwise force them into categories with which they did not identify. So long as there is one option open which an individual considers acceptable, freedom of choice can serve as a criterion for deciding what good racial relations would be. It is convenient to go back to the case of the person of Jewish origin who rejects the Jewish faith. He or she should be free to identify as a member of the Jewish minority or as a member of the majority. The American male with a brown complexion is not free to choose between being an Afro-American and being a majority member because, whatever his wishes, whites will assign him to a racial category. His freedom is restricted by others' definitions as well as by the consequences of any choices he has made.

It is very difficult to determine which choices are free unless they can be measured against an independent standard. For example, were a person able to choose his group before birth he would have no reason for not choosing to be born into the most privileged group. In reality some people will discover as they grew up that they have been born into racially disadvantaged groups. Most will identify with their ancestral group and seek to make membership of it a matter of pride. This will feel like a decision freely made and there may be few members of the disadvantaged group who take advantage of any opportunity to transfer to membership of the privileged one. Yet so long as any individual is forced to belong to a racial category with which he or she does not identify there is a denial of freedom.

The prime motivation behind the actions of those who mark off physically distinguishable people as constituting separate racial categories is the defence of privilege, though the privilege is not necessarily economic; people who draw a psychological satisfaction from a feeling of belonging to a group could not draw so much satisfaction if everyone could be a member. Social exclusiveness can create a privilege irrespective of whether the group is economically privileged, indeed exclusiveness on the part of a minority can be important to an ethnic revaluation movement. The question whether people should be encouraged or discouraged from drawing psychological satisfactions from group membership is not of importance to discussions of social policy; but economic privilege is another matter, since economic inequalities, if they are allowed to get too large, occasion disruption if not revolution. If the economic inequalities between racial groups are reduced, there will be less incentive to maintain racial categories. People will have more freedom to gain entry to groups on their individual merits rather than on their complexion, and competition will be more on an individual rather than a group basis. In such circumstances people of a light-brown skin colour might find it easier to gain entry to white social groups than people of a darker complexion. Colour would still be an element in the assessment of an individual's claims to status but it would be just one item among many and, as has happened in Brazil and Puerto Rico, a dark complexion would be noticed less readily in a rich man than a poor one because class considerations were dominant. Change would be slower in respect of a physical characteristic like colour than a cultural one because colour is transmitted genetically and identifies one generation with its predecessor. In most parts of the United States a substantial measure of intermarriage would have to occur before colour could lose its salience.

If this process were carried to its logical conclusion every adult could seek membership of any group, just as he or she can change his or her religion and seek recognition by others who profess his or her chosen faith. The only groups (at any rate groups of this general kind, since other considerations arise with respect to families) would then be voluntary groups resulting from inclusive processes. Chapter 6 presented ethnic groups as groups of this kind, in which beliefs about a common heritage are used to create identities. It is therefore possible to answer the question that has just been posed, by replying that good racial relations would be ethnic relations.

Strategies for governments

The policy implications for the majority society of the rational choice analyses of racial and ethnic discrimination advanced in earlier chapters are simple and clear. They underline the case for governmental action to promote fair competition by eliminating restrictive practices and monopolistic organization. Such action has to be reviewed continuously and modified to respond to changes in the behaviour that is to be controlled. By showing how racial discrimination is threaded into the broader fabric of social inequality, the analyses indicate that action against discrimination will be more effective if it is part of a general policy for regulating social inequality. These prescriptions are relatively uncontentious, for there is widespread agreement in very many societies that it is the duty of governments to promote fair competition and penalize people who discriminate on grounds of race, nationality or religion.

Governments in the United States have been the pioneers in the use of legal measures to combat discrimination. For example, the state of Massachusetts in 1946 established a Fair Employment Practice Commission which, after the enactment of laws against discrimination in housing, became the Massachusetts Commission Against Discrimination. It was empowered to investigate complaints, hold hearings, and issue orders, if these were not obeyed the Commission could obtain court orders for their enforcement. Particularly in the first decade, the Commission's policy stressed processes of conciliation by which parties against whom justified complaints had been lodged were brought to change their practices without feeling that they had done so under duress (Mayhew, 1968). The difficulty with using formal methods to regulate new areas of behaviour – as everyone familiar with 'work to rule' modes of industrial action will know – is that they are of limited effect when people do not feel morally bound and look for ways in which they can sabotage the law's intent without leaving themselves open to punishment. Whenever there is a reasonable hope that persuasion will succeed, it is to be preferred to force.

The policy followed by the Massachusetts Commission Against Discrimination can be defended as appropriate for that era and as having helped to build up a wider agreement that racial discrimination had to be stopped. Its impact was limited because the Commission took action only on the receipt of complaints and not all of these opened up situations strategically important to the attack on prevailing practices. The typical complaint about discrimination in employment alleged unequal treatment on the job. It was brought by a working-class Afro-American and, perforce, related to a firm which already employed a certain number of blacks. There were fewer complaints about firms which rejected black job-applicants and so the complaints that came forward for investigation rarely had much strategic value. The position was different in housing where the typical complaint was brought by a middle-class Afro-American against someone who had refused to rent an apartment. In employment it could be assumed that employers were primarily concerned with profitability and resistance to the unemployment of blacks was seen in terms of expediency rather than principle. In housing, discrimination was more flagrant, the justice of a complaint was easier to prove and, if proven, could be resolved more simply. Relations at work can be impersonal, but they entail continuing contacts. Relations between tenants or between a landlord and a tenant do not usually require much give-and-take between the parties, so that although resistance to integration may be greater in this field the actual transactions are more easily regulated.

When in the 1960s dissatisfaction mounted over the slowness of reform the Commission had to move beyond complaint-initiated procedures and take more initiatives itself. The first big step in this direction is for such bodies to have the legal powers and the resources to investigate practices in the areas they consider important without having to wait for complaints. The next big step is for them, or some other body, to impose quotas. A company – or, for example, a police department – may be ordered to recruit one minority employee for every majority person engaged until it has attained a stipulated quota of minority employees. In support of such actions it can be argued that statistical discrimination in hiring (as this was described in the last chapter) can rarely be modified by the investigation of individual complaints. It is a malady which requires a statistical remedy even if the treatment has some undesired side-effects. Whether it is necessary, or morally justifiable, for governments to authorize the imposition of quotas – and indeed whether such policies are actually effective in attaining their goals – have been matters of bitter dispute.

Broadly speaking, there are two contrasting arguments, one future-orientated and one past-orientated, for policies extending preferences to members of designated minorities. A future-oriented argument might say that members of a minority suffer peculiar disadvantages such that without special assistance they will not catch up within the foreseeable future. In some circumstances it could go on to maintain that since many (but not all) young people in that group are unable to compete effectively, they take to anti-social behaviour and to crime. Their anti-social behaviour damages the reputation of their group, lowers morale, increases friction within their group, and in many ways makes it more difficult for other members of the minority to compete effectively with majority members. Their criminal behaviour necessitates greater expenditure on the police, the courts, the probation service, the prisons, and all the social agencies that assist the dependants of people in prison and help prisoners on release. Their criminality also entails costs for the victims, increases insurance rates and so on. These costs are the greater because the criminal justice system is labour-intensive and cannot benefit as much as some other sectors from the savings that result from technological advances. On such grounds it can be maintained that it is cheaper to spend money on programmes that will prevent anti-social behaviour and crime than on dealing with their consequences. Such programmes could be either discretionary – such as spending more money on schooling in particular localities – or be based upon a legally enforceable rule – such as one stating that only employers with a particular quota of minority employees will be eligible to tender for government contracts. The distinctive characteristic of the argument is that such a policy is justified by the case for achieving a particular future outcome.

A past-oriented argument might say that members of a particular minority are at a disadvantage because of past injustices to them which have had a cumulative effect in reducing their competitive ability. As a consequence many, but not all, young people in that group take to anti-social behaviour and to crime, with the results just mentioned. To rectify the disadvantages suffered (though not evenly) by the minority as a group, they should be compensated for past exploitation (in the way, for example, that Germany was required to pay reparations to the Allies after the First World War). Compensation might take the form either of payments or of preferential policies designed to permit minority members to recover from past disadvantage.

Each of these two kinds of argument has its special difficulties. One based upon the desirability of attaining a particular state in the future is dependent upon very unreliable estimates about the amount of expenditure required, and about the probability of that expenditure having the desired result. It is far from easy for politicians to put such a policy before an electorate since members of the public are being asked to bear short-term costs for speculative long-term benefits. They are likely to see members of the minority as morally undeserving of preferential treatment.

Where a future-oriented argument is based upon the interest of the public in bringing about a new state of affairs, a past-oriented argument can appeal to the duty of the public to make good past injustice. It can benefit from the sense of guilt many members of the majority feel about features of their society's history and at the same time promise to bring about a better state of affairs in the future. Yet such a policy encounters two special difficulties: firstly, that of deciding how much recompense is sufficient; and secondly, that of establishing a transfer mechanism consistent with the rationale of the policy. In the United States, objections have been raised to policies which require the descendants of immigrants who entered in the twentieth century to pay for injustices committed to Afro-Americans in earlier historical periods. On the same grounds it is suggested that benefits should be made available only to those minority members who can show that they have been disadvantaged by the historical injustices.

The federal government in the United States started at least as early as 1941 to pursue policies based upon the future-oriented argument and to promote equality of opportunity. Executive orders issued by Presidents Kennedy and Johnson used the expression 'affirmative action' without defining it, but in contexts which suggested that employers should advertise that they were equal-opportunity employers, should seek out qualified job applicants from all likely sources, and should treat them without discrimination. In 1968 the Department of Labor started to require every major contractor and sub-contractor for federal contracts to submit an affirmative action compliance program, showing what they were doing to utilize minority-group personnel. These requirements were progressively tightened. For the federal government's purposes not all ethnic groups counted as minorities. Jews, for example, had higher than average incomes and lower unemployment so their human resources were not 'under-utilized' and they needed no special protection. Because state and local governments and other bodies throughout the South resisted the implementation of the Civil Rights Act of 1964 and the Voting Rights Act of 1965 the federal government had to issue more guidelines about the kind of action that was necessary in order to comply with the law. In due course the legality of such guidelines was tested in the courts and frequently upheld. Thus in the important case of *Griggs v. Duke Power Company* in 1971 the Supreme Court upheld the Equal Employment Opportunity Commission's guidelines as to the kinds of testing of the abilities of job recruits which met the standard of non-discrimination. In this way the federal courts were increasingly involved in themselves setting standards about the hiring and promotion of employees, qualifications for being able to register as voters, and the adequacy of plans to desegregate schooling (Glazer, 1975:43–66). Such a development is possible only because in the United States the federal courts are the guardians of the country's constitution. In a country such as Great Britain without a written constitution and where parliament is supreme in legislative matters (apart from commitments to the European Convention on Human Rights and to the European Community) the role of the courts is more limited. It is also important to note that in the arguments before the United States Supreme Court and in the judgements of the justices, past discrimination has often been urged as a rationale for preferential policies in the present.

Affirmative action policies started as the promotion of equal opportunity but, as a result of the vigorous modes of enforcement developed by federal agencies, they became something different. The courts were the more ready to accept arguments based upon the statistics of voter registration and minority employment because these offered a more objective foundation for inferring a history of discrimination and assessing the adequacy of remedial plans. Thus a discretionary policy of showing preference to minority job applicants whose qualifications were comparable with those of majority applicants changed into one by which employers had to be able to show that they had taken all reasonable steps to meet targets for employing given quotas of minority employees. Equality of opportunity gave place to a test which required equality of results or outcomes.

How effective the new policies have been is a matter of bitter debate. The position of middle-class Afro-Americans has been improving. Previously black–white differentials in earnings were greatest at the top of the economic ladder, but in recent years black earnings have been improving relative to those of whites and the increase has been greatest for the better educated blacks. This improvement may be due in part to a lessening in white prejudice and better black schooling, and post 1964 anti-discrimination policies seem to have been crucial since the subsequent increase in the incomes of the black elite cannot be accounted for in terms of previous trends, cyclical booms, or increased black educational attainment. Discussing the possible causes, Richard B. Freeman (1976:130) attributes particular significance to the policies of corporations like IBM in evaluating their managers on their success in hiring competent minority employees and in selecting personnel on a basis of ethnic quotas. A subsequent study (Smith and Welch, 1978) concluded that, up to 1974, official quota policies had no effect beyond that which had already been achieved by the earlier equal-opportunity policies. On the other hand supporters of affirmative action point to cases such as that of the American Telephone and Telegraph Company who, because they were brought to court, increased their percentage of minority employees substantially. As part of the settlement this Company increased the pay of nearly 10 per cent of its employees at an annual cost of $35 million and paid $18 million compensation to those who were regarded as having been paid substandard wages. Over the period 1973–8 the percentage of appointments to management positions obtained by black males rose from 2.3 to 4.9; by black females from 2.9 to 6.0; and by white females from 34.4 to 37.4. More recent figures show that white females have been the principal beneficiaries, but the action certainly assisted blacks (Northrup and Larson, 1979:228–9). Surely, it is asked, affirmative-action enforcement of this character cannot be insignificant in promoting racial equality?

All parties to the debate seem agreed, however, that neither equal-opportunity policies nor quota policies have helped the black poor. This should be no surprise, since their problems are so much more complex. In 1978 74 per cent of all poor black families had female heads and, as has been mentioned already, this family form is less able to foster social mobility. It is also worth repeating the statement that among blacks who failed to pass army I.Q. tests three-quarters were from families of four or more children and one-half from families of six or more children. No policy package is likely to have much impact upon such a set of conditions unless it can improve male employment, relieve poverty, and promote family stability.

In recent decades it has become more difficult in all industrial societies to maintain stable family relations during the years which are important to the psychological development of children. In the conditions in which most poor Afro-American children grow up, the parents' problems are magnified by the incidence of crime (of which blacks are most often the victims) and the glamour which seems to attach to many deviant life-styles. If it is the accumulation of human capital that enables immigrant minorities to climb the ladder, what is to happen in connection with drug addicts and criminals who, far from accumulating any capital themselves, only destroy that which is accumulated by others? If processes of exchange are of particular importance to the development of group identities, how do they bear upon the growth of anti-social behaviour?

It is consistent with a rational-choice approach if social control is seen as a property of social relations, rather than as something imposed from outside. Relationships are maintained only as long as they are rewarding to the parties. If one party, who can be called Ego, makes too great a demand upon the other, Alter, then Alter signals displeasure. Ego then has to choose between the alternatives of either conciliating Alter, by indicating that he or she will in future respect Alter's views more carefully, or of ignoring the signal, in which case Alter may break off the relationship. So long as the relationship is in being, Ego and Alter are controlled by one another's expectations and behind them is a sanction. Either party will reduce or terminate the relationship if he or she is no longer getting a return from it equivalent to its cost. Benefits and costs are assessed against an implicit scale of social values or preferences and the nature of those values cannot be explained by the exchanges that take place within any one relationship. Just where these values come from is a complex problem; but many of them are inculcated during infancy in the development of relations between the child and other members of the household, particularly the mother. These are very unequal relationships in which the child receives great benefits without giving very much in return, though the parents may obtain great emotional satisfaction if their child grows up in the culturally approved manner and this may contribute to their reputation in the eyes of others. Children respond to the social patterns they see around them as they grow up. If the rewards and punishments which regulate behaviour in their neighbourhood reflect those in the wider society, they will go out equipped to compete in that society.

The desire of individuals for a good reputation among their peers is perhaps the most potent influence upon human behaviour, but it operates only within relatively small circles. As societies grow in size and complexity the formal controls of codes, courts and constables are expanded though they are never quite as effective as the informal controls. They can restrain deviant behaviour but they rarely bring people to un-learn the lessons they learned about social relations during their early years. The criminal justice system is supposed to constitute a framework permitting exchanges to take place freely between individuals, by providing and enforcing sanctions upon people who break the rules about what may be exchanged and how. If it were as it is supposed to be, the criminal justice system would not itself be part of the pattern of transactions between individuals that constitutes society. It would simply prescribe and enforce the rules for the inter-generational relay race. In practice, however, laws often reflect the interest of particular groups within society: the laws about slavery in the United States reflected the interests of the slave-owners and not the slaves. The judges who interpret and enforce the laws are members of the society and they are likely to sympathize with the views prevailing in the groups from which they are recruited and among the persons with whom they associate. Similar observations can be made with respect to the police, who are more vulnerable to political pressure and bribery than the judges. There is, indeed, ample evidence of the full force of criminal justice administration being employed to enforce highly unequal contracts of employment, especially in places experiencing rapid economic development like late-nineteenth-century Queensland.

The criminal justice system can be used both to protect and to undermine minority interests. The civil courts can be used, as they have been in the United States, to solve problems about the distribution of resources which elsewhere would be considered problems for the politicians, but they can contribute little to policies directed to the wantonly anti-social and criminal behaviour that has characterized several immigrant groups at early stages of their settlement in urban areas. In the United States that problem is more acute at the present time because of the ready availability of deadly weapons, the lower level of informal social control and the greater pressures of a more competitive social order. It may now be more difficult for a group to emerge from a stage in which it contributes disproportionately to criminality than used to be the case. In New York City in the 1970s a minority of Afro-Americans and a minority of Cubans followed crime as a way of life with a callousness that has little precedent. Of every twenty criminal homicides for which a black person is responsible, in nineteen cases the victim is another black. Afro-American communities are terrorized and gravely handicapped by the violence in their midst. The people who live in them will not be able to improve their economic position until the level of violence has been greatly reduced and they have some expectation that they will be able to enjoy the fruit of their labours. A past-oriented policy based on a rationale of compensation is insufficient in this realm. A future-oriented policy would present crime as a threat no matter what the historical background may be to the disproportionate involvement of particular ethnic groups in criminality. Measures to reduce that threat and assist those who have been disproportionately subject to it are a form of social defence and should help increase national productivity.

Minority criminality is in no sense a racial problem. Indeed the very idea of a 'racial problem' (which was a product of the Typological Theory) is an obstacle to clear thinking. Research has demonstrated over and over again that the problems which have been loosely called racial are economic, social, psychological and political problems, each one of which is to be analysed in ways appropriate to its peculiar character. Policies for dealing with these problems do not have to be of a special kind.

Strategies for minorities

No minority has to contend with precisely the same problems as any other, if only because they differ in their internal resources. The alternatives before them also vary, and it is difficult to generalize about factors which may make one more attractive than another. However, they do have to contend with the two main kinds of discrimination on the part of the majority which have earlier been described as price discrimination and exclusion. Minority members may be able to secure employment only by working for lower pay or by being more accommodating to an employer's demands. In the respect of housing, they may be able to rent the rooms or buy the properties they want only by paying a premium (referred to earlier as a 'colour tax'), that is, paying more than a member of the majority would have to. Minority members can also be excluded altogether from certain kinds of employment, by either employers or unions, irrespective of wage levels. In the public sector, official policies may neglect their interests or administrators use discretionary powers to their disfavour. In the private sector, vendors, real-estate agents, finance companies and landlords can combine to exclude them from certain residential neighbourhoods while any family that slips through the net can be subject to intimidation. Though this distinction between price discrimination and exclusion does not fit the educational sector so well, it can be applied there too. Black parents may have to spend more than white parents to obtain for their children an education of the same quality, because in a segregated system less money is spent on black schools. In other cases blacks have been excluded from white educational institutions without any provision being made for their wants.

In general, a low-profile strategy will be best for countering price discrimination and a high-profile strategy for countering exclusion. Examples of low-profile strategies are provided by the middlemen minorities referred to in Chapter 8. Another instance is that of Britain's Jewish minority which has never organized as a political group. Jews have entered all political parties; they have held more seats in the House of Commons than might have been expected on the basis of their proportion in the total population and have often attained high office, Benjamin Disraeli being an early example of such success. In so far as Jews are an ethnic group they have presented that ethnicity as a characteristic relevant in the private domain of social contacts, but irrelevant in the public domain of civil rights and responsibilities, and of access to jobs and public positions. The adoption of such a stance was least likely to evoke antagonism from the majority, something they had good reason to fear and which was whipped up in Nazi Germany despite the tendency of the Jewish minority there to move closer to majority cultural patterns than in any other country with a significant Jewish population.

The most striking example of a high-profile strategy is that followed by the black political movement in the United States during the mid and late 1960s. It was directed primarily towards Afro-Americans, trying to mobilize them politically and persuade them to abandon attitudes of deference towards whites and of resignation to subordination. The movement could best appeal to young blacks by excluding white sympathizers (on which see Levy, 1967) and adopting a fierce and threatening posture towards white society. It declared, in effect, that blacks had to be more proud of being black and that they had to attain a position of political and economic equality before they could relax the call for solidarity and start competing with whites on a more individual basis.

Any strategy's chance of success will be affected by the extent to which the majority regards minority ethnicity as a legitimate basis for pressing a political claim. Majorities often see themselves as committed to universalist values and deny claims which they interpret as particularistic and sectional. It is difficult for majority representatives in the United States to argue in such a vein given the long history of legal discrimination against blacks and the legitimacy that has been accorded to white ethnic organizations.

In Great Britain, as in most European countries, the argument from universalism can be more persuasive. Ethnic minority organization in England, as by the Scots, Welsh and Irish as well as the Jews, is regarded as legitimate and expected in the social sphere. It is not used as a basis for claims to resources. The whites can make use of a potent past-oriented argument which presents the country as the historical patrimony of a white English nation. This constrains any attempt on the part of the ethnic minorities to follow the political example of the black movement in the United States since, apart from the difference in size of the two minorities, any use of a high-profile strategy has to be based upon moral claims of a kind that the majority cannot successfully deny.

When minority members follow a low-profile strategy, they present themselves as individuals ready to compete with others on equal terms and do nothing which attracts attention to their membership of a distinctive group. They assume that the more competitive a market becomes the less room there will be for ethnic discrimination. There will be some non-discriminatory employers or sellers in the market, or, at the very worst, some who discriminate less than others. Non-discriminators will then make greater profits and oblige the others to compete with them. As majority people become acquainted with minority members any disposition to discriminate purely on a group basis can be expected to decline. Where individual competition can hold out the prospect of success, it has the advantage of minimizing hostility towards the minority as a group.

When minority members follow a high-profile strategy they present themselves as members of a group rather than as individuals. They draw attention to any injustices from which their group has suffered and which still handicap them. They know that by so doing they are likely to increase hostility from some sections of the majority but assume that these costs will be outweighed by the likely long-run benefits. Since they are being excluded from the possibility of equal competition there is little chance of their being able gradually to prove themselves, so there is little attraction in continuing as they have been doing. They have to take political action, threatening to increase costs to the majority by disruptive activity unless the rules on which the market operates are changed. This can be done most easily by a fairly powerful minority whose members do not feel that they have too much to lose by running the risks that come from raising the political temperature.

Bibliography

Adam, Heribert, and Giliomee, Hermann (1979) *Ethnic Power Mobilized: Can South Africa Change?* New Haven: Yale University Press.

Adams, Barbara, Okely, Judith, Morgan, David, and Smith, David (1975) *Gypsies and Government Policy in England: a study of the travellers' way of life in relation to the policies and practices of central and local government.* London: Heinemann.

Alba, Richard D. (1981) The Twilight of Ethnicity Among American Catholics of European Ancestry. *The Annals of the American Academy of Political and Social Science*, 454:86–97.

Allardt, Erik (1979) *Implications of the Ethnic Revival in Modern Industrialized Society.* Helsinki: Commentationes Scientiarum Socialum, 12.

Anwar, Muhammad (1979) *The Myth of Return: Pakistanis in Britain.* London: Heinemann.

Arrow, Kenneth J. (1972) Models of Job Discrimination, pp. 83–102 in Pascal, Anthony H., editor, *Racial Discrimination in Economic Life.* Lexington, Mass.: Heath.

Ashenfelter, Orley (1973) Discrimination and Trade Unions, pp. 88–112 in Ashenfelter, Orley and Rees, Albert, editors, *Discrimination in Labor Markets.* Princeton: Princeton University Press.

Ballard, Catherine (1979) Conflict, Continuity and Change: Second-Generation South Asians, pp. 109–29 in Khan, Verity Saifullah, editor, *Minority Families in Britain.* London: Macmillan.

Ballard, Roger (1973) Family Organisation Among the Sikhs in Britain. *New Community*, 2:1–13.

Ballard, Roger and Ballard, Catherine (1977) The Sikhs: The Development of South Asian Settlements in Britain, pp. 21–56 in Watson, James, editor, *Between Two Cultures: Migrants and Minorities in Britain.* Oxford: Blackwell.

Banton, Michael (1957) *West African City: A Study of Tribal Life in Freetown.* London: Oxford University Press.

Banton, Michael (1967) *Race Relations.* London: Tavistock, and New York: Basic Books.

Banton, Michael (1972) *Racial Minorities.* London: Fontana.

Banton, Michael (1977) *The Idea of Race.* London: Tavistock, and Boulder, Col.: Westview.

Banton, Michael (1979) Gender Roles and Ethnic Relations. *New Community*, 7:323–32.

Banton, Michael (1983) Categorical and Statistical Discrimination. *Racial and Ethnic Studies*, 6: 269–283.

Banton, Michael (forthcoming) The Influence of Colonial Status upon Black–White Relations in England, 1948–58, 17: 546–59.

Banton, Michael and Harwood, Jonathan (1975) *The Race Concept*. Newton Abbott: David and Charles, and New York: Praeger.

Barker, Anthony J. (1978) *The African Link: British Attitudes to the Negro in the Era of the Atlantic Slave Trade, 1550–1807*. London: Frank Cass.

Barrera, Mario (1979) *Race and Class in the South West*. South Bend: University of Notre Dame Press.

Barry, Brian (1970) *Sociologists, Economists, and Democracy*. London: Collier-Macmillan.

Barth, Fredrik, editor (1969) *Ethnic Groups and Boundaries: The Social Organization of Cultural Difference*. London: Allen and Unwin.

Beck, E. M. (1980) Discrimination and White Economic Loss: A Time Series Examination of the Radical Model. *Social Forces*, 59:148–68.

Beck, E. M., Horan, Patrick M. and Tolbert, Charles M. (1980) Industrial Segmentation and Labor Market Discrimination. *Social Problems*, 28:113–30.

Becker, Gary S. (1957) *The Economics of Discrimination*. Chicago: University of Chicago Press.

Benedict, Ruth (1942) *Race and Racism*. London: Labour Book Service, 1942. (First published as *Race: Science and Politics*. New York: Modern Age Books, 1940.)

Benjamin, Geoffrey (1976) The Cultural Logic of Singapore's 'Multi-racialism', pp. 115–33 in Hassan, Riaz, editor, *Singapore: Society in transition*. Kuala Lumpur: Oxford University Press.

Berlin, Ira (1974) *Slaves Without Masters: The free Negro in the Antebellum South*. New York: Vintage Books.

Bermuda (1978) *Report of the Royal Commission on the 1977 Disorders*. Hamilton, Bermuda: Cabinet Office.

Biddiss, Michael D. (1971) The Universal Races Congress of 1911. *Race*, 13:37–46.

Biddiss, Michael, editor (1979) *Images of Race*. Leicester: Leicester University Press.

Blalock, Hubert M. (1967) *Toward a Theory of Minority Group Relations*. New York: Wiley.

Blalock, Hubert M. and Wilken, Paul H. (1979) *Intergroup Processes: A Micro-Macro Perspective*. New York: The Free Press.

Bloch, F. E. (1977) Discrimination in Non-referral Unions, pp. 105–20 in Bloch, F. E., *et al., Equal Rights and Industrial Relations*. Madison: Industrial Relations Research Association.

Böhning, Roger (1972) *The Migration of Workers in the United Kingdom and the European Community*. London: Oxford University Press.

Bonacich, Edna (1972) A Theory of Ethnic Antagonism: The Split Labor Market. *American Sociological Review*, 37: 547–59.

Bonacich, Edna (1973) A Theory of Middleman Minorities. *American Sociological Review*, 38:583–94.

Bonacich, Edna (1979) The Past, Present, and Future of Split Labor Market Theory. *Research in Race and Ethnic Relations*, 1:17–64.

Bonilla, Frank and Campos, Ricardo (1981) A Wealth of Poor: Puerto Ricans in the New Economic Order. *Daedalus*, Spring:133–76.

Brotz, Howard (1977) *The Politics of South Africa: Democracy and Racial Diversity.* London: Oxford University Press.

Bryce, James (Viscount) (1902) *The Relations of the Advanced and Backward Races of Mankind.* Romanes Lecture. Oxford: Clarendon Press.

Burridge, Kenelm (1969) *New Heaven and New Earth: A Study of Millenarian Activities.* Oxford: Blackwell.

Butler, David and Stokes, Donald (1969) *Political Change in Britain: Forces Shaping Electoral Choice.* Harmondsworth: Penguin.

Butler, Richard and Heckman, James J. (1977) The Government's Impact on the Labor Market Status of Black Americans: A Critical Review, pp. 235–81 in Bloch, F. E. *et al., Equal Rights and Industrial Relations.* Madison: Industrial Relations Research Association.

Carey, A. T. (1956) *Colonial Students.* London: Secker and Warburg.

Cashmore, Ernest (1979) Rastaman: *The Rastafarian Movement in England.* London: Allen and Unwin.

Cashmore, Ernest (1981) After the Rastas. *New Community,* 9:173–81.

Castles, Stephen (1981) Review of *Transnational Production* in *Race and Class,* 22:409–17.

Catterall, Helen Tunnicliff (1926) *Judicial Cases Concerning American Slavery and the Negro.* 5 vols. Washington D.C.: Carnegie Institution of Washington.

Chafe, William H. (1980) *Civilities and Civil Rights: Greensboro, North Carolina, and the Black Struggle for Freedom.* New York: Oxford University Press. Galaxy Book edition 1981.

Challoner, W. H. and Henderson, W. O. (1975) Marx/Engels and Racism *Encounter* (1):18–23 and correspondence 45(5):94–96, 46(3):92–94, 46(4):92–94.

Chiswick, Barry (1980) The Earnings of White and Coloured Male Immigrants in Britain. *Economica.* 47:81–7.

Churchill, Sir Winston (1956–8) *A History of the English-Speaking Peoples.* 4 vols. London: Cassell.

Civil Rights, United States Commission on (1980) *The State of Civil Rights: 1979.* Washington, D.C.: Government Printing Office.

Clammer, John (1982) The Institutionalization of Ethnicity: the culture of ethnicity in Singapore. *Ethnic and Racial Studies,* 5:127–39.

Cohen, Brian G., and Jenner, Peter J. (1968) The Employment of Immigrants: A Case Study Within the Wool Industry. *Race,* 10:41–56.

Cohen, Ronald, and Middleton, John, editors (1970) *From Tribe to Nation in Africa: Studies in Incorporation Processes.* Scranton, Pennsylvania: Chandler.

Collard, David (1970) Immigration and Discrimination: Some Economic Aspects, pp. 65–87 in Wilson, Charles, *et al., Economic Issues in Immigration.* London: Institute of Economic Affairs.

Collard, David (1973) Price and Prejudice in the Housing Market. *Economic Journal,* 83:510–15.

Committee on the Rent Acts (1971) *Report.* Cmnd 4607. London: Her Majesty's Stationery Office.

Coser, Lewis A. (1956) *The Functions of Social Conflict.* New York: The Free Press.

Cox, Oliver C. (1948) *Caste, Class and Race: A Study in social dynamics.* New York: Monthly Review Press.

Dahya, Badr (1973) Pakistanis in Britain: Transients or settlers? *Race.* 14:241–77.

Dahya, Badr (1974) The Nature of Pakistani Ethnicity in Industrial Cities in Britain, pp. 77–118 in Cohen, Abner, editor, *Urban Ethnicity*. ASA monograph 12, London: Tavistock.

Daniel, Pete (1972) *The Shadow of Slavery: Peonage in the South, 1901–1969*. New York: Oxford University Press.

Daniel, W. W. (1968) *Racial Discrimination in England*. Harmondsworth: Penguin.

Darwin, Charles (1859) *The Origin of Species, or The Preservation of Favoured Races in the Struggle for Life*. New York: Mentor Books.

Davis, Allison, Gardner, Burleigh B. and Gardner, Mary (1941) *Deep South: A Social Anthropological Study of Caste and Class*. Chicago: University of Chicago Press.

Davis, Kingsley (1941) Intermarriage in Caste Society. *American Anthropologist*, 43:376–95.

Davis, Kingsley (1948) *Human Society*. New York: Macmillan.

Davison, R. B. (1962) *West Indian Migrants: Social and Economic Facts of Migration from the West Indies*. London: Oxford University Press.

Deakin, Nicholas (1975) Harold Macmillan and the Control of Commonwealth Immigration. *New Community*, 4:191–4.

Degler, Carl N. (1971) *Neither Black Nor White: Slavery and Race Relations in Brazil and the United States*. New York: Macmillan.

de Kiewiet, C. W. (1941) *A History of South Africa: Social and Economic*. Oxford: Clarendon Press.

Deloria, Vine (1981) American Indians, Blacks, Chicanos and Puerto Ricans. *Daedalus*, Spring:13–27.

Dench, Geoff (1975) *The Maltese in London: A Case Study in the Erosion of Ethnic Consciousness*. London: Routledge.

Dobb, Maurice (1973) *Theories of Value and Distribution Since Adam Smith*. Cambridge: Cambridge University Press.

Dobyns, Henry F. (1966) Estimating Aboriginal American Population: An Appraisal of Techniques With a New Hemispherical Estimate. *Current Anthropology*, 7:395–416.

Dollard, John (1937) *Caste and Class in a Southern Town*. New York: Harper; 3rd edn, New York: Doubleday (Anchor), 1957.

Dollard, John (1938) Hostility and Fear in Social Life. *Social Forces*, 17:15–26.

Donnan, Hastings (1976) Inter-Ethnic Friendship, Joking and Rules of Interaction in a London Factory, pp. 81–99 in Holy, Ladislav, editor, *Knowledge and Behaviour*. The Queen's University Papers in Social Anthropology: 1, Belfast.

Dorris, Michael A. (1981) The Grass Still Grows, The Rivers Still Flow: Contemporary Native Americans. *Daedalus*, Spring:43–69.

Douglas, Mary (1967) Primitive Rationing: A Study in Controlled Exchange, pp. 119–47 in Firth, Raymond, editor, *Themes in Economic Anthropology*. ASA Monograph 6, London: Tavistock.

Drake, St Clair (1956) The 'Colour Problem' in Britain: A Study in Social Definitions. *Sociological Review*, N.S. 3:197–217.

Drake, St Clair and Cayton, Horace R. (1945) *Black Metropolis*. New York: Harcourt Brace. London: Cape, 1946 (the London edition was published with the authors' names in reverse order).

Dumont, Louis (1966) *Homo Hierarchicus: the Caste System and its Implications*. London: Weidenfeld and Nicolson.

Easthope, Gary (1976) Religious War in Northern Ireland. *Sociology*, 10:427–50.

Eggington, Joyce (1957) *They Seek a Living*. London: Hutchinson.

Elster, Jon (1979) *Ulysses and the Sirens: Studies in Rationality and Irrationality*. Cambridge: Cambridge University Press.

Elston, R. (1971) The Estimation of Admixture in Racial Hybrids. *Annals of Human Genetics*. 35:9–17.

Essien-Udom, E. U. (1962) *Black Nationalism: A Search for Identity in America*. Chicago: University of Chicago Press.

Estrada, Leobarda F., Garcia, F. Chris, Macias, Renaldo Flores, and Maldonaldo, Lionel (1981) Chicanos in the United States: A History of Exploitation and Resistance. *Daedalus*, Spring:103–31.

Evans, Raymond, Saunders, Kay, and Cronin, Kathryn (1975) *Exclusion, Exploitation and Extermination: Race Relations in Colonial Queensland*. Sydney: Australia and New Zealand Book Co.

Farley, Reynolds, Bianchi, Suzanne and Colasanto, Dianne (1979) Barriers to the Racial Integration of Neighborhoods: the Detroit Case. *The Annals of the American Academy of Political and Social Science*, 441:97–113.

Farmer, Mary (1982) Rational Action in Economic and Social Theory: Some Misunderstandings. *European Journal of Sociology*, 23:179–97.

Fenton, Mike (1976) Price Discrimination Under Non-monopolistic Conditions. *Applied Economics*, 8:135–44.

Fenton, Mike and Collard, David (1977) *Do Coloured Tenants Pay More?* Bristol: SSRC Research Unit on Ethnic Relations, Working Paper 1.

Field, Simon, Mair, George, Rees, Tom and Stevens, Philip (1981) *Ethnic Minorities in Britain*. Home Office Research Studies, 68. London: Home Office.

Firth, Michael (1981) Racial Discrimination in the British Labor Market. *Industrial and Labor Relations Review*, 34:265–72.

Fitzgerald, Jeffery M. (1975) The Contract Buyers League and the Courts: A Case Study of Poverty Litigation. *Law and Society Review*, 5(2):165–95.

Fitzpatrick, Joseph P. (1971) *Puerto Rican Americans: The Meaning of Migration to the Mainland*. Englewood Cliffs, N.J.: Prentice-Hall.

Flett, Hazel (1977) *Council Housing and the Location of Ethnic Minorities*. Bristol: SSRC Research Unit on Ethnic Relations, Working Paper 5.

Flett, Hazel (1979) Bureaucracy and Ethnicity: Notions of Eligibility to Public Housing, pp. 135–52 in Wallman, Sandra, editor, *Ethnicity at Work*. London: Macmillan.

Fogel, Robert William and Engerman, Stanley L. (1974) *Time on the Cross: The Economics of American Negro Slavery*. Boston: Little, Brown.

Foner, Nancy (1979) West Indians in New York City and London: A Comparative Analysis. *International Migration Review*, 13:284–97.

Frazier, E. Franklin (1957) *Race and Culture Contacts in the Modern World*. Boston: Beacon Press.

Fredrickson, George M. (1971) *The Black Image in the White Mind: The Debate on Afro-American Character and Destiny, 1817–1914*. New York: Harper and Row.

Fredrickson, George M. (1981) *White Supremacy: A Comparative Study in American and South African History*. New York: Oxford University Press.

Freeman, Richard B. (1974) Labor Market Discrimination: Analysis, Findings, and Problems, pp. 501–69 in Intriligator, Michael D., and Kendrick, David A., editors, *Frontiers of Quantitative Economics, II*. Amsterdam: North-Holland Publishing Co.

Freeman, Richard B. (1976) *Black Elite: The New Market for Highly Educated Black Americans*. New York: McGraw-Hill.

Freund, W. M. (1976) Race in the Social Structure of South Africa, 1652–1836. *Race and Class*, 18:53–67.

Furnival, J. S. (1948) *Colonial Policy and Practice: A Comparative Study of Burma and Netherlands India*. Cambridge: Cambridge University Press.

Gaertner, Samuel L. (1976) Nonreactive Measures in Racial Attitude Research: A Focus On 'Liberals', pp. 183–211 in Katz, P. A., editor, *Towards the Elimination of Racism*. New York: Pergamon.

Gaertner, Samuel L. and Bickman, Leonard (1971) Effects of Race on the Elicitation of Helping Behaviour: The Wrong Number Technique. *Journal of Personality and Social Psychology*, 20: 218–22.

Galenson, David W. (1981) The Market Evaluation of Human Capital: The Case of Indentured Servitude. *Journal of Political Economy*, 89:446–67.

Gaskell, George, and Smith, Patten (1981) 'Alienated' Black Youth: An Investigation of 'Conventional Wisdom' Explanations. *New Community*, 9:182–93.

Geiger, Theodor (1962) *Arbeiten zur Soziologie*. Berlin: Neuwied.

Gerson, Louis L. (1964) *The Hyphenate in Recent American Politics and Diplomacy*. Lawrence: University of Kansas Press.

Glazer, Nathan (1975) *Affirmative Discrimination: Ethnic Inequality and Public Policy*. 2nd edn 1978. New York: Basic Books.

Glazer, Nathan and Moynihan, Daniel Patrick (1963) *Beyond the Melting Pot: The Negroes, Puerto Ricans, Jews, Italians, and Irish of New York City*. Cambridge, Mass.: The MIT Press and Harvard University Press. 2nd edn 1970.

Glazer, Nathan and Moynihan, Daniel Patrick (1975) *Ethnicity: Theory and Experience*. Cambridge, Mass.: Harvard University Press.

Gluckman, Max (1940) Analysis of a Social Situation in Modern Zululand. *Bantu Studies*, 14:1–30, 147–74. Reprinted as Rhodes-Livingstone Paper no. 28. Manchester: Manchester University Press, 1958.

Gluckman, Max (1969) The Tribal Area in South and Central Africa, pp. 373–409 in Smith, M. G., and Kuper, Leo, editors, *Pluralism in Africa*. Berkeley: University of California Press.

Gordon, Milton M. (1964) *Assimilation in American Life: The Role of Race, Religion and National Origins*. New York: Oxford University Press.

Goren, Arthur A. (1980) Jews, pp. 571–98 in Thernstrom, Stephan, editor, *Harvard Encyclopedia of American Ethnic Groups*. Cambridge, Mass.: Harvard University Press.

Gould, Julius and Kolb, William L. (1964) *Dictionary of the Social Sciences*. London: Tavistock.

Greene, John C. (1959) *The Death of Adam: Evolution and its Impact on Western Thought*. New York: Mentor Books.

Gwynn, Stephen (1932) *The Life of Mary Kingsley*. London: Macmillan. Page no. of citation refers to Penguin Books edition, 1940.

Hall, Douglas (1972) Jamaica, pp. 193–213 in Cohen, David W. and Greene, Jack P., editors, *Neither Slave nor Free: The Freedmen of African Descent in the Slave Societies of the New World*. Baltimore: Johns Hopkins University Press.

Hall, Gwendolen Midlo (1972) Saint Domingue, pp. 172–92 in Cohen, David, W., and Greene, Jack P., editors, *Neither Slave Nor Free: The Freedmen of African Descent in the Slave Societies of the New World*. Baltimore: Johns Hopkins University Press.

Halliday, R. J. (1971) Social Darwinism: A Definition. *Victorian Studies*, 14: 389–405.

Hancock, Ian F. (1980) Gypsies, pp. 440–5 in Thernstrom, Stephan, editor, *Harvard Encyclopedia of American Ethnic Groups*. Cambridge, Mass.: Harvard University Press.

Hancock, W. Keith (1968) *Smuts*. 2 vols. Cambridge: Cambridge University Press.

Hansen, M. L. (1938) *The Problem of the Third Generation Immigrant*. Rock Island, Illinois: Augustana Historical Society.

Harper, Edward B. (1968) Social Consequences of an 'Unsuccessful' Low Caste Movement, pp. 36–65 in Silverberg James, editor, *Social Mobility in the Caste System in India*. Comparative Studies in Society and History, Supplement 3. The Hague: Mouton.

Harris, Marvin (1964a) *Patterns of Race in the Americas*. New York: Walker.

Harris, Marvin (1964b) Racial Identity in Brazil. *Luzo-Brazilian Review*, 1:21–8 (reprinted, Bobbs-Merrill reprint series, no. BC-128).

Harris, Rosemary (1972) *Prejudice and Tolerance in Ulster: A Study of Neighbours and 'Strangers' in a Border Community*. Manchester: Manchester University Press.

Harris, Rosemary (1979) Community Relationships in Northern and Southern Ireland: A Comparison and a Paradox. *Sociological Review*, 27:41–53.

Heath, Anthony (1976) *Rational Choice and Social Exchange*. Cambridge: Cambridge University Press.

Hechter, Michael, Friedman, Debra and Appelbaum, Malka (1982) A Theory of Ethnic Collective Action. *International Migration Review*, 16:412–34.

Helweg, Arthur H. (1979) *Sikhs in England: The Development of a Migrant Community*. Delhi: Oxford University Press.

Herskovits, Melville J. (1930) *The Anthropology of the American Negro*. Columbia University Contributions XI. New York: Columbia University Press.

Higgs, Robert (1977) *Competition and Coercion: Blacks in the American Economy, 1865–1914*. Cambridge: Cambridge University Press.

Higgs, Robert (1978) Race and Economy in the South, 1890–1950, pp. 89–116 in Haws, Robert, editor, *The Age of Segregation: Race Relations in the South, 1890–1945*. Jackson: University Press of Mississippi.

Hill, Herbert (1968) The Racial Practices of Organized Labor: The Contemporary Record, pp. 286–357 in Jacobson, Julius, editor, *The Negro and the American Labor Movement*. New York: Doubleday, Anchor Books.

Hill, Mozel C. (1944) Social Status and Physical Appearance among Negro Adolescents. *Social Forces*, 22:443–8.

Hodson, H. V. (1950) Race Relations in the Commonwealth. *International Affairs*, 26:305–15.

Hodson, H. V. (1956) The Study of Race Relations. *Optima*, 5:52–4.

Hoetink, H. (1973) *Slavery and Race Relations in the Americas: Comparative Notes on their Nature and Nexus*. New York: Harper.

Hollis, Martin (1978) *Models of Man: Philosophical Thoughts on Social Action*.

Cambridge: Cambridge University Press.

Holmes, Colin (1975) Violence and Race Relations in Britain, 1953–1968, *Phylon*, 36:113–24.

Horowitz, Donald (1983) Ethnic Groups in Conflict: Theories, Patterns, Policies. *Forthcoming.*

Hostetler, John A. (1968) *Amish Society.* Baltimore: Johns Hopkins University Press. (First published 1963.)

Hostetler, John A. (1980) Amish, pp. 122–5 in Thernstrom, Stephan, editor, *Harvard Encyclopedia of American Ethnic Groups.* Cambridge, Mass.: Harvard University Press.

Hughes, Everett Cherrington, and Hughes, Helen McGill (1952) *Where Peoples Meet: Racial and Ethnic Frontiers.* Glencoe, Ill.: Free Press.

Hunter, G. K. (1967) Othello and Colour Prejudice. *Proceedings of the British Academy*, 53:139–63.

Hutchinson, Harry W. (1952) Race Relations in a Rural Community of the Bahian Recôncavo, pp. 16–46 in Wagley, Charles, editor, *Race and Class in Rural Brazil.* Paris: UNESCO.

Huxley, Julian S. and Haddon, A. C. (1935) *We Europeans: A Survey of 'Racial' Problems.* London: Cape.

Illsley, Raymond (1955) Social Class Selection and Class Differences in Relation to Stillbirths and Infant Deaths. *British Medical Journal*, 1520–33.

Jackson, Harold (1972) The Two Irelands: The Problem of the Double Minority, pp. 187–216 in Whitaker, Ben, editor, *The Fourth World: Victims of Group Oppression. Eight Reports from the Field Work of the Minority Rights Group.* London: Sidgwick and Jackson.

Jeffery, Patricia (1976) *Migrants and Refugees: Muslim and Christian Pakistani Families in Bristol.* Cambridge: Cambridge University Press.

Jenkins, David (1975) *Black Zion: Africa, Imagined and Real, as Seen by Today's Blacks.* New York: Harcourt Brace Jovanovich.

Johnson, Charles S. (1943) *Patterns of Negro Segregation.* New York: Harper.

Johnstone, Frederick A. (1976) *Race, Class and Gold: A Study of Class Relations and Racial Discrimination in South Africa.* London: Routledge.

Jones, Eldred (1965) *Othello's Countrymen: The African in English Renaissance Drama.* London: Oxford University Press.

Jones, Peter R. (1982) Ethnic Intermarriage in Britain. *Ethnic and Racial Studies*, 5:223–28.

Jordan, Winthrop D. (1968) *White Over Black: American Attitudes Towards the Negro, 1550–1812.* Chapel Hill: University of North Carolina Press.

Kain, John F. and Quigley, John M. (1975) *Housing Markets and Racial Discrimination: A Microeconomic Analysis.* New York: National Bureau of Economic Research.

Kerckhoff, Alan C. and Campbell, Richard T. (1977) Race and Social Status Differences in the Explanation of Educational Ambition. *Social Forces*, 55:701–14.

Kessler-Harris, Alice and Yans-McLaughlin, Virginia (1978) European Immigrant Groups, pp. 107–37 in Sowell, Thomas, editor, *American Ethnic Groups.* Washington, D.C.: The Urban Institute.

Keyes, Charles F. (1976) Towards a New Formulation of the Concept of Ethnic Group. *Ethnicity*, 3:202–13.

Khan, Verity Saifullah (1976) Purdah in the British Situation, pp. 224–45 in

Barker, Diana Leonard and Allen, Sheila, editors, *Dependence and Exploitation in Work and Marriage*. London: Longmans.

Killian, Lewis M. (1981) Black Power and White Reactions: The Revitalization of Race-thinking in the United States. *The Annals of the American Academy of Political and Social Science,* 454:42–54.

Kilson, Martin (1975) Blacks and Neo-Ethnicity in American Political Life, pp. 236–66 in Glazer, Nathan, and Moynihan, Daniel Patrick, editors, *Ethnicity: Theory and Experience*. Cambridge, Mass.: Harvard University Press.

Kilson, Martin (1976) Whither Integration? *The American Scholar*, 45:360–73.

Kilson, Martin (1981) Black Social Classes and Intergenerational Poverty. *The Public Interest*, 64:58–78.

Kirzner, Israel M. (1973) *Competition and Entrepreneurship*. Chicago: University of Chicago Press.

Kitano, Harry H. L., Yeung, Wai-Tsang, Chai, Lynn, and Hatanaka, Herbert (1982) Asian–American Interracial Marriage, *forthcoming* in *Marriage and Family Review*.

Kitzinger, Sheila (1978) West Indian Adolescents: An Anthropological Perspective. *Journal of Adolescence*, 1:35–46.

Kosmin, Barry (1979a) Traditions of Work Amongst British Jews, pp. 37–68 in Wallman, Sandra, editor, *Ethnicity at Work*. London: Macmillan.

Kosmin, Barry (1979b) J. R. Archer (1863–1932): A Pan-Africanist in the Battersea Labour Movement. *New Community*, 7:430–6.

Kuper, Leo (1974) *Race, Class and Power: Ideology and Revolutionary Change in Plural Societies*. London: Duckworth.

Kuper, Leo (1977) *The Pity of It All: Polarization of Racial and Ethnic Relations*. London: Duckworth.

Lawrence, Daniel (1974) *Black Migrants, White Natives: A Study of Race Relations in Nottingham*. Cambridge: Cambridge University Press.

Lawrence, Daniel (1978) Prejudice, Politics and Race. *New Community*, 7:44–55.

Le Lohé, M. J. (1975) Participation in Elections by Asians in Bradford, pp. 84–122 in Crewe, Ivor, editor, *The Politics of Race* (British Political Sociology Yearbook 2). London: Croom Helm.

Levy, Charles (1967) *Voluntary Servitude: Whites in the Negro Movement*. New York: Appleton-Century-Crofts.

Leyton, Elliot (1974) Opposition and Integration in Ulster. *Man*, 9:185–98.

Leyton, Elliot (1975) *The One Blood: Kinship and Class in an Irish Village*. (Newfoundland Social and Economic Studies No. 15.) Newfoundland: Memorial University.

Lincoln, C. Eric (1974) *The Black Church Since Frazier*, published with Frazier, E. Franklin, *The Negro Church in America*. New York: Schoken Books.

Little, Kenneth L. (1948) *Negroes in Britain: A Study of Racial Relations in English Society*. London: Routledge.

Litwack, Leon F. (1979) *Been in the Storm So Long: The Aftermath of Slavery*. New York: Random House, Vintage Books.

Long, Edward (1774) *History of Jamaica, or, General Survey of the Ancient and Modern State of That Island*. 3 Vols. London. Reprinted, London: Frank Cass, 1970.

Lorimer, Douglas A. (1978) *Colour, Class and the Victorians: English Attitudes to the Negro in the Mid-nineteenth Century*. Leicester: Leicester University Press.

Lowry, Ira S. (1982) The Science and Politics of Ethnic Enumeration, pp. 42–61 in Van Horne, Winston A. and Tonnesen, Thomas V., editors, *Ethnicity and Public Policy*. Madison: University of Wisconsin System American Ethnic Studies Co-ordinating Committee/Urban Corridor Consortium, vol. 1.

Lustgarten, Laurence (1980) *Legal Control of Racial Discrimination*. London: Macmillan.

McClelland, David C. (1961) *The Achieving Society*. Princeton: Van Nostrand.

McConahay, John B. (1982) Self-Interest Versus Racial Attitudes as Correlates of Anti-Busing Attitudes in Louisville: Is it the Buses or the Blacks? *Journal of Politics*, 44:692–720.

McKay, David H. (1977) *Housing and Race in Industrial Society: Civil Rights and Urban Policy in Britain and the United States*. London: Croom Helm, and Tottowa, N.J.: Rowan and Littlefield.

Macmillan, W. M. (1949) *Africa Emergent: A Survey of Social, Political and Economic Trends in British Africa*. Harmondsworth: Penguin.

McPherson, James Alan (1972) In My Father's House There Are Many Mansions ... *The Atlantic*, 229(April):51–82.

McPherson, Klim and Gaitskell, Julia (1969) *Immigrants and Employment: Two Case Studies in East London and in Croydon*. London: Institute of Race Relations.

Makabe, Tomoko (1981) The Theory of the Split Labor Market: A Comparison of the Japanese Experience in Brazil and Canada. *Social Forces*, 59:786–809.

Markus, Andrew (1979) *Fear and Hatred: Purifying Australia and California, 1850–1901*. Sydney: Hole and Iremonger.

Marshall, Ray (1968) The Negro in Southern Unions, pp. 128–54 in Jacobson, Julius, editor, *The Negro and the American Labor Movement*. New York: Doubleday, Anchor Books.

Martinez-Allier, Verena (1974) *Marriage, Class and Colour in Nineteenth Century Cuba: A Study of Racial Attitudes and Sexual Values in a Slave Society*. Cambridge: Cambridge University Press.

Mason, Philip (1962) *Prospero's Magic: Some Thoughts on Race and Class*. London: Oxford University Press.

Mason, Philip (1983) *A Thread of Silk*. London: Deutsch.

Mathias, Charles McC. (1981) Ethnic Groups and Foreign Policy. *Foreign Affairs*, Summer: 975–98.

Matthews, Basil (1924) *The Clash of Colour: A Study in the Problem of Race*. London: Edinburgh House Press.

Mayhew, K. and Rosewell, B. (1978) Immigrants and Occupational Crowding in Great Britain. *Oxford Bulletin of Economics and Statistics*, 40: 223–48.

Mayhew, Leon H. (1968) *Law and Equal Opportunity: A Study of the Massachusetts Commission Against Discrimination*. Cambridge, Mass.: Harvard University Press.

Mayr, Ernst (1972) The Nature of the Darwinian Revolution. *Science*, 176:981–9.

Meade, James E. (1973) *Theory of Economic Externalities: The Control of Environmental Pollution and Similar Social Costs*. Geneva and Leiden: Sijthoff.

Miles, Robert (1980) Class, Race and Ethnicity: A Critique of Cox's Theory. *Racial and Ethnic Studies*, 3:169–87.

Miles, Robert and Phizacklea, Annie (1977) Class, Race, Ethnicity and Political Action. *Political Studies*, 25:491–507.

Miles, Robert and Phizacklea, Annie (1978) The TUC and Black Workers, 1974–76. *British Journal of Industrial Relations*, 16:197–207.

Miller, Carol (1975) American Rom and the Ideology of Defilement, pp. 41–54 in Rehfisch, Farnham, editor, *Gypsies, Tinkers and Other Travellers*. London: Academic Press.

Mills, C. Wright (1962) *The Marxists*. Harmondsworth: Penguin.

Milne, R. S. (1981) *Politics in Ethnically Bi-Polar States: Guyana, Malaysia and Fiji*. Vancouver: University of British Columbia Press.

Mitchell, J. Clyde (1956) *The Kalela Dance: Aspects of Social Relationship Among Urban Africans in Northern Rhodesia*. Manchester: Manchester University Press.

Montagu, M. F. Ashley, editor (1964) *The Concept of Race*. London: Collier-Macmillan.

Mörner, Magnus (1967) *Race Mixture in the History of Latin America*. Boston: Little, Brown and Co.

Myrdal, Gunnar (1944) *An American Dilemma: The Negro Problem and Modern Democracy*. New York: Harper.

National Advisory Commission on Civil Disorders (Chairman: Otto Kerner) (1968) *Report*. New York: Bantam Books.

Newman, Jerry M. (1978) Discrimination in Recruitment: An Empirical Analysis. *Industrial and Labor Relations Review*, 32:15–23 (and see 33:543–50).

Northrup, Herbert R. and Larson, John A. (1979) *The Impact of the ATT and T-EEO Consent Decree*. Labor Relations and Public Policy Series no 20. Philadelphia: Industrial Research Unit, University of Pennsylvania.

Oaxaca, Ronald L. (1973) Sex Discrimination in Wages, pp. 124–51 in Ashenfelter, Orley and Rees, Albert, editors, *Discrimination in Labor Markets*. Princeton: Princeton University Press.

Oaxaca, Ronald L. (1977) Theory and Measurement in the Economics of Discrimination, pp. 1–30 in Bloch, F. E. *et al., Equal Rights and Industrial Relations*. Madison: Industrial Relations Research Association.

Oldham, J. H. (1924) *Christianity and the Race Problem*. London: Student Christian Movement Press.

Olson, Mancur (1965) *The Logic of Collective Action: Public Goods and the Theory of Groups*. Cambridge, Mass.: Harvard University Press.

Page, Benjamin I. (1977) Elections and Social Choice: The State of Evidence. *American Journal of Political Science*, 21:639–68.

Park, Robert Ezra (1950) *Race and Culture*. New York: The Free Press.

Park, Robert E., and Burgess, E. W. (1921) *Introduction to the Science of Sociology*. Chicago: University of Chicago Press.

Parsons, Talcott (1968) The Problem of Polarization on the Axis of Color, pp. 349–69 in Franklin, John Hope, editor, *Color and Race*. Boston: Houghton Mifflin (reprinted from *Daedalus*).

Parsons, Talcott (1975) Some Theoretical Considerations on the Nature and Trends of Change of Ethnicity, pp. 58–83 in Glazer, Nathan and Moynihan, Daniel Patrick, editors, *Ethnicity: Theory and Experience*. Cambridge, Mass.: Harvard University Press.

Pascall, Anthony H., and Rapping, Leonard A. (1972) The Economics of Discrimination in Organized Baseball, pp. 119–56 in Pascall, Anthony H., editor, *Racial Discrimination in Economic Life*. Lexington, Mass.: Heath.

Patterson, Orlando (1968) West Indian Migrants Returning Home. *Race*, 10:69–77.

Patterson, Orlando (1975) Context and Choice in Ethnic Allegiance: A Theoretical Framework and Caribbean Case Study, pp. 309–49 in Glazer, Nathan and Moynihan, Daniel Patrick, editors, *Ethnicity: Theory and Experience.* Cambridge, Mass.: Harvard University Press.

Patterson, Sheila (1957) *The Last Trek: A Study of the Boer people and the Afrikaner Nation.* London: Routledge.

Paul, Diane (1981) 'In the Interests of Civilization': Marxist Views of Race and Culture in the Nineteenth Century. *Journal of the History of Ideas* 42:115–38.

Paul, J. B., editor (1901) *Accounts of the Lord High Treasurer of Scotland,* Vol III, 1506–7. Edinburgh: H.M. General Register House.

Peach, Ceri (1968) *West Indian Migration to Britain: A Social Geography.* London: Oxford University Press.

Peterson, John H. (1971) The Indian in the Old South, pp. 116–33 in Hudson, Charles M., editor, *Red, White and Black: Symposium on Indians in the Old South.* Southern Anthropological Society Proceedings, no 5. Athens: University of Georgia Press.

Peterson, William (1971) *Japanese Americans: Oppression and Success.* New York: Random House.

Peterson, William (1978) Chinese Americans and Japanese Americans, pp. 65–106 in Sowell, Thomas, editor, *American Ethnic Groups.* Washington, D.C.: The Urban Institute.

Pettigrew, Joyce (1972) Some Observations on the Social System of Sikh Jats. *New Community,* 1:354–63.

Pettigrew, Thomas F. (1981) Race and Class in the 1980s: An Interactive View. *Daedalus,* Spring: 233–55.

Phillips, U. B. (1918) *American Negro Slavery: A Survey of the Supply, Employment and Control of Negro Labor as Determined by the Plantation Regime.* Baton Rouge: Louisiana State University Press reprint.

Philpott, Stuart B. (1973) *West Indian Migration: The Montserrat Case.* London: Athlone Press.

Phizacklea, Annie and Miles, Robert (1980) *Labour and Racism.* London: Routledge and Kegan Paul.

Pienaar, S. and Sampson, Anthony (1960) *South Africa: Two Views of Separate Development.* London: Oxford University Press.

Piliavin, Irving M., Rodin, Judith and Piliavin, Jayne Allyn (1969) Good Samaritanism: An Underground Phenomenon? *Journal of Personality and Social Psychology,* 13:289–99.

Pitt-Rivers, Julian (1969) Mestizo or Ladino? *Race,* 10:463–77.

Pitt-Rivers, Julian (1971) On the Word 'Caste', pp. 231–56 in Beidelman, T. O., editor, *The Translation of Culture: Essays Presented to E. E. Evans-Pritchard.* London: Tavistock.

Pitt-Rivers, Julian (1973) Race in Latin America: The Concept of 'Raza'. *European Journal of Sociology,* 14:12–31.

Pollard, Paul (1972) Jamaicans and Trinidadians in North London. *New Community,* 1:370–7.

Popper, Karl R. (1972) *Objective Knowledge: An Evolutionary Approach.* Oxford: Clarendon Press.

Pryce, Kenneth (1977) *Endless Pressure: A Study of West Indian Life-Styles in Bristol.* Harmondsworth: Penguin.

Rabushka, Alvin and Shepsle, Kenneth A. (1972) *Politics in Plural Societies: A*

Theory of Democratic Instability. Columbus, Ohio: Merrill.

Reed, T. Edward (1966) Caucasian Genes in American Negroes. *Science*, 165:762–8.

Reinders, Robert C. (1968) Racialism on the Left: E. D. Morel and the 'Black Horror on the Rhine'. *International Review of Social History*, 13:1–28.

Rex, John (1968) The Sociology of a Zone of Transition, pp. 211–31 in Pahl. R. E., editor, *Readings in Urban Sociology*. Oxford: Pergamon.

Rex, John (1971) The Concept of Housing Class and the Sociology of Race Relations. *Race*, 12:293–301, reprinted at pp. 32–42 in Rex, John, *Race, Colonialism and the City*. London: Routledge and Kegan Paul, 1973.

Rex, John (1982) West Indian and Asian Youth, pp. 53–71 in Cashmore, Ernest and Troyna, Barry, editors, *Black Youth in Crisis*. London: Allen and Unwin.

Rex, John and Moore, Robert (1967) *Race, Community and Conflict: A Study of Sparkbrook*. London: Oxford University Press.

Rex, John and Tomlinson, Sally (1979) *Colonial Immigrants in a British City: A Class Analysis*. London: Routledge and Kegan Paul.

Reynolds, Henry (1981) *The Other Side of the Frontier: An Interpretation of the Aboriginal Response to the Invasion and Settlement of Australia*. Townsville, Queensland: History Department, James Cook University.

Reynolds, Vernon (1976) *The Biology of Human Action*. Oxford: W. H. Freeman. 2nd edn, 1980.

Richmond, Anthony H. (1955) *The Colour Problem: A Study of Racial Relations*. Harmondsworth: Penguin.

Richmond, Anthony H. (1967) *Post-War Immigrants in Canada*. Toronto: Toronto University Press.

Robertson, H. M. (1934–5) 150 Years of Economic Contact Between Black and White: A Preliminary Survey. *South African Journal of Economics*, 2:403–25 and 3:3–25.

Rose, E. J. B. *et al.* (1969) *Colour and Citizenship: A Report on British Race Relations*. London: Oxford University Press.

Rose, Harold M. (1976) *Black Suburbanisation: Access to Improved Quality of Life or Maintenance of the Status Quo?* Cambridge, Mass.: Ballinger.

Rose, Peter I. (1968) The Subject is Race: *Traditional Ideologies and the Teaching of Race Relations*. New York: Oxford University Press.

Rowe, William L. (1968) The New Cauhāns: A Caste Mobility Movement in North India, pp. 66–77 in Silverberg, James, editor, *Social Mobility in the Caste System in India*. Comparative Studies in Society and History, supplement 3. The Hague: Mouton.

Saldanha, P. H. (1962) Race Mixture Among Northeastern Brazilian Populations. *American Anthropologist*, 64:751–9.

Scarman, Lord (1981) *The Brixton Disorders, 10–12 April 1981*. Cmnd 8427. London: Her Majesty's Stationery Office.

Schelling, Thomas (1972) A Process of Residential Segregation: Neighborhood Tipping, pp. 157–84 in Pascal, Anthony H., editor, *Racial Discrimination in Economic Life*. Lexington, Mass.: D. C. Heath.

Schelling, Thomas (1978) *Micromotives and Macro Behaviour*. New York: W. W. Norton.

Schlemmer, Lawrence and Webster, Eddie, editors (1978) *Change, Reform and Economic Growth in South Africa*. Johannesburg: Rowan Press.

Searle, G. R. (1971) *The Quest for Efficiency: A Study in British Politics and Political Thought, 1899–1914*. Oxford: Blackwell.

Shugg, Roger W. (1939) *Origins of Class Struggle in Louisiana*. Baton Rouge: Louisiana State University Press.

Shyllon, Folarin (1977) *Black People in Britain, 1553–1833*. London: Oxford University Press.

Sillitoe, Ken (1978) Ethnic Origin: The Search for a Question. *Population Trends*. 13:25–30.

Simons, H. J. and Simons, R. E. (1969) *Class and Colour in South Africa 1850–1950*. Harmondsworth: Penguin Books.

Simons, Sarah E. (1901) Social Assimilation. Part 1. Principles. *American Journal of Sociology*, 6:790–822.

Siu, Paul C. P. (1952) The Sojourner. *American Journal of Sociology*, 58:34–44.

Sivanandan, A. (1974) *Race and Resistance: The IRR Story*. London: Race Today.

Sivanandan, A. (1977) Race, Class and the State: The Black Experience. *Race and Class*, 17:347–68.

Smith, David J. (1977) *Racial Disadvantage in Britain*. The PEP Report. Harmondsworth: Penguin.

Smith, Graham A. (1980) Jim Crow on the Home Front 1942–5. *New Community*, 8:317–28.

Smith, J. P. and Welch, Finis (1978) *Race Differences in Earnings: A Survey and New Evidence*. Santa Monica, California: Rand Corporation.

Smith, M. G. (1965) *The Plural Society in the British West Indies*. Berkeley: University of California Press.

Sofer, Cyril (1954) Working Groups in a Plural Society. *Industrial and Labor Relations Review*, 8:68–78.

Sollors, Werner (1980) Literature and Ethnicity, pp. 647–65 in Thernstrom, Stephan, editor, *Harvard Encyclopedia of American Ethnic Groups*. Cambridge, Mass.: Harvard University Press.

Southall, Aidan (1975) General Amin and the Coup: Great Man or Historical Inevitability? *Journal of Modern African Studies*, 13:85–105.

Sowell, Thomas (1975) *Race and Economics*. New York: David McKay.

Sowell, Thomas (1978) Race and I.Q. Reconsidered, pp. 203–38 in Sowell, Thomas, editor, *American Ethnic Groups*. Washington, D.C.: The Urban Institute.

Sowell, Thomas (1981a) *Ethnic America: A History*. New York: Basic Books.

Sowell, Thomas (1981b) *Markets and Minorities*. New York: Basic Books.

Spiller, G., editor (1911) *Papers on Inter-Racial Problems Communicated to the First Universal Races Congress*. London: P. S. King.

Stuckert, Robert P. (1964) Race Mixture: The African Ancestry of White Americans, pp. 192–7 in Hammond, Peter B., *Physical Anthropology and Archaeology*. New York: Macmillan.

Stymeist, David H. (1975) *Ethnics and Indians: Social Relationships in a Northwestern Ontario Town*. Toronto: Peter Martin Associates.

Sutherland, Anne (1975) *Gypsies: The Hidden Americans*. London: Tavistock.

Tambs-Lynch, Harald (1980) *London Patidars: A Case Study in Urban Ethnicity*. London: Routledge and Kegan Paul.

Tanenbaum, Frank (1947) Slave and Citizen: *The Negro in the Americas*. New York: Knopf.

Tanner, R. E. S. (1965) European Leadership in Small Communities in Tanganyika Prior to Independence: A Study of Conflicting Social and Political Interracial Roles. *Race*, 7:289–302.

Taylor, D. Garth, Sheatsley, Paul B. and Greeley, Andrew (1978) Attitudes Toward Racial Integration. *Scientific American*, 238(6):42–9.

Tessler, Mark A. (1981) Ethnic Change and Nonassimilating Minority Status: Jews In Tunisia and Morocco and Arabs in Israel, pp. 154–97 in Keyes, Charles, editor, *Ethnic Change*. Seattle: University of Washington Press.

Thernstrom, Stephan F. (1964) *Poverty and Progress: Social Mobility in a Nineteenth Century City*. Cambridge, Mass.: Harvard University Press.

Thomas, Piri (1967) *Down These Mean Streets*. New York: Knopf.

Thompson, Edgar T., editor, (1939) *Race Relations and the Race Problem: A Definition and an Analysis*. Durham: Duke University Press.

Thompson, Marcus (1974) The Second Generation – Punjabi or English? *New Community*, 3:242–8.

Thorne, Christopher (1974) Britain and the Black G.I.s: Racial Issues and Anglo-American Relations in 1942. *New Community*, 3:262–71.

Thurow, Lester (1969) *Poverty and Discrimination*. Washington: Brookings Institute.

Thurow, Lester (1975) *Generating Inequality: Mechanisms of Distribution in the US Economy*. New York: Basic Books.

Tomlinson, Sally (1979) The Educational Performance of Ethnic Minority Children. *New Community*, 8:213–34.

Trosper, Ronald L. (1976) Native American Boundary Maintenance: The Flathead Indian Reservation, Montana, 1860–1970. *Ethnicity*, 3:256–74.

Tuck, Mary and Southgate, Peter (1981) *Ethnic Minorities and Policing: A Survey of West Indian and White Experiences*. Home Office Research Studies, 70. London: Home Office.

Turner, Jonathan H. and Bonacich, Edna (1980) Toward a Composite Theory of Middleman Minorities. *Ethnicity*, 7:144–58.

Turner, Ralph H. (1960) Sponsored and Contest Mobility and the School System. *American Sociological Review*, 25:855–67.

van den Berghe, Pierre L. (1981) *The Ethnic Phenomenon*. Amsterdam: Elsevier.

van Jaaresveldt, F. A. (1964) *The Afrikaner's Interpretation of South African History*. Capetown: Simondium.

Wagley, Charles (1959) On the Concept of Social Race in the Americas, pp. 403–17 in *Actas del XXXIII Congresso Internacional de Americanistas*. San José, Costa Rico. Reprinted in Wagley's *The Latin American Tradition*. New York: Columbia University Press, 1968, Ch. 5.

Wallace, Anthony F. C. (1956) Revitalization Movements. *American Anthropologist*, 58:264–81.

Wallerstein, Immanuel (1960) Ethnicity and National Integration in West Africa. *Cahiers d'études africaines*, 1:129–39.

Walvin, James (1971) *The Black Presence: A Documentary History of the Negro in England*. London: Orbach and Chambers.

Walvin, James (1973) *Black and White: The Negro and English Society 1555–1945*. London: Allen Lane.

Ward, Robin (1978) Race Relations in Britain. *British Journal of Sociology*, 29:464–80.

Ward, Robin (1979) Where Race Didn't Divide: Some Reflections on Slum Clearance in Manchester, pp. 204–22 in Miles, Robert and Phizacklea, Annie, editors, *Racism and Political Action in Britain*. London: Routledge and Kegan Paul.

Ward, Robin and Sims, Ron (1981) Social Status, the Market and Ethnic Segregation, pp. 217–34 in Peach, Ceri, Robinson, Vaughan and Smith, Susan, editors, *Ethnic Segregation in Cities*. London: Croom Helm.

Warner, W. Lloyd and Srole, Leo (1945) *The Social Systems of American Ethnic Groups*. New Haven: Yale University Press.

Watson, George (1977) Race and the Socialists, pp. 120–34 in Watson, George, *Politics and Literature in Modern Britain*. London: Macmillan.

Watson, Graham (1970) *Passing for White: A Study of Racial Assimilation in a South African School*. London: Tavistock.

Watson, James L. (1977) Chinese Emigrant Ties to the Home Community. *New Community*, 5:343–52.

Wattenburg, Ben J., and Gergen, David (1980) Attitudes, pp. 21–6 in Cousins, Norman, editor, *Reflections of America: Commemorating the Statistical Abstract Centennial*. Washington, D.C.: Bureau of the Census.

Weatherford, Willis D. and Johnson, Charles S. (1934) *Race Relations: Adjustment of Whites and Negroes in the United States*. Boston: D. C. Heath.

White, Robin M. (1979) What's in a Name? Problems in Official and Legal Uses of 'Race'. *New Community*, 7:333–49.

Wilder-Okladek, F. (1969) *The Return Movement of Jews to Austria After the Second World War*. (Publications of the Research Group for European Migration Problems, XVI). The Hague: Nijhoff.

Williams, Glyn (1975) *The Desert and the Dream: A Study of Welsh Colonization in the Chubut, 1865–1915*. Cardiff: University of Wales Press.

Wilson, Monica and Thompson, Leonard (1971) *The Oxford History of South Africa*. 2 Vols. London: Oxford University Press.

Wilson, William Julius (1978) *The Declining Significance of Race: Blacks and Changing American Institutions*. Chicago: University of Chicago Press.

Winter, John (1974) The Webbs and the Non-White World. *Journal of Contemporary History*, 9:181–92.

Wirth, Louis (1945) The Problem of Minority Groups, pp. 347–72 in Linton, Ralph, editor, *The Science of Man in the World Crisis*. New York: Columbia University Press.

Wispe, Lauren G. and Freshley, Harold B. (1971) Race, Sex, and Sympathetic Helping Behaviour: The Broken Bag Caper. *Journal of Personality and Social Psychology*, 17:59–65.

Wolpe, Howard (1972) Capitalism and Cheap Labour-power in South Africa: From Segregation to Apartheid. *Economy and Society*, 1:425–56.

Woodward, C. Vann (1957) *The Strange Career of Jim Crow*. Revised Edn. New York: Oxford University Press.

Wright, Harrison M. (1977) *The Burden of the Present: Liberal–Radical Controversy over Southern African History*. Capetown: David Philip; London: Rex Collings.

Wright, Harrison M. (1980) The Burden of the Present and its Critics. *Social Dynamics*, 6:36–48.

Wright, Peter L. (1968) *The Coloured Worker in British Industry, with Special Reference to the Midlands and North of England*. London: Oxford University Press.

Author index

Subject index